District Gazetteers of India Series 64

CENTRAL PROVINCES DISTRICT GAZETTEERS

AKOLA

(DESCRIPTIVE)

District Gazetteers of India Series 64

CENTRAL PROVINCES DISTRICT GAZETTEERS

AKOLA

(DESCRIPTIVE)

A. E. NELSON, C. BROWN

30 VOLUMES (IN 33 BINDINGS)

(1st, Vol. A)

GYAN

Published by

Gyan Publishing House
5, Ansari Road
Daryaganj, New Delhi-110002
Phone: 011-47034999, 9811692060
E-mail: books@gyanbooks.com

Distribution Network
gyanbooks.com
India, USA, Canada, UK, Australia, France

ISBN: 978-93-6208-539-9 (Set) 30 Volumes (In 33 Bindings)
978-93-6208-172-8 (PB)

First Published, 1910

2nd Impression 2024

Printed at: Gyan Press, Delhi.

CENTRAL PROVINCES DISTRICT GAZETTEERS (1st, Vol. A)
Author: A. E. NELSON, C. BROWN

LIST OF VOLUMES

S. NO.	ISBN NO.	VOLUME	TITLE	AUTHOR	PRICE	PAGES
			ASSAM DISTRICT GAZETTEERS			
1	9788121285926	1st	Cachar	B. C. Allen	600	300
2	9788121285919	2nd	Sylhet	B. C. Allen	750	378
3	9788121285902	3rd	Goalpara	B. C. Allen	400	203
4	9788121285896	4th	Kamrup	B. C. Allen	675	344
5	9788121285889	5th	Darrang	B. C. Allen	725	364
6	9788121285872	6th	Nowgong	B. C. Allen	560	280
7	9788121285865	7th	Sibsagar	B. C. Allen	675	343
8	9788121285858	8th	Lakhimpur	B. C. Allen	690	347
9	9788121285841	9th	Naga Hills and Manipur	B. C. Allen	580	294
10	9788121285834	10th	The Khasi And Jaintia Hills, The Garo Hills And The Lushai Hills	B. C. Allen	675	363
11	9788121285827	11th	The Sadiya and Balipara Frontier Tract	B. C. Allen	375	190
			BENGAL DISTRICT GAZETTEERS			
12	9788121218672	1st	Angul	L. S. S. O'Malley	340	168
13	9788121259637	2nd	Bakarganj	J. C. JACK	970	194
14	9788121218696	3rd	Balasore	L. S. S. O'Malley	450	228
15	9788121259590	4th	Bankura	L. S. S. O'Malley	1000	199
16	9788121218375	5th	Bhagalpur	J. Byrne	390	194
17	9788121218290	6th	Birbhum	L. S. S. O'Malley	300	150
18	9788121259651	7th	Eastern Bengal and Assam - Bogra	J. N. Gupta	940	188
19	9788121218351	8th	Burdwan	J. C. K. Peterson	450	227
20	9788121259538	9th	Calcutta District Gazetteer - Statistics, 1901 - 02		340	68
21	9788121218313	10th	Champaran	L. S. S. O'Malley	410	205
22	9788121259613	11th	Eastern Bengal District Gazetters - Chittagong	L. S. S. O'Malley	1080	216
23	9788121259552	12th	Chota Nagpur Tributary		130	26
24	9788121259415	13th	The Cooch Behar Gazette: Statistics		1460	292
25	9788121218412	14th	Cuttack	L. S. S. O'Malley	490	248
26	9788121261357	15th	Eastern Bengal District Gazetteers Dacca	B. C. Allen	400	207
27	9788121218436	16th	Darbhanga	L. S. S. O'Malley	360	180
28	9789362089335	17th	Darjeeling	L. S. S. O'Malley	500	248
29	9788121259453	18th	Eastern Bengal District Gazetteers - Dinajpur	F. W. Strong	890	178
30	9788121259392	19th	Faridpur	L. S. S. O'Malley	700	140
31	9788121218474	20th	Gaya	L. S. S. O'Malley	540	270
32	9788121214032	21st	Bihar and Orissa District Gazetteer: Hazaribagh	E. Lister	715	234
33	9788121218337	22nd	Hooghly	L. S. S. O'Malley	680	340
34	9788121218191	23rd	Bengal District Gazetteer Howrah	L. S. S. O'Malley	390	199
35	9788121259293	24th	Eastern Bengal and Assam - Jalpaiguri	John F. Gruning	890	178
36	9788121259279	25th	Jessore	L. S. S. O'Malley	960	192
37	9788121259231	26th	Khulna	L. S. S. O'Malley	1100	220
38	9788121259217	27th	Malda	G. E. Lambourn	670	134
39	9788121267854	28th	Manbhum	H. Coupland	600	313
40	9788121218498	29th	Midnapore	L. S. S. O'Malley	500	252
41	9788121218597	30th	Monghyr	L. S. S. O'Malley	560	280
42	9788121259156	31st	Murshidabad	L. S. S. O'Malley	1250	250
43	9788121259576	32nd	Bengal District Gazetteers - Muzaffarpur	L. S. S. O'Malley	940	188
44	9788121259132	33rd	Mymensingh	F. A. Sachse	960	192
45	9788121259118	34th	Nadia	J. H. E. Garrett	1070	214
46	9788121259095	35th	Eastern Bengal and Assam - Noakhali	J. E. Webster	580	115
47	9788121218450	36th	Feudatory States of Orissa	L. E. B. Cobdenramsay	790	395
48	9788121259071	37th	Pabna	L. S. S. O'Malley	710	142
49	9788121218511	38th	Palamau	L. S. S. O'Malley	380	190
50	9788121218634	39th	Patna	L. S. S. O'Malley	500	250
51	9788121218535	40th	Puri	L. S. S. O'Malley	650	328
52	9788121218757	41st	Purnea	L. S. S. O'Malley	440	220
53	9788121258937	42nd	Rajshahi	L. S. S. O'Malley	1080	216
54	9788121256681	43rd	Bihar and Orissa District Gazetteers: Ranchi	M. G. Hallett	1350	278
55	9788121258913	44th	Eastern Bengal and assam - Rangpur	J. A. Vas	890	178
56	9788121218559	45th	Sambalpur	L. S. S. O'Malley	480	242
57	9788121214056	46th	Santal Parganas	L. S. S. O'Malley	940	308
58	9788121218610	47th	Saran	L. S. S. O'Malley	380	190
59	9788121218658	48th	Shahabad	L. S. S. O'Malley	380	190
60	9788121256704	49th	The Gazetteer of Sikhim	H. H. Risley	960	481
61	9788121218573	50th	Singhbhum, Saraikela And Kharsawan	L. S. S. O'Malley	560	280
62	9788121259439	51st	Eastern Bengal District Gazetteers - Tippera	J. E. Webster	730	146
63	9788121259033	52nd	24 Parganas	L. S. S. O'Malley	1420	284

S. NO.	ISBN NO.	VOLUME	TITLE	AUTHOR	PRICE	PAGES
			CENTRAL PROVINCES DISTRICT GAZETTEERS			
64	9789362081728	1st, Vol. A	Akola (Descriptive)	A. E. Nelson, C. Brown	870	436
65	9789362085481	2nd, Vol. A	Amraoti (Descriptive)	S. V. Fitzgerald, A. E. Nelson	1050	524
66	9789362089267	3rd,Vol. A	Balaghat (Descriptive)	R. V. RUSSELL	430	216
67	9789362083494	4th, Vol. A	Betul (Descriptive)	R. V. RUSSELL	610	306
68	9789362085146	5th, Vol. A	Bhandara (Descriptive)	R. V. RUSSELL	580	292
69	9789362088390	6th, Vol. A	Bilaspur (Descriptive)	R. V. RUSSELL	870	434
70	9789362086044	7th, Vol. A	Buldana (Descriptive)	A. E. Nelson	1090	543
71	9789362089014	8th, Vol. B	Chanda (Descriptive)	R. V. RUSSELL	470	234
72	9789362086938	9th	Chhattisgarch Feudatory State	E. A. De Brett	880	440
73	9789362082961	10th	Chhindwara (Descriptive)	R. V. RUSSELL	550	274
74	9789362089342	11th, Vol. A & B	Damoh (Descriptive and Statistical Tables 1891-1901)	R. V. RUSSELL	830	414
75	9789362081230	12th, Vol. A	Durg (Descriptive)	A. E. Nelson	460	232
76	9789362086037	13th, Vol. A	Hoshangabad (Descriptive)	R. V. RUSSELL	860	430
77	9789362086792	14th, Vol. A	Jubbulpore (Descriptive)	A. E. Nelson	950	474
78	9789362089663	15th, Vol. A & B	Mandla (Descriptive and Statistical Tables 1891-1901)	R. V. RUSSELL	370	186
79	9789362086419	16th, Vol. A	Nagpur (Descriptive)	R. V. RUSSELL	790	394
80	9789362080646	17th, Vol. A	Narsinghpur (Descriptive)	R. V. RUSSELL	510	257
81	9789362084835	18th, Vol. A	Nimar (Descriptive)	R. V. RUSSELL	600	299
82	9789362087737	19th, Vol. A	Raipur (Descriptive)	A. E. Nelson	790	396
83	9789362080264	20th, Vol. A	Saugor (Descriptive)	R. V. RUSSELL	570	285
84	9789362081117	21st, Vol. A	Seoni (Descriptive)	R. V. RUSSELL	460	232
85	9789362084965	22nd, Vol. A	Wardha (Descriptive)	R. V. RUSSELL	600	302
86	9789362083401	23rd, Vol. A	Yeotmal (Descriptive)	R. V. RUSSELL	550	277
87	9789362080325	24th, Vol. I, Pt. I	Gwalior (Text and Tables)	R. V. RUSSELL	980	489
88	9789362087133	24th, Vol. I, Pt. II	Gwalior (Maps)	R. V. RUSSELL	400	198
89	9789362086341	24th, Vol. I, Pt. III	Gwalior (Village List)	R. V. RUSSELL	810	406
90	9789362085467	24th, Vol. I, Pt. IV	Gwalior (Photos)	R. V. RUSSELL	1400	698
91	9789362087393	25th, Vol. II	Indore (Text and Tables)	C. E. Luard	1050	524
92	9789362084422	26th, Vol. III	Bhopal (Text and Tables)	C. E. Luard	540	272
93	9789362086815	27th, Vol. IV	Rewah (Text and Tables)	C. E. Luard	500	250
94	9789362087584	28th, Vol. V, Pt. A	Western States - Malwa (Text)	C. E. Luard	1520	762
95	9789362087300	29th, Vol. VI, Pt. A	Eastern States - Bundelkhand (Text)	C. E. Luard	930	463
96	9789362082169	30th, Vol. VI, Pt. B	Eastern States - Bundelkhand (Tables)	C. E. Luard	830	417
			GAZETTEER OF THE BOMBAY PRESIDENCY:			
97	9788121283441	1st, Part I	History of Gujarat	Ed.: James M. Campbell	3220	644
98	9788121285582	1st, Part II	History of the Konkan Dakhan and Southern Maratha Country	Ed.: James M. Campbell	4200	840
99	9788121285568	2nd	Gujarat, Surat and Broach	Ed.: James M. Campbell	2990	598
100	9788121285544	3rd	Kaira and Panch Mahals	Ed.: James M. Campbell	1690	339
101	9788121285520	4th	Ahmedabad	Ed.: James M. Campbell	1860	372
102	9788121285506	5th	Cutch, Palanpur, and Mahi Kantha	Ed.: James M. Campbell	2390	478
103	9788121285483	6th	Rewa Kantha, Narukot, Cambay, and Surat States	Ed.: James M. Campbell	1450	290
104	9788121285469	7th	Baroda	Ed.: James M. Campbell	3260	652
105	9788121285445	8th	Kathiawar	Ed.: James M. Campbell	3790	758
106	9788121285421	9th, Part I	Gujarat Population - Hindus	Ed.: James M. Campbell	3170	636
107	9788121285407	9th, Part II	Gujarat Population - Musalmans and Parsis	Ed.: James M. Campbell	1520	304
108	9788121285384	10th	Ratnagiri and Savantvadi	Ed.: James M. Campbell	2500	501
109	9788121285360	11th	Kolaba and Janjira	Ed.: James M. Campbell	2550	513
110	9788121285346	12th	Khandesh	Ed.: James M. Campbell	3190	638
111	9788121285322	13th Part I	Thana	Ed.: James M. Campbell	2050	413
112	9788121285308	13th Part II	Thana	Ed.: James M. Campbell	1770	357
113	9788121285285	14th	Thana - Places of Interest	Ed.: James M. Campbell	3290	659
114	9788121285261	15th Part I	Kanara	Ed.: James M. Campbell	2340	348
115	9788121285247	15th Part II	Kanara	Ed.: James M. Campbell	1740	348
116	9788121285223	16th	Nasik	Ed.: James M. Campbell	3490	698
117	9788121285209	17th	Ahmadnagar	Ed.: James M. Campbell	3860	772
118	9788121285186	18th Part I	Poona	Ed.: James M. Campbell	2930	586
119	9788121285162	18th Part II	Poona	Ed.: James M. Campbell	2680	537
120	9788121285148	18th Part III	Poona	Ed.: James M. Campbell	2500	503
121	9788121285124	19th	Satara	Ed.: James M. Campbell	3450	692
122	9788121285100	20th	Sholapur	Ed.: James M. Campbell	2730	547
123	9788121285087	21st	Gazetteer of the Bomaby Presidency: Belgaum	Ed.: James M. Campbell	2570	514
124	9788121285063	22nd	Dharwar	Ed.: James M. Campbell	4200	841
125	9788121285049	23rd	Gazetteer of the Bombay Presidency:Bijapur	Ed.: James M. Campbell	3550	712
126	9788121285025	24th	Kolhapur	Ed.: James M. Campbell	2250	450

S. NO.	ISBN NO.	VOLUME	TITLE	AUTHOR	PRICE	PAGES
127	9788121285001	25th	Botany	Ed.: James M. Campbell	2040	408
128	9788121284981	26th, Part I	Materials Towards a Statistical Account of the Town and Island of Bombay - History	Ed.: James M. Campbell	2500	504
129	9788121284967	26th, Part II	Materials Towards a Statistical Account of the Town and Island of Bombay - Trade and Fortifications	Ed.: James M. Campbell	2690	538
130	9788121284943	26th, Part III	Materials Towards a Statistical Account of the Town And Island of Bombay - Administration	Ed.: James M. Campbell	2450	702
131	9788121284929	27th	General Index	Ed.:R. E. Enthoven	2190	428

MADRAS DISTRICT GAZETTEERS

S. NO.	ISBN NO.	VOLUME	TITLE	AUTHOR	PRICE	PAGES
132	9788121258814	1st	Anantapur	W. Francis	1140	227
133	9788121258555	2nd	Malabar	C. A Innes & F. B Evans	3010	602
134	9788121258791	3rd	Bellary	W. Francis	1890	377
135	9788121258777	4th	Statistical Appendix For Chingleput		280	56
136	9788121258753	5th	Coimbatore	K. N. Krishnaswami Ayyar	3420	628
137	9788121232814	6th	Madras District Gazetteers District Gazetteer Cuddapah	C. F. Brackenbury	1120	285
138	9788121258715	7th	Statistical Appendix For Ganjam		370	73
139	9788121256766	8th, Vol. 1st	Godavari District Gazetteer	F. R. Hemingway	650	320
140	9788121256803	8th, Vol. 2nd	Godavari District Gazetteer	F. R. Hemingway	160	83
141	9788121258678	9th	Statistical Appendix For Kistna		640	127
142	9788121258654	10th	Statistical Appendix For Kurnool		270	54
143	9788121258616	11th	Madura	W. Francis	1900	379
144	9788121258579	12th	Statistical Appendix For Madura		740	148
145	9788121258630	13th	The Nilgiris	W. Francis	2190	437
146	9788121234276	14th	Madras District Gazetteers Gazetteer Of The Nellore District Brought Upto 1938		1150	386
147	9788121258517	15th	North Arcot		590	118
148	9788121258494	16th, Vol. 1, Part I	Salem	F. J. Richards	1710	343
149	9788121258593	16th, Vol. 1, Part II	Salem	F. J. Richards	1800	360
150	9788121258456	17th	South Arcot	W. Francis	2400	480
151	9788121258470	18th	Statistical Appendix For South Canara		400	80
152	9788121258432	19th, Vol. 1st & 2nd	Tanjore: Main Volume and Statistical Appendix		2070	401
153	9788121258395	20th	Tinnevelly	H. R. Pate	2740	547
154	9788121258418	21st	Statistical Appendix For Tinnevelly		320	64
155	9788121258371	22nd, 1st & 2nd	Trichinopoly: Main Volume and Statistical Appendix	F. R. Hemingway	2440	487
156	9788121241953	23rd	Vizagapatam District Gazetteer	W. Francis	760	385

PUNJAB DISTRICT GAZETTEERS

S. NO.	ISBN NO.	VOLUME	TITLE	AUTHOR	PRICE	PAGES
157	9788121255943	1st	Ambala District 1883-84		620	124
158	9788121255967	2nd	Amritsar		1180	236
159	9788121255981	3rd	Delhi		1300	260
160	9788121256001	4th	Ferozepore		950	188
161	9788121256025	5th	Faridkot		350	70
162	9788121256049	6th	Gujranwala 1893-94		1270	254
163	9788121256063	7th	Gujrat	C. E. Luard	1140	228
164	9788121256087	8th	Gurdaspur 1891-92		1260	252
165	9788121256100	9th	Gurgaon 1883-4		1020	203
166	9788121256124	10th	Hazara	H. D. Watson	2290	458
167	9788121256148	11th	Hissar district and Lohar State		1840	367
168	9788121256162	12th	Hoshiarpur		1420	283
169	9788121256186	13th	Jhang		1070	213
170	9788121256209	14th	Jhelam		1010	202
171	9788121256223	15th	Jalandhar District 1883-84		540	108
172	9788121256247	16th, Vol. XIV-A	Jullundur District, with maps and Kapurthala		1990	398
173	9788121256261	17th, Pt. I	Kangra (Proper)		1450	290
174	9788121256285	17th, Pt. II	Kangra (Kulu, Lahual, Spiti)		1800	357
175	9788121256308	18th	Karnal		1930	386
176	9788121256322	19th	Kohat		1540	307
177	9788121256346	20th	The Lahore District 1883-84		1220	244
178	9788121256384	21st	Ludhiana and Maler Kotla		1680	335
179	9788121256407	22nd	Lyallpur		735	147
180	9788121256421	23rd	Mianwali		1170	234
181	9788121256445	24th	Montgomery	P. J. Fagan	1590	318
182	9788121258364	25th	Multan (1901-02)	E. D. Maclagan	2400	480
183	9788121258708	26th	The Rohtak District 1883-84		980	196
184	9788121258746	27th, Vol. III A	Dujana State 1904		500	16
185	9788121256483	28th	Shahpur District		1780	356
186	9788121256506	29th	Simla District		800	159

S. NO.	ISBN NO.	VOLUME	TITLE	AUTHOR	PRICE	PAGES
187	9788121256520	30th	The Chamba State		2040	408
188	9788121256544	31st	The Chenab Colony 1904		1550	310
189	9788121256568	32nd	Kalsia State		270	53
190	9788121256582	33rd	Suket and Mandi		770	154
191	9788121256605	34th	Phulkian States, Patiala Jind And Nabha 1904		2070	414
192	9788121256643	35th	Simla Hill States		2220	443
193	9788121256667	36th	Sirmur		920	183
			RAJPUTANA DISTRICT GAZETTEERS			
194	9789362088994	1st, Vol. I-A & B	Ajmer-merwara (Text and Statistics Tables)	C. C. Watson	1230	246
195	9789362080882	2nd. Vol. II-A & B	Mewar Residency (Text and Statistics Tables)	K.D. Erskine	1700	339
196	9789362088444	3rd, Vol. III-A & B	The Western Rajputana States Residency And The Bikaner Agency	K.D. Erskine	3590	718
			UNITED PROVINCES OF AGRA AND OUDH DISTRICT GAZETTEERS			
197	9789362087560	Vol. I	Agra	H. R. Nevill	2260	452
198	9789362082466	Vol. II	Aligarh	H. R. Nevill	1300	260
199	9789362089779	Vol. III	Allahabad	H. R. Nevill	2050	409
200	9789362081346	Vol. IV	Almora	H. G. Walton	1670	333
201	9789362085658	Vol. V	Azamgarh	D. L. Drake Brockman	1750	349
202	9789362080547	Vol. VI	Bahraich	H. R. Nevill	1410	281
203	9789362085214	Vol. VII	Ballia	H. R. Nevill	1750	350
204	9789362084668	Vol. VIII	Banda	D. L. Drake Brockman	1750	349
205	9789362086518	Vol. IX	Bara Banki	H. R. Nevill	1720	344
206	9789362084101	Vol. X	Bareilly	H. R. Nevill	1640	327
207	9789362086631	Vol. XI	Basti	H. R. Nevill	1610	321
208	9789362083814	Vol. XII	Benares	H. R. Nevill	2290	458
209	9789362086105	Vol. XIII	Bijnor	H. R. Nevill	1820	363
210	9789362081674	Vol. XIV	Budaun	H. R. Nevill	1890	378
211	9789362086891	Vol. XV	Bulandshahr	H. R. Nevill	2100	419
212	9789362081520	Vol. XVI	Cawnpore	H. R. Nevill	2210	442
213	9789362088031	Vol. XVII	Dehra Dun	H. G. Walton	1710	342
214	9789362088710	Vol. XVIII	Etah	E. R. Neave	1600	320
215	9789362082992	Vol. XIX	Etawah	D. L. Drake Brockman	1390	277
216	9789362082220	Vol. XX	Farrukhabad	E. R. Neave	1620	324
217	9789362083869	Vol. XXI	Fatehpur	H. R. Nevill	1890	377
218	9789362085962	Vol. XXII	Fyzabad	H. R. Nevill	1700	339
219	9789362087997	Vol. XXIII	Garhwal	H. G. Walton	1270	254
220	9789362089892	Vol. XXIV	Ghazipur	H. R. Nevill	1600	320
221	9789362085436	Vol. XXV	Gonda	H. R. Nevill	1650	330
222	9789362080271	Vol. XXVI	Gorakhpur	H. R. Nevill	1890	378
223	9789362086129	Vol. XXVII	Hamirpur	D. L. Drake Brockman	1390	277
224	9789362087638	Vol. XXVIII	Hardoi	H. R. Nevill	1680	336
225	9789362081636	Vol. XXIX	Jalaun	D. L. Drake Brockman	1180	236
226	9789362084309	Vol. XXX	Jaunpur	H. R. Nevill	1750	350
227	9789362084187	Vol. XXXI	Jhansi	D. L. Drake Brockman	1960	391
228	9789362089168	Vol. XXXII	Kheri	H. R. Nevill	1650	330
229	9789362086778	Vol. XXXIII	Lucknow	H. R. Nevill	1760	352
230	9789362088635	Vol. XXXIV	Mainpuri	H. R. Nevill	1740	348
231	9789362080424	Vol. XXXV	Meerut	H. R. Nevill	2170	434
232	9789362081087	Vol. XXXVI	Mirzapur	D. L. Drake Brockman	2430	486
233	9789362085443	Vol. XXXVII	Moradabad	H. R. Nevill	1900	380
234	9789362082763	Vol. XXXVIII	Muttra	D. L. Drake Brockman	2140	428
235	9789362089915	Vol. XXXIX	Muzaffarnagar	H. R. Nevill	2260	451
236	9789362086143	Vol. XL	Naini Tal	H. R. Nevill	1890	377
237	9789362086761	Vol. XLI	Partabgarh	H. R. Nevill	1560	312
238	9789362081124	Vol. XLII	Pilibhit	H. R. Nevill	1570	314
239	9789362084453	Vol. XLIII	Rai Bareli	H. R. Nevill	1610	322
240	9789362088284	Vol. XLIV	Rampur	H. R. Nevill	1170	234
241	9789362083654	Vol. XLV	Saharanpur	H. R. Nevill	2190	438
242	9789362083142	Vol. XLVI	Shahjahanpur	H. R. Nevill	1510	302
243	9789362083623	Vol. XLVII	Sitapur	H. R. Nevill	1590	317
244	9789362089939	Vol. XLVIII	Sultanpur	H. R. Nevill	1330	266
245	9789362080851	Vol. XLIX	Unnao	H. R. Nevill	1530	305

CENTRAL PROVINCES AND BERAR DISTRICT GAZETTEERS

AKOLA DISTRICT

VOLUME A—DESCRIPTIVE

BY

C. BROWN, I.C.S.

General Editor and Supdt. of Gazetteer } A. E. NELSON, I.C.S.

CALCUTTA

PRINTED AT THE BAPTIST MISSION PRESS

1910

PREFATORY NOTE.

Chapter II, History and Archæology, is by Major W. Haig, and Chapter IX, General Administration, by Mr. F. L. Crawford, Deputy Commissioner of the District. Chapter VII, Famine, is abstracted from the reports for Berār as a whole and from those by Mr. Rustomji Faridoonji for Bāsim in 1896—1897 and Akola in 1899—1900 and by Mr. F. W. Prideaux for Bāsim in 1899—1900. The greater part of the sections on Botany, Wild Animals, and Forests is taken from notes by Mr. R. H. Cole, Divisional Forest Officer, and the medical paragraphs are largely based on notes by Major P. F. Chapman, I.M.S., Civil Surgeon of Akola. The paragraphs on the Kānadi, Gopāl, Pāthrat, and Lonāri castes in Chapter III represent information collected in the District by Mr Adūrām Chaudhri, clerk in the office of the Superintendent of Gazetteer; and most of the local traditions given in the Appendix were recorded by my clerk, Mr. Mādhorao Rangnāth Shembekar, when I was on tour in the District. Information has been taken freely from Sir A. C. Lyall's Gazetteer for the Hyderābād Assigned Districts (1870), the Settlement Reports, and other official records. The reports for the original settlement were written by Major P. A. Elphinstone and Mr. R. R. Beynon, and those for the revision settlement by Major R. V. Garrett and Mr. F. W. Francis. Enquiries on some curious beliefs and customs were suggested by "Indian Folk Tales (Bilaspore)" by the Reverend E. M. Gordon, and many interesting points were mentioned by Mr. Padithyum Shankar Dās, Hospital

Assistant. I have tried to make no statements about creed or practice without either substantiating them by personal enquiry or else quoting my authority in the text. A large proportion of the book is based on information gathered in a special tour of the District, when several hundred people, representing all classes, were consulted either individually or in small groups. Capable critics have kindly revised the press copy, generally with approval. In practically every instance information was given with great cordiality; I must gladly acknowledge the kindly spirit shown.

The representation of vernacular terms has caused some difficulty. As far as possible these have been transliterated directly from Marāthi. In many cases, however, a word has already appeared in a Hindi form in other Gazetteers of this series; in such cases the Hindi form has generally been adopted. In other instances the local form differs from that of classical Marāthi, or a word has different local forms; it has then been necessary to select a form according to the particular circumstances. The cerebral letter which is transliterated by *r* in Hindi words has, according to a common and convenient practice, been represented by *d* in Marāthi words. The long accent has been omitted over capital initial vowels, generally over final vowels, and often over *i* and *u*.

C. B.

AKOLA:
The 6th March, 1909.

AKOLA DISTRICT GAZETTEER.

CONTENTS.

LIST OF MAPS AND PHOTOGRAPHS.

PARAGRAPH INDEX.

CHAPTER I.—GENERAL DESCRIPTION.

CHAPTER II.—HISTORY AND ARCHÆOLOGY.

CHAPTER III.—POPULATION.

CHAPTER IV.—AGRICULTURE.

CHAPTER V.—LOANS, PRICES, WAGES, MANUFACTURES, TRADE, AND COMMUNICATIONS.

CHAPTER VI.—FORESTS AND MINERALS.

CHAPTER VII.—FAMINE.

CHAPTER VIII.—LAND REVENUE ADMINISTRATION.

CHAPTER IX.—GENERAL ADMINISTRATION.

APPENDIX.—GAZETTEER OF TALUKS, TOWNS, IMPORTANT VILLAGES, RIVERS, AND HILLS.

Name of Place—

List of Deputy Commissioners who have held charge of the Akola District, with the dates of their periods of office.

		Names.	Period.	
			From	To
Berār.	1.	Mr. T. H. Bullock ..	1853	13- 9-1857
	2.	Captain Meadows Taylor	14- 9-1857	End of Feb. 1858
		Mr. T. H. Bullock ..	End of Feb. 1858	End of Dec. 1858
	3.	Captain J. G. Hamilton	Jan. 1859	....
	4.	Lieutenant J. G. Bell ..	1861	....
	5.	Captain J. Stubbs ..	1862	20- 5-1864
		Captain J. G. Bell ..	21- 5-1864	26-11-1864
	6.	Mr. J. G. Cordery ..	27-11-1864	23- 1-1866
	7.	Captain J. T. Bushby ..	24- 1-1866	10- 5-1866
		Mr. J. G. Cordery ..	11- 5-1866	8- 4-1867
	8.	Lieutenant R. Hudleston	9- 4-1867	28- 8-1868
	9.	Lieutenant R. Bullock	29- 8-1868	3-11-1868
		Lieutenant R. Hudleston	4-11-1868	24- 3-1869
	10.	Dastur Bymonji Jamasji	25- 3-1869	28- 3-1869
	11.	Mr. C. Hordern ..	29- 3-1869	21- 4-1869
	12.	Captain K. J. L. Mackenzie	22- 4-1869	23- 7-1869
		Mr. C. Hordern ..	24- 7-1869	3- 9-1870
	13.	Captain R. H. Salkhed	4- 9-1870	5- 9-1870
		Captain K. J. L. Mackenzie	6- 9-1870	25-11-1870
		Captain R. Hudleston ..	26-11-1870	7- 3-1872
	14.	Captain A. Farrer ..	8- 3-1872	10- 3-1872
	15.	Captain J. FitzGerald ..	11- 3-1872	7-11-1872
		Major J. G. Bell ..	8-11-1872	16- 3-1873
		Captain R. Bullock ..	17- 3-1873	3-11-1873
		Major J. T. Bushby ..	4-11-1873	18- 3-1874
		Major J. G. Bell ..	19- 3-1874	9- 4-1874

	Names.	Period.	
		From	To
	Captain K. J. L. Mackenzie	10- 4-1874	23- 8-1874
	Captain R. Bullock ..	24- 8-1874	16-11-1875
	Major J. G. Bell ..	17-11-1875	12- 3-1876
	Captain R. Bullock ..	1-33-1876	1- 4-1876
	Major D. W. Laughton ..	2- 4-1876	20- 4-1876
	Major R. Hudleston ..	21- 4-1876	12- 5-1876
16.	Major D. W. Laughton	13- 5-1876	12- 6-1876
	Major R. Hudleston ..	13- 6-1876	3- 3-1877
17.	Lieut.-Col. C. T. O. Mayne	4- 3-1877	23- 6-1878
	Captain A. Farrer ..	24- 6-1878	18- 7-1878
	Captain R. Bullock ..	19- 7-1878	31- 3-1879
	Major D. W. Laughton	1- 4-1879	22-10-1879
18.	Mr. E. J. Kitts ..	23-10-1879	2- 2-1880
	Major J. FitzGerald ..	3- 2-1880	3-10-1881
19.	Mr. A. J. Dunlop ..	4-10-1881	3-11-1881
	Major J. FitzGerald ..	4-11-1881	2- 5-1883
20.	Mr. H. S. Nicholetts ..	3- 5-1883	15- 7-1883
	Lieut.-Col. J. FitzGerald	16- 7-1883	10- 9-1884
21.	Colonel F. W. Grant ..	11- 9-1884	12-11-1884
	Lieut.-Col. J. FitzGerald	13-11-1884	4- 4-1885
22.	Mr. R. D. Hare ..	5- 4-1885	10- 5-1885
	Mr. H. S. Nicholetts ..	11- 5-1885	15- 2-1886
23.	Colonel H. De P. Rennick	16- 2-1886	17-12-1886
	Colonel F. W. Grant ..	18-12-1886	11- 4-1888
24.	Mr. A. Elliott ..	12- 4-1888	8- 8-1888
25.	Mr. R. Obbard, I.C.S. ..	9- 8-1888	24-10-1888
	Colonel F. W. Grant ..	25-10-1888	6- 7-1889
26.	Mr. C. A. W. Davies ..	7- 7-1889	9- 7-1889
	Mr. R. D. Hare ..	10- 7-1889	17- 3-1890
	Mr. C. A. W. Davies ..	18- 3-1890	20- 4-1890
	Mr. H. S. Nicholetts ..	21- 4-1890	2- 6-1890
27.	Muhammad Yasin Khan	3- 6-1890	2- 7-1890
	Mr. H. S. Nicholetts ..	3- 7-1890	3-12-1891
28.	Mr. H. Godwin-Austen	4-12-1891	6- 9-1892
29.	Mr. R. A. Simpson ..	7- 9-1892	12- 9-1892
30.	Captain J. G. Morris ..	13- 9-1892	27-10-1893
	Mr. R. D. Hare ..	28-10-1893	18- 3-1896
	Mr. R. A. Simpson ..	19- 3-1896	27- 5-1896
31.	Captain O. G. Ievers ..	28- 5-1896	8- 6-1896

	Names.	Period.	
		From	To
	Mr. R. A. Simpson ..	9- 6-1896	27- 7-1896
32.	Mr. F. W. A. Prideaux	28- 7-1896	20-10-1897
	Mr. R. D. Hare ..	21-10-1897	4-11-1897
	Mr. F. W. A. Prideaux	5-11-1897	17- 2-1898
	Mr. R. D. Hare ..	18- 2-1898	12- 3-1898
	Mr. F. W. A. Prideaux	13- 3-1898	25-10-1898
33.	Mr. Rustomji Faridoonji	26-10-1898	31- 3-1901
34.	Kumar Shri Harbhamji Rawaji	1- 4-1901	1- 5-1902
35.	Mr. A. C. Currie ..	2- 5-1902	6- 7-1902
	Kumar Shri Harbhamji Rawaji	7- 7-1902	23- 3-1903
	Mr. Rustomji Faridoonji	24- 3-1903	20-11-1903
36.	Major R. P. Colomb ..	21-11-1903	15- 6-1904
37.	Major F. R. M. C. de R. Mauduit	16- 6-1904	13- 9-1904
	Mr. Rustomji Faridoonji	14- 9-1904	28- 4-1906
	Major F. R. M. C. de R. Mauduit	29- 4-1906	27- 6-1907
38.	Mr. K. S. Jatar	28- 6-1907	25- 3-1908
39.	Mr. J. A. Bathurst, I.C.S.	26- 3-1908	7- 6-1908
40.	Mr. F. L. Crawford ..	8- 6-1908	....

AKOLA DISTRICT

CHAPTER I.

GENERAL DESCRIPTION.

BOUNDARIES AND PHYSICAL FEATURES.

General.

Akola District has an area of four thousand square miles and a population of three-quarters of a million, and pays twenty-five lākhs of rupees as land revenue. It is tenth in regard to size, and fourth in population, among the Districts of the Central Provinces and Berār. The Districts which have a larger population are Raipur, Amraoti, and Bilāspur; Nāgpur is slightly less in population and considerably less in area. Akola occupies roughly the middle of Berār, and is perhaps the most typical of the Berār Districts. The greater part of it is fertile plain country, but the Sātpurā plateau rises abruptly on its northern border and a range of steep hills runs across the middle of the southern tāluks. The people everywhere belong mostly to true agricultural castes long settled in the country, so that Kunbis form one-third of the whole population, but there are a certain number of more aboriginal descent, besides numerous recent immigrants; a few castes have pronounced criminal traditions.

Position and boundaries.

2. The District lies between latitudes 21° 16′ N. and 19° 51′ S. and longitudes 77° 44′ E. and 76° 38′ W.; its area is 4,110 square miles. Its length, measuring due north and south, varies at different points between 80 and 90 miles, and its breadth, taken east and west, is about 30 miles across Akot tāluk in the north, 60 across the middle of the District, and 45 across Bāsim tāluk in the south. Across the northern border lies the Melghāt tāluk of Amraoti District; on the east are the Daryāpur, Amraoti, and Chāndur tāluks of Amraoti District, and the Dārwhā and Pusad tāluks of Yeotmāl District; the Nizām's Dominions lie to the south; and the Mehkar, Chikhli, Khāmgaon, and Jalgaon tāluks of Buldāna District occupy the west. The border is marked on the north by the Sātpurās, and on half of the south by the Penganga river, but elsewhere no physical feature, as a rule, distinguishes it. The District is divided into six tāluks; Akot occupies the area between the Sātpurā ghāts and the Pūrna river; Bālāpur (on the west), Akola, and Murtizāpur (on the east), lie immediately south of the Pūrna, with the Nāgpur branch of the Great Indian Peninsula Railway running through them; and Bāsim and Mangrul lie to the south again.

Physical features.

3. The chief hills are the Sātpurās in the north and parts of the Ajantā system toward the south. The Sātpurā plateau bounds the view to anyone travelling north from Akola. It appears from a little distance as a long broken ridge springing precipitously from the plain; the sides are in fact generally very steep, but there is an intermediate strip of small foot-hills, with numerous valleys or gorges running up into the hills. A legend recounted in the classics about the Vindhyādri or Vindhyan

range is told locally about these hills. They are personified as a being who, in jealousy of the heavenly Mount Meru, raised himself in such gigantic bulk that neither could sunlight reach men nor prayers and sacrifices reach the gods; he now lies prostrate at the bidding of his spiritual guide Agastya, waiting only till that sage and his wife, ingenious pair, returning from Benāres, shall free him from this humility. The boundary of the District lies as a rule along the foot of the plateau, but a narrow strip runs three miles into the hills to Narnāla, where a large ancient fort is situated. The Sātpurās form the northern sides of a great valley, or small plain, 40 or 50 miles in breadth, called the Pāyanghāt; the river Pūrna flows westward through the midst of it. South of this plain lies the Bālāghāt, a region hilly in most parts but containing some considerable expanses of plain. In Akola District the southern wall of hills runs along just where Bāsim tāluk, on the south, meets Bālāpur and Akola on the north; it then passes eastward in distinguishable ranges through Murtizāpur and Mangrul tāluks. These hills are by no means on the scale of the Sātpūras, but they rise in many parts in *ghāts*, that is almost in precipices; for instance, the road from Akola to Bāsim climbs, in the south of Bālāpur tāluk, a steep ascent of more than a mile in length cleverly cut along a recess in the line of hills. In the south-east of Mangrul tāluk the hills form two very abrupt ranges with the river Arnāwati flowing between them; the ground on the south, where Mangrul and Pusad tāluks meet, is especially rugged, and forms a great obstacle to traffic. Hills again occupy the south-east and south-west of Bāsim tāluk, and run northwards at a few points into Bālāpur, and along the east of Akola tāluk, while the north-east of Murtizāpur is also hilly. Bāsim tāluk, lies mostly on high ground, which seems to extend, though without any marked ridge, north-east between Mangrul and Akola tāluks and past Kāranja town in Murtizāpur tāluk. This forms one of the great watersheds of the Indian continent. Streams on the northwest flow north to the Pūrna and are carried by it west to the Tāpti and thence into the Gulf of Sūrat in the Indian Ocean; those on the south and east flow into the Penganga, which joins the Godāvari and flows into the Bay of Bengal. The great plain of the Pāyanghāt, occupying most of the northern half of the District, consists chiefly of rich black soil, though as the hills in any direction are approached the ground begins to become rough and stony and the soil gets shallow and light; however, the western part of the middle of Bāsim, which is by far the largest of the tāluks, and the level parts of Mangrul have also good black soil. The plain country again is not entirely flat but forms very broad and gentle undulations. *Rabi* was formerly grown on a large scale in the good land, but cotton and jawāri are now the most common crops in all parts; rice is grown in the poor land in the east of Akola tāluk. In the north-east, about Dahihanda, Kutāsa, and Ghusar, salt-wells used to be worked, but the industry has now died out. Trees and groves are found in certain neighbourhoods all over the District, but there is also a great deal of unshaded ploughed land, especially in the rich soil which extends for ten miles or more north and south of the Pūrna. Thin forest covers most of the ridges of the Sātpurā and Ajanta hills.

4. Rivers. The Pūrna is the chief river of the District; it flows all the year but is not navigable. It rises in Amraoti District and flows due west across Akola into Buldāna. It forms the northern boundary of Murtizāpur, Akola, and Bālā-

pur tāluks, and the southern boundary of Akot. Its channel is in many places 100 feet deep and 200 yards wide; the banks are of soft earth but generally resist further encroachments successfully; trifling erosion, however, takes place at several points. The Penganga, which flows south-east across Bāsim tāluk, maintains its current throughout the year, and is the chief channel by which water is conveyed toward the south-east; it has a very considerable channel in parts but does not, within this District, attain to the size of the Pūrna. A good general description of the smaller streams is given in the Berār Gazetteer of 1870, p. 36: 'First as the waters 'leave the hills they run under one bank or both banks 'of scarped rock, sometimes 100 feet high. Then the 'undulated light soil tract at the foot of the hills is 'passed, sometimes with banks overhung with trees, at 'others through quite bare rock and *muram*. Further 'on, the banks are bordered with gardens and vegetation. 'Lastly, the stream gets into the region of the deep black 'soil; the banks are hence rugged and unsightly; the bed 'is sandy, and usually with a deep black mud fringe.' All the streams of the northern part of the District flow into the Pūrna. At one time the Shāhānur on the northern bank was of some importance, but during the famine of 1896-1897 it was diverted at Dahihanda in the south-east of Akot tāluk so that it joined the Pūrna almost immediately after entering the District. The results of the diversion are somewhat disquieting but are not yet fully apparent; the new channel carries off the water so rapidly that it is always dry except in brief intervals of violent flood; it is proposed to turn the stream back into the old channel. The chief tributaries of the Pūrna on the south bank are the Pedhi, Uma, Kātepurna, Lonār, Morna, Nirguna, and Man. Almost all of these, like the old Shāhānur, bend to the west just before joining it. The Pedhi flows across the north-eastern corner, and the Uma through the centre, of Murtizāpur tāluk, a well-watered area. The Kātepurna, which is the largest of all the tributaries, rises within a few miles of Bāsim and flows across the eastern side of Akola tāluk and the north-western corner of Murtizāpur; in its upper course, in the north of Bāsim tāluk, it passes through broken hilly country with some striking views. The Lonār flows through the northern half of Akola tāluk and is interesting because of an old suggestion to form a large tank upon it. The Morna rises in Bāsim tāluk and flows northward through Akola tāluk a few miles from the western border, passing also across the extreme south-eastern and north-eastern corners of Bālāpur tāluk. Akola town stands upon the Morna, and the wells of the town are probably much benefited by two dams which, though small, hold up the water of the river for three or four miles. The Nirguna river rises in Bāsim and flows north through Bālāpur tāluk, being called Bhuikund in its lower course. The Man rises in the Chikhli tāluk of Buldāna District and flows through Bālāpur tāluk, the town of Bālāpur standing at a point where the Mhais, on the west, joins the Man. Three miles further north the Bhuikund also unites with it, and the combined stream is known as the Man; this, for most of the rest of its course, forms the boundary between Bālāpur and Khāmgaon tāluks. The rivers formed additional defences for the old fort at Bālāpur, but now they interrupt the communications of the town, the Bhuikund in particular cutting it off from its railway station at Pāras. All these southern tributaries hold water throughout the year, though the Pūrna itself is the only river in the northern system which maintains constantly a good running stream. The Adān, Arnāwati, and Pus rise in Bāsim tāluk and flow through parts of Mangrul, finally joining the Penganga. The two former pass through the whole length of Mangrul, but neither attains an important size before passing beyond its borders. The Penganga has numerous small tributaries which hold water for about four months in the year and are used to a slight extent for irrigation. The Bembala river nominally rises at a holy spot in Kāranja town, in the south of Murtizāpur tāluk; after flowing north through half of the tāluk it turns to the east and finally passes into the Wardha in Yeotmāl District. The line of the Ajanta watershed can be traced for nearly 70 miles from Bāsim town north to Shelu, north-east to Kāranja, north again to Kāmargaon, and north-east past Kuram; at many points neighbouring watercourses could be found, the water of which flows into opposite seas.

Elevation.

5. The elevation of the plain portion of the District seems to vary between 900 and 1100 feet, but full information is not available; Akola is said to be 925 feet above sea-level, while Kuram, further east beside the railway, is 1013. Bāsim tāluk in the south forms a plateau, the least heights recorded being 1560 feet at Wādi and 1582 at Khedkhed, in the north; the ground level at Bāsim circuit-house is 1840 feet; the greatest height recorded is 1877 at Jāmbrun in the middle, while other hills in the north of the tāluk are also more than 1800 feet high. Mangrul tāluk is also high, the least height recorded being 1393 feet at Kārli in the east; the higher parts of the tāluk vary between 1407 and 1800 feet. The hilly land in the south of Akola and Bālāpur tāluks varies from 1200 to 1600 feet, land in Māhān and Rudrama in the former being 1206 and 1384 respectively, while in the latter Khānāpur is 1521 and Gāwandgaon 1579. In the east of Murtizāpur are points of less than 1100 feet elevation, such as Bapori (1011), Hinganwādi

(1041), and Pimpri (1087); the greatest height given in the tāluk is 1500 feet at Kāmatwāda in the south-east.

GEOLOGY.

Geology.

6. The geology of Akola District is very simple. Hills of Deccan trap run along the northern border and across the southern half of the District, and trap constantly appears through the soil in most other parts. The Pūrna river or some ancient lake has, however, deposited a belt of alluvial soil which stretches completely across the northern half of the District, and the other rivers are bordered by similar black soil. The Pūrna alluvium extends roughly from the hills in the north to the railway, but the soil further south, though it does not completely conceal its bed of trap, is largely alluvial. Calcareous conglomerate or concrete is of common occurrence in every part of the alluvium. Fragments of bone or fossil teeth of ruminants are occasionally found in it, but apparently no large accumulation, or even large fragment, of these fossils has been discovered, nor are flints found. Much of the alluvium produces effluorescences of salts of soda and, especially on the north of the river, wells were formerly sunk to obtain salt; some of these wells near Dahihanda in the south-east of Akot tāluk were considerably over 100 feet in depth. The trap in the tract south of Akola contains all the usual varieties of amygdaloid, zeolithic, columnar, hard, gray, and softer traps; their stratification is always nearly horizontal and very perceptible; but no peculiarities have been noted worthy of mention.

BOTANY.

Botany.

7. The District is not well wooded, especially in the fertile plain country through which the Pūrna flows, but a fair number

of trees and groves are scattered over it. The main tract of forests runs along a range of hills which passes from east to west across the middle of the District about 20 miles south of Akola. There are also a few *bābul bans*, containing scarcely anything but *bābul*, a few areas of mixed growth, and other areas reserved chiefly for the supply of grass. The growth in all the forests except the *bābul bans* is deciduous, containing a variety of species. The most valuable species is teak (*Tectona grandis*) which is largely used for the posts and rafters of buildings. The tree unfortunately seldom grows to a large size in this District. It is generally unsound, over-matured, and stag-headed, and is thus useless as timber. The species next in value to teak is *ain* (*Terminalia tomentosa*), and the next again are *dhawara* (*Anogeissus latifolia*), *lenda* (*Lagerstrœmia parviflora*), and *bijāsāl* (*Pterocarpus Marsupium*) These are also used for building by the poorer classes in villages. *Beherā* (*Terminalia belerica*) and *harrā* (*Terminalia Chebula*) are valued for their fruit, but the latter is not found in sufficient quantities for exportation. *Nīm* (*Melia Azadirachta*), mango (*Mangifera indica*), *karan* or *karanji* (*Pongamia glabra*), and some of the *Ficus* species are often seen along roadsides and, being evergreens, provide most valuable shade during the hot weather. *Salāi* (*Boswellia serrata*) is a common tree, but is not much used either for fuel or for timber. The fruit of the *bel* (*Aegle Marmelos*), *tembhurni* (*Diospyros melanoxylon*), *chār* (*Buchanania latifolia*), and the various species of *Zizyphus* are eaten by the poorer classes. Mahuā (*Bassia latifolia*) is largely used for the manufacture of country spirit. Other species found in the forests are *ganher* (*Cochlospermum Gossypium*), *katsāwar* (*Bombax malabaricum*), *kad* or *ghuyarā* (*Sterculia urens*), *bāharukh* (*Ailantus excelsa*), *rohan* (*Soymida febrifuga*), *kusam* (*Schleichera trijuga*)—though this is very scarce—*moi* (*Odina Wodier*), *bhilāwa* or *bība* (*Semecarpus Anacardium*), *tiwas* (*Ougeinia dalbergioides*) *amaltās* or *bādha* (*Cassia Fistula*), *haldū* (*Adina cordifolia*), *kalamb* (*Stephegyne parvifolia*), *kahu* (*Terminalia Arjuna*), and some *Grewia* and *Albizzia* species.

The principal shrubs are *parijātak* (*Nyctanthes Arbor-tristis*), which bears a sweet-smelling flower, largely used for garlands, *umar* or *sheng* (*Helicteres Isora*), *ber* (*Zizyphus nummularia*), *dhaiti* (*Woodfordia floribunda*), and *nirgudi* or *shembālu* (*Vitex Negundo*). No large species of creepers are found, but the most common kinds are *mālkāmni* (*Celastrus paniculata*), *palās* (*Butea superba*), and the Indian sarsaparilla (*Hemidesmus indicus*). Various grasses are found, including *rosa* or *tikhādi*, from one variety of which *rūsa* oil, very valuable for the preparation of scent, is extracted, *kusali*, *muselsurya*, *khansa*, *lona*, *pawana*, and *shāhāda* ; the two last are especially valued for grazing. The Forest Department is considering a project largely to develop the industry of extracting *rūsa* oil ; careful regulation is needed to safeguard the purity of the oil, or the industry would be shortlived. Bamboo is very scarce and the supply is not equal to the demand ; a few clumps of *Dendrocalamus strictus* are found.

WILD ANIMALS, ETC.

Wild animals, etc.

8. The Berār Gazetteer of 1870 contains an account of the wild animals of Akola District which is interesting both in itself and for purposes of comparison : 'Wild animals abound-'ed when this District first came into British hands ; 'large waste tracts covered with jungle gave them ample 'shelter. Now a single tiger may be occasionally heard 'of in the undulating tracts north and south, whither 'they venture under shelter of the hills and jungle.

'Leopards are very uncommon indeed, while panthers 'are comparatively plentiful in the rugged country along 'the hills; they live and hunt in families. Hyenas and 'wolves are not uncommon, but they do not exist in 'sufficient number to cause uneasiness to the people. 'Jackals, foxes, and wild cats continue to be numerous. 'They are not disturbed except by the Pārdhis (hunting 'tribe) for their sinews; they are tolerated by the agri-'culturists for the good they do in keeping down field 'rats and such-like vermin destructive to crops and 'grain, and in removing carrion. Black bears are to be 'found in the coverts bordering the hills; during the rains '(the rutting season) they are said to grow bold and to 'be met with in some numbers; while the crops are on 'the ground they are seldom to be seen, but during the 'hot weather they are to be found near the waterpools; 'these failing they make nightly excursions down to the 'valley and may be intercepted at early dawn returning 'to their lairs gorged with roots, nuts, and the day's sup-'ply of water. The moist coolness of the gardens of the 'betel and plantain attracts tigers during the hot weather. 'The gardeners are reluctant to inform against a tiger or 'panther who may have taken up his quarters in their 'plantations, for they have a superstition that a garden 'plot ceases to produce from the moment one of these 'animals is killed there....Our stock of 'ruminantia' 'is not to be slighted, considering the immense strides 'cultivation has made. We have the sāmbhar and the 'spotted deer, with three kinds of antelope--the common 'antelope, the *chikāra*, and the *nīlgai*. Wild boar in 'herds are to be heard of everywhere in the District; for-'merly they used to be seen everywhere. The snaring 'Pārdhi commits great havoc among the antelope and '*chikāra*. Provided with a trained bullock which pre-'tends to graze constantly without doing so, and a small 'blind (an earth-coloured rag stretched over four sticks) 'the Pārdhi goes, seen, round and round the animal or 'birds he intends to take, fixing his snares in a regular 'maze. The prepared sinews of animals and birds are the 'materials used. The snares are running nooses fixed on 'pegs, which are all connected. I (Mr. J. H. Burns) have 'witnessed four antelopes thrown at once, and ten pea-'fowl out of a dozen captured in a single setting. In 'game birds there are the bustards (*Otis Edwardsii*) in 'great plenty. Peafowl are to be found in plenty along 'the hills and where there are gardens. Florican (*Syphe-'otides auritus*, not to be confused with the Bengal flori-'can) inhabit the *ramnās*, grass lands. The curlew, both 'black and white, is a very common bird. There are two 'varieties of partridges in great plenty—the black species 'is to be found in the ripe wheat fields—and there are 'several sorts of quails. Ducks of various kinds, and teal, 'are to be found in the Pūrna, mostly to the westward, in 'large flocks. The alligator is to be found in all the deep-'er pools of the Pūrna and Kātepūrna rivers. The 'rivers abound in fish. Mr. Nicholetts, Assistant Com-'missioner, says, "The fishermen are very great adepts at 'netting. They drag with great precision; sometimes 'they meet with an active old stager, but by signals they 'indicate his course to each other and will make a capture 'of a large fish that had passed four or five of them in a 'regular hunt." In respect to nets Mr. Nicholetts enu-'merates—"First, the large stationary net, to which the 'fish are driven down by a number of men getting in the 'water and advancing towards the net. Second, the drag 'net, enclosing gradually any pool where fish are known 'to stay. Third, a peculiar kind of large shrimping-net, 'which is placed at the mouth of a rapid where there is 'little water; the mouth of the net is kept open by means 'of a small stick three feet long, which falls and lets it 'shut when the fish (enter). Fourth, the cast net similar 'to the English one. Fifth, the shrimping-net, a bag-like 'net fixed to three sticks forming a triangle. The fisher-'men are principally Bhois. The *maral* is constantly 'shot during the heat of the day; they come to the sur-'face and skim about for hours; a tree overhanging a 'pool is the best place to shoot from." During freshes 'the fish flock up every nala and are easily captured. 'River-fish become in a manner stupefied during high 'floods and come gasping towards the banks, where they 'are knocked on the head.'

Cultivation has now (1909) extended so much and there is so little forest that wild animals are comparatively scarce. All kinds of game, but especially sāmbhar, suffered very severely in the famine of 1899-1900. A "Narnāla tiger" is sometimes to be found near the ancient fortress of that name in the extreme north of Akot tāluk, or a stray tiger may enter the south of the District, but this is all. Panthers (*Felis pardus*), *M. bībat*, *H. tendua*, are fairly common, especially near the belt of forest which runs across the middle of the southern part of the District; they cause considerable loss of small cattle, and are generally thought to have very little fear of men. The fat of a tiger or panther is almost universally valued as a cure for rheumatism and paralysis. It is sometimes said that panthers like to drink the blood of their prey before it gets cold but to leave the flesh till next day. Panthers, wolves, and hyenas are all said occasionally to carry off children from villages; but the deaths from wild animals in the last three years have in fact amounted only to five. Wolves (*Canis pallipes*), *M. lāndga*, *H. bheriya*, are rare but are known all over the District. A forest official says he has seen a single wolf hide behind a bush while the rest of the pack drove a herd of buck past him. According to popular tradition this is a frequent stratagem, but the solitary wolf is half buried in the ground, and if he fails to make a capture is torn to pieces by the rest of the pack. Two wolves hunting together are similarly said to show marvellous skill in halving their prey. A few castes kill wild animals for the sake of the Government reward; Pāl Pārdhis, for instance, would snare several wolves at a time and beat them to death with long sticks, perhaps not escaping unwounded themselves. The jackal (*Canis aureus*), *kolhā*, is common throughout the District and is a valuable scavenger. The wild dog (*Cyon Dukhunensis*), *M. jangli kutrā*, *H. kol kuttā*, *son kuttā*, has increased of late years and is very destructive to game. Hyenas (*Hyaena striata*), *taras*, are common but very shy. The wild cat (*Felis chaus*) is common everywhere and very destructive to feathered game; it often hides in cactus or in stacks of *kadbi*; some people keep its testicles, which have an odour resembling musk. The common fox (*Vulpes Bengalensis*), *khokad*, the mongoose (*Herpestes mungo*), *mungus*, and the hare (*Lepus ruficaudatus*) are all common; Pārdhis say that a mongoose when fighting with a snake frequently stops and sniffs the ground. The black bear (*Melursus ursinus*), *M. aswal*, *H. bhālu*, *rīchh*, is fairly common in the denser forests, especially in Bālāpur tāluk. It is popularly said to be deaf, and its fat is supposed to alleviate pain and to promote the growth of hair; a vicious beast is occasionally known to have killed two or three human beings. The wild boar (*Sus cristatus*) is scattered everywhere, and causes much damage to crops. Only two kinds of monkeys are found, the black-faced *Semnopithecus entellus*, and the red-faced *Macacus rhesus*; the former is common, but the latter very rare. They cause a great deal of harm to the roofs of houses, so that in some places corrugated iron is preferred to other materials for roofing because it suffers less from them. A young monkey sometimes delights to swing to and fro between two branches just out of reach of an excited dog barking below. The monkeys at Kherda Buzruk, on the main road from Murtizāpur to Kāranja, have become tame enough to take food from the hands of people passing. Monkeys are regarded as sacred by Hindus throughout the District. Among deer and antelopes, the sāmbhar (*Cervus unicolor*) has become so rare that it is almost extinct. The *chītal* or spotted deer (*Cervus axis*) is fairly common, especially on river banks and in scrub jungle. The *nīlgai* (*Boselephas tragocamelus*), *rohi*, and especially the black buck (*Antelope cervicapra*), *haran*, are very common and cause great harm to the crops. Both the four-horned deer (*Tetracerus quadricornis*), *mendal*, *chausing* or *chaurang*, and the barking-deer (*Cervulus muntjac*) are occasionally found; and the *chikāra* is common in some parts. The iguana, *ghodpad*, lives in burrows on the banks of streams. It is said to take such a firm hold of the sides of the burrow that it can hardly be pulled out. Its skin is used for making a kind of drum called *khanjiri*, and its flesh is not only eaten by some castes but is considered a good tonic for horses.

The chief edible game-birds are the peafowl (*Pavo cristatus*), which is chiefly found near streams, sand grouse (*Pterocles exustus*), grey partridge (*Ortygornis Ponticerianus*), and the common quail, which are found, though not plentifully, in all parts. The green pigeon (*Crocopus Chlorigaster*) is found when the *Ficus* species are in fruit. The blue rock-pigeon (*Columba intermedia*) frequents temples and wells, and the bustard (*Epodotis Edwardsii*) is sometimes seen. Among water-birds are different species of wild duck and teal, plover, snipe, the *sāras*, crane, curlew, and *kullung*

Among fish are the *maral*, *bām* or *wāhir*, *rahu*, *pāhādin*, *dokadā*, *tām*, *nain*, *khekadā*, *kāso* or *kachhwā*, *kāwasi* or *kālosi*, *tewarā*, *bhātmachhi*, *tepari*, *bhārki*, *chāl*, *pāpta*, *sāndkol*, *malgannā*, *katarnā*, and *jhingā*.

RAINFALL AND CLIMATE.

Rainfall and climate.

9. The records of rainfall and climate are incomplete and somewhat untrustworthy; for instance, the rain-gauges away from headquarters are often full of stones through the dry months. Available statistics show, however, that the average rainfall for Akola District for the 14 years ending in 1908 was—June 4 inches, July 9½, August 6½, September 4½, October 1, and for each of the remaining months ¼ or less, the total being 27 inches; it is possible that this is unduly low on account of the extraordinary deficiency of the famine year 1899-1900. Records for the 29 years ending in 1906 show that the average fall of the old Akola District was 32 inches, while the 27 years ending in 1904 gave Bāsim District an average of 39 inches. The Berār Gazetteer of 1870 estimates the fall in the plain tāluks of the Province at 27 inches and that of the country above the ghāts at over 30 inches, but this was admittedly uncertain. It is said all over the District that the rainfall has greatly decreased during the last two generations; such a tradition is of doubtful value but is partly supported by the fact that *kharīf* crops have been largely substituted for *rabi*, uncertain rainfall being one of the reasons for this. The spread of cultivation has involved the removal of a number of large trees and a great deal of scrub jungle, and the introduction of some deliberate drainage; on the other hand the fields are covered with young crops soon after the beginning of the rainy season, the surface of

the ground is kept soft and permeable, and drainage is often checked to prevent soil being carried away.

10. The rains are traditionally expected to break in *Mrig nakshatra*, in the beginning of June. A fairly heavy downpour is then preferred, especially for such occasional fields of cotton as in the south are sown before rain comes; if the first fall is scanty and is succeeded by a break of several days the seeds germinate but again wither away. However, cotton is generally sown only after the first rain has fallen; it is important then that there should be repeated breaks of some days, partly because the crops are injured by constant wet weather, partly because weeding is almost impossible except in such breaks—the bullock hoe cannot be put in. The hire of labourers for weeding rises so high when a break is long delayed that poor cultivators have occasionally to let their fields be choked with grass just because it costs too much to have them cleared. The time and degree of the late rains make all the difference between the *kharīf* crops being very good and very poor. Cultivators divide the *Hasta nakshatra*, about a fortnight in September or October, into four *chiran*, parts, called respectively iron, brass (*tāmbal-pitalche*, copper-brass), silver, and gold, according to the value of rain falling in them; rain in the next *nakshtara*, *Swāti*, is better still, and is called pearl-rain. *Rabi* crops are generally sown in September and October, wheat a fortnight later than the others. They require a fairly heavy aggregate rainfall but are not quite so much affected by its time, nor are *rabi* crops by any means as important as *kharīf*. Rain during the rest of the year is scanty and of little importance; heavy rain or hail may knock off the bolls of cotton, but this rarely occurs; timely showers may help *rabi* crops, but upon the whole dry weather is likely to

The rainy season.

be most useful during seven or eight months of the year; cotton is said to be injured by overcast, cloudy weather. For agricultural purposes, at least in regard to *kharīf* crops, the timeliness of the rain is of far more importance than its quantity; a year of light but well-distributed rainfall would be far better than one of heavy rain concentrated in a short period (though again it was shown in 1907-1908 that if fair rain continues till near the end of August there is no danger of a total failure of the *kharīf* crops). On the other hand if the total fall is deficient for successive monsoons the supply of drinking water for man and beast becomes inadequate in many villages. Differences in depth and slope of soil, or in the nature of a water-supply, also cause variations in the requirements of individual villages.

Temperature.

11. Statistics of temperature for Akola town are available for 38 years between 1868 and 1908. According to the average of the extremes of that period, it appears that the temperature in the shade varies in January between 44 and 92½, in May between 73 and 114½, in August between 70 and 91½, and in November between 48 and 93. The lowest temperature on record in January is 37 degrees in 1873; only 4 years are recorded in which the thermometer fell below 40 degrees in that month. The highest temperature for May is 120 degrees in 1868; 117 degrees or more have been recorded in eight years. During the first half of the hot weather the temperature of Akola often heads the daily list for Western India, with Nāgpur and Amraoti usually a little below; changes in the roof under which the thermometer is kept may have caused some variations in the readings. The climate in the plain tāluks is always hot by day; occasional nights in December, January, and February feel cold, but frost is almost unknown. The increasing

heat is usually noticeable during February, and the hot season seems to set in during the last ten days of March; but a good breeze almost always prevails during the hot weather and, where no buildings obstruct it, makes the nights comparatively cool and comfortable. The hill tāluks, Bāsim and Mangrul, have a slightly heavier rainfall and slightly cooler climate than the others. The rains are by far the least healthy season, but the District as a whole is by no means unhealthy. Numerous reports remark on the easygoing way in which the native of Berār works, and this may be in part a concession to the demands of an exhausting climate; but officials of different races discover that hard work is by no means impossible.

CHAPTER II.

HISTORY AND ARCHÆOLOGY.

W. HAIG.

HISTORY.

Hindu period.

12. It is not possible to compile a connected historical account of an area which, until little more than half a century ago, was never a distinct political entity; and the history of the Akola District must therefore be, in the main, a chronicle of noteworthy events which have occurred at various places within its present boundaries. The District, with the rest of Berār, must have formed part of the kingdom of Vidarbha in heroic times, if the kingdom described under that name in the Mahābhārat ever existed, which may be doubted.

Berār formed part of the empire of Asoka Maurya (B.C. 272—231), but before the disruption of that empire in 184 A.D. was governed by an independent ruler referred to as the rājā of Vidarbha. Neither his name nor his dynasty is mentioned, but we may perhaps assume him to be one of the Sakas, Pahlavas, or Yavanas, who made extensive conquests in the northern Deccan, Berār. If this assumption be correct we may identify him with the Saka satrap Rudradāman or his successor. It is probable, however, that southern Berār, including part of the Akolā District, was within the dominions governed by Pulumāyi II, the twenty-fourth king of the Andhra dynasty. This dynasty came to an end about 236 A.D., and from this time to 550 we know very little of the history of the Deccan; but Berār, with the rest of Mahārāshtra, was probably governed during a great part of this period by princes of the Rāshtrakūta or Ratta clan, which in the middle of the eighth century became the leading power in the Deccan. There is, however, some trace of another dynasty, that of the Vākātakas, whose capital is conjectured to have been in the present Chānda District of the Central Provinces, and who probably ruled over the whole of Berār, but their dates, unfortunately, are at present so uncertain that a recapitulation of their names cannot be said to add to our knowledge of local history. In 550 the Chālukya dynasty was founded, and in the early days of its existence its dominions included Berār and several States to the north. In the middle of the eighth century Dantidurgā the Rāshtrakūta extinguished the western branch of this dynasty and made himself supreme in the Deccan, which his successors ruled for two centuries and a quarter. In 973 a descendant of the Chālukyas overthrew the last of the Rāshtrakūtas but was not able at once to establish his authority in the northern provinces of the kingdom which had been ruled by them, and Berār remained part of the dominions of the rājā of Mālwā until the Chālukya reconquered it in 995. In the latter half of the twelfth century the power of the Chālukyas was broken by rebellions, and towards the end of that century the northern provinces of their dominions were seized by the Yādavas of Deogiri.

Muhammadan invasion of the Deccan.

13. The last independent rājā of Deogiri was Rāmachandra, styled Rāmdeo by Muhammadan historians, who was defeated in 1294 by Alā-ud-dīn, the nephew and son-in-law of Jalāl-ud-dīn Fīroz Shāh Khiljī of Delhi, and became a tributary of the emperors of Delhi. Rāmachandra was succeeded in 1309 by his eldest son Shankar, who rebelled, but was defeated and slain, his dominions being annexed to the empire. The Akola

District thus came for the first time directly under Muhammadan administration. In the confusion which followed the death of the emperor Alā-ud-dīn and the assassination of his minister Malik Naib in 1316, Harpāl, a son-in-law of Rāmachandra, seized on his father-in-law's kingdom and ruled it for a short time as an independent king; but in 1318 he was defeated by Kutb-ud-dīn Mubārak Shāh of Delhi, who caused him to be flayed alive, and placed his head above one of the gates of Deogiri.

Muhammadan period.

14. Kutb-ud-dīn Mubārak Shāh was assassinated in 1321 and the usurper who ascended his throne was defeated and slain before the end of that year by the Turkī governor of the Punjab, who was raised to the imperial throne under the title of Ghiyās-ud-dīn Tughlak Shāh. In his reign and in that of his son Muhammad-bin Tughlak, who succeeded him in 1325, the District was frequently traversed by expeditions from Hindustān to the Deccan, and in 1339 Muhammad-bin Tughlak transferred the capital of the empire from Dehli to Deogiri, which he re-named Daulatābād.

Rebellion of the amīrs of the Deccan.

This measure, which probably invested Berār, and especially its western districts, with an artificial and fleeting importance, was afterwards revoked, and before the end of Muhammad's reign Delhi was once more the capital of India, while the oppressive rule of this most eccentric emperor provoked insurrections in all outlying provinces of the empire. In 1347 the centurions of the Deccan rebelled and elected one of their number as their king. Muhammad marched southwards and defeated them, but their king, Ismail Fateh, an aged Afghān who had taken the title of Nasīr-ud-dīn [1] Shāh,

[1] Or, according to some authorities, Nāsir.

took refuge in Daulatābād, and there held out until the emperor was called northwards by news of a rebellion in Gujarāt, when the centurions of the Deccan fell upon the imperial troops which had been left to invest Daulatābād, defeated them, and proclaimed Hasan, entitled Zafar Khān, king of the Deccan in place of the aged Ismail, who abdicated on finding that kingship had its responsibilities as well as its delights. Hasan assumed royal power in the Deccan under the title of Alā-ud-dīn Bahman[1] Shāh, and made Gulbarga, where he had held a *jāgīr* before he was called to the throne, his capital.

The Bahmanis.

15. Bahman Shāh divided his kingdom into four *tarafs* or provinces, each under the governorship of a *tarafdār* or provincial governor, whose powers were very extensive. These four provinces were Berār, Daulatābād, Bīdar and Gulbarga. Muhammad Shāh Bahmanī, who succeeded his father in 1358, elaborated the organization of the four provinces and bestowed on each *tarafdār* a distinctive title, that of the governor of Berār being *Majlis-i-Ali*.

Rebellion in Daulatābād.

16. In 1366, while Muhammad Shāh Bahmanī was waging war against Vijayanagar, Bahrām Khān Māzandarāni, the deputy governor of Daulatābād, rebelled at the instigation of a Marātha named Kondbā Deva, and was joined by many of the nobles of Berār who were related to him. The rebellion was suppressed and the leaders made good their escape into Gujarāt. At about this time highway robbery was rife in the Deccan, and Muhammad Shāh found it necessary to adopt stringent measures for its suppression. The male-

---

[1] This was his correct title as a contemporary inscription and legends on coins show. The fantastic titles ascribed to him by most historians have their origin in foolish traditions.

factors were beheaded and their heads were sent to the capital, where the tale of heads collected amounted to 20,000. We may assume that Berār contributed its share, and that the " proud and refractory Hatgars " of Bāsim, afterwards mentioned in the Ain-i-Akbarī, had their share both in the depredations and in the punishment which followed them.

Famine.

17. Akolā suffered with the rest of Berār from the severe famine which occurred in the reign of Muhammad Shāh,[1] the fifth king of the Bahmani dynasty, who reigned from 1378 to 1397, but no details of the extent of the suffering in this particular tract of Berār have been handed down.

Ahmad Shāh visits Berār and repairs Narnāla.

18. In 1425 Ahmad Shāh, the ninth king of the dynasty, was compelled to visit his northern province owing to the invasion of eastern Berār by the Gonds. After driving the intruders from his dominions he halted for a year at Ellichpur, and while there built the fort of Gāwīl and repaired that of Narnāla in the Akolā District. These expressions, which are used by Firishta in connection with the two forts, have been understood to mean that the antiquity of Narnāla is superior to that of Gāwīlgarh, but they were probably used loosely, for there is no building in Narnāla which can be assigned with any certainty to a period earlier than that of Ahmad Shāh's sojourn in Ellichpur, and the evidence for the supposition that the covered cisterns in the fort were the handiwork of Jains of prae-Muhammadan times is most unsatisfactory.

[1] Some writers, in deference to Firishta, who is obstinately mistaken regarding this king's name, style him Mahmūd in spite of the evidence of coins, inscriptions, and other historians. Mahmūd was his father's name—*vide Journal of the Asiatic Society of Bengal*, vol. lxxiii, part I, extra number, 1904, pp. 6, 7

War between the Deccan and Khāndesh.

19. Ahmad Shāh died in 1435 and was succeeded by his eldest son Alā-ud-dīn Ahmad II, who had married the daughter of Nasīr Khān Fārukī, ruler of Khāndesh. Alā-ud-dīn Ahmad neglected his lawful wife for a Hindu maiden, the daughter of Rainal rājā of Sangameshwar in the Konkan, and the *malika-i-jahān*, or 'queen of the world,' as the principal queen of the Bahmani kings was always styled, wrote to her father and complained of her husband's conduct. Nasīr Khān was not strong enough to attack his powerful son-in-law single-handed and therefore his first step was to detach the nobles of Berār from their allegiance. In this he succeeded to a great extent by setting forth the religious merit which would be acquired by fighting for a descendant of the Khalīfah Umar al-Fāruk, though he did not scruple to enlist the aid of infidel Gonds, and apparently Korkūs also, against a brother Muslim Having thus corrupted many of the nobles of Berār, Nasīr Khān invaded the province, while the treacherous officers plotted to capture the Khān-ī-Jahān, the governor of Berār, who remained faithful to his master. He, perceiving their design, retired to Narnāla, where he was besieged by the rebels, but contrived to send a message to Alā-ud-dīn Ahmad Shāh informing him of the state of affairs. Khalaf Hasan Basrī, governor of Daulatābād, was ordered to march northwards and meet the invader, and the Khān-ī-Jahān succeeded in escaping from Narnāla and joined Khalaf Hasan at Mehkar. It has been mentioned that Nasīr Khān had obtained a promise of assistance from the "Gonds," and Khalaf Hasan, in order to prevent these allies of the enemy from ravaging Berār and falling on his flank, despatched some of the Deccani officers and troops who were with him to Bālāpur and Ellichpur. From the situation of these two places it

appears likely that the "Gonds" mentioned as Nasīr Khān's allies were in fact Korkūs of the Melghāt, for the Muhammadan historians, like the British officers first appointed to administer Berār, fell into the error of believing the Korkūs to be Gonds.

Defeat of the Sultān of Khāndesh.

20. Khalaf Hasan defeated Nasīr Khān at Rohankhed and drove him out of Berār and, having defeated him once more in the neighbourhood of his capital, returned to the Deccan with much plunder.

War between Mālwā and the Deccan.

21. In 1462, the year after the accession of the boy king Nizām Shāh, the twelfth of the Bahmanids, Mahmūd Shāh of Mālwā invaded the Deccan, entering the Bahmani dominions by the route followed by Nasīr Khān in 1436, and occupied Berār. He defeated the Deccanis at Kandahār, about 70 miles north of Bīdar, which Ahmad Shāh Bahmani had made his capital, advanced on Bīdar, captured the city, and laid siege to the citadel. Mahmūd Shāh of Gujarāt now advanced to the frontier of Berār with 80,000 horse in order to support Nizām Shāh, and Mahmūd Gāwān, an officer of Nizām Shāh's, busied himself in raising troops until, after receiving aid from Mahmūd of Gujarāt, he was able to take the field with 40,000 Deccani and Gujarāti horse. He sent 10,000 Deccani horse into Berār to clear the province of the intruders and to harass Mahmūd of Mālwā on his retreat, and hastened southwards towards Bīdar, where he compelled Mahmūd of Mālwā to raise the siege. The army of Mālwā retreated northwards through eastern Berār and the Melghāt, in which latter tract it was led astray and almost destroyed by the Korkūs, and Mahmūd Shāh of Mālwā reached Māndū, his capital, with much difficulty and with the mere remnant of an army. In the following year, however, he again invaded the

Bahmani dominions, and advanced through Berār as far as Daulatābād, but, on hearing that Mahmūd Shāh of Gujarāt was again marching to the aid of Nizām Shāh, he repented of his enterprise and returned to his capital.

Famine.

22. In 1471 Muhammad Shāh, who had succeeded his brother, Nizām Shāh, in 1463, appointed Fateh-ullāh Imād-ul-Mulk to the governorship of Berār, and two years later Berār suffered from a terrible famine which destroyed large numbers and caused wholesale emigration to Gujarāt and Mālwā.

Redistribution of the provinces of the Deccan.

23. In 1480 Muhammad Shāh divided the four original *tarafs* of the Bahmani kingdom into eight provinces and under this arrangement Berār was divided into the two provinces of Gāwīl in the north and Māhur in the south. The position of the line of demarcation between these two has not been recorded, but it is probable that it followed the line of the northern face of the plateau of the Bālāghāt, and that the tāluks of Bāsim and Mangrul were included in the province of Māhur while the rest of the District was included in Gāwīl. This measure, which was most distasteful to some of the older *tarafdārs* whose powers it curtailed, led to a plot against its originator, Khāja Mahmūd Gāwān, against whom the conspirators fabricated evidence to support a false charge of treason. Muhammad III, while under the influence of wine, ordered the execution of his faithful minister without inquiring into the charge against him. The innocence of the Khāja became apparent after his death, and Muhammad Shāh bitterly repented his swiftness to punish, but repentance was powerless to avert the consequences of the crime, which destroyed the confidence of the principal *amīrs* of the kingdom in their king and

alienated their affection from him. Chief among those who openly showed their disapproval of the unjust act were Yūsuf Adil Khān, who afterwards founded the Adil Shāhi dynasty of Bījāpur, Fateh-ullāh Imād-ul-Mulk of Gāwīl, and Khudāwand Khān of Māhur. These *amīrs*, though they still openly professed obedience to the Bahmani king, regarded him with suspicion and were not slow to justify acts of disobedience of his authority by open expressions of that suspicion.

Imād-ul Mulk repairs Narnāla.

24. In the reign of Mahmūd Shāh, the son and successor of Muhammad III, the assumption of supreme power in Bīdar by Kāsim Barīd, a Turk, disgusted the *tarafdārs*, whose allegiance to Mahmūd was, after the year 1487, merely nominal. Fateh-ullāh Imād-ul-Mulk, who retained to the end an affectionate regard for Mahmūd Shāh, was resolved not to be the servant of the Turkish upstart, and now began to pave the way for an open declaration of his independence by repairing and strengthening his forts. The inscriptions over the beautiful *Mahākāli* or *Muhammadī* gate of the fortress of Narnāla, though they contain exaggerated expressions of respect for the *roi fainéant* Mahmūd, record the fact that the gate, which is the strongest in the fort, was built by Fateh-ullāh in 1487.

The Imād Shāhi dynasty of Berār.

25. In 1490 Malik Ahmad Nizām-ul-Mulk, *tarafdār* of Daulatābād, who had founded Ahmadnagar, sent envoys to Yūsuf Adil Khān of Bījāpur and Fateh-ullāh Imād-ul-Mulk, urging them to join him in assuming the royal title. They consented and eliminated the name of Mahmūd Shāh from the *khutba*, which they henceforward caused to be read in their own names. Fateh-ullāh seems to have been chary of using the title of Shāh, although he had formally proclaimed himself inde-

pendent as governor of Berār, and it does not appear that he found it necessary to assert his authority over Khudāwand Khān of Māhur, who always remained on the best of terms with him and measured his conduct by his. There is nothing of interest connected with the Akola District to record during the reign of Fateh-ullāh Imād Shāh, who died at a great age in 1504 and was succeeded by his son Alā-ud-dīn Imād Shāh.

War between Berār and Ahmadnagar.

26. In 1510 Alā-ud-dīn, at the instigation of some foreign nobles of Ahmadnagar who took refuge with him after an unsuccessful attempt to oust from power the Deccani party in that kingdom and represented affairs there as being in great confusion, invaded the dominions of Burhān Nizām Shāh, the young king of Ahmadnagar. He was defeated and fled to Ellichpur, and thence to Burhānpur, while the enemy occupied and ravaged the whole of south-western Berār, including the Akola District. With some difficulty Adil Khān of Khāndesh, to whom Alā-ud-dīn Imād Shāh had appealed for help, brought about a treaty of peace, and Burhān Nizām Shāh retired from Berār.

Death of Alā-ud-dīn Imād Shāh.

27. Alā-ud-dīn Imād Shāh, after taking the false step of inviting Bahādur Shāh of Gujarāt to assist him against Ahmadnagar, was forced, as the price of getting rid of his inconvenient ally, to have the *khutba* read in his name in Berār. Very shortly after Bahādur Shāh's return to his own country Alā-ud-dīn died in 1529, and was succeeded by his son Daryā Imād Shāh, who died in 1561 after a reign during which no events of sufficient importance to be chronicled occurred in the Akola District. He was succeeded by his son Burhān Imād Shāh, who was seized early in his reign by his minister, Tufāl Khān, and confined in the fortress of Narnāla.

Invasion of Berār by the Sultāns of Bījāpur and Ahmadnagar.

28. Tufāl Khān, who was now *de facto* ruler of Berār, refused to join the great confederacy of the Mahmmadan kings of the Deccan which in 1654 destroyed the Hindu empire of Vijayanagar, and in the following year Murtazā Nizām Shāh of Ahmadnagar and Alī Adil Shāh I of Bījāpur united to punish him for this refusal. The allies invaded Berār from the south and south-west and devastated it with fire and sword as far as Ellichpur. They remained in the province, wasting the country and slaughtering its inhabitants, until the approach of the rainy season, when Tufāl Khān, by means of an enormous bribe, enlisted the sympathies of Alī Adil Shāh, who succeeded in persuading Murtazā that it would be wise to retire before the rains rendered the black cotton soil impassable for troops with their heavy baggage. Berār was then left in peace, but not for long.

Murtazā Nizām Shāh invades Berār.

29. In 1572 Alī Adil Shāh entered into a treaty with Murtazā Nizām Shāh, in accordance with the terms of which the latter was to be allowed to annex Berār and Bīdar without objection from Bījāpur, while the latter was to possess himself of so much of the dismembered territories of Vijayanagar as should be equal in revenue to those two provinces. Murtazā lost no time in taking advantage of his arrangement with Bījāpur, and encamped at Pāthri with the object of invading Berār. As a pretext for this aggression he pretended sympathy with Burhān Imād Shāh and sent a letter to Tufāl Khān calling upon him to release his sovereign, to be obedient to him in all things, and to refrain from interfering in the government of Berār. The letter concluded with a threat that disobedience would entail swift punishment. Tufāl Khān took counsel of his son,

Shamshīr-ul-Mulk, who had a reputation for valour and was astute enough to perceive that Murtazā's real object was the annexation of Berār, and not the release of Burhān from confinement. He advised his father to rely on the resources of Berār and to return no answer to the letter. Murtazā Nizām Shāh, on hearing of the dismissal of his envoy, set out from Pāthri for Ellichpur. The army of Berār was defeated in a hotly contested battle, and Murtazā Nizām Shāh, before advancing further, took steps to attach the Hindu revenue officials to his cause. He then pursued Tufāl Khān and Shamshīr-ul-Mulk through the Melghāt. The former fled and attempted to take refuge with Mīrān Muhammad II of Khāndesh, but Murtazā Nizām Shāh informed that ruler by letter that his country would be invaded if he gave shelter to Tufāl. Mīrān Muhammad sent the letter on to Tufāl Khān without comment, and the latter understood that he was no longer safe in Khāndesh and returned to Berār, where he took refuge in Narnāla, while Shamshīr-ul-Mulk shut himself up in Gāwīlgarh. Murtazā Nizām Shāh at once marched to Narnāla and laid siege to the fort. When the siege had progressed for some months Murtazā Nizām Shāh, who was already weary of campaigning, received news that a son had been born to him in Ahmadnagar, and proposed to return to his capital and celebrate the auspicious event, but his energetic minister, Changīz Khān, exerted all his influence to prevent his master from taking his hand from the plough. The effeminate Murtazā soon began to despair of ever capturing Narnāla, when chance placed a weapon in Changīz Khān's hands. A merchant arrived in camp with horses and merchandise which had been ordered by Tufāl Khān from Lahore, and besought Changīz Khān that he might be allowed to enter the fort and conclude his bargain with the nominal ruler of

Berār. Changīz Khān granted this request on condition that the merchant should, on his return, enter the service of Murtazā Nizām Shāh, adding that he could see he possessed both valour and acumen. The merchant, beguiled by this flattery, readily accepted the condition, and Changīz Khān caused a large sum of money to be hidden in a bale of merchandise, with which he sent one of his own followers with instructions to do all in his power to corrupt the defenders. The agent laid out his money well and succeeded in leaving the fort at nightfall and rejoining his master. Changīz Khān, having thus established secret communications with Tufāl Khān's nobles, succeeded in detaching large numbers of them from their allegiance, and night after night Berāri officers with their followers secretly left the fort and joined Murtazā Nizām Shāh's army, until there remained in Narnāla no more than twelve men able to work guns. Asad Khān and Rūmi Khān, who commanded the artillery of Ahmadnagar, now drew their guns up as close as might be to the walls, and soon made a practicable breach in one of the bastions and its curtain. The defenders of the fort were now so few that the result of an attempt on the breach was a foregone conclusion. The attack was made by night, and Changīz Khān's trumpeter went in advance of the attacking party and sounded his trumpet in the fort. Tufāl Khān, aroused from sleep, fled through the northern gate into the hills of the Melghāt, but was pursued by Saiyid Hasan Astrābādi, who captured him on the third day after the fall of Narnāla. Murtazā Nizām Shāh found Burhān Imād Shāh in the fort and made him his prisoner, and also took possession of a large quantity of treasure. Shamshīr-ul-Mulk surrendered Gāwīlgarh on hearing of the capture of Narnāla. Burhān Imād Shāh, Tufāl Khān and Shamshīr-ul-Mulk, with their families and followers, numbering about forty souls, were sent to a fortress in the Ahmadnagar kingdom, where, after a short time, they perished, probably by suffocation. The Imād Shāhi dynasty was thus utterly extinguished in 1572, and Berār was annexed to Ahmadnagar, Khudāwand Khān and Khursaid Khān being appointed to govern it.

Berār a province of the kingdom of Ahmadnagar.

30. Murtazā Nizām Shāh having annexed Berār marched towards Bīdar, but was recalled by news of an attempted revolution in favour of the son of Burhān Imād Shāh's foster-mother, who was set up by Mīrān Muhammad II of Khāndesh as a son of Daryā Imād Shāh. The Sultān of Khāndesh was defeated and the rebellion was quelled.

Invasion of Berār by the Mughals.

31. After the suppression of this rebellion no historical event of any importance occurred in the Akola District until 1584, when the Mughals made their first appearance in the Province. The cavalry of the Khān-i-Azam, Akbar's foster-brother and governor, invaded Berār from the north, plundered Ellichpur, and then moved on into the Akola District, where they plundered Bālāpur, then second only to Ellichpur in importance. The activity of Murtazā Nizām Shāh's troops and of Rājā Alī Khān of Khāndesh, who had not yet been won over to the imperial cause, and the dissensions of the Mughal officers, rendered the raid abortive, and the cavalry left Berār as rapidly as they had entered it. In 1590 chance provided Akbar with a pretext for interfering in the affairs of the Deccan. Shāhzāda Burhān, who had plotted unsuccessfully against his brother, Murtazā Nizām Shāh, had been compelled to flee for refuge to Akbar's court. In 1588 Murtazā died and was succeeded by his son Husain Nizām Shāh II, who was put to death after a reign of two months. Ismail, the

young son of the fugitive Burhān, was then raised to the throne, whereupon Akbar made preparations for assisting Burhān to obtain the throne, to which he had an undoubted right. The assistance of Rājā Alī Khān of Khāndesh was enlisted, and he helped Burhān to defeat the adherents of Ismail and to ascend the throne of Ahmadnagar. Burhān Nizām Shāh was thus placed under an obligation which was regarded by Akbar as giving him a right to interfere in the affairs of the Deccan, but active interference was delayed for some years.

Sultān Murād invades the Deccan.

32. Towards the end of 1595 party strife in Ahmadnagar reached such a height that one of the disputants invited Sultān Murād, Akbar's fourth son, who was then in Gujarāt with a commission to invade the Deccan whenever a favourable opportunity should present itself, to assist him. The opportunity was seized, and Murād marched to Ahmadnagar and besieged the city. He did not succeed in capturing it, but was not to be bought off by any less price than the cession of Berār to the empire.

Berār a province of the Mughal empire.

33. Henceforward Berār was a province of Delhi, and the Mughals, who ever kept in view the prospect of a general advance on the Deccan, made Bālāpur, which lay near the road between Burhānpur and the Rohankhed ghāt, then regarded as the highway between Hindustān and the Deccan, their headquarters, and maintained an advanced post at Jālna. For some time after this, Bālāpur was in fact, though not in name, the capital of Berār and the residence of its governor. Here the Mughals maintained their largest garrison, and here, even when the greater part of the province was overrun by the Deccanis, as often happened, they

contrived to maintain a military post. From Ahmadnagar Murād retired to Bālāpur and at a distance of some twelve miles from the town he built himself a palace at a village which he re-named Shāhpur, where the ruins of his residence may still be seen.

Quarrels between the imperial officers.

34. Although Berār had been formally ceded to Akbar, its principal fortresses had not been surrendered, and Gāwīlgarh and Narnāla were still held by officers of the king of Ahmadnagar. Meanwhile the Khān-i-Khānān, who was the real commander-in-chief of the Mughal forces in the Deccan, had established himself at Jālna and engaged on the banks of the Godāvari in a campaign which is not immediately connected with the history of the District, while Murād spent his time in debauchery and excessive drinking in Shāhpur. In 1598 a quarrel occurred between the prince and the general. Murād proposed to complete the conquest of the Ahmadnagar kingdom by capturing its capital and taking possession of its other provinces, but the Khān-i-Khānān insisted that the first thing to be done was to render Berār secure by capturing Gāwīlgarh and Narnāla. The result of the quarrel was that the Khān-i-Khānān was recalled and Abul Fazl was sent to the Deccan. He captured the two great fortresses of Berār, but complaints that he had failed to support the Mughal governor of Bīr when he was hard pressed reached the ears of Akbar, and Abul Fazl was recalled. It was now recognized that the Khān-i-Khānān was the only one of Akbar's officers who was fit to have charge of affairs in the Deccan, and his only disqualification was his intolerance of the drunken and slothful Murād. Murād solved the difficulty by dying in Shāhpur in 1599 from drink and the effects of incontinence, and Sultān Dāniyāl, Akbar's youngest son, was appointed nominal governor

of the Deccan under the tutelage of the Khān-i-Khānān. He had not reached Berār when Akbar, in consequence of a report received from Abul-Fazl, set out from Agra for the Deccan, but discovered as he advanced that his presence would not be required in Ahmadnagar. He therefore laid siege to and captured Asīrgarh, the principal fortress of Khāndesh, sending Dāniyāl and the Khān-i-Khānān on to Ahmadnagar, which place fell into their hands later in the same year (1599), when Bahādur Nizām Shāh was captured and sent to Akbar at Burhānpur. Akbar then returned to Agra, leaving Dāniyāl as governor of the three provinces of Berār, Khāndesh, now re-named Dāndesh, and Ahmadnagar.

The Ain-i-Akbari.

35. The account of Berār in the Ain-i-Akbarī was added to that work in 1596-97. The greater part of the Akola District was included in Akbar's *sarkār* or revenue district of Narnāla, but some of the parganas of this *sarkār* are now included in Buldāna, while Akola, on the other hand, includes three parganas of Akbar's revenue district of Bāsim. The whole revenue demand for the area now included in the Akola District seems to have been nearly twenty-four lakhs of rupees. The only special notice of any places in the District has reference to Bālāpur, Shāhpur, and Bāsim. 'Near Bālāpur,' says Abul Fazl, 'are two streams, about the borders of which are found various kinds of pretty stones, which are cut and kept as curiosities. Six *kos* distant were the headquarters of Sultān Murād, which grew into a fine city under the name of Shāhpur.' Of Bāsim he writes, 'About Bāsim is an indigenous race, for the most part proud and refractory, called Hatgars: their forces consist of 1000 cavalry and 5000 infantry.' He adds that the Hatgars are Rājputs, which is a mistake, for they are a branch of the Dhangar caste. It is strange

that according to the figures of the census of 1901 Hatgars were exceptionally weak in numbers in the late Bāsim District.

Death of Akbar.

36. After the fall of Ahmadnagar Bālāpur was still the principal garrison town of Berār, but Dāniyāl preferred Burhānpur, where he died of drink in 1605, as his viceregal capital. The death of his favourite son was a severe shock to Akbar, who survived Dāniyāl only for a few months, and died in October 1605, when he was succeeded by his eldest son Salīm, who took the title of Jahāngir.

Malik Ambar in Berar.

37. In 1609 Jahāngir appointed his second son Parvez to the governorship of the Mughal provinces of the Deccan, and the prince chose Burhānpur as his headquarters. Owing partly to his lack of enterprise and partly to dissension between his officers, over whom he had little real control, the administration of Parvez was a dismal failure. In 1610 Malik Ambar, the African, who still supported a representative of the Nizām Shāh dynasty in Ausa, attacked Ahmadnagar, repulsed Parvez when he advanced to its relief, and overran the greater part of Berār. A Mughal garrison was still maintained in Bālāpur, but for some time its principal occupation was to look to its own safety, and its sphere of influence did not extend far beyond the walls of the town. So small a part had the Mughals in the administration of Berār that Malik Ambar introduced a settlement of the land, and, though the imperial officers probably succeeded in collecting some revenue from the northern parganas of the province, the garrison at Bālāpur was the only evidence of the emperor's nominal sovereignty. This state of affairs lasted until the beginning of 1616, when the prestige of the Mughal arms was somewhat restored. Dissensions in Malik Ambar's camp drove some of his

officers to offer their services to Shāhnawāz Khān, a gallant officer who at this time commanded at Bālāpur. Shāhnawāz Khān, taking advantage of Malik Ambar's difficulties, marched from Bālāpur with such troops as he could collect and, after defeating the Deccanis in the field, laid waste Ambar's capital, Khirkī, afterwards known as Aurangābād, but was not strong enough to maintain a permanent hold on any of Ambar's dominions beyond Berār, and fell back again to Bālāpur. This raid, however, restored for a time the authority of the Mughals in Berār, and the Akola District was now in fact, as well as in name, in the hands of Shāhnawāz Khān.

Drunkenness of the imperial officers.

38. The climate of Bālāpur had an unfortunate effect on the Mughal officers. Akbar's son Murād had already died there from the effects of drink, and in 1617 Rājā Mahān Singh, a distinguished and valued officer of Jahāngir's, died there from the same cause. Shāhnawāz Khān succumbed to the same fate a few years later.

Shāhjahān appointed to the Deccan.

39. Early in 1617 the prospects of the imperial army were improved by the removal of the indolent Parvez and the appointment of the enterprising Khurram, Jahāngir's third son, to the command in the Deccan. This appointment produced an immediate effect on the Deccanis, who surrendered to the imperial officers many of their recent conquests and ceased to molest Berār. Later in the year Khurram was recalled to Māndu, where the emperor was then in camp, and was honoured with the title of Shāhjahān, under which he afterwards ascended the throne. At the same time the Khān-i-Khānān, the father of Shāhnawāz Khān, who now held the position of governor of Berār and

Ahmadnagar, was appointed viceroy of the Deccan. Two years later Shāhnawāz Khān, to the emperor's great grief, died of drink in Burhānpur. His younger brother, Darāb Khān, succeeded him as governor of Berār and Ahmadnagar, and took up his residence in Bālāpur.

In 1620 Malik Ambar took advantage of Jahāngīr's absence in Kashmīr to besiege Khanjar Khān, the Mughal commandant of Ahmadnagar, while he also drove in the commanders of military posts in the Bālāghāt of Akola and Buldāna and forced them to take refuge with Darāb Khān in Bālāpur. Darāb Khan collected his forces, advanced into the Bālāghāt, and thence to Ahmadnagar, where he fell upon and dispersed the besiegers. But supplies were scarce and dear, and the Mughal army could not maintain itself in the Ahmadnagar country. Darāb therefore retired on Bālāpur, where he encamped until supplies should be collected. A force of the Deccanis hung on the rear of the retreating army and followed it as far as Bālāpur, where the intruders were defeated by Rājā Narsingh Deo, who captured and beheaded Mansūr, one of Ambar's African officers. This trifling success did not suffice to stay the progress of the Deccanis. The siege of Ahmadnagar was vigorously pressed forward, and most of the fortified posts in the Ahmadnagar country and Berār were captured from the imperialists, while the enemy ravaged nearly the whole province of Berār and burnt the standing crops. Malik Ambar's strength increased with his prestige, and he was now able to put into the field 60,000 horse, including the contingents furnished by the kings of Bijāpur and Golconda. Darāb Khān made an effort to check Ambar's further advance by moving from Bālāpur to Mehkar, where he remained for three months, but in spite of his successes against the Deccanis in the field their Marātha horse succeeded in cutting off his supplies until he was compelled to fall back once more on Bālāpur The enemy followed him and repeated at Bālāpur the tactics which had compelled him to leave Mehkar. The activity and mobility of the Marāthas enabled them to destroy the crops and to intercept all supplies until the imperial troops were reduced to such straits that numbers of them deserted daily to the enemy. Darāb Khān had now no choice but to retreat to Burhānpur, and the fortunes of the Mughals were at a lower ebb than at any time since their first interference in the affairs of the Deccan. Malik Ambar even ventured to besiege the imperial troops in Burhānpur and to cross the Nerbudda and ravage the southern districts of Mālwā, but early in 1621 Shāhjahān was again sent to the Deccan. He drove the Deccanis from the neighbourhood of Burhānpur, and pressed on through Berār to Khirkī, which he demolished. Malik Ambar, now in dire straits, agreed to a humiliating treaty of peace, one of the articles of which was to the effect that the southern frontier of the empire should be advanced thirty miles to the south. This provision secured Berār for the emperor, the southern tracts of the Akola District were again brought under the management of Mughal officers, and Bālāpur was again garrisoned.

Rebellion of Shāhjahān.

40. In 1622 Shāhjahān rose against his father and was in rebellion for three years, during which period the imperial cause in the Deccan suffered much, though the Mughals never again lost their hold on Bālāpur and the Akolā district. After Shāhjahān's submission to his father Pīrā Lodi, an Afghān who held the high title of Khān-i-Jahān and was one of the principal nobles of the empire, was appointed governor

of Berār. The Afghān betrayed his trust with a shamelessness which eclipsed all former dealings of the Mughal officers in Burhānpur with Malik Ambar. Their traffic with the enemy had at least been carried on under the cloak of secrecy, and their treason was never unveiled; but the Khān-i-Jahān openly sold the Bālāghāt of Berār, which comprised the southern parganas of the Akola District, to Murtazā Nizām Shāh, the creature of Malik Ambar, for twelve lākhs of rupees, and insisted on the fulfilment of his bargain by his subordinates, compelling all commanders of posts in the Bālāghāt to return to Bālāpur. This was the situation of affairs in Berār when Shāhjahān, early in 1628, ascended the imperial throne in Delhi. The new emperor ignored the nefarious bargain of Pīrā Lodī and ordered Murtazā Nizām Shāh to vacate the military posts in the Bālāghāt, and the latter did not venture to disobey the command. Pīrā Lodī was summoned to court and, discovering on his arrival there that his treachery was well known and was likely to be punished, fled towards the Deccan, where he was harboured by Murtazā Nizām Shāh, who refused to surrender him. Shāhjahān now prepared for war and advanced to Burhānpur.

Invasion of the Deccan.

41. Early in 1630 three imperial armies invaded the Bālāghāt, and Rao Ratan with 10,000 horse was sent to occupy the valley of the Penganga near Bāsim, there to await an opportunity of advancing into Telingāna. A marauding force of the Deccanis succeeded, however, in evading him and, having entered Berār, committed extensive ravages. Rao Ratan was inclined to turn back aud pursue them, but received orders to stand fast in Bāsim while Vazīr Khān was sent from Burhānpur in pursuit of the invaders and dispersed them. Later in the year Rao Ratan, who was deficient

in enterprise, was relieved in Bāsim by Nasīri Khān. The war was now carried beyond the confines of the Akola District and calls for no further notice here.

Famine.

42. In 1630 the rains failed, and a severe famine which affected the whole of Berār was the result. The province had been for many years the scene of hostilities and neither of the hostile armies was in the habit of respecting the rights of private property, while the invariable tactics of one of them consisted in the destruction of crops with the object of depriving the other of supplies. It is therefore not surprising that the famine was more severe than any which has occurred in recent years. The official chronicler of Shāhjahān's reign describes it in the following terms :—' Buyers were ready to give a life for a ' loaf, but seller was there none. The flesh of dogs was ' sold as that of goats and the bones of the dead were ' ground down with the flour sold in the market, and the ' punishment of those who profited by this traffic pro- ' duced yet more dreadful results. Men devoured one ' another and came to regard the flesh of their children ' as sweeter than their love. The inhabitants fled afar to ' other tracts till the corpses of those who fell by the way ' checked those who came after, and in the lands of ' Berār, which had been famous for their fertility and ' prosperity, no trace of habitation remained.' Some mention is made of measures of relief, but it is very clear that these were utterly inadequate.

Operations in Telingāna and against Daulatābād.

43. In 1632 Shāhjahān returned to Agra and Mirzā Isā Tarkhān was appointed governor of Ellichpur while Yamīn-ud-daulah was viceroy of the Deccan. The viceroy directed two campaigns, one in Telingāna which ended with the fall

of Kandahār, and the other in the Daulatābād country which ended with the fall of Daulatābād in 1633. Bāsim was the base of operations in the former campaign and Bālāpur in the latter.

Reorganization of the Mughal conquests in the Deccan.

44. Towards the end of 1634 Shāhjahān issued a *farmān* redistributing his conquests in the Deccan. Hitherto Khāndesh, Berār, and the conquests from the Nizām Shāhi dominions had formed an unwieldy *sūbah* under one *sūbahdār*. This arrangement was now changed. Berār, Khāndesh and the Ahmadnagar kingdom were divided into two *sūbahs*, the Bālāghāt on the south and the Pāyanghāt on the north. The line of demarcation between the two new *sūbahs* was the edge of the plateau of southern Berār, and the Akola District was thus divided between the two, the tāluks of Akola, Akot, Bālāpur and Murtizāpur lying in the Pāyanghāt and those of Bāsim and Mangrul in the Bālāghāt. The new arrangement was not of long duration. In 1636 Shāhjahān appointed his third son Aurangzeb, viceroy of the Deccan, which was divided into the four *sūbahs* of Daulatābād, Telingāna, Khāndesh, and Berār.

Accession of Aurangzeb (Alamgīr).

45. No event worthy of note occurred in the District during the remainder of the reign of Shāhjāhān, and in 1658 Aurangzeb, after a fratricidal struggle, ascended the throne of Delhi under the title of Alamgīr. There is nothing to chronicle during his long reign, towards the end of which Akola was held in *jāgīr* by his prime minister Asad Khān, whose local agent was Khāja Abdul Latīf. This officer built the walls of Akola, which he named Asadgarh in compliment to his master, and the *īdgāh* to the north of the town.

Accession of Bahādur Shāh.

46. In 1707 Aurangzeb died and was succeeded by his eldest surviving son, Shāh Alam, who took the title of Bahādur Shāh.

Recognition of *chauth* and *sardeshmukhī*.

47. In 1718, during the reign of the wretched Farrukhsiyar, a regular system of buying off the Marātha marauders was inaugurated, and was sanctioned by the emperor's advisers. In consideration of refraining from ravaging the six *sūbahs* of the Deccan these freebooters were to be allowed to collect, under the name of *chauth*, blackmail amounting nominally to one-fourth of the revenue; and to indemnify them for their trouble in collecting *chauth* they were to be permitted to collect a cess, known as *sardeshmukhī*, amounting to a tenth of the revenue. This disgraceful compact amounted to no more than an imperial confirmation of a practice which had for some years past been usual among the slothful *amīrs* of the Deccan. Its effects on the wretched cultivators of Berār must have been disastrous, and are briefly described by Sir Alfred Lyall in the Gazetteer of Berār as follows: 'Wherever the 'emperor appointed a *jāgirdār* the Marāthas appointed 'another, and both claimed the revenue, while foragers 'from each side exacted forced contributions; so that 'the harassed cultivator often threw up his land and helped to plunder his neighbour.'

Campaign of Bālāpur.

48. In 1720 the two Saiyid brothers of Bārha, Abdullah Khān and Husain Alī Khān, who had long held all real power at Delhi, began to conspire against their most dangerous rival, the brave and astute Chīn Kilīz Khān, better known by his titles of Nizām-ul-Mulk and Asaf Jāh. Asaf Jāh was appointed *sūbahdār* of Mālwā in the hope that he would be defeated and

perhaps lose his life in attempting to quell disturbances sedulously fostered from Delhi, or that he would be entrapped into some overt act of rebellion which would expose him to attack by the imperial army from Delhi under the command of the brothers and by the army of the Deccan under the command of their nephew, Alam Alī Khān. Asaf Jāh, however, held his own at Burhānpur, where he was joined by his uncle Iwaz Khān, the *sūbahdār* of Berār, and by most of the principal officers in Mālwā. The Saiyids now repented of having allowed him to strengthen himself in Mālwā, and Husain Alī Khān prepared to oust him from his appointment and to assume it for himself. Alam Alī Khān was ordered to attack him from the south while Saiyid Alī Khān, another member of the family, was sent from Delhi with instructions to attack him from the north should success appear probable, or to avoid him and join Alam Alī Khān without risking an action. Meanwhile Asaf Jāh had been attacked by and had defeated and slain at Ratanpur, within forty miles of Burhānpur, Dilāwar Alī Khān, another relative of the Saiyid brothers. Husain Alī Khān, who had intended to march in person against Asaf Jāh, was detained at Delhi, but Alam Alī Khān marched from Aurangābād into Berār. Asaf Jāh sent the corpse of Dilāwar Alī to Alam Alī for burial, informing him at the same time that he might retire with his family to Hindustān without molestation. Alam Alī Khān, however, was not disposed to give up the Deccan without a struggle, and Asaf Jāh marched towards the Pūrna river, the south bank of which was now held by Alam Alī Khān. The rains were heavy, the river was in flood, there were no boats, and the country was well nigh impassable owing to the deep mire. Asaf Jāh accordingly moved eastwards along the bank of the river until he heard of a ford in the direction of Bālāpur. With the assistance of Iwaz Khān and the local zamīndārs he crossed the river and awaited the arrival of Alam Alī Khān at Shegaon. Here his army suffered great discomfort. Rain fell incessantly, supplies could not be obtained, and the Marāthas hung around the camps so that the baggage animals could not be sent out for grass. Many of the rank and file deserted and fled to their homes and many of the horses and baggage animals, standing up to their girths in mud, died of exhaustion and disease. As soon as the rain ceased Asaf Jāh marched from Shegaon towards Bālāpur. The Marāthas molested his army on its march but were attacked and defeated. The army then halted at a deserted village six miles from Bālāpur and some supplies were collected, but Asaf Jāh was compelled to bury some of his heavy guns at this place as the debilitated bullocks could not drag them through the mud. The army then pressed on to Bālāpur, where supplies were plentiful. Here they encamped, and Asaf Jāh selected a defensive position within six miles of the town. Alam Alī Khān had been following him as rapidly as the state of the country permitted, and Asaf Jāh had no more time at his disposal than was necessary for the selection of his position and the preparation of his troops for battle.

Battle of Bālāpur.

49. The armies met on August 12th, 1720. In the artillery combat which preceded the actual conflict Asaf Jāh had the advantage, but this advantage was nullified by the vigour with which Alam Alī's men delivered their attack. Asaf Jāh's first line was broken, but Alam Alī, in pursuing his advantage, pressed on at such a pace that his companions could not keep up with him. He fought valiantly and was once repulsed, but returned to the attack, while the defence was weakened by the necessity

for detaching a force to deal with the Marāthas, who had already plundered some of Asaf Jāh's treasure. Alam Alī at length fell, covered with wounds, and his army was defeated and dispersed with comparatively small loss to Asaf Jāh, who now became supreme in the Deccan. The families of Dilāwar Alī Khān and Alam Ali Khān fled to Daulatābād, where they took refuge, and shortly after this the Saiyid brothers were destroyed and Muhammad Shāh was freed from their domination.

Asaf Jāh independent of Delhi.

50. In 1724 Asaf Jāh defeated at Shakarkheldā in the Buldāna District Mubāriz Khān, the *sūbahdār* of Hyderābād, who was instigated to attack him by intriguers at Delhi, and henceforth ruled Berār and the Deccan virtually as an independent sovereign, though he never formally proclaimed his independence.

The Nizāms of Hyderābād.

51. The status of the Marāthas in the imperial provinces of the Deccan has already been explained, and during the rule of the Nizāms of Hyderābād these freebooters tightened their grip on the land. The Bhonslas of Nāgpur acquired a recognized position as *mokāsadārs*, or assignees of a share of the revenues of Berār, and maintained an establishment of revenue collectors, and before the death of Asaf Jāh in 1748 they had become possessed of the Melghāt and its two fortresses, Narnāla and Gāwīlgarh. These they held nominally as feudatories of the Nizām, but actually as a guarantee for their share of the revenue, and they retained possession of them until the close of the third Marātha war.

The Akola campaign.

52. In 1758 Nizām Alī Khān, *sūbahdār* of Berār, took the field against his brother, the Nizām Salābat Jang, marched from Burhānpur, his headquarters, towards the Deccan, and halted during the rainy season at Bāsim, leaving his

lieutenant, Shaikh Amīn Ahmad, at Burhānpur to organize and equip his artillery train. Salābat Jang succeeded in gaining over to his cause Jānojī Bhonsla of Nāgpur, who, as soon as the cessation of the rains rendered field operations possible, raided Berār. The first care of Nizām Alī, who had spent the rainy season in Bāsim, was to draw the claws of Jānojī Bhonsla, and he was preparing to march against him when he heard that his artillery park in Burhānpur was ready to join him, but that Bāpu Karandiya, Bhonsla's lieutenant, was only waiting for it to leave Burhānpur in order to fall upon it. Nizām Alī therefore wrote to Shaikh Amīn Ahmad bidding him be upon his guard and cautioning him against leaving Burhānpur until he was joined by his master. Nizām Alī followed his letter by way of Akola, beyond which place he had to fight his way to Burhānpur. The Marāthas opposed him in the field on each day of his march and were daily repulsed. Jānojī, seeing that his lieutenant was no match for Nizām Alī, marched to his assistance, and the Marāthas so harassed Nizām Alī on his march that his troops had rest neither by day nor by night At last, when Nizām Alī had reached the bank of the Pūrna, probably in the vicinity of Pātharda, he saw and seized his opportunity. The Marāthas had encamped for the night, when Nizām Alī directed Sīdī Ambar Khān and Kādir Sāhib to fall upon them. The night attack was successful and both Jānojī Bhonsla and Bāpū Karandiya fled in confusion. Jānojī succeeded in rallying a force sufficient to harass Nizām Alī and so keep him on the alert, but the spirit of the Marāthās was broken and they would not face the Mughals in the field. Jānojī now forsook Salābat Jang and threw in his lot with Nizām Alī, whom he advised to march on Hyderābād. The advice was followed and in 1761 Nizām Alī deposed his brother and took his place as Nizām.

Battle of Argaon.

53. The history of the District is uneventful from this period till the time of the second Marātha war. The battle of Assaye was fought on September 23rd, 1803, and Major-General Arthur Wellesley and Colonel Stevenson, after much marching and countermarching occasioned by the movements of Daulat Rao Sindhia and Raghujī Bhonsla, met on November 28th and marched to Pātharda on the Pūrna with the object of attacking the Marāthas, now awaiting them at Argaon (Argaum) in the Akot tāluk. The Marātha armies, though nearly as numerous as at Assaye, were neither so well disciplined nor so well appointed, and their artillery consisted of no more than thirty-eight guns. Their position was thus described by Wellesley in his despatch to his brother, the Governor-General :—

'The enemy's infantry and guns were in the left of 'their centre, with a body of cavalry on their left. 'Sindhia's army, consisting of one very heavy body of 'cavalry, was on the right, having upon its right a body 'of Pindāris and other light troops. Their line extended 'above five miles, having in their rear the village and 'extensive gardens and enclosures of Argaum; and in 'their front a plain, which, however, was much cut by 'water-courses, etc.'

The troops engaged at Argaon were the King's 19th Light Dragoons, 74th Highlanders, 78th Highlanders (Ross-shire Buffs), and 94th Foot, the Company's artillery, the 3rd, 4th, 5th, 6th, and 7th Madras Native Cavalry and the following battalions of Madras Native Infantry :—1st battalion 2nd (now the 62nd Punjabis), 2nd battalion 2nd (now the 80th Carnatic Infantry), 1st battalion 3rd (now the 63rd Palamcottah Light Infantry), 1st battalion 4th (now the 64th Pioneers), 1st battalion 6th (now the 66th Punjabis), 2nd battalion 7th (now the

79th Carnatic Infantry), 1st battalion 8th, 2nd battalion 9th, 1st battalion 10th, 1st battalion 11th (now the 81st Pioneers), and 2nd battalion 12th (now the 84th Punjabis). The infantry were drawn up in one line with the 78th on the right, having the 74th on its immediate left and the 94th on the extreme left of the line. The cavalry were formed in a second line, the regular cavalry being on the right and the Mughal and Mysore horse on the left. The right of the line was somewhat thrown forward in order that the first blow might be struck at the enemy's left.

As the lines were forming at a distance of about 1200 yards from the enemy the latter opened a cannonade which did no actual damage but threw nearly three entire battalions of native infantry, which had behaved admirably under a much heavier fire at Assaye, into confusion. They took refuge in a village behind which the cavalry were halted prior to deployment, leaving the Highlanders and the artillery alone in the field on the right. Fortunately Wellesley was close at hand and was able to rally these battalions, but much valuable time was wasted. When the line was reformed the troops advanced in perfect order, the march of the 78th being directed against a battery of nine guns on the enemy's left. As this battery was approached a body of about 800 infantry, supposed to have been Persians, but more probably Arabs, which had been sheltered behind it, charged with the apparent intention of breaking through the interval between the 74th and the 78th. These two regiments, however, closed the interval and pressed on with ported arms to meet the enemy. A deep muddy nullah unfortunately prevented them from closing with the bayonet, but they maintained a steady fire until their assailants, who displayed the most obstinate courage, were entirely destroyed. Sindhia's cavalry charged the 6th

Native Infantry on the left of the line, next to the 94th, but were repulsed, and the Marātha army then broke and fled in confusion, leaving the whole of their artillery and ammunition in the hands of the victors. The British cavalry pursued them for many miles, destroying great numbers and capturing many elephants and camels and much baggage, and the Mughal and Mysore cavalry continued the pursuit with much slaughter. Wellesley wrote that had there been one hour's more daylight not a man of the enemy would have escaped, and the delay caused by the unaccountable panic of some of his best native infantry was a great disappointment to him. The Marāthas were, however, completely demoralized. Vithal Pant, who commanded Bhonsla's cavalry, was killed and Gopāl Bhau, who commanded Sindhia's cavalry, was wounded. After this signal victory Wellesley marched towards Ellichpur for the purpose of attacking Gāwīlgarh.

Maladministration of Berār.

54. After the close of the Marātha war of 1803 the Akola District was nominally at peace, but the people suffered much from the depredations of the Pindāris and from the results of maladministration. Extravagance at the capital led to wholesale borrowing, and the approved method of satisfying creditors was the farming to them of Districts in Berār. The lessee's term was uncertain, for a more importunate creditor sometimes obtained a lease over his head, with authority to oust him, and it was therefore to his interest to make as much money as he could in the shortest time possible, without regard to the fate of the cultivators. Pūran Mal, a great moneylender of Hyderābād, in this way held most of Berār in farm. In 1839 he was ousted by Pestonji and Company, an enterprising Pārsi firm whose methods with the cultivators contrasted very

favourably with those of other farmers. Pestonji, however, was deprived of his lease in 1845, in spite of his plea that forty lākhs were still due to him, and his revenue collectors were forcibly ejected, not without bloodshed, from Akola and Bālāpur. They were succeeded in Akola by a rapacious *tālukdār* who robbed the people without protecting them from other robbers and drove many of them to Amraoti for refuge.

The Assignment. Boundaries of the District.

55. In 1853 the Akola District, with the rest of Berār, was assigned to the East India Company. The province was at first divided into the two Districts of East and West Berār, Akola being the headquarters of the latter, which included the present Akola District, except the tāluk of Murtizāpur, the Buldāna District, and the Pusad tāluk of the Yeotmāl District. In 1864 the Buldāna District, at first called the South-West Berār, and afterwards the Mehkar, District, was formed, and in 1875 the Bāsim District, which had for some years been an independent subdivision, was separated from Akola. In August 1905, when the six Districts of Berār were reconstituted, the limits of the Akola District, which had till then consisted of the five tāluks of Akola, Akot, Bālāpur, Khāmgaon, and Jalgaon, were extensively modified. Murtizāpur was received from Amraoti, Khāmgaon and Jalgaon were transferred to Buldāna, and Bāsim and Mangrul were received from the Bāsim District, which was broken up.

Progress since the Mutiny.

56. The Mutiny did not affect the Akola District, the history of which is, since that time, merely a record of steady progress, broken only twice by famine. The nature of the administration before the Assignment has already been described. Its effect was, in very

many cases, to drive the cultivators from their holdings The establishment of British rule was the signal for the repopulation of the province, and the Akola District, which contains some of the richest land in Berār, was one of the first tracts to welcome back the cultivator. The opening of the Nāgpur branch of the Great Indian Peninsula Railway established railway communication with Bombay and greatly increased the cotton trade, which was enormously stimulated by the American Civil War. Since that time both agriculture and commerce have progressed steadily.

ARCHÆOLOGY.

Pātur caves.

57. The oldest archæological remains in the Akola District are probably two caves hewn in the rocky side of a low hill just west of the town of Pātur Shaikh Bābu in the Akola tāluk. These are simple *vihāras* with heavy square pillars and a verandah. The inscriptions on the pillars and architraves have not yet been deciphered, and the caves are otherwise unadorned and contain no images except a portion of a seated figure with the legs crossed, which has been held to be a Jain relic but may be a Buddhist image. A local legend exists to the effect that the flat rock above the verandah of the caves bore a ong Sanskrit inscription, but that the inscribed portion parted from the hill, fell before the caves, and was shivered.

Temple at Bārsi Tākli.

58. Next in order of age is the blackstone temple of Bhawāni at Bārsi Tākli, twelve miles south-east of Akola. 'It consists of a shrine and *mandap*, or hall, both being freely decorated upon the exterior with bands of mouldings and figures. The *mandap* is curiously arranged with regard to the shrine, being

attached, as it were, sideways to it, the open side of the *mandap* with its entrance being on one side, or at right angles to the doorway of the shrine. The plan of the *mandap* is rectangular, while that of the shrine is star-shaped. Four decorated pillars support the central ceiling of the hall. The principal figures around the outside of the temple, excepting Ganpati, are females, Mahākāli and Mahishāsuramardinī occupying important positions. The temple is not free from indecent figures. The ceiling is particularly well-decorated.'[1] Within the temple, engraved upon the back wall, is a long Sanskrit inscription, unfortunately very much damaged. It bears the date Shaka 1098 (A.D. 1176) which Mr. Cousens, Superintendent of the Archæological Survey of Western India, takes to be the date of the construction of the temple.

Sirpur temple.

59. At Sirpur in the Bāsim tāluk stands the old temple of Antariksha Pārsvanātha, belonging to the Digambara Jain community. This temple, which appears to be unfinished, bears an abraded inscription over its eastern doorway, to one side, with a date which has been read as Samvat 1334 (A.D. 1406), and the name Antariksha Pārsvanātha. Mr. Cousens inclines to the opinion that the temple was begun during the early Muhammadan invasions of the Deccan, at least a hundred years before the date of the inscription, and that the work was abandoned lest the iconoclastic zeal of the invaders should be excited, and subsequently resumed when their zeal had subsided into the tolerance of rulers, at which time, probably, the image of Pārsvanātha Antariksha was installed. He also suggests that the old temple was finally abandoned after the commencement, but before the completion, of the brick *sikhar* in hybrid style, and

---

[1] Progress Report of the Archæological Survey of Western India for the year ending June 30th, 1902.

owing to the insecurity of temples during the contests of rival Muhammadan powers in the Deccan. The plan of the shrine is star-shaped and the walls are decorated with bands of arabesque, no images being carved except in the three principal niches, these figures being loose and detachable if necessary. Mr. Cousens suggests that the people of the Deccan had heard before the arrival of the Musalmāns of their hatred of images and that Hindu temple-builders of this period introduced bands of arabesque and plain mouldings as an exterior decoration in place of the profusion of images which formerly prevailed in order that there should be nothing outside to excite the enmity of the Musalmāns. The entrance doorway of the hall is elaborately carved and images occur here, but they would have been hidden by the porch, had it been completed. On either side of the doorway are nude Jain figures and over the lintel is a small seated Jina. In the shrine are two small marble Jinas, neither of them being Pārsvanātha.

Narnāla fort.

60. The largest monument of antiquity in the District is the fine hill fort of Narnāla, standing upon an isolated hill of the Sātpurā range. The whole series of fortifications consists of three distinct forts stretching in a line from east to west,—Jafarābād on the east, Narnāla, the principal fort, in the centre, and Teliyāgarh on the west. The forts are enclosed, except in those places where the natural escarpment of rock renders artificial defences unnecessary, by crenellated stone walls, well and strongly built. The bastions are numerous and the gates number twenty-two in all, but this number includes wicket gates and separate gateways situated on the same main entrance to the fort. The main entrances to the fort are but four in number, the Delhi *darwāza*, the Sirpur *darwāza*, the Akot *darwāza*, and the Shāhnūr

darwāza. None of the entrances, save the last, calls for any special mention. The Shāhnūr entrance consists of three separate gateways on the same path. The outer most is the Shāhnūr gate proper, the first and main gate of the fort, and a very plain structure. Mr. Cousens concludes from its style that it is prae-Muhammadan, but doubts whether it is Gond or not. The ornaments on this gateway are two lions, facing inwards, just as they are found on the old Gond fort of Chānda. Firishta says that Ahmad Shāh Walī, the ninth king of the Bahmani dynasty, when he halted at Ellichpur in 1425 "built" the fort of Gāwīl and "repaired" that of Narnāla, from which it may perhaps be concluded that fortifications already existed on the Narnāla hill, though the words of a somewhat inaccurate historian must not be construed too literally. We certainly have no reason to believe that the Gonds ever bore sway in the Melghāt, and there is not, perhaps, sufficient ground for the belief that the Shāhnūr gateway is prae-Muhammadan. 'It 'is flanked by walls and bastions built of cyclopean 'masonry, some of the great blocks being over six feet 'long. These are laid upon one another with very clean 'joints and their surfaces are cleanly dressed. Some of 'the *kangūras* or merlins of the battlementing are of 'single stones, one that was measured being four feet 'five inches high by three feet seven inches broad. A 'curtain wall of this same heavy masonry projects upon 'the outer side of the gateway and thus screens and 'protects it from below.' This description would apply generally to prae-Muhammadan architecture, but it is not mentioned that the gateway itself consists of a simple Pathān arch instead of the post and lintel doorway which we should have expected to find. That this outer gateway is of earlier date than the innermost gateway of the same entrance is evident, but there is no reason to believe that it was not constructed by Ahmad Shāh's builders in 1425. The second gateway of this entrance is the Mehndī *darwāza*, which calls for no special notice, but is probably of the same date as the outer gateway. The third and innermost gateway is the best piece of work in the fort. Hindus have named it the Mahākāli gateway, though there is nothing Hindu in its architecture or its surroundings, except a heap of rough stones daubed with red pigment and oil in one of its galleries and locally known as 'Rājā Ilāl,'—a possible reference to the eponymous Rājā Il of Ellichpur. The gateway is wholly Muhammadan and was built by Fath-ullāh Imād-ul-Mulk in 1487, a year before he repaired the companion fort of Gāwīl. It consists of the great entrance archway, nineteen feet from the ground to the apex of the arch and ten feet six inches wide. The whole height of the gateway is thirty-seven feet three inches. Above the lower arch ring is a second, with an inscription in Arabic between them. Above this again are several horizontal courses, one being corbelled forward, forming, with their vertical jambs or pilasters, a recessed framework round the archway. Over these again is a very large inscription, stretching across the gateway and surmounted by a line of ornamental *kangūras* or battlements. The gateway is flanked upon either side by galleries and rooms, probably the original guard-rooms; but the most striking feature of all is the overhanging balconied windows, two on either side. These are beautifully wrought, being supported by corbels or brackets below, and having deep cornices and eaves' boards protecting them above. A couple of little pillars and corresponding pilasters, with panels of perforated screen-work between, add to the general pleasing effect. The gateway must be regarded as being in the main ornamental, for it is weak in itself and adds nothing to the strength of the entrance, which is defended by the Shāhnūr and Mehndī gateways. In front of the gateway a quadrangle has been added at a later date, surrounded by guard-rooms, but the workmanship of these additions is rough and coarse, and they have been built up against the gateway on either side, covering up much of its work.

The upper inscription on the gateway runs as follows :—

"On the date of victory. Saith the Lord God Most High and Exalted, 'Whosoever entereth herein is safe from fear.' The year 892 (A.D. 1487).

"Far removed from imperfections is God. There is no God but the one God and Muhammad is the Prophet of God. May God bless and save him and may God bless all the prophets and apostles and the favoured angels Praised be the Lord God, the Ruler of the universe. Lord have mercy on the legitimate *khalīfahs*, the rightly guided, exalted over others of the believers and Muslims, namely, Abū Bakr the Truthful, Umar the Discriminator, Uthmān, and Alī the approved of God, and Hasan-ur-Radhā, and Husain, and all the martyrs of Karbalā, and Hamzah, and Abbās, and all those who accompanied the Prophet in his emigration to Madinah, and all those who helped him there. May the acceptance of God be on them all. (Written by Muhammad Abdullāh.)"

The lower inscription runs as follows :—

"In the reign of the great and exalted *Sultān*, the *Ghāzī*, Shahāb-ud-dunyā Wa'd-dīn, Mahmūd Shāh, the son of Muhammad Shāh, the son of Humāyūn Shāh, the son of Ahmad Shāh, the son of Muhammad Shāh, the ruler, the Bahmanid ; may God prepetuate his rule, his kingdom, and his *khilāfat*. Written by Kamāl Jang."

It is not clear what victory is referred to in the beginning of the first inscription, for no victory was gained by Fath-ullāh Imād-ul-Mulk in 1487. The expression used may perhaps be regarded as a rhetorical flourish, with a reference to Fath-ullāh's name and to the fact that he was already virtually independent. The rest of the inscription indicates his orthodoxy as a Sunnī. The pedigree of Shahāb-ud-dīn Mahmūd Shāh in the second inscription is full of errors, but corroborates more valuable evidence which refutes Firishta's obstinate assertion that the name of the fifth king of the Bahmani dynasty was Mahmūd, and not Muhammad.

On a knoll in the fort is the large gun known as the *nau-gazī top*, or nine yard gun, built of rods and rings on the fagot system. Engraved on it is a Persian inscription of which the following is a translation :—" He (God) is the Everlasting One. The emperor Aurangzeb Alamgīr. This is the nine-yard gun which was made during the rule of the Deccanis. Now Atlū Beg, the slave of the imperial court, having come to the fort of Narnāla in the month of Jamādī-ul-awwal, in the year 1091 of the holy Hijra, has mounted the above mentioned gun by the grace of His Majesty, the lord of the earth and the age, ruler of the world and its inhabitants, the true spiritual guide. Written by Pahlād Dās the Kāyath. It is 150 years since this gun was captured, and nobody has mounted it till now."

The three forts contain between them twenty-two tanks, most of which are in the central fort. The system of water-supply in this fort was admirable. Of the old water-works there still remain a part of the old aqueduct and some of the stone drains constructed for conveying the surface water into the cisterns and the overflow from one cistern into another. From the fact that some of the cisterns are covered it has been surmised that they are the handiwork of Jains, but there is not sufficient ground for this belief.

The *Jāmi masjid* or principal mosque is in ruins. It occupies a commanding position and was perhaps an imposing structure, but what is left of it does not enable us to form an opinion on this point. A local historian tells us that it was built in A.H. 915 (A.D. 1509) by one Mahābat Khān, and that it bears an Arabic inscription to this effect, but of this no trace now remains.

Upon the hill, close beside the *ambār khāna*, now converted into a residence, is a neat and substantial little mosque in good repair, with three arches and a high Pathān dome. It is disfigured by an inscription recording the visit of a Hyderābād noble in 1873. This should be removed. Other buildings are the mint, *sarrāf khāna*, arsenal, and elephant stables. There are also the ruins of a *mahal* erected for one of the Bhonsla rājās of Nāgpur, and in Teliyāgarh is a small mosque The ruins of two gun foundries also remain.

Shrine at Pātur.

61. At Pātur is the shrine of the saint Shaikh Bābu, in the interior of which is the chronogram giving as the date of the saint's death A.H. 791 (A.D. 1388). A slab above the arch of the outer gate of the shrine bears the following inscription :—

"This building was erected in the time of the Khān-i-Khānān, the son of Bairam Khān, and by means of the liberality of that successful and exalted man."

"He was a ruler who was kind to *darveshes*. A.H. 1015 (A.D 1606-07)."

The shrine is not of much architectural interest.

The inscriptions above the gates in the walls of Pātur are now illegible.

Akola town.

62. The walls and gates of Akola bear several inscriptions, but none of them is important. They show that the walls, as well as the *īdgāh* without the town, were first built in

the latter part of the reign of Aurangzeb, Akola being then held in *jāgīr* by his prime minister Asad Khān, for whom it was managed by Khāja Abdul Latīf. Additions to the fortifications were made in the reigns of later Mughal emperors.

63. The fort at Bālāpur is interesting rather by means of its structure than of its age, but is a building well worth preserving. It crowns the high ground between the two branches of the river on which Bālāpur stands, and its walls and bastions, which are very lofty, are built entirely of the best brickwork of the period to which the fort belongs. The outer or lower fort is a decagon, with a bastion at each angle, and above it rises, by the whole height of its walls, the inner fort, which is a pentagon, each angle terminating with a bastion, as in the lower fort. Both the outer and the inner forts are entered by fine Mughal gateways, above the former of which is an inscription, now illegible, which formerly recorded the building of the fort in 1757 by Ismail Khān, Nawāb of Ellichpur. On the bank of the river stands the *chhatrī*, or kiosk, of Rājā Jai Singh,—a graceful building on a high plinth, resembling in plan what is called by heralds a cross quadrate, that is to say, the four arms of a cross issuing from the four sides of a square. It is surmounted by five Pathān domes, one large one in the centre, over the square, surrounded by four small ones. The superstructure is supported by twenty pillars and lintels. The ornament is principally of the leaf and dart pattern, with conventional lotus flowers, and the interior of the domes is fine. A flight of steps formerly led from the pavilion down to the river, but these have disappeared.

Bālāpur.

A fine *havelī* in the town was built by a local saint, Saiyid Amjad, and an inscription over the principal gateway, a good specimen of Mughal architecture, conveys the information that it was built in A.H. 1115 (A.D. 1703).

The mosque in Kāsārpura is a fair specimen of later Mughal architecture, but the arches are too squat to be graceful; a long and somewhat bombastic inscription, exceedingly well executed and well preserved, gives as the date of the construction of the mosque the year A.H. 1150 (A.D. 1737). The mosque is known as the *Rauzah Masjid*, for it contains the tomb of a local saint, Maulvī Masūm Shāh.

CHAPTER III.

POPULATION.

STATISTICS OF POPULATION.

Area and population.

64. Akola District was absolutely reconstituted in 1905. It had formerly consisted of five tāluks, of which it now retained three, Akola, Bālāpur, and Akot, but it lost the other two, Khāmgaon and Jalgaon. At the same time it received three more, Murtizāpur, Bāsim, and Mangrul. The six tāluks have a total area of 4110 square miles, and their population in 1901 was 754,804, placing Akola 10th in area and 4th in population among the Districts of the Central Provinces and Berār; its density is 184 persons to the square mile as against an average of 120 for the whole territory. According to the Census Report of 1901 the tāluks contained 11 towns, that is places with a population of over 5000, 27 villages with a population of over 2000, 111 villages with something between 1000 and 2000, and 1325 with less than 1000, the majority of these having less than 500. The towns were Akola (29,289), Akot (18,252), Kāranja (16,535), Bāsim (13,823), Bālāpur (10,486), Bārsi Tākli (6288), Murtizāpur (6156), Hiwarkhed (6143), Pātur (5990), Wādegaon (5825), and Mangrul (5793). The villages with a population between 2000 and 5000 varied greatly in different tāluks. In Akot there were 10—Mundgaon (3329), Adgaon (3131), Dahihanda (2847), Belkhed (2698), Telhāra Buzruk (2528), Akolkhed (2525), Pāthardi (2402), Dānāpur (2126), Mālegaon (2115), and Akoli Jāgīr (2089). Akola had 5—Borgaon Manju (3861), Pinjar (2565), Ugwa (2473),

Kurankhed (2316), and Māhān (2239). Bāsim also contained 5—Risod (3923), Sirpur (3809), Medsi (3615), Rājura (2122), and Ansing (2087). Murtizāpur had 4—Sirso (4503), Kuram (3293), Kāmargaon (2346), and Mānā (2172). Bālāpur had 3—Alegaon (2848), Pāras (2764), and Wyāla (2460). Mangrul had no villages of this class. In some cases, however, the census figures are misleading. Murtizāpur is shown as having a population of 6156, and Sirso as having 4503; this is true as far as the revenue areas so named are concerned, but a settlement called Mubārakpur, technically attached to Sirso, is practically a part of Murtizāpur, and the transference of its population would give Murtizāpur over 9000 and Sirso only about 1500. Again, Telhāra Buzruk in Akot tāluk had only 2528 inhabitants, but the name Telhāra is commonly applied to the whole of an unbroken inhabited area which falls for revenue purposes into 5 different villages; the whole taken together had a population of 5160. Yet again, Kutāsa in Akot tāluk had only 1866 residents on the night of the census, but the people say that the permanent population was over 2000; it happened that one or two very largely attended weddings were in progress in neighbouring villages and scores of families had gone to them. Akola town is said to have gained through a number of country people being detained by a heavy hailstorm on the night of the census. Municipalities have been instituted in Akola, Akot, Bāsim, and Kāranja. The total urban population was 124,580, or 17 per cent. of the total, this proportion being the third largest in the amalgamated Provinces. (Nāgpur has 32 per cent. and Amraoti 22 per cent.). Combining the latest figures available for cropped area and population, those for 1907-1908 and 1901 respectively, the cropped area per head of population was 2½ acres. The figures for area, population, and density of the tāluks are—

Tāluk.	Area sq. ms.	Population.	Density.
Akot	517	137,683	266
Bālāpur ..	569	104,495	184
Murtizāpur ..	610	118,022	193
Mangrul ..	630	91,062	145
Akola	738	150,222	204
Bāsim	1046	153,320	147

Akot has therefore much the greatest density; it is a wealthy part, with an unusual number of large villages, situated mostly in the northern half; though the smallest tāluk in the District it has the reputation of providing more revenue and criminal work than any other in Berār. Bāsim is far larger than any other tāluk in the District, though several tāluks in other parts of Berār are larger again, but its density is low. Mangrul is very hilly and not very large, and has the thinnest population in the District; the headquarters town (5793) is the only place with as much as 2000 people. However even Mangrul has a much higher density than some Berār tāluks and is 20 per cent. above the provincial average.

Growth of population.

65. A census of the District has been taken on four occasions, in 1867 (a provincial census), 1881, 1891, and 1901. The boundaries of the tāluks were not quite the same in 1867 as they have been later, but the differences were of a kind which admit of some general comparisons being fairly made; for instance,

the greater part of Mangrul tāluk was then included in Bāsim, but the table given above shows that at least in regard to density the two parts are very similar. In 1867 the density of the different areas now included in the District varied from 100 to 257 per square mile; in 1881 from 120 to 278; in 1891 from 130 to 266; and in 1901 from 145 to 266. The fall in maximum density in the decade ending in 1891 is not explained in the Census Report, but at that time there was a slight fall in several of the plain tāluks of Berār and a great rise in all the hilly and remote tāluks; it is possible that there was a general movement to take up virgin soil in the only parts where it was then available. The rise in minimum density in the famine decade ending in 1901, combined with the steadiness of maximum density, is very satisfactory, but was possibly assisted by immigration from Pusad tāluk. The variation in the larger towns, those with a population of more than 10,000, was:—

Town.	1867	1881	1891	1901
Akolā ..	14,606	16,614	21,470	29,289
Akot ..	14,006	16,137	15,995	18,252
Bālāpur ..	12,631	11,244	10,250	10,486
Kāranjā ..	11,750	10,923	14,436	16,535
Bāsim ..	8,625	11,576	12,389	13,823

Thus Akola has doubled in size, Kāranja and Bāsim have increased by 50 per cent., Akot has risen by 30 per cent., and Bālāpur alone has declined. It is significant that Akola alone is on the railway, Kāranja, Bāsim, and Akot are served by good metalled roads, but the communications of Bālāpur are seriously interrupted by awkward river crossings. Important roads running north and south meet at Murtizāpur station just as they do at Akola, but to get a just idea of the growth of population it is necessary to combine the totals for Murtizāpur and Sirso; in 1891 these amounted to 6930, in 1901 to 10,659.

Taking all the towns now having a population of more than 5000, it appears that every place except Kāranja and Bālāpur increased in the fourteen years ending in 1881; seven declined, but three large towns and Mangrul increased, in the decade ending 1891; all except Hiwarkhed, Pātur, and Wādegaon increased again in the decade ending in 1901. In the decade 1881 to 1891 there was an increase of 3 per cent. in the total population, whereas the urban population increased by 6 per cent.; some large towns grew, but there was perhaps a general movement from fully cultivated neighbourhoods to parts where land was available for cultivation. The average number of persons per house in the five tāluks of the old Akola District was 5½ in 1881, 4 in 1891, and 4½ in 1901; while in the same years in the three tāluks of Bāsim District it was 6, 5½ and 5. In 1901 the average was about 4½ in Akot and about 5 in each of the other tāluks of the present District.

Migration.

66. The tables of migration given with the Census Report are probably unreliable, but the percentage of immigrants to total population shown by them in 1901 was 31 in Murtizāpur, 25 in Akola and Mangrul, 20 in Bāsim, 16 in Akot, and 10 in Bālāpur. Immigrants are attracted by different features within the District—its agriculture, commerce, finance, general labour, and so on. A great

deal of movement within the District and between adjoining Districts has been due to cultivators moving to thinly-settled neighbourhoods in order to take up land on advantageous terms. Female immigrants are generally more numerous than males because wives are often brought from villages which happen to lie across the tāluk border, but immigrants from a long distance seldom bring womenfolk with them. Many of the clerks first employed by the British Government, and many of the early pleaders, came from Bombay Presidency. Hindus from northern India are commonly called Pardeshis; both Hindus and Muhammadans from the south are known as Dakhanis. These two large classes are mostly engaged in labour, especially driving carts or working as *hamāls*, porters, at cotton factories; they are therefore most common in towns; sometimes, however, a colony of Dakhanis settles in a village by the side of a metalled road and finds employment upon it. Scattered over the southern tāluks are a number of Jhādiwālas, or people from the Central Provinces, mostly engaged in agriculture; they are said to have come during a famine about 35 years ago. In most of the villages in the extreme north of Akot tāluk are other Jhādiwālas, working as field labourers or petty artisans, who have been gradually drifting into the neighbourhood for several years. They come on foot through the plain country and then seem to strike north till they are stopped by the Sātpūra plateau. Mārwāris, engaged chiefly in money-lending and, when they are rich enough, in cotton and grain speculation, are found in almost every village; a large settlement at Telhāra in the west of Akot tāluk owns a great deal of land, occupies houses with handsome fronts of carved wood, and is served by artisans of all kinds from Mārwār; Dhanaj, in the east of Murtizāpur tāluk, is the scene of a settlement on a smaller scale. Petty money-lending, at very high rates, is carried on by Muhammadans from the frontiers; they are known as Rohillas, are readily distinguished by their dress, and are generally feared on account of their truculence. Pilgrimages and other religious interests cause a further constant trickle of migration; one may meet in the remote Mangrul tāluk a little party of Bundelkhand Brāhmans begging their way to Rāmeshwar (at the end of Adam's Bridge in the extreme south of India) without knowing anything about its whereabouts except that it is in the Deccan; their return journey will be easier because they will carry "Ganges water" (from the sea) and *tilakchhāp*, sectarian marks, to sell as relics. A wandering Muhammadan may be a *Maulvi-mullā* from Ajmer, or perhaps only a local *fakīr* with his wife.

Medical statistics.

67. Medical statistics for the area forming the present District are available only from 1905 to 1908. Difficulties in diagnosis and imperfections in recording occur here as elsewhere, but according to the reports the average annual number of deaths is 37,000 (49 per 1000); of which dysentery and diarrhœa caused 8500, fevers 6500, plague 3200, respiratory diseases 3100, cholera 1400, injuries 300, smallpox 300, measles and chickenpox 200, and miscellaneous causes 13,700. The total number of deaths varied between 26,000 (35 per 1000) and 44,000 (58 per 1000). Nearly all the deaths from cholera occurred in the single year 1906 (5000); plague rose to 6200 in 1907 and fell to 500 in 1908; other causes vary to a less extent.

Diseases.

68. The heat is considerable in the cold weather and intense in the hot weather, but the rainfall is not heavy, a cool breeze generally prevails at night, and the climate is not

on the whole unhealthy. The rate of mortality in the "salt tract" appears to be slightly higher than that elsewhere; this is an area extending for some miles on each side of the Pūrna river in the north-east of the District. One theory is that this region was once a great salt lake, and that when its waters found an outlet and the Pūrna drained the valley the saline deposits remained in the soil. However this may be, the water is so impregnated with soda salts as to be almost undrinkable. Sweet wells are in fact often found close beside brackish ones, but there is no means of knowing whether good or bad water will be found. The higher death rate in this tract seems to be chiefly due to bowel diseases, but the birth rate is as high as elsewhere in Berār and the neighbourhood is not seriously unhealthy.

In Akola District, as over the greater part of India, the months of July, August, and September form the most unhealthy period; malaria and bowel diseases are most prevalent then. Infant mortality is high and is chiefly due to these causes. The malaria is chiefly of the "benign" and "malignant" tertian types. It is naturally most common toward the end of the rains and in the beginning of the cold weather, because the anopheles mosquitoes have at that time the best chance of breeding in the pools. The District, however, suffers much less than some others in the Provinces from malaria, and the parasite is curiously hard to find. Enlarged spleen in children, which is common in malarious regions, is comparatively rare here—the endemic index is low. Mortality from bowel diseases is high throughout Berār and is naturally highest in the rains. The District has always been subject to violent outbreaks of cholera; these occur at short intervals and cause enormous mortality; thus in 1906 the deaths from this cause alone amounted to close upon 5000, a ratio of 6½ per mille. The outbreaks seem generally to be due to importation, especially from such gatherings as the Pandharpur fair, but there can be no doubt that cholera is endemic throughout Berār. For some unascertained reason which must be sought in the life history of the organism the disease lies dormant or shows only a little activity, and then for some equally unknown reason it breaks out again. The town of Akola has of late years been given a pipe water supply brought from Kāpsi, 10 miles away, and this has certainly provided an irresistible weapon against severe epidemic outbreaks in the town itself. As this water supply is improved it may be hoped that Akola town will be practically freed from cholera. Smallpox has always been prevalent, but its ravages have decreased considerably of late years; vaccination is efficiently carried out, 3½ per cent of the population being protected every year. Neither cataract nor stone is very common.

Plague.

69. Plague first appeared in 1902 and has recurred every year. The chief outbreak in Akola town was in 1905, when the deaths amounted to 1468. In 1907 the total number of deaths in the District from plague was 6160, or 8 per mille. The people are very slow to have recourse to inoculation, only 1700 being done in the 7 years from 1902 to 1908; villages are evacuated fairly promptly when the discovery of dead rats shows that plague is coming, but villagers say that the idea of inoculation is still too novel for them. On the other hand a Teli in the north of Berār who a few years ago professed without any qualifications to protect from plague soon had a large following; but the disease broke out among the crowds who attended him, and he ran away. Dur-

ing January and February 1909 about 1600 people were inoculated in Akola town, and this may possibly mark a turning-point in the public attitude, but much of the enthusiasm was certainly due to the fact that R. 1 was being given to each patient; when the payment was reduced to As. 8 about 500 people who were waiting in the hospital compound turned without a word and walked away; one hears of people trying to squeeze the serum out of their arms when they have received their reward. The greater part of the population is at present (February 1909) living outside the town and coming in daily for business; well-to-do families have put up small bungalows of tin, or with tiled roofs; 195 deaths from plague have occurred within the two months, but only one case, and that not fatal, has happened among those inoculated. An energetic campaign against rats has been carried on since 1907, but it is impossible to give accurate statistics; for instance, for 100 poisoned baits laid down it is very rare for more than 3 dead rats to be found, but one municipality reported that nearly 6000 rats were collected for 7000 baits; it was afterwards explained that 6000 baits had disappeared and were considered equivalent to so many dead rats found. People of the middle class, the large numbers who are not very poor but are not highly educated, are far less willing in Akola District than in other Provinces to accept skilled medical advice; the very poor are generally less reluctant, but a beggar who has been blind from his infancy will sometimes not permit a simple operation which would probably restore his sight.

Medical practices.

70. Enquiries made in several villages about infant mortality showed that it is quite common for 20 per cent. of children to die in the first year, while over 50 per cent. sometimes

die. When a child is born it is not put to the breast for two or three days, but is fed on *sulāche pāni*, sugared water, *sahad*, honey, and the like, and a few drops of castor oil are given it; the mother does not take any food for a day or two. A child is generally suckled for a year, and often, if there is no other claimant, for two or three years, and sometimes longer still. When it is weaned it is given cow's or goat's milk by well-to-do people, but the bulk of the people give it no further milk; it is fed on jawāri bread, alone or mixed with *tūr* flour, and on rice, sugar, sweetmeats, and so on. Medical knowledge is very scanty. People with broken limbs usually go now to a hospital, but they used to call in a Dhangar who might have gained experience in binding up the legs of his flocks and herds. It is said that he would apply bamboo splints for about a week, and then remove them permanently, having the leg rubbed with *tilli* or castor oil. The process was apt to be unsatisfactory, but the principle is akin to that of very recent surgery. A mortified finger may be plunged into boiling oil; cobwebs are used to stop excessive bleeding, and *chunā*, lime, and leaves are applied to cure a wound; but magic is largely relied on to give the motive power of healing—a string with a certain number of knots being tied, for instance, round the neck, and *mantras* recited meanwhile, to prevent tetanus. Sometimes people's eyesight is ruined by the application of absurd remedies. A kind of fever called *kāpsi mātā*, cotton disease, is mentioned in all parts of the District; something that looks like cotton fluff is said to collect at night under the patient's bed; the disease generally occurs in the cold weather, but its real nature is not clear. Native doctors, *vaidyas*, of various degrees of pretention are found in the larger villages; they are generally very ignorant and sometimes deliberate impostors; they not infrequently secure payment in advance. Their medicines are usually pills, which are dissolved in honey or the juice of a lime, an onion, or wet ginger; powders are taken in cow's milk or hot water; and infusions are occasionally brought. *Vaidyas* like to recite *shlok*, texts, from various sources and make a great point of feeling the pulse, though without using a watch. Men who have been compounders in a Government hospital sometimes make great profit out of their fallacious knowledge.

71. The writer has met two or three men who are almost certainly centenarians; Hāji Ghasumiya of Akot has an invitation written for his Bismillah ceremony when he was four years and four months old and bearing a date in the first half of 1207 Fasli, that is 1797 A.D.; this seems to prove that he is now 116 years old. A patel of more than 40 says that his grandfather, who died 25 years ago at a great age, spoke of Ghasumiya as a schoolfellow. It is said universally that men in general are much smaller and weaker than they were two or three generations ago. The first explanation offered by villagers is often that food is dearer and people are more worried by debt and competition. Everyone however readily admits that far more comfort prevails now than before, and some serious and common causes of anxiety have been removed. Another explanation, originally kept in reserve from motives of delicacy, is then almost invariably given and the first is dropped. In most castes the husband used generally to be 8 or 10 years older than the wife, and 5 years difference was absolutely the minimum; the last difference, by the way, is given as the average in the Census Report of 1881. The parents took simple precautions to keep the wife apart from her husband till she attained puberty. For

Physique.

many years the difference in age has been decreasing, and parental strictness has greatly relaxed, and this has caused a serious decline in the physique of the middle castes, Kunbis and the like. Tradition is extraordinarily untrustworthy; one hears of days when the husband was 30 and the wife 12, when men commonly lived to be 100 and drove cattle every day 20 miles to pasture; but the widespread insistence on this particular point may have some significance. The idea is illustrated by the fact that the Mārwāris, who permit adult marriages, recently held a great meeting about caste matters and formally instituted a rule that the husband must be at least three years older than the wife.

Occupation.

72. Statistics of occupation are given in the census reports only by Districts, not by tāluks, but probably the percentages suggested by a combination of the figures for the old Akola and Bāsim Districts would be very nearly true for the area forming the present Akola District. In 1901 the proportion of the population engaged in agriculture was 71 per cent. in Akola District and 76 in Bāsim, the industrial population 14 per cent. in Akola and 11 in Bāsim, the commercial 2 per cent. in each, and the professional 2 per cent. in Akolā and 1 in Bāsim. Thus three-quarters of the population were engaged in agriculture; a large proportion of industrial workers again were engaged in work subsidiary to agriculture, such as the making of carts and agricultural implements. Hand industries had never been very important, because for many years before the Assignment very few people in Berār had dared to show any signs of wealth, but those that formerly existed declined with the introduction of better, or much cheaper, articles from outside. In 1901 Akola contained only 3,384 cotton weavers, including dependents, and Bāsim only 1,223. Cotton factories

have however given increasing mechanical employment; the number of workers, without dependents, in 1891 was—in Akola 1,933, Bāsim 76; in 1901 it was—Akola 5,727, Bāsim 340. The present District consists of 6 tāluks in place of 8 in the two old Districts, but according to the only reports obtainable for the last few years it now contains over 8,000 factory-hands. Among the agriculturists in 1901 about 48 per cent. of the whole population were returned as labourers, three-quarters of them being actual workers; about 23 per cent. were landholders and tenants, not quite a half being workers. The circumstances, however, show that it must be very difficult to get such returns made correctly; it is very common for a man to be both landholder and labourer and not to know which to call himself, while the women-folk of quite well-to-do landholders work as labourers; in an ordinary village there are very few families in which the women think it beneath them to do field work. In 1901 village service was returned as engaging or supporting 3 per cent. of the population. Government officers numbered 39 in the two Districts combined, clerks and inspectors were 450, constables and warders 1,575 (each supporting 2 dependents); teachers were 750. Akolā had 29 pleaders with 160 dependents and Bāsim 9 with 57 dependents; the large proportion of dependents in this class throws into strong relief the fact that women and youths in most classes are to a large extent workers, though much of the field-work they do is brief in time and light in nature. Mendicants and their dependents, religious and otherwise, were reported as numbering 21,500 in the two Districts, that is 2 per cent. of the whole.

Criminal population.

73. Most of the population, especially the Hindus, are on the whole quiet and law-abiding, but there are some people

whose caste tradition makes them the object of more or less suspicion. Kaikāris number 734, scattered all over the District; some of them support themselves by taking contracts for road repair and for work on public buildings, but many are habitual thieves and the police find it hard to decide who are honest. Tākankārs or Takāris are found chiefly in the northern tāluks; they number altogether 2,911; old men speak of them as the chief robbers of former times. Pārdhis are, like most of these castes, divided into several sub-castes; the Langoti Pārdhis are commonly given to petty thefts from fields or houses, and the old men can hardly talk to a Government officer without endless demands that if they do not speak the truth (which they do not) they may be hanged, transported, blown from a gun, or the like. Sarodis make a temporary encampment which is given up by day to the women and the children, with babies swinging in cradles of rope; the men wander from village to village leading perhaps a bull with showy trappings and jingling bells; the man beats a drum, begs in the name of his bull-god, and watches for opportunities of theft. A small proportion of the Pardeshi and Dakhani immigrants are criminals. The Muhammadan Gaolis of Kāranja concert road-crimes along with their relatives at Dārwhā. The Pātharkāds located here and there near the Pūrna river, like most castes whose occupation involves much wandering, are strongly suspected of thefts of various kinds. Muhammadan rowdies are sometimes hired to help in a quarrel about a field; Rohillas bring more than legal pressure to bear, sometimes, on their debtors; the poorer classes are often tempted to steal crops at night (and honest people may profess to be afraid to catch them); gangs from outside may include the District in a very large field of operations, or parties of a wandering caste pass through it; and crime is committed by individuals of miscellaneous castes.

Language.

74. Marāthi is the common language of the great bulk of Hindus throughout Berār; it differs little from the standard Dakhani Marāthi of Poona. Some variations occur between the different Districts within Berār, but these again are too slight to cause any difficulty in conversation. Educated people speak in a more refined way, so that they sometimes term their own speech Brāhmani as distinguished from the Kunbi or Kunbau of the mass of the people, but it is difficult to formulate such differences as would constitute distinct dialects. However certain variations can be pointed out as arising in common speech. Even the educated generally say *Māhādeo* instead of *Mahādeo*, and *Yejurveda* instead of *Yajurveda*. It is very common to substitute *a* for *e* in the termination of neuter bases, *e.g*, *khālcha* for *khālche*, *lower*; the Konkani dialect spoken on the far side of the Deccan tract has also this characteristic. Villagers often interchange *i* with *e* and *ya*, saying *dilla*, *della*, or *dyalla*, *given*. Initial *e* is sometimes pronounced *ye*, thus *ek* and *yek*, *one*; and *v* is sometimes slurred or dropped before *i* or *e*, thus *vechne*, *echne*, or *yechne*, *to pick* (*cotton*). The cerebral *l* is sometimes softened into *y* or perhaps *r*, *māli*, *māyi*, *gardener*, and cerebral *n* is sometimes changed to plain *n*, *kon*, *who*, *pāni*, *water*. In case-suffixes the dative is sometimes formed by adding *le* instead of *lā*, *bāpāle*, *to the father*, while the plural may be *bāpāhīs* or *bāpāns*, *to the fathers*. Pronouns sometimes take peculiar forms in declension, *tyā* for *twā*, *by thee*, *māhā* for *mājhā*, *my*, and *tuhā* for *tujhā*, *thy*; the nominative singular feminine of the demonstrative pronoun is *te* instead of *ti*, *she*; *lā* is sometimes inserted before

the plural termination of pronouns, *tyālāchā* instead of *tyāchā*, *his*. In verbs the form *mi marto*, *I die*, might be used by either man or woman, when the standard feminine form is *mi marte*, and in the third person the neuter form may be used instead of the masculine, *porgā khelte* instead of *porgā khelto*, *the boy plays*. The second person singular takes the same form as the third, *tu āhe* instead of *tu āhes*, *thou art* ; just as the second and third persons plural of the past tense coincide, *tumhi gele*, *you went*, and *te gele*, *they went*. The habitual past becomes an ordinary past, especially in the expression *to mhane*, he said. In the future tense *n* and *l* are interchanged, giving the forms *mi mārīl*, *tu mārsīn*, and *te mārtīn* instead of *mi mārīn*, *tu mārshīl*, and *te mārtīl*, *I will*, *thou wilt*, and *they will strike* ; *tumhi mārsān* is also substituted for *tumhi mārāl*, *you will strike*. The form *sanyā* is sometimes added to the conjunctive participle, *khāūn sanyā*, *having eaten* ; Kunbis from both Nāgpur and Sholāpur say *shani* instead of *sanyā*. Trifling differences also occur in the use of words and the genders ascribed to them ; thus in some parts the ordinary word for *woman* is *bāiko*, in others it is *lakshmi*, while an educated man might say *strī* ; *rastā*, *road*, and *gānw*, *village*, should be masculine and neuter respectively, but are neuter and masculine in some neighbourhoods ; some Sanskrit words are commonly used, thus *indhan* instead of *sarpan*, *fuel* ; also *tutāri* instead of *kāthi*, *goad* ; Urdu words are also adopted, *sapīlī*, *saphīl*, *town-wall* ; and common words sometimes take peculiar forms, *kothā* instead of *gothā*, *cattle-shed* ; while some terms are said to be peculiarly Berāri, such as *vetāl*, *quarter* (*of a town*). Numerous other petty differences occur ; the speech of remote and hilly tracts being perhaps most markedly different because of its additional roughness, but local variations are in fact seldom striking. Caste variations are much more considerable. The great points in regard to them are that immigrants on the one hand, and the more aboriginal castes on the other, retain more or less of their original tongue, so that a Mahār from the south may say that his father talks Telugu, but he himself does not; and that castes with criminal traditions have their own private vocabularies, generally based on Gujarāti. These two causes account for the recognition in the census of 1901 of 16,000 people speaking Banjāri, 15,000 Mārwāri, 7,000 Gujarāti, 5,000 Telugu, and 3,000 Gondi; the figures, by the way, must be inexact because people very commonly fail to distinguish as separate languages the varying forms in which they communicate with different acquaintances, and because criminals like to keep their own speech secret. Muhammadans almost invariably speak dialects which they would call either Urdu, Hindi, Hindustāni, or Musulmāni; the Muhammadans of the District number 54,000, and according to the last census Urdu was spoken by 65,000 people, and Hindi by 16,000. They generally consider that there is a difference between these two forms of speech, but it seems to consist simply in the extent to which Persian and Sanskrit sources are drawn upon for vocabulary, and in the grammatical finish of the construction. Musalmāni is a loose term applicable to both Urdu and Hindi. The Hindutāni of the District is in fact very corrupt when compared with that of northern India. Practically all the Marāthi-speaking population know enough Hindustāni to carry on a conversation in it with Muhammadans, who generally understand Marathi but seldom condescend to speak it. A man at a loss for a word in either language is very often safe in using the corresponding word of the other language. Mārwāris speak Hindustāni in their dealings with people in general, though those that live in small villages are often fluent in Marāthi also. English was in 1901 the language of 115 persons.

RELIGION.

75. General. To give a correct sketch of the religion of the Hindus of the District is impossible. One constantly comes across ideas drawn from the ancient classical teachings of India, but these not only seem vague and confused but are often buried under the habitual worship of local saints or divinities and under a mass of superstition. Religion touches every detail in the life of a Hindu, sometimes with admirable effect but sometimes in mere formalism. In almost every village new temples are being built, but old men of the middle castes say—" A man's heart is the proper temple. Nowadays people make a show of buildings of brick but there is no temple in their hearts." The Bhagavad-Gīta would be readily acknowledged as a religious authority, and sometimes one sees traces of its description of a Brāhman's ideal (Lesson XVIII, 42) — "Restraint of spirit and sense, mortification, purity, patience, uprightness, knowledge, discernment, and belief are the natural Brahma-works"; but the standard is a very high one. The Kshatriya ideal, given in the next verse, brings this curiously into accordance with English ideas—" Valour, heroic temper, constancy, skill, steadfastness in strife, largesse, and princeliness are the natural Knightly works" ; but these are virtues far beyond the ambition of the ordinary Hindu. In a small village one may hear the teaching of the Vedānta, the greatest, perhaps, of the Indian philosophies; the following story, told with no trace of irony, seems at least to belong to a popular exposition of that school. " Once when a Brāhman was offering rice and other food to Mahādeo a rat came and

ate the sacrifice, whereon the Brāhman concluded that the rat must be the god himself. He placed it in a cage therefore and fed it with the best of everything, but by a series of accidents a cat ate the rat, a dog worried the cat, his wife beat the dog, and he beat her, and so, transferring his worship constantly to the conqueror, he realised that he himself was the god." On the other hand a Brāhman of some education from Akola itself may be ignorant of both the sound and the idea of the fundamental *Tat tvam asi*, Thou art That, of the school; in fact very few people pretend to any thought of philosophy. The ordinary intelligent but practically uneducated Hindu would apparently consider both that there are many gods and that there is only one god, but would humbly abstain from a definite theory to reconcile the two ideas. He believes in an absolute *karma*, whereby act and consequence attend the soul in earth and heaven and hell remorselessly through an endless cycle of births but sometimes he holds that bad means are justified by a good end, or he trusts to the expiatory sacrifice of *prāyaschitta* or some other protection. Indeed he must often feel that fate dictates not only the punishment but the very evil that is to be punished. In his religious thought *bhakti* occupies a very large place, with the meanings apparently of faith, worship, and the reaching out of the human to the divine. People in remote villages say that it is chiefly on account of this vague *bhakti* that red *shendur* is applied to prominent stones or trees. The patel of a small hilly village said that for the same reason goats were sacrificed to different local *Asrās* when a marriage took place—"We feel that we must do an act of worship." An educated Hindu will say that an offering of rice and curds, under the name of *bona*, is always made to the goddess *Asrā*—who is generally represented by a stone daubed with red on the bank of a river—so that nothing may occur to prevent the ceremony, but the more primitive worshipper seemed merely to be reaching out to the unknown God. One seems to see worship done sometimes for definite material ends and sometimes as the unqualified expression of a powerful instinct.

Religious practices.

76. In the actual performance of religious duties a combination of correct ritual with faith is apparently imperative. Certain ceremonies are daily performed in the house, and a pious man might also go to the temple every day. A Brāhman of the older generation and of only moderate education would daily repeat in Sanskrit a selection from the Vedas or the whole of the Bhagavad-Gīta, or perhaps only the very important 15th chapter, though he might have no knowledge of the language; thus there is a great deal of uncomprehending worship. The same religion however produces very distinct practical consequences. Hinduism seems to be as a rule extraordinarily tolerant, permitting both the greatest variations of creed within its own limits and viewing with calmness yet other ideas in other religions. It enjoins a very wide charity, so that travellers can almost always secure food and lodging and support is almost always provided for the destitute and afflicted. Brāhmans have of course the first claim; one may meet a little party, more than half of them women or infants, making a four months' pilgrimage on foot from Allahābād to Nāsik and living wholly on charity. Asked how they manage about expense, the reply comes simply, "We are Brāhmans," though the complaint may be added that nowadays hardly more than one person in ten gives to them. All religious mendicants share in this charity, and sometimes in a village two or three wait at doors a few yards apart till their dole is given. Sometimes there is a rest-

house especially set aside for pious wanderers; occasionally a wealthy man supports all such comers, and Bairāgis, Sanyāsis, Gosāins, and the like come to stay in peace for a month or two at his rest-house amid their travels. Sometimes a holy man who has settled near a village collects subscriptions to build or repair a temple, or he is pressed to come and take charge of one, and become its *pujāri*, worshipper, and the *guru*, religious guide, of the people. People show an extraordinary degree of respect to a man who has given up all worldly interests and devotes himself entirely to what is considered a religious life; to go naked is perhaps one of the most compelling proofs of devotion. The popular attitude must offer some temptation to the hypocritical, but on the other hand anyone living in a small village is under very close scrutiny; hypocrisy would be discovered except in a constant wanderer. In former times this wandering religious element was far more striking. Naked Gosāins, Bairāgis wearing only a *langoti*, and Mānbhaus in plain black would come in bodies of perhaps five hundred, with horses and camels, and pass slowly through the country at the cost of the people. Such pomp has now departed, though various orders have still their characteristic garbs and individuals are sometimes distinguished by wearing a red Mephistopheles cap or some such mark; one *sādhu* in the neighbourhood, Gājanan Mahārāj of Shegaon, is so deeply reverenced that a Brāhman of position and education bows his forehead to the dust before him and does not dream of an acknowledgment. Gradually miraculous stories come to be told about distinguished *sādhus* and some of them are worshipped even before their death. (A *chelā*, disciple, is bound to worship his teacher while yet alive; occasionally he does so by putting up an image of him). Tombs at which saints are worshipped are scattered all over the District and are very numerous in Akot tāluk; the traditions of several are given in the Appendix. The chief forms of worship seem to be, firstly to vow some small offering in case a certain prayer is granted, and secondly to attend an annual festival in honour of the saint. Different tombs have reputations for different kinds of virtue, some curing snake-bite, some fever, and some possession by an evil spirit; an extraordinary variety of miracles is attributed to these saints; and Hindus feel no reluctance to worship at a Muhammadan tomb. Among lesser saints stands the labourer of Wyāla who, according to present tradition, was canonised for the two reasons that he once collected thorns for a fence by setting his bare foot upon them without being hurt and that he was seen worshipping at the same time in two temples five miles apart; the virtue inherited from him enabled his son to cast out evil spirits. Among the greater is Narsingboa of Akot, whose casual word is said to have preserved a corpse from dissolution for four years, at the end of which time it ate a piece of bread. Shāh Dāwal of Gowardha has a characteristic, though mixed, reputation. Nothing is known of his life except that he was one of a trio of Muhammadan *awalyās* (*awalyā*, honorific plural of *wali*, saint) who settled respectively at Gowardha, Uprāi in Daryāpur tāluk, and Burhānpur. A man desirous of begetting a son goes to Gowardha and ties a stone to a string fastened around the inside door of the tomb. Later he brings the child, cuts his hair, distributes sweetmeats of the weight of the hair, and finally ties it up instead of the stone. Men possessed of demons and men and women suffering from various diseases come and live here till they are relieved, though *chudhels* are apparently not expelled from women. The cure may take a month or more, but the patients must live meanwhile by begging from door to door with the cry, "*Dam, dam, Shādalboāchi gadā!*" or "*Dom! Dom!*", a well-known call of pilgrims. Resident *mujāwars*, attendants, are in charge of the tomb and worship every day, a fair attended by all castes is held every Thursday, and Kolis come on pilgrimage from a distance. The worship of these saints takes a large place in the life of an ordinary family; it is impossible to say exactly how far the stories about them are accepted, but there is certainly a great deal of religious credulity.

Religious organisation.

77. Various figures besides that of the *sādhu* stand out in such efforts at organisation as can be traced amid the general confusion. A really important place, such as the headquarters of a tāluk, would contain one or more Shāstris and perhaps an Agnihotri. Some Shāstris are Vedic, knowing one or more of the Vedas (either by heart or by meaning), and some are Dharma shāstris, knowing other *granths*, sacred writings; they have an unequalled knowledge of the demands of religion. A Kunbi might become a Dharmashāstri, though in fact he never does so, but it is not permitted to teach him the Vedas. An Agnihotri performs three times a day the sacrifice of the *homa*; he is distinguished by various characteristics, but need not be learned. In the rains a Shāstri, *purānik*, or perhaps the local schoolmaster, is often engaged in the largest villages to recite and explain some *purāns*; in the town of Akolā there are often 10 or 12 such courses in different temples, a *purān* appropriate to the particular god or season being generally chosen. Sometimes a *haridās* or *kathekari* conducts a *kathā*, a preaching service diversified with music and the calling of "Rām, Rām," "Krishna, Krishna," and the like. (In a third service called

bhajan, the congregation has no official leader; they chant a series of texts, each man keeping time with a pair of *jhānja, tāl*, cymbals; in villages two *dindi*, parties, are formed, of which one leads and the other responds). Brāhmans have also a *dharmādhikāri*, who is a final authority on questions of religion, and a *shankarāchārya* with power to punish for breaches of caste rule and the like; the *dharmādhikāri* holds his office by hereditary right, but should take skilled advice if he is himself unlearned; there are nine representatives in the single town of Bāsim; the *shankarāchārya* requires to be personally qualified for his post. The middle castes, such as Kunbis, have Brāhman *joshis* to conduct most of their ceremonies; these are hereditary officers and need to know only a single *granth*, the Shūdra Kamalākar. They are supported partly by fees for the particular ceremonies and partly by *haks*, annual contributions, from their people. A *joshi* on the Pūrna river told the writer that some of the Kunbis in his neighbourhood were beginning to do without a *joshi* at their ceremonies, but this was probably a trivial movement due to personal disagreement. Beside these officers there are *pujāris*, worshippers, attached to many tombs and temples. They are often Brāhmans from different parts of India, sometimes having the hereditary title of *swasthānik*, but more frequently Gosāins. In the latter case it is usual for the worshipper who is getting old to take a boy, perhaps a Kunbi, and train him to the succession. The temple buildings are likely to include a walled compound enclosing a *pinda*, shrine of the god—who is very likely Mahādeo worshipped under some such local name as Kāteshwar—a dwelling-house for the worshipper, and ten or a dozen tombs of former worshippers, the main building being called *math*. No attempt is made, however, to follow any particular plan; the *math* occasionally occupies part, or the whole, of an ordinary village-fort. These Gosāins both perform daily worship of the god on behalf of the village—bathing, feeding, and adoring him—and are called *guru* by the people. They almost always recognise the Mahant of Māhur, on the Penganga in the Nizām's Dominions, as their head, and both they and their flocks make pilgrimages to Māhur, to Sahasrakund near by, and perhaps to Umagdeo 20 miles further east.

Practices at festivals.

78. Festivals again are an important feature of the ordinary Hindu religion. They are very frequent, are given considerable religious value, and are enjoyable social events. They may be divided roughly into two classes; in the former are the anniversaries of local gods or saints, when pilgrimages, great or petty, are made to particular temples or tombs; in the latter class are the greater festivals of Hinduism. Pandharpur is the place of pilgrimage most frequented by Berāris; pilgrims wear a necklace of beads made from the root of the *tulsi* plant; during the festivals caste restrictions are set aside in the one detail that no one is defiled by being touched by a man of low caste. An annual fair is held at the tomb of every saint whose memory has any vitality and at a great many temples, the number of visitors varying from a few score to some thousands. There might be half a dozen, or a dozen, of these annual festivals in a village that had no tomb or temple of any note. At some villages the festival has some such special feature as fire-walking, or the apparent relics of human sacrifice or self-torture. Fire-walking appears to be very rare, but is said to exist in at least three of the four Berār Districts. The only case in this District which has come to the writer's notice is that of Malsud, in the south of Bālāpur tāluk. An account of

it was given by the village officers of Malsud and some neighbouring villages. The village contains a temple dedicated to Supoba, an *ansha*, incarnation, of Mahādeo, and a Dāndi-Punao festival is held in February-March during the fifteen days which end at Shivrātra. On the first Friday a *dongar* (a kind of *mandap*, *phātā*, or *mandir*), booth or pavilion, is made. Two days of worship follow, and on the Monday a *lahād*, pit, is dug five cubits in length, one in breadth, and a span or two in depth. This is filled with wood (of all kinds), oil, contributed by all the villagers according to their means, is poured upon it, and the whole is set on fire. The priests of the temple are Hatkars, and they walk the length of this pit while the fire is still burning. If a man has a wife by *lagna* marriage she accompanies him, but a wife by *mohatir* (also called *pāt* or *gandharwa*) marriage does not. Last year, 1908, five couples performed the ceremony, walking slowly along the pit to the temple, praying, and then returning. The chief narrator of this account was the (Hatkar) patel of the village. He said the devotees were preserved from harm only by faith, and that it was believed that if anyone but them attempted the feat his family would die out. The ashes of the fire are considered to cure snake-bite without any *mantras* being recited. The chief day of the festival is however a Friday, when *bhandāra*, a religious meal, is given. Then the worshippers, forming groups of perhaps 50 at a time, hold out their hands with the backs upwards, and the chief *pujāri* of the temple gives five blows with a *sat*, whip of cord, to those near him, and is considered to have struck them all. On certain occasions practices which appear to be relics of human sacrifice or self-torture are done, and middle-aged men in some villages can remember seeing self-torture done in earnest. People take small children before the goddess Asra at Donad on the Kātepurna river in Akola tāluk. A good swimmer swims about the river with the child in a cradle, and finally the child is taken out and the cradle is allowed to float down the stream; people say that the child used at one time to be drowned. In some places a childless couple vow that if a child is granted them it shall be devoted to the goddess Devi. In fact, they take it before the shrine dressed in good clothes and leave the garments alone there. *Gal pūja*, hook-worship, used to be done at Hiwarkhed and Chandkāpur in Akot tāluk, at Bālāpur, and at some other villages. One or two iron hooks were thrust into a man's back and he was either swung or made to pull carts. Even now lemons are fastened on a man's middle, hooks are put into them, and with the help of the crowd the man pulls four or five carts along by a cord attached to the hooks, the people meanwhile shouting '*Hagraj*.' At Sawandal in Akot tāluk two strings used to be drawn through the muscle just above a man's thighs, one friend would take the strings in front and another behind, and the three would go around the village. As the strings were pulled the victim danced, and the performance was called *nādegal*, the hook-dance. These things were done in Akot tāluk on Chaitra Shuddh Pūrnima in honour of Devi, but in some places Khandoba is said to have been the divinity honoured. The victims were not devotees but merely casual villagers who offered to endure the pain in gratitude for some benefit received from the god; perhaps they were specially prepared for the ordeal by drugs or a long course of massage. At Kurankhed in Akola tāluk people used to make a vow to the goddess Devi in the village, and if their prayer was granted would cut off the tip of an index finger and offer it to her. An image made of kneaded flour is sometimes, especially by Mahārs and other low-caste people, laid before Marimā, the goddess of cholera. The writer quite recently noticed in a field the remains of half a dozen little clay bullocks, the model of a cart, the heads of two dolls, and a lime in the ruins of what may have been a model house. The actual object was apparently unknown to the headmen, but the variety of their conjectures showed that there were many occasions on which some one or other might think such symbolism of value.

Besides the festivals with a chiefly local interest there are those that celebrate the great days of the Hindu calendar. It may be remarked here that every day of the week is not merely named in connection with the same heavenly body in India as in England but it is also sacred to a particular god and has to some extent a character of its own. A list given in the south of Bālāpur tāluk showed that Sunday was dedicated to Nārāyan, Monday to Mahādeo and his local incarnation Supoba, Tuesday to the goddesses Devi, Bhawāni, and Asra, and among Brāhmans to Graha (planet), Wednesday to Wālkeshwar (a name of Mahādeo), Withoba, and Datta, Thursday to Guru or Shāhdāwal Pir, a Muhammadan saint whose limbs were buried at different villages, Friday to Bālāji, Khandoba, and Supoba again, and Saturday to Māroti. Some pious people fast on their particular god's day, and if they worship equally more than one god may fast four days in the week. Coming unexpectedly to a school on Tuesday forenoon one may find the headmaster absent; he is fasting on account of his *graha*. Every Brāhman has his own unlucky day of the week, called *ghātwār*, *warjawār*, day of loss or prohibition, told in the horoscope cast at birth. Besides this there are two days unlucky for everyone, Tuesday and Saturday. A man should not get shaved then, and fever beginning on one of these days is thought especially dangerous.

The local form of the great Hindu festivals is much the same in Akola as in other Berār Districts; no description can be given here on account of lack of space.

General beliefs about the supernatural.

79. It is perhaps unfair to speak of all the local ideas about the supernatural as religious, but it is impossible to draw exact lines between those that are really religious and those that would more fittingly be called magical. It is equally impossible to say how far particular beliefs are still held. The degree of belief varies greatly from one individual to another and the details differ equally. Some of the ideas and observances to be described in the following sections are held almost universally while others are said to have died out; perhaps no individual, and no village, knows them all, yet all have been collected within the District and many others must exist. People are generally reluctant to discuss some of them, partly because they are ashamed of being thought superstitious and partly, it would appear, from a positive fear of black magic. A number of people profess a universal scepticism of the superstitious as distinguished from the religious, but it is generally easy to find wide joints in their armour; sometimes men of position and intelligence first make a general denial but presently give an earnest exposition of some of the most extreme ideas. A few religious and magical ideas are therefore mentioned with no attempt at distinguishing the two.

Beliefs about disease.

80. In regard to illness perhaps the most prominent point is the way in which small-pox is regarded. It is hardly looked on as a disease at all but as a personal visitation of the goddess Devi, or Māta. In her honour the patient and his family are all dressed

in white, a *lotā*, vessel, containing water and *nīm* leaves is fetched by a man who has just bathed and is set at the door for everyone who enters the house to sprinkle himself. In the evenings *gharās* of water are carried to the shrine of Devi and ashes are brought thence and applied to the patient's forehead. Whatever the sick person says is regarded as the word of the goddess. He is in fact only given milk to drink, but if he should ask for some unreasonable food it would be brought and set before him. Every morning all the members of the family ask each other whether the Māta has spoken to anyone in the night, for sometimes she comes in a dream and says that she has taken care of the patient so long but that on a certain night she will leave and they must beware of any other spirit taking possession of him. Music is then kept up every night till, seven or nine days later, the ceremony of recovery is performed. Formal bathing is done on a Tuesday because that is the day sacred to Devi; the goddess is ceremoniously sent away in a curtailed form directly after the recovery and more fully some months later. The simplest form of the earlier ceremony is to give sugar and balls of jawāri flour to a few boys and to sprinkle water containing *nīm* leaves over them. The final ceremony is that which would be used for any distinguished human visitor. In cases where so much elaboration is not known one gets at least the central idea of the presence of the goddess; in very few even of the most educated families would any medicine be accepted beyond the water in which sacred *nīm* leaves were soaking. Cholera is supposed to be brought by the same goddess but is not so much linked up with religious ceremonies as smallpox; people in the larger villages will take medicine for it. When a village is threatened people may sacrifice or turn loose a goat, perhaps cutting off one of its ears as a token of its being sacrificed to the goddess. Sometimes the people collect a subscription and gather in a distant part of the village lands. Someone, generally a woman and not infrequently a Murli, dancing-girl, presently declares that the goddess has entered her body, has been wronged in some way, and demands a sacrifice of cocks and goats. The sacrifice is killed by a strong man of good caste on behalf of the patel, the headman of the village, and water is taken from the place of sacrifice and sprinkled on every house to keep cholera away. No religious traditions seem to have gathered about plague: the difference in the religious significance of the three diseases perhaps reflects the difference in the duration and extent of their ravages in the country. At delivery people put a cane at the head of the bed, an old shoe at the foot, and an iron knife and sickle underneath. The ordinary cure for snake-bite is to have *mantras* said by someone learned in such matters, who may be of practically any caste. He sometimes blows upon the wound and sometimes uses water; and it may be necessary to perform further ceremonies on Nāgpanchmi, the snake festival. A few shrines, however, exist about the efficacy of which to cure snake-bite no one in the neighbourhood has the least doubt: leading people will examine with interest one of Sir Lauder Brunton's lancets and even volunteer the statement that permanganate of potash is wonderfully effective in easing the pain of a scorpion-sting, but they explain that with such a shrine at hand they have no need of any other remedy. The procedure at the different shrines varies. That at Narnāla and at Shiupur near Bordi is described in the Appendix; other such shrines exist at Golegaon in the south of Bālāpur tāluk and at Kawatha in Murtizāpur tāluk. The sacred place at Golegaon is the ruinous tomb of Supoba; it is effective both for man and beast. If there is doubt whether a cow has been bitten by a poisonous snake or not one pulls out a hair from her tail. When the hair comes out readily it is a sign that she has been bitten, and *vice versa*. If similar doubt is felt about a man four tests can be applied; pepper, leaves of the sour lime, those of the *nīm* tree, or *pānāchā vidā*, a roll of betel leaves, is put into his mouth. Any-one bitten by a poisonous snake is supposed not to distinguish the taste of either of the first three, while the fourth when chewed by him fails to turn red. A man at the moment of being bitten puts a stone upon his head and starts for the tomb. If his road passes the temples of Māroti at Alegaon or Golegaon he must go behind, not in front of, them. If he cannot walk he may be carried, but not lying on his back. Arrived at the tomb he must go around it five times against the sun, with the stone still on his head. Then he lies on his face and must pass water and if possible vomit, which empties him of the poison and leaves him cured. One informant, who had himself been through the cure, said that one or two people were bitten every year, but in 60 years only four people had died. An intelligent informant, by the way, had himself come across a snake with two heads; ten kinds of snake could be mentioned but no one had any knowledge about what species of snakes were poisonous.

Beliefs about agriculture.

81. A long list of practices and beliefs is naturally connected with agriculture, but these again vary greatly in different parts. In the southern tāluks, at least, a white onion and some parched jawāri are sometimes applied to cotton seed before sowing it, the idea being apparently that the cotton boll may burst like the opened grain with cotton as white as the onion. In the

same part it is thought unlucky to take jawāri to the field in a bamboo basket (though this is done in Akot tāluk); it is placed in an earthen pot, white-washed, and having tied to it with the hair of a woman a large white onion and a piece of leather. Some people merely apply cow's urine to the seed, saying this will prevent the grain turning black; some say that if at the time of sowing the oxen step across the *dhussa*, drill, blackness will result. The invocation of Khat Deo, literally the Manure God, is widely practised. When the sowing of jawāri is finished the cultivator and his men build a little platform of earth and place upon it five white-washed stones to represent Khat Deo, and to these they offer vermilion, turmeric, sandal paste, and rice. Five holes are dug in front of the god, seed grain is put into them and covered with earth, and the god is earnestly invoked to bestow fertility. Some people also sow a few handfuls of grain in the name of evil spirits and of wild animals, saying "*Ek bhāg ghe, vīs bhāg de*—take one part, give me twenty." Before cotton-picking begins unwidowed females take two or three plants and form them into a cradle; they put into this an idol of earth, to which they offer curds, boiled rice, and incense. Before til is harvested boiled rice and curds are thrown out on all four sides of the field. When the *med*, pole, is to be put up in a threshing-floor bread and water are first put in the hole dug for it. The pole itself is often ornamented with a green bough and peacock's feathers, the latter more particularly for *rabi* grains. In the evening when the first heap of threshed jawāri is to be measured the master himself should take the *tokri*, basket, walk once round the heap with the sun, and burn incense before the first full basket. Silence should always be kept while jawāri is being measured. A scheme called *wārshul* dictates what directions a man may and may not face when sitting to measure jawāri. He is forbidden on Saturday and Monday to face east, on Tuesday and Wednesday north, on Friday and Sunday west, and on Thursday south. When all the grain has been threshed and stacked a goat is sacrificed and its flesh eaten at the threshing-floor. A man without a head-dress, a woman who is ceremonially unclean, *vitālshi*, *asparsha*, or any one who has ridden on an elephant or sat in a creaking *jhula*, swing, at a fair, should not enter a threshing-floor. When til has been cut the plants are first tied in small *pendya*, *pulya*, bundles, and then equal numbers of these are—to prevent the grain being wasted—bound in large bundles, *kothal*. When the crop is large these *kothal* are in some places made of 40 or 50 *pendya* each, but often they contain only three or four. If the outturn of the second *kothal* is greater than that of the first it is believed that some demon has taken possession of the grain and that the life of the cultivator is in danger. To avert the evil the grain is sometimes flung out beside the threshing-floor, or burnt, and the work is postponed till the next day. Some people when threshing keep the spirit at a distance by eating *badas*, made of lumps of ground pulse fried in *ghi* or oil. If the outturn of any crop is amazingly high people sometimes sacrifice a goat, but they complain that the circumstances very seldom arise. When til is very good the sacrifice is sometimes made by goats being turned loose in the field: they are said to die on account of the *daitya*, the evil in the crop, but no doubt they also suffer from over-eating. Finally, though the floor is carefully hardened and care is taken to prevent uncleanness some of the jawāri becomes mixed with earth. This is cleaned and kept and eaten in the family of the cultivator because it brings *barkat*, the spring of prosperity.

Rain charms.

82. Rain charms are numerous, most of them being intended to bring rain, but some to prevent it. To bring rain women, or in some parts girls, make a doll, *bhāwali* or *bāhuli*, of cloth, tie it to the frame of a door, take off their clothes, and beat the doll with a broom (a magical implement). Again a brass pot, *pitalyāche bhānde*, is filled with water and covered with a bag of the plant called *akao*, swallow-wort. A woman quickly turns the pot upside down and puts it on the head of an image of the god Māroti, telling it to fall either on Meskai (a demon goddess) or Māroti ; rain will fall if water comes out from the pot but not otherwise. A frog is sometimes tied to a stick, covered with *nīm* leaves, and taken around the village by scantily clad men and boys. They beg at every house, chanting some such couplet as—

"*Dhondi, dhondi, pāni de*
Arkya paili jawāri de

Dhondi, Dhondi, give rain and let jawari sell at 10 cowries (one-twenty-fifth of an anna) a paili." (Dhondi may refer to the month Dhonda or Adhik, which occurs once in three years and is sometimes said to bring deficient rain, or may have some less obvious meaning.) Sometimes the frog itself is addressed, or a different couplet is sung, perhaps ending—

"*Dhonga bhar bhar pān de*

Give rain enough to float a boat." The people throw pots of water over the party and give them jawāri, which they take to a well and boil and eat there. Another plan is to hold a *nāmasapla*, a seven day's service ; *bhajan*, chanting to the clashing of cymbals, is kept up day and night for seven days. Again, every hole in a temple of Mahādeo may be blocked and the temple be filled with water so that no part of the idol appears above the surface, and this is kept up for four or seven days; or the villagers may simply unite to bring vessels of water and pour them out in the temple. Different again is the worship of Gowardhan, in which the whole population of a village goes in a body to any hill near by and there worships Gopāl Krishna. Gowardhan was, according to one story, the mountain in Vrindāvana which Krishna induced the cowherds and cowherdesses to worship instead of Indra, whereon the latter sent a deluge to wash them away, but Krishna supported the hill with all the people for seven days on his little finger so that they were saved. A gruesome charm by which grain dealers tried to prevent rain is also told by an officer of experience. An imitation spinning wheel is made of the bones of a woman who died in child-birth, and an old and barren woman is made to turn it against the sun on the bank of a dry watercourse.

Spirits.

83. There seems to be a universal belief in a supernatural will o' the wisp, *chalāwa*. A most sceptical man will tell how he was attended by one through a whole night's journey but was protected from harm by the fact that he never lost courage, while others tell of a near relative losing his sanity and dying through the sight. Lights in a graveyard are spirits dancing. A *bābula*, dusty whirlwind, is a spirit, and there is a formula to keep it off a house. A spirit called *chakwa*, which may take any form, loves to mislead people at night. The victim wanders round and round, utterly incapable of seeing the object of his journey, though close to it. If he is thirsty the *chakwa* may throw him into a well. One remedy is to take off one's turban and shoes, stand on the former, and apply a little urine to one's eyes. Otherwise one should simply stand still and wait for morning. (Ordinary people used to wear very little that was capable of being markedly turned inside out.) A curious

account was given of an educated man going from Buldāna to Chikhli, fourteen miles, and being misled the whole night by the voice of his servant, only to find in the morning that the latter had not stirred outside the house. Elsewhere *chakwi* is an ailment of very rare occurrence in which people, especially young men, leave their homes and wander without sense in the jungle for days. Even by day a spirit might want the food one was carrying, and therefore a prudent man would throw a morsel aside at once to satisfy it and prevent further troubles. Brāhmans when eating their food often throw a little aside for the same reason. Possession by a spirit, *bhūt* in the case of a man, and *chudhel*, woman who died in child-birth, in the case of a woman, is generally believed in. The spirit finds easy entrance into the body of anyone whose hair is loose, and for this reason both men and women are generally careful to keep their hair plaited. A story told to the writer by a retired schoolmaster will perhaps best illustrate the nature of this belief. He said he had never credited such things till eighteen months ago, when his daughter-in-law became possessed in his own house. She had for some time been very weak and almost wholly unable to eat, but she had just done a long journey in his company. Suddenly, at midnight, her whole manner changed, and she became full of energy and ravenously hungry. She declared that she did not know any of the family, gave a detailed description of herself as a woman of another village whom none of them knew, and when given food ate enormously, swallowing handful after handful in the twinkling of an eye. Occasional visitations of this sort continued for some months, the girl sometimes lying absolutely rigid for hours and then suddenly raving. The spirit at various times gave particulars of its history, but these were unfortunately never tested. It was a woman who had died in child-birth and whose husband, after promising to remain single, had taken another wife, and it had entered the body of this girl one day on the journey mentioned when her hair was loose. The father-in-law was advised by some to beat her with a shoe and drive the spirit out by force, but did not do this. He took the girl to Mānbhau shrines, where she generally became very obstreperous and refused the consecrated food which was given her, and the possession continued for six months. Finally his wife remarked that while he had been going to strange gods he had failed to appeal to the god of his own family, Wyenkatesh Bālāji; so for four Fridays he offered special prayer to this god, and it happened that the girl then recovered; she died a year later. Some say that not every woman who dies in child-birth becomes a *chudhel*, but only those whose character has been bad. A *chudhel* can take absolutely any form, but one hears repeatedly that its power, and perhaps even its existence, depend wholly upon the mind of the spectator. If he becomes terrified he is lost; a courageous man might, on the other hand, persuade the *chudhel* to let him cut some of its hair, upon which it would remain in absolute subjection to him as long as the hair was in his possession. Seeing that a *chudhel* has unlimited supernatural powers this might be made a source of great profit and enjoyment.

The virtues of oil.

84. Various beliefs centre in the Teli. He never sells any oil of the kinds used for condiments while it is actually in process of being expressed, some saying that to do so would cause his own ruin, some that the oil would have magical efficacy to entice people away. These edible oils are not bought or sold on a Saturday (in some places Monday), and a pretty explanation is given. In the war

of the Mahābhārata, Aswasthāma, son of Drona, was caught by the Pāndavas and a very precious jewel was taken out of his head, leaving a terrible wound to which he applied oil. He is immortal and, still needing the oil, goes begging for it on Saturdays; anyone, man, woman, or child, coming on that day may be Aswasthāma, from whom no one would demand payment. Another reason given is that *Shani*, Saturn, is the god of oil and therefore it must not be sold on his day, *Shanwari*, Saturday. He has a shrine in Akolā where people, though they worship every day, offer oil on Saturday. His planet is the star of evil and brings to every one the *sāde sāti*, seven and a half years of misfortune, which every villager expects. The horoscope cast at birth shows one's *rās*, zodiacal sign, the relation then subsisting between the moon and the planets. When Saturn is passing through the *graha*, house, so formed and the houses on each side this *sāde sāti* of misfortune will attend the man.

Magic.

85. The skull either of a Teli or of a woman, preferably of the Dhobi caste, who died in child-birth, is much valued for magical purposes; limes, cocoanut, *sendur* (oxide of mercury), camphor, betelnut, sweetmeats, the liver of an unborn kid, and other things are applied to it with the proper formulas. The stone in a river at which Dhobis wash clothes has curious magical properties; to attain supernatural powers the disciple is taken there on *amawāsya*, the last day of a dark fortnight, and mysterious ceremonies are gone through; fear or any mistake makes the adventurers the prey of the spirits who surround such a stone. A Dhobi woman, a young girl, and a she-ass have peculiar properties for the healing of venereal diseases. A magician is called *jādugār*, or *jānāra*, "one who knows," or *mut mārnār*, fist-striker, because when bringing evil upon any one he shakes his fist towards

his enemy as if he were striking him. People sometimes say the profession has died out, but admit that a member is called in to lay the spirit of a woman who dies in child-birth, limes and other objects being bound up in the clothes in which she is buried, or to exorcise such a spirit. In one method of exorcism, whether of a *bhūt* or a *chudhel*, the *jādugār* makes a heap of various articles worth altogether Rs. 30 or Rs. 40, and puts the family to sit around it. The limbs of the patient—generally a woman—are tied and her eyes covered, and various ceremonies are performed. Presently she is made to eat a little rice, and is unbound and beaten, upon which she runs till she is exhausted. The *jādugār* buries a nail and bursts a lime at the spot where she falls, so confining the spirit to that spot; or he may shut it up in a bottle. The bodies of children born dead, or dying within a few hours of birth, used to be buried close to their parents' house, possibly to prevent *jādugārs* getting hold of them. For the magician is said to go on a dark night to the grave of a small child and place around it in a continuous line grains of urad over which he has chanted *mantras*, this forming a fence which the disembodied spirit cannot surmount. Still chanting *mantras*, he digs up the body, cuts off some of its hair, and places *ūd*, incense, in its mouth. After a time the corpse becomes alive, when it is made to promise to obey the orders of the magician in future. The head is severed from the body with a single stroke of a sword or knife, and the hair and incense are taken to the magician's house; if he burns a little of them at any time the spirit appears and executes all his commands.

Treasure and the *pāyālu*.

86. By one branch of the black art called *kushi* a witch can cause any quantity of grain or money to be transported to her own house; when she combs

her hair a spirit appears and obeys her orders. A *pāyālu*, a boy born feet foremost, especially if he is the eldest son of his mother, has also magical powers; this belief is most widely repeated. He is constantly watched and pursued by evil spirits, to circumvent whom a little *bibha*, marking-nut, is kept applied to his body. When he reaches the age of puberty he has the faculty of seeing where treasure is buried. The chief method seems to be for him to look at some *anjan*, lamp-black, placed in his hand by a *jādugār*; by another device the *jādugār* sacrifices the *pāyālu* to the earth-god (a snake) and applies some of the fat to his own eyes; the service roll of a retired police inspector shows that a youth was killed in 1891 with the object of discovering hidden treasure. Such treasure, *dhan*, is the subject of many other beliefs, almost every village having perhaps its own story; in fact money is constantly being buried in small quantities. It is a well-known practice to make the image of a snake or a demon out of wheat-flour and set it to protect the money; but buried treasure is said sometimes supernaturally to become invisible even to the owner. Some people in the District are said to know of wealth buried in their houses but to be afraid to dig it up because of the spirits that guard it. Sometimes on the other hand it calls to a passer-by, "*Yeu*, *yeu*, come, come"; if he listens it will probably bargain, promising to come to him if he will give it his son or some other prized object. Should he agree the son is to be placed on a certain night in the doorway of his house, when suddenly the floor will be covered with gold, but the son will fall dead. A story is told of a cunning man who made the bargain, but set up instead of his son a figure made of wheat-flour; a shower of gold fell in the room and the figure toppled over on the ground, but the spirit immediately discovered the fraud and the gold turned to coal. The image of Māroti in a deserted village is said often to have treasure hidden under it; people go at the proper time and with suitable sacrifices to search, but success is difficult of attainment. People tell of the wrong man trying to take treasure and finding that he had thrust his hand into a nest of snakes and scorpions.

Animals.

87. Animals are the subject of numerous ideas. To see crows mating causes one to die within six months, but the penalty is escaped if the relatives think one dead and mourn accordingly; accordingly a false report of death may be sent by post, or companions may hurry at once to the village and, concealing the facts, say that the man or woman in question has just been bitten by a snake. It is a sign of calamity for an owl to cry at night over a house; one should avoid shouting a name at night lest the owls hear and repeat it. A clod of earth, or even a stone, thrown at an owl is carried by it to a stream and left there to dissolve, the life of the thrower wasting as the clod shrinks. The feather of an owl or the quill of a porcupine if put in a house, especially under the bed, will cause husband and wife to quarrel. A magical drum can be made from the skin of the *hudhud*, hoopoe; if it is beaten at a feast all the other drums will burst. If a child's teeth do not come quickly the tusk of a wild boar may be dipped in water and rubbed on a stone and then applied to the gum. The fat of a boar or tiger is applied to the legs of a child who does not learn to walk quickly (or the mechanical support of a *pāngul-gāda*, cradle-cart, might be given). A cat is so holy that if it entered and even died in a temple a Brāhman praying there would not be defiled but might himself put it outside. Tremendous, though rather vague, penalties are imposed on anyone who kills a cat; he should make one of gold, and if possible throw it into the sea; else he might

take it to Manjirath (apparently in the north of the Nizām's Dominions). If a dog, which knows no better, kills a cat it need not be punished.

Miscellaneous.

88. Various love charms are practised, some by no means cleanly. The *mohoni* is a complicated affair in which one must first obtain the ashes of a sacrifice by a special ceremony, and then sit naked in cold water at the Dhobi's stone, all the time reciting *mantras* and exposed to the most terrible dangers from spirits. One either puts the magical product on one's eyes or throws it towards the person to be influenced, upon which he or she will immediately fall hopelessly in love. If cobras are mating and a cloth is thrown over them it becomes a potent charm for love and fertility. Love mixtures are so readily given with betel leaves that men are advised never to accept these from a woman. When a lamp is brought in at dusk—for this should not be left till night has completely fallen—people often salute first the light and then each other and perhaps utter a laudatory formula ; a common explanation is that men once longed to see God and he appeared in the form of light, *agni deota, dīpak*. People also salute the sun in the morning, and on seeing the new moon salute both it and each other ; at that time they also tear their old clothes and offer a piece to the moon in the hope of getting new ; rags are with the same object sometimes tied to particular trees, or to a branch set up on a mound, in the name of Chindhya Devi. It is said that father and son, two brothers, three Brāhmans, or nine women should never go on business together ; thus they would be advised to go separately to a marriage ; husband and wife may ride in the same cart but should never try to cross a river in the same boat.

Finally two little stories may be told ; they come

from the Hyderābād direction, but seem quite in sympathy with the thought of the District. A certain young man used to keep watch at night in a field, and every evening a strange woman came to spend the night with him. His elder brother's wife saw that his health was failing and managed to discover his secret; she warned him that the stranger was no ordinary mortal and instructed him in a stratagem. Accordingly he omitted one evening to go to the field; next night, when the stranger reproached him, he falsely declared that she, or someone exactly like her, had come to him in the village. The woman believed him and pointed out a certain tree, saying that if last night's visitor came again he should hold up a twig of that tree. The next night she herself came, but he pretended to think it was her imaginary double, brandished the twig, and was for ever delivered from her power. Again, small-pox broke out in a village, and a man put his children in a bag and tried to carry them away secretly. He stopped at a distance and released them, but his wife saw there another woman who asked her to come and look for lice on her head. The wife did so, but discovered that the stranger's head was covered with eyes. The stranger said, "You thought I had only two eyes and could only see what was before me, but now you see that my sight is unlimited and you cannot by any attempt at secrecy escape me." They begged her forgiveness and returned to their village, for she was the goddess of small-pox herself.

Muhammadan belief and organisation.

89. It is not necessary to describe at length the Muhammadanism of the District. It is in essentials the true Islām of three continents, but it bears the marks of long contact with a very powerful but kindly idolatry. Hindus worship largely at the tombs of Muhammadan saints, and Muhammadans have borrowed

some Hindu marriage customs and touches of their religious prejudices. Their philosophy is perhaps summed up in the phrases, "*Hama u'st, hama ba u'st, hama az u'st*, He is all, all is for Him, all is from Him." They attribute to all phenomena reality and even life, though only as emanations from God, so differing from the common Hindu view. The Muhammadan *fakīr* believes merely that the differences in value ordinarily made by the world are unreal, the Hindu *sādhu* that only unreality and illusion surround him; but both live in fact very much the same life. The organization of Muhammadanism includes several figures. Above all stands the Mufti, the final authority on matters of religion, who alone can give *fatwā's* thereon. In a Muhammadan country he would be appointed by the king, but here a great public ceremony among Muhammadans might be sufficient; Berār is said by some to contain two Muftis, the Maulvis of Bālāpur and Ellichpur, but others say that it is incorrect to apply the title to anyone in the Province. In a lower grade, though of much importance, are the *maulvi*, *kāzi*, and *mashā-ikh* (called also *pirzādā*, and *pirpādre*). The *maulvi* should answer *maslā*, questions, put to him; the *kāzi* holds the *sharī'at kām*, order-work, telling the plain layman simply what commands God has laid upon him; the *mashā-ikh* instructs his *murīd*, disciple, in the *tariqāt*, *ma'rifāt*, and *haqīqat*, the deeper mysteries of the "way, knowledge, and reality" about God. Another classification might be made to include the different officers in charge of individual *masjids*, mosques. Here may be *kāzi*, *naib-kāzi*, *khatīb*, *pesh imām*, *muazzan*, and *mullā*, the exact staff varying according to the means of the worshippers. The peculiar duties of the *kāzi* are to decide on questions of religion and to give judgment in religious cases brought before him; final authority in regard to the mosque also rests with him. He may act either personally, or through a *naib-kāzi*, or even through the *naib* of a *naib*; or a *pesh-imām*, temporary or permanent, may take the place of both *kāzi* and *khatīb*. The *khatīb* should read the prayers; the *muazzan*, in the larger mosques, gives the *azān*, call to prayer, and is also caretaker; the *mullā* is generally the officer who lays out the dead and, muttering the consolatory and sanctifying *bismillah*, kills animals for the sellers of meat; but the offices below the rank of *kāzi* are often combined in different ways. An annual gathering called *urus* is often held in memory of a local saint and is attended by both Muhammadan and Hindus; *urus* literally means *nuptials*, but the bride of the saint is death.

Bohrās.

90. Practically all the Muhammadans of the District are Sunnis except the few Bohrās who are found in the largest villages; these belong to a heterodox sect of Shiahs. Mr. E. Kitts, in the Berār Census Report of 1881, adds that the 'Bohrās believe in eight Imāms only, and 'say that the last has come and is gone. They follow a 'fifth rejected version of the sacred text. They are gen'erally traders but occasionally agriculturists. Burhān'pur is said to be their *fons et origo*, and all the good 'Bohrās desire to lay their bones there. They are not 'uniform in their worship; some evince a tendency to'wards the Sunni creed. In prayer they differ both from 'Shiahs and Sunnis in that they follow their *mullā*, pray'ing aloud after him, but without much regularity of 'posture. The times for commencing their devotions are 'about five minutes later than those observed by the 'Sunnis. After midday and the sunset supplications they 'allow a short interval to elapse, remaining themselves 'in the mosque meanwhile; they then commence the 'afternoon and evening prayers, and thus run five ser-

'vices into one.' They shave their heads, wear long beards, cut their moustaches close, and wear a turban, a shirt falling below the knee, loose trousers, and long shoes called *ujjaini*. They are said to cleanse their dead with morbid thoroughness, even using a syringe and sprinkling over the food or tobacco of the funeral feast some of the last water used. Both Bohrās and Cutchis often close their shops in the rains and take an annual holiday of two months or more.

Birth, marriage, and death among Muhammadans.

91. In ordinary Muhammadan families the *azān*, the declaration of faith in Allah and His Prophet, is whispered into a child's ear either immediately it is born or at some time on that or the next day; some whisper the *azān* into the right ear, and the *akāmat*, which should be slightly differently worded, into the left. On the 7th, 14th, or 21st day *akika* is performed, when the child's hair is shaved and the weight in silver given to *fakīrs*; goats are sacrificed—two at least for a boy and one for a girl—and their flesh is distributed among relations and the poor. The mother may do her ordinary household work but is otherwise apparently unclean for 40 days, during which time she may not even offer prayers. Marriages are seldom celebrated before the parties have attained the age of puberty, but may take place when the boy is only ten and the girl only seven or eight years of age. The *meher* is an important feature in marriage negotiations; it is a sum which the bridegroom settles on the bride but does not actually pay at the time of the marriage. It varies in amount from Rs. 100 to perhaps Rs. 25,000, and its existence largely protects the wife against the power of divorce enjoyed by the husband; she can remit the debt if she likes. A dowry, *jehez*, is also given by the bride's father; it usually takes the form of land, houses, cattle, jewel-

lery, furniture, or clothes. The cost of the marriage ceremony is scarcely ever below Rs. 100 or Rs. 150, and may rise to an enormous sum in a wealthy family. At death the corpse of either man or woman ought to be covered with a white cloth, but a practice has grown up of laying above this an upper red cloth in the case of a woman who dies before her husband. Hymns are chanted as the funeral procession passes to the graveyard. The body is generally placed in the grave lying on its back with its feet to the south, but *bagli* burial is also known; in this form the corpse is placed in a sitting posture in a recess at the side of a grave, and the earth is hollowed above its head to leave room for a turban to be tied when the trumpet of Azrael first sounds, lest the deceased be late when the dead rise on the day of judgment. If a tombstone, *tāwīz*, is put on the grave it is cut with a rounded top for a man and with a flat and slightly hollowed top for a woman. Funeral feasts and alms are given to an amount which usually varies from Rs. 25 to Rs. 500, and mourning is observed for three days. Further ceremonies are performed on the third day, *siyum* or *fateha*; the tenth, *daham*; twentieth, *bastam*; and fortieth, *chihilam*; and then annually, *barsi*; the expense of the different days varying. Muhammadans of low standing are somewhat infected with Hindu ideas about the supernatural; they say also that no epidemic disease ever occurs in Muharram; they talk of fairies, *pari*, living in any pretty garden; and their magicians are said to differ from Hindus only in using Hindustāni instead of Marāthi for the formulas.

Christians.

92. The Christians of the old Akola and Bāsim Districts numbered 495 in 1881, 393 in 1891, and 847 in 1901. Of these the numbers of Europeans, Eurasians, and natives were given respectively in 1881 as 94, 209, 192; in 1891 as

82, 68, and 243; and in 1901 as 98, 50, and 699; the distinction of race is not applied closely. The chief divisions enumerated in 1901 were Presbyterian (246), Anglican (185), Methodist (181), and Roman Catholic (168). The District is in the charge of the Chaplain of Berār, resident at Amraoti. The missions are the Alliance and Roman Catholic Missions at Akola, and the Methodist Episcopal Church Mission at Bāsim. The Alliance Mission is an American undenominational organisation described for convenience only as Presbyterian; it began work shortly before the famines of 1896 and 1899, and its energies were largely devoted to the care of an orphanage of famine waifs; it has an excellent workshop for carpentering and iron-work.

CASTE.

93. Principal castes. The total population of the District in 1901 was 754,804. Kunbis were by far the most numerous caste, forming 32 per cent. of the whole. Marāthās, a name sometimes used interchangeably with Kunbi but sometimes distinctively, formed 1 per cent. Mālis, engaged like Kunbis chiefly in cultivation, formed 7 per cent. Mahārs support themselves chiefly by agricultural labour but also form in practically every village a most important class of public servant; they amounted to 14 per cent. Māngs, who besides working as labourers supply most of the local musicians and midwives, formed 2 per cent.; but both Mahārs and Māngs sometimes hold land. Andhs are a comparatively aboriginal tribe and are found mostly in the hilly villages of the south; they constituted 2 per cent. of the whole. Kolis, who may be early immigrants, numbered 1 per cent. These are all engaged mainly on agricultural work. The Brāhmans of this part of India are often employed on work for which

a little education is required, while those from northern India are often coolies; but Brāhmans are found to some extent in almost every occupation; they amounted altogether to 3 per cent. All the Hindus together formed 87 per cent. of the total. Muhammadans, who undertake all employments but are often a poor community, formed 9 per cent.; Jains made 1 per cent.

Kunbis form by far the largest caste in the District but are sufficiently described in other Berār Gazetteers. Notes of some length are given on the Brāhman, Koli, Mahār, Gondhali, Jhingābhoi, and Pāl Pārdhi castes because of various points of interest or importance connected with them, and of the Bedar, Gopāl, Pāthrat, and Lonāri castes because they are more numerous in Akola than in any other Berār District. Brief remarks are also made about several other castes in a final miscellaneous paragraph. The selection of castes had to be made in a somewhat arbitrary way. The information was in every case gathered from members of the caste in question, but the questions involved are very complicated and customs differ from place to place, so that there are bound to be some mistakes.

94. Brāhman. The Brāhmans of the District number 21,000, or 3 per cent. of the whole population. A twofold division exists among them, the one depending chiefly on their country of origin and the other on the Veda they follow, besides numerous minor distinctions. The great bulk are Deshasth Brāhmans, natives of this particular country, but Konkanasth, Karhāda, Gujarāti, Mārwāri, Telangi, and Golak Brāhmans are also found, and the Konkanasthas are increasing in number. Each of the four Vedas has its own followers in different parts of India, but practically none are found in Akola District except Rigvedī and Yajurvedī Brāhmans, the latter being the

8

more numerous. One small division of the Yajurvedīs, called Taittirīya or Apastambh, do not intermarry with the rest of the main body but only with Rigvedīs. With this exception the members of the different groups may all eat together but may never intermarry. Two further points of subdivision may be noted which do not break *soyarepana*, the right of intermarriage—Rigvedī Brāhmans are subdivided into two equal bodies, Shākal and Bāshkal, and Yajurvedī Brāhmans are similarly subdivided into Shukla and Krishna. Most Brāhmans are engaged in worldly affairs and are therefore called Laukika or Grihasth, no distinction being recognised between the two. Another class called Bhikshu consists of men who have devoted themselves to the study of holy writings and are therefore especially worthy of receiving alms, but they do not actually beg alms. The name Konkanasth refers to the Konkan, that is the west coast of India, and includes the Chitpāwans. Karhāda refers apparently to the town of Karad at the junction of the Krishna (Kistna) and Koyna near Sātāra, though some derive it from *kar*, ass, and *hād*, bone, and recount a legend about a magician creating the caste from the bones of asses or camels Gujarāti Brāhmans include a subdivision of water-carriers. Mārwāri Brāhmans are generally employed as the priests of Mārwāri Baniās. Telangi or Telugu territory actually enters Berār in Yeotmāl District. Golaks are Brāhmans of illegitimate descent and are considered much inferior to the others. They are called Kund Golak if the husband of the woman was alive at the time of the illegitimate birth and Rānd or Rend Golak if the mother was a widow. The Brāhman is of course regarded with great though, it is said, decreasing veneration. His ideal differs in some important respects from that of the Englishman, and perhaps it has been somewhat coarsened during the recent years of commercial activity.

He is the most intellectual member of the community and often shows an admirable patience in his work, but perhaps when judged by a high standard he seems to lack balance or even weight of thought—though in view of his wonderful traditions he is naturally not readily conscious of the defect.

Koli.

95. The District contains 8556 Kolis out of a total of 28,038 for the whole of Berār. Kolis are to be found in numerous villages all over the north of the District, a settlement of them occasionally forming the bulk of the population and including the patel. In the north-east of Akola tāluk twelve very small villages near together are Koli settlements of this sort and are called, as one whole, Bārula. According to legend they were all at one time inhabited by *rākshasas*, giants or demons. At Apa Tāpa in particular three demon brothers called Atapi, Wātapi, and Ilwāla used to practise a trick by which they killed numbers of wayfarers, especially Brāhmans. Ilwāla used to take the form of a Brāhman and sit by the wayside, and when any traveller of that caste appeared would invite him home to dine. Atapi then took the form of food and Wātapi that of water and both were taken into the stomach of the traveller. Finally Ilwāla called upon them by name and they took their own form in the man's belly and forced their way out, thus killing him. It chanced that Agastya Rishi passed that way and swallowed the fateful food, but he realised in time what had happened and by passing his hand to and fro upon his belly caused the giants he had swallowed to turn to ashes, so that they could not come when their brother called. Ilwāla was terrified and fled, with Agastya in pursuit. Seeing no other resource the demon plunged into the ocean, but again Agastya followed and by soaking up all the water destroyed Ilwāla. The sage

finally discharged the water in the form of urine, which has caused the sea for ever to remain salt. The story has perhaps some real value because it gives exact locality to an incident mentioned in both the Mahābhārata and the Rāmāyana. According to the epics Agastya dwelt in a hermitage on Mount Kunjara which was situated in a most beautiful country to the south of the Vindhya mountains, while the demon brothers lived in the Dandaka forest. The main caste of Kolis is said to include seven subdivisions, Kshatriya, Rāj, Pān, Fisherman, Begging, Watandār, and Naik or Nāwik Kolis. Most of the Kolis in this District belong to what is called the Kshatriya division, though they are considered Shūdras by Hindus in general. On the day a child is born sugar and betel leaves are distributed. On the third day a mixture of *kanis*, jawāri heads, and *tāk*, buttermilk, called *penjan*, is distributed to boys; on the sixth or seventh day the period of impurity, *vitāl*, comes to an end. *Jaula*, the first hair-cutting, may be done at any time within five years. The age of marriage is from 9 to 15 for boys and from 5 to 12 for girls. The customs of Kolis are in general just the same as those of Kunbis. The different subdivisions may not marry together, though some of them take food from one another. According to some people the local Kolis came from the hills, according to others from the Pandharpur direction. Kshatriya Kolis are those who belong to deshmukh, patel, or patwāri families, while the rāja, royal, subdivision includes the Rāja of Jawhār in Bombay Presidency. Pān Kolis are water-carriers and are only found further south; the fishing caste live by the sea and the begging caste near Manmād in Bombay Presidency. Watandārs are found in Jalgaon tāluk and in Khāndesh, doing village service but superior to Mahārs. When a festival in honour of Mahādeo is held at Mahābleshwar the feast begins by food being set before two Watandār Kolis. Nāwik Kolis are boatmen and are chiefly found near Pandharpur. The Kolis of the north-east of Akola tāluk worship two *pīrs* who are buried at Gowardha in Akot tāluk and Uprāi in Daryāpur tāluk. They go on pilgrimage to these tombs, and the whole affair is minutely regulated. Firstly both men and women buy new clothes, all of white, and don them on a Monday. Next they call in a *fakīr*, who repeats sayings which they call *mantras*. Then they make two and a half cakes of wheat mixed with *gur* and *ghī* and dedicate them, *naivedya dākhwine*, at home in the name of the *pīr*, and take food in company with the *fakīr*. On the following day they set out for the tomb, which they must not leave till the buried *pīr* himself gives them permission. This he does either by appearing in a dream to one of the members of the party, by letting loose one of their bullocks, or by beating them in their sleep; he keeps them from a day to a week. Permission to go having been received they give a rupee or two to the *mujāwar* who is in charge of the tomb, and offer the two and a half cakes already mentioned. To make the offering the whole party, men and women, stand in a row praying to the *pīr*, the men having to loosen the back folds, *kāsotā*, of their *dhotras*. The *mujāwar* of the tomb returns small pieces of the cakes as *prasād*, a holy gift, the party distribute sweetmeats, prostrate themselves before the *pīr*, take their food, and start home. At every village on the way back the party halts; one member is left in charge of the cart: the rest take in their right hands sticks of the *ber* tree coloured red, and in their left pieces of dried gourd, *wālalelya bhopdyāche takkar*, and go to a few houses without distinction of caste, standing in the doorway and repeating *Dam, Dam, Shādal Sāhebāchi gadā*, in praise of the saint Shādal, whereupon the householder gives them a handful of jawāri. On reaching their own village they do the same and then fix a day for a ceremony called *kandori*, which must take place within three weeks. All the connections, *soyara*, of the family are invited to this ceremony, *udi*, cowdung ashes, being sent with the invitation. Every visitor brings garments such as a *dupatta* or *shela* for the head of the family and a *choli* for his wife. A *fakīr* who is present repeats *mantras* and kills a goat or two, or even four for a great feast, and the company eat its flesh along with bread made from the jawāri collected on the way back from the tomb, the men eating first and the women afterwards. The head of the goat is not cooked, but is placed on a stick which has been coloured red with chalk, *geru*, and set up in the name of the *pīr*. The white robes of the pilgrimage are then laid aside, to be used later for ordinary wear, and the visitors go home.

Mahār.

96. The Mahārs of the District number 105,306, or 14 per cent. of the whole population. The Mahārs of Berār belong to three sub-castes, Somonche, Lādwāde, and Andhwan, of which the first-named are much the most numerous, but in the largest villages there are immigrants from the Central Provinces belonging to several other sub-castes. All Berāri Mahārs may eat together, but no one may marry out of his own sub-caste. They worship Bāp Sāheb and some local saints, often Muhammadan *fakīrs*, and swear in the law-courts by the Black Dog, an oath the breach of which is supposed to be punished by outcasting. Their religious traditions are very vague and their practices are often dictated merely by commonsense. They have five principal holy places, Dombegir, Mehona, Wādegaon, Gawandhāla, and Pimpardol, besides Muhammadan tombs at Sirpur in Bāsim tāluk and Burhānpur, to which they go on pilgrimage either on account of some sin or from pure religious feeling.

The five places are said to be sacred to five gods, brothers, whose names were Dego, Mego, Dombya, Jhabrāyan, and Ajrāyan, but it is not clear with which spot each god is associated. Dombegir, which is situated on the bank of the Godāvari river near Rākshasban in the Nizām's Dominions, is the most sacred place and is immediately connected with the worship of Bāp Sāheb, the Lord Father. Some Mahārs say that the reason they have no temples is that Bāp Sāheb forbids it—he dwells in the sky, not in any earthly building—but the idea seems not to be common. A man who has returned from the pilgrimage builds a wall or shed and sets up a flag coloured red, white, or green, and the Mahārs of the village come to worship. The pilgrim should not take food or drink from a woman for a month or a month and a quarter. *Pūja* at the wall is done to Dego Mego, but thereby Bāp Sāheb is also honoured. A sacrifice of *ūd*, frankincense, and of camphor, is made every day, but Wednesday is a particularly sacred day. Women take no part in worship or in the great pilgrimages, though they go to Sirpur with their husbands. If husband and wife are childless the husband vows to give gold to God—and sends it to the *guru* at Dombegir—or to send the child on a long pilgrimage. Mehona is often visited on the way to Dombegir. The path to the shrine at Mehona passes along a dangerous ridge in the hills; formerly there was also risk from wild beasts. The pilgrim ties strings of *nāthe* on a large rock called Dhondibali, visits the holy place stark naked, washes his face and hands and drinks at a *jhira*, shallow well, dresses again and does *tīrth*, bathing. Wādegaon is in Bālāpur tāluk, eight miles south of Bālāpur. The sacred place is a rough platform with several tombs upon it, at the top of a high wall which was apparently built to strengthen the bank of the river. A *guru*, who wears a yellow cloth on his shoulders as insignia of office, lives here but also makes long pastoral rounds receiving such petty contributions as his people can afford. The present incumbent is called Pagdu Mānāji. He and other Mahārs of Wādegaon say that the principal tomb there, which they call by the Persian name of *turamat*, is that of Dego Mego. This god was once a man with the power of commanding rain and thereby brought a grievous famine to an end. Previously Mahārs had received *haks*, dues, by custom only, but the Emperor of the time thereupon made the claims definite and enforced payment. Rain about to fall is regarded as Dego, and fallen rain as Mego. Of the other places of pilgrimage Gawandhāla is in the Khāmgaon tāluk and Pimpardol in the Jalgaon tāluk of Buldāna District. The latter is at the end of a tank belonging to a large fort now deserted, parts of which look very old. Here, as at Mehona, strings are tied round a large stone by the path. People go on these pilgrimages at various times, but the great festivals are Akhāji for Mehona, Wādegaon, and Gawandhāla and Polā for Pimpardol; pilgrims reach Dombegir about a week after visiting Mehona. Akhāji is the great festival of the caste but other Hindu festivals are also observed. The Black Dog seems to be an evil spirit but is a curiously vague conception. Some Mahārs worship Khandoba, or Bhairao, who is attended by a black dog. The caste, though higher than Māngs and some others, is a very low one, and seems to correspond with the Pariahs (as the Māngs with the Chaklas) of Madras. A Mahār may not enter the house, much less the temple, of an ordinary Hindu, or use the same well, and the Kunbis of Wādegaon openly regard their holy place with amused contempt; but some say a Mahār is the proper priest of Marimāta. In every village some Mahārs by hereditary right, confirmed by Government appointment, perform numerous public menial services and are paid by contributions in grain, *haks*. They also remove the carcasses of dead animals and in payment receive their flesh to eat and skins to sell. Mahārs eat the flesh of cows and all other domestic animals except the pig. dog, donkey, and horse, and that of all wild animals except the pig, wolf, and bear. Their caste prejudices are few, but they are emphatically forbidden to touch either the wild or the domestic pig, or the body of a dead dog, especially if it is a black one; a sweeper may remove it. Sometimes they are given to drink. Mahārs, apart from the individuals employed in the public service of the village, are almost always labourers, though a very few are shopkeepers and still fewer landholders. One of the latter, Jānu Kachrya of Pāras, who died about six years ago, started a boarding-house at Akola so that boys of the caste coming from the villages might have the benefit of the good schools at head-quarters. A night-school for adults, attended at present by 28 pupils, has also been in existence at Akola for about a year ; the expenses are chiefly paid from subscriptions by men of other castes. No objection seems to be felt in any part of the District to Mahārs being employed as yearly servants or being given any particular agricultural work. In some villages, however, Mālis, or some sub-divisions among them, and in some places most Hindu castes other than Kunbis, are unable to work at the same plough with a Mahār. The position of Mahārs has immensely improved in the last two generations and they generally have a fair supply of ornaments, usually of glass and silver but sometimes of gold. Widows must dress plainly, not wearing shoes or an expensive *sāri*, and removing the red *tīka*, spot, from their foreheads.

Gondhali.

97. A few Gondhalis, 1324 in all, are scattered about the District. They say that about 100 families live at Tuljāpur, in the Nizām's Dominions, where there is a large temple

of Devi, but none can be found east of Māhur on the Penganga or in Hindustān, and they are very rare in Khāndesh; their total number in Berār is 3107. They are a caste of some slight dignity, as it is their peculiar function, without the help of any other official, to offer a noisy sacrifice to conciliate Devi and avert smallpox. They do this for anyone by whom they are summoned, but the materials of the sacrifice and their own payment vary somewhat according to the client. Some people have the sacrifice done just before marriage, some soon afterwards, and some when recovering from the disease, while very many people neglect it altogether; it is performed at the door of the house which is to be protected. The Gondhalis' account of their origin goes back to the stories about Parashurām. Sahasrārjuna, king of Māhishmati, coveted the wonderful cow Kāmadhenu, the granter of desires, given by Indra to the sage Jamadagni, and killed the latter. Jamadagni's wife Renuka mounted the funeral pyre and ordered her son Parashurām to avert his gaze till she was consumed, but he looked too soon and so part of her head was not burnt; he set it up at Māhur and performed the first *gondhal* ceremony.

Jhingābhoi.

98. The Jhingābhois speak of themselves as quite a separate caste but are not distinguished from Bhois in the Census Reports. Members of the caste say they have no fixed home but divide themselves into small parties and wander about selling medicines, each party having a definite area assigned for its operations. Their chief deity is the goddess Kātmāramma or Sarkāramma, but they also worship Mariamma or Mātamma. They have no temple of their own but Hindus allow them to worship in village temples. They wear a hair-knot, *shendi*, and a moustache and a kind of goatee, but shave the rest of their heads. They profess to be of Berāri origin, but

those interrogated, while understanding Marāthi, spoke Hindustāni. Five days after the birth of a child a *panchāyat* of four is called and a name is given. The mother is supposed to be able to carry the child thenceforth as she goes about her ordinary work. Ten days after birth the child's abdomen is seared with a heated needle, an unfixed number of lines being drawn; the object is to protect the infant from disease. The dead are not burnt but are buried in a grave about six feet deep. The body is taken to the place of burial wrapped in old clothes and is buried naked, in a squatting posture, facing north, with the hands brought palm to palm upon the breast. The family are unclean for ten days. A silver image of the deceased about two inches in length is made by an ordinary village goldsmith and is kept by any member of the family and worshipped on the anniversary of the death. The spirit of the dead man attaches to this image as a shadow goes with a living man, and the relatives are left in peace, but if the image was not made the spirit would become a wandering malevolent ghost, *bhūt*, and give all kinds of trouble, *satānā*, to the living relatives. In each party there is one family in which a similar image of Kātmār-amma is kept, and if any member of the band thinks himself supernaturally afflicted he makes a small offering, the image is brought, and the goddess is invoked to set him right.

Pāl Pārdhi.

99. Men among the Pāl Pārdhis often wear numerous strings of glass beads, *pot*, around their necks; headmen, *naik*, may wear also a locket, *tāīt*, dedicated to Khandobā. Khandobā is the chief god, and Mariammā, Mhānkāli (Mahānkāli), and Bhawāni are important goddesses. An educated Hindu considers these three as different incarnations of Pārvati, wife of Siva, but the Pāl Pārdhis think them separate goddesses. When a child,

whether boy or girl, is five days old its hair is cut and the cuttings are offered at some shrine of Khandobā. A boy's hair is cut once more when he reaches the age of puberty, but a girl's hair is never cut again. A cock is vowed to Mhankāli when a child is ill; Mariammā sometimes receives the sacrifice of a young male buffalo, but Bhawāni's offerings seem not to involve the taking of life. Dasrā (Dasahra) is the great festival of the year. On that day all married women have to undergo an ordeal to test their chastity, *īmān*. Three stones are set up so as to support a. cooking-vessel, *karhai*; a fire is lit underneath, *ghī* is boiled in the *karhai*, and a pice is dropped into the boiling *ghī*. A crowd of perhaps one or two hundred of the caste remain around the fire, and the married women are called in one by one from a distance. Each woman has to take the coin out of the *ghī* and touch her forehead with it. It is believed that if she has been faithful to her husband during the year she will suffer no harm, but that otherwise she will be scalded. A *naik* of the caste says that at a recent Dasrā gathering six women out of about fifty failed to pass the test; they had not been suspected previously. Pāl Pārdhis do not eat the flesh of cows, buffaloes, beasts of prey, or domestic pigs, but eat most other flesh, including that of wild pig. At death they bury a body lying at full length on its back, and lay upon it a new cloth, *dhotra*, of the value of five or six rupees, a large sum to the ordinary Pāl Pārdhi. A dead man who has not been properly buried is liable to turn into a malevolent ghost, *shaitān*, and offerings have to be made and worship must be done to quiet him.

Bedar.

100. The Bedars of the District number 2075, the bulk of them living in Akolā tāluk; the Census Reports also mention Berads, who numbered 20 in 1901, and identify them

with the Bedars; this identification was also made by Tod, but prominent Bedars now say it is a mistake. A distinction must also be made between Marāthā, Telanga, and Kanarese Bedars. The leading Marātha Bedars, such as Rao Sāhib Dhonji Kondji of Akola, retired Inspector of Police, say that it is a mistake to speak of a Bedar caste; the name is merely a title. They say that the true Bedars belong to a caste called in Kanarese Beāradu; it is largely represented in Sholāpur State, the Rājā of which belongs to it; it is on the same level as the Marātha Kunbi caste. Colonel Meadows Taylor was in charge of Sholāpur during the minority of the Rājā; he gives the Bedars a character for bravery and chivalry, if also for lawlessness. It is said that the ancestors of the present Marātha Bedars entered military service and presently joined the Pindhāri bands; they were given their name because they were 'without fear.' Tipu Sultān converted some to Muhammadanism, and others consented to eat in small parties out of one dish in order to divert his suspicions. Under early English rule they were afraid to give a true account of themselves lest they should be punished for sharing in the Pindhāri raids. For the one reason they were put out of caste by their old caste-fellows, for the other they formally described themselves as Bedar Dhers (Mahārs) and by other false names. Now they suffer the penalty that other Hindus are inclined to look down upon them, though in fact these Marāthā Bedars are given spiritual instruction and admitted into the temples in a way always impossible to a Mahār or anyone of similar standing; moreover, people of really very low caste who wish to enter police or military service falsely take the name which the true Bedars have made respected. This is felt as a great grievance, and the leading Marātha Bedars wish that the term

Bedar could be dropped as a caste name. The writer cannot give a final opinion about the historical question involved, but there is no doubt that the Marātha Bedars include men of high character, ability, and position. Besides these Marāthas are Telanga and Kanarese Bedars. The Marāthas have a Brāhman from northern India to officiate at their ceremonies, while the others call in a Jangam from the south. In the marriage ceremony all three sub-castes follow the ordinary Marātha ritual, according to which the bride and bridegroom stand on opposite sides of an *antarapat*, curtain. The priest recites *mantras* and concludes with the word *sāwadhān*, be careful, whereon the guests throw rice or jawāri dyed yellow on the couple. Cremation is said to have been practised at one time, but since going to the wars the caste bury their dead. Directly life departs water and basil leaves are placed in the mouth of the corpse, and it is washed with lukewarm water and covered with a new cloth. As it is taken to the burial ground music accompanies the procession. The body is placed in the grave in a sitting position, facing the east and with its hands on its knees. When the grave has been filled in the mourners go to a river and bathe, return to the house of the deceased and look at a lighted lamp, and then disperse. On the third day the grave is again visited and such intoxicants as the deceased used to drink are placed upon it. On that day the widow is taken to the grave and her glass bangles and *mangal-sūtra*, the 'string of fortune' with gold strung on it worn by a married woman, are broken, her toe-rings are removed, and the *kunku* marriage spot, is wiped off her forehead. On the tenth day *pinda*, oblations, are offered to the deceased, and on the thirteenth a caste feast is given, and some food is laid before a cow and some thrown on the roof for crows.

Mourning for small children is only observed for three days. Most Bedars worship Devi and Mahādeo, but some are followers of Kabīr, who preached religious equality. When a man of the Marātha Bedars is caught in criminal intimacy with a woman his tongue is branded with a bar of hot gold; a woman so discovered is put out of caste permanently. Bedars drink strong liquors and eat the flesh of fowls, goats, and the wild pig. Telanga and Kanarese Bedars are given a low place among Hindus and are mostly engaged as daily labourers. Some Bedars, however, are engaged in trade and agriculture, while others form a considerable fraction of the police force of the District.

Kānadī.

101. The Kānadi caste numbers 1181 here and only 1407 in the whole of Berār. They say they came from the Kanarese country ten generations ago and were named accordingly. They now speak Marāthi as their mother-tongue. Their chief employment is growing betel leaves, like the Bāris, but they claim to be Lingāyat Baniās of the Pancham subdivision. Their septs are not identical with those of the undoubted Lingāyat Baniās, and this throws some doubt on their assertion. Their betrothal ceremony, *sākhar puda*, consists in washing the girl's feet, applying vermilion to her forehead, and giving her new clothes. It is performed in the presence of the Jangam, spiritual adviser, and is said to be inviolable. Infant marriage is the prevailing practice; the favourite months for marriages are Māgh, Phālgun, Chaitra, and Vaishākh, while Paush is very inauspicious. The first day of the ceremony is called *haldi*, turmeric being then applied to the bride and bridegroom. On the second day the bridegroom is carefully dressed, a *bāsing*, wreath, of flowers is placed on his head, and he sets out in a procession which the women of the family accom-

pany to the bride's village. Her father is informed of their approach and comes outside the village to meet them. The parties greet each other with the word *sharnāth*, and apply *gulāl*, red powder and sandalwood, to each other's foreheads. The procession moves on to the temple of Māroti, where the bridegroom bows before the image. The people of the bride's house then bring a pot of water called *rukhmat kā gharā* and he drops a rupee into it. Next, riding on a horse or in a palanquin, he comes to the *māndhawa*, marriage booth. Someone here drops on him from above the booth water in which turmeric has been dissolved, and the marriage ceremony is performed according to the ordinary Marāthā ritual. After this the couple are seated on an earthen platform where a brass pot full of water is placed. The guests pass one by one, dip a mango leaf in the pot, and sprinkle water with it on the feet, knees, shoulders, and then the heads of the pair; finally the parents come and drop a rupee in the pot; the whole ceremony is called *kalas chadhane*. On the third day the ceremony of *pāi ghadi chauk ṇhān* is performed. A cloth is laid on the road to form a pathway along which the mother of the bridegroom walks, to seat herself presently on a board. The mother of the bride then comes and washes her feet and applies vermilion to her forehead, repeating the action two or three times. On the fourth day comes the *tāmbul* ceremony, new clothes and ornaments being given to the boy and girl. Widow re-marriage and polygamy are practised. On the seventh day after a child is born the Jangam ties the symbol of a *linga* to its arm, and the mother unties the *linga* and keeps it till the infant is able to walk. As in many other castes a dying man is removed from his bed and placed on the ground to breathe his last. Immediately after death the corpse is placed in a sitting position against the wall of the house and cotton-wool is placed in its nose and ears, after which it is taken into the courtyard and very carefully washed. Next a silken cloth is thrown over it and a rupee, which becomes the perquisite of the Jangam, is tied to its forehead, and the Jangam worships the corpse and places the *linga* in its right hand. The dead are buried, in a sitting posture, the *linga* being again worshipped at the funeral. After the grave has been filled in the Jangam stands on it and, blowing a conch shell, declares that the spirit of the deceased has reached *kailās*, the paradise of Siva. The chief mourner takes hold of his hand to assist him to come down from the grave, and without such help he would not come down. No explanation is given by the Kānadis, but perhaps the Jangam is supposed to have mounted to heaven with the spirit. Kānadis are pollut-ed by a death for one day only.

Gopāl.

102. The Gopāls in the District number 1266, mostly in Bāsim and Murtizāpur tāluks, out of a total of 2150 in Berār. Mr. E. J. Kitts wrote in the Census Report of 1881: 'Of 'the Gopāls who appear to have entered Berār from Nimār 'and Indore, and who from their occupation are some- 'times known as Boriawālas, there are five distinct divi- 'sions, allowing no intermarriage and each having 12½ sub- 'divisions. They are the Vīr, Pāngul or Pāngoh, Pahal- 'wān, Khām, and Gujarāti Gopāls. The Vīr Gopāls live 'in leaf huts, made from the date palm, which they set up 'outside villages: they remain in one place two or three 'years at a time and then move on. The Pahalwāns live 'in small tents or *pāls*; they are wrestlers and gymnasts. 'The Khām Gopāls are wanderers hailing from the north- 'ern portion of the Nizām's Dominions; they perform 'feats with a long pole. The Gujarāti Gopāls are the 'lowest division in the social scale; other Gopāls will not

'dine with them. All five divisions have the reputation 'of being confirmed cattle-lifters and occasional house-'breakers.' The Gopāls of Murtizāpur tāluk are now partly employed as herdsmen but have not lost their bad reputation. They include exogamous septs with such names as Dhangar, Hatkar, Sonār, Yādava, and Sindhe, so that it is possible that they were formed originally of people from different castes, though they now no longer admit outsiders. In the marriage ceremony the bride and bridegroom stand facing each other and a cotton thread is wound five times round the neck of the former and seven times round that of the bridegroom, and at the end jawāri dyed yellow is thrown over the pair. Widow marriage is allowed, and a widow price of Rs. 40 or Rs. 60 is paid to the woman's guardian. The dead are always buried, the corpse being placed in a sitting posture with its face to the east. Mourning is observed for three days only, and a caste feast is given on the third day. The Gopāls begin to train their boys to acrobatic exercises from the age of seven, daily practice being given. The dress of the caste is like that of Kunbis, but Gopāl women do not wear nose-rings. The women are tattooed with one dot on the forehead, one on the right cheek, and one on the chin. Food is taken from a Kunbi, Sonār, or Sutār, but not from a Teli, Rangāri, or any of the low castes. Ordinary Hindu festivals are observed; the special god of the caste is Khandobā, whose aid is invoked at the beginning of a performance.

Pāthrat.

103. Pāthrats number less than 1000 in the whole of Berār and 596 in this District, being found chiefly in Bālāpur and Murtizāpur tāluks. The name is said to be a contraction of Pātharwat, stone-dresser, and the caste is chiefly engaged in making small mill-stones for different purposes. They have a legend that in old days one father

had five sons, of whom the eldest took to dressing stones and became a Pāthrat, the second to working in iron and became a Khāti, smith, the third was a carpenter, the fourth, as a Kasār or Tāmbatkār, worked in brass and copper, and the youngest became a Sonār. The story may be an exposition of the brotherhood of the arts, or perhaps a record of the successive stages of their development. A widow is allowed to take one husband, but if he dies she may not marry a third time; no such restriction applies to a man. Among Kunbis and similar castes a man can marry a cousin to whom he is related only through females but not an agnatic relative, and can only marry the second of two sisters if it is the elder to whom hei s already married. The Pāthrats, perhaps on account of the difficulty of arranging marriages in a small caste, recognise neither of these restrictions. The age of marriage is from 20 to 25 years for the man and from 10 to 15 for the girl. The dates for the different rites are fixed by a Brāhman. The first day of the marriage is called *haldi*, because turmeric is then applied, and three ceremonies are performed upon it. At about noon the families bring cotton stalks from a field and weave a *tatti*, set it up on five posts and scatter leaves of the *jāmun* or *umbar* tree over it; this is called the *toran tatti* ceremony. Next comes the *deo pūja*, in which the family deities, embossed on a piece of silver, are worshipped—the sacred silver being washed and having sandal paste, rice, and turmeric placed before it. Thirdly comes the *jeonār*, in which the goddess Meskai is worshipped. For this ceremony a lighted lamp is placed in a new bamboo basket at about sunset and covered with a few stalks of jawāri and a blanket. An unwidowed woman takes the basket on her head and a brass dish with vermilion, turmeric, and rice in her hand and goes to the place of worship, the father of the bridegroom taking an axe on his right shoulder and following her. Next a goat is killed at the bridegroom's house and its flesh served up at a caste-feast, at which liquor is freely provided. Meanwhile a marriage booth has been erected at the bride's house. The second day is called *lagna*, marriage. The bridegroom is first taken to the shrine of Māroti in his own village to worship there, whence he goes to the village of the bride; a message is sent to the bride's father, who comes out to receive him. The bridegroom, seated on a horse or bullock, is conducted to the marriage booth and the actual wedding is performed according to the ordinary Marāthā fashion. On the next day the mother of the bridegroom, riding in a *pālki*, visits the bride's house, where the mother of the latter gives her a lighted lamp in an earthen pot. This lamp is kept constantly burning day and night and carried before the married couple till they reach the house of the bridegroom; it would be very unlucky for the lamp to be extinguished. Divorce is said not to be allowed under any circumstances, but a woman found in criminal intimacy with a man of any caste whatever is permanently outcasted. A widow-price of about Rs 9 is paid for a second marriage. The dead are sometimes burnt and sometimes buried, the body in the latter case being laid on its back with its head to the south and feet to the north. Pāthrats can take food from a Sutār or Kumbhār but not from a Teli or Dhobi. Imprisonment, the killing of a cow, or criminal intimacy of a man with a woman of another caste is punished by temporary outcasting, re-admission involving a fine of Rs. 4 or Rs. 5. The chief deity is the Devi of Tuljāpur and the chief festival Dasahra, but other gods and saints, such as Dāwal Mālik, are also worshipped, and other festivals observed. The implements of the caste are worshipped twice a year, on Gudhi Pādwa and Diwāli. Pāthrats have a large belief in witchcraft, and often employ a *jādugār*. The males dress like Kunbis, wear sect-marks on their foreheads, and are not tattooed. The women wear a *choli* tied in a knot in front and a *lugdā* passed between the legs and tucked in at the back, one end being drawn over the right shoulder, but it is said that the tucking in of the *lugdā* is a recent innovation. Women are tattooed with a crescent between the eye-brows and dots on the right side of the nose, the right cheek, and the chin, and a basil plant or peacock is drawn on their wrists.

Lonāri.

104. Less than 1000 Lonāris are found in the whole of Berār, and 436 in Akola District, mostly in Akot tāluk. Their traditional occupation was the preparation of salt from the wells in the Pūrna valley, and they are sometimes called Mīt-Lonāri, Salt Lonāris (though *lonār* itself means salt). If a man who has never been married wishes to marry a widow he must first go through a ceremony with a ring, and if he should at any time lose the ring, funeral ceremonies ought to be performed. Divorce is practised upon a deed of separation being given. Lonāris take food from a Kunbi, but not from a Sonār, Sutār, or Lohār.

Miscellaneous.

105 A few miscellaneous notes are added about various castes. Hatkars follow as a rule the same customs as ordinary Hindu castes but do not shave their moustache when a death occurs in their family. The only occasion when they remove their moustache is on a pilgrimage to the temple of Mahādeo at Malkārjun near Rāmeshwara in the extreme south of India. They never burn their dead but bury them, sitting with hands on knees and facing north. In the south of the District are both Wanjāris

and Banjāras. The two are absolutely distinct. Wanjāris are a single caste divided into four subdivisions which intermarry. They are scarcely distinguishable from other ordinary Hindus in religion or customs, but the men frequently, though not universally, wear side-whiskers. They hold the *patelki* of 16 villages in the north of Bāsim tāluk, all owning a kind of allegiance to a Naik, the patel of Rājura. Cremation is practised in his family but memorials are erected to the dead. Banjārās are divided into twelve-and-a-half sub-castes which do not intermarry. They are in many respects a peculiar people, but cannot be described here. The name Marātha is sometimes given as a caste name, especially by families holding rights of *deshmukhi* or *patelki*. Such people almost always admit that there is no distinction of caste between themselves and ordinary Kunbis but that the different name is taken on account of their higher position. In a very few cases, however, they claim that the castes are distinct, sometimes explaining that the Marāthas condescend to intermarry with Kunbis merely because their own caste-folk are few in Berār. In one village men of some position said that they were Marāthas and were accustomed even to call themselves Rājputs but that they intermarried with plain Kunbis. The title deshmukh is sometimes given as a caste name, or taken as a surname. Mālis are very similar to Kunbis but are inclined to marry their children younger. The boy must be older than the girl, and the ordinary age is from 10 to 12 for him and from 5 to 7 for her, but the girl may be only one year of age. Among Kunbis the least age for a girl is three years, and that is thought exceptionally young. Mālis generally refuse to work at the same plough with a Mahār, while Kunbis will always do so, but Mālis seem always to allow widow-remarriage while some Kunbi families do not. Mālis have the reputation of working very hard on irrigated land

and making their wives and children work harder than other castes do. Members of one sub-caste of Kaikāris take up contracts of several hundred rupees for road repair and similar work, and manage the carriage of material by means of droves of donkeys looked after by their wives and families; one may see a score or two of loaded donkeys in charge of a little boy and girl. The caste has a bad name, but Major E. J. Gunthorpe ("Notes on Criminal Tribes") wrote that in 1882 only a few of the subdivisions were traditionally criminal; this employment may be of use to the others. A Muhammadan who had taken such a contract would very likely hire grown-up Bhois with their donkeys, or might employ carts, which would clearly put him at a disadvantage. Bhois sometimes undertake brick-making on a large scale, willingness to use donkeys again giving them an advantage. Among Muhammadans a few relics of a previous faith can be found. In some villages one deshmukh out of three or four is a Muhammadan and can even say in what reign the conversion occurred. In any case he and his Hindu colleagues would probably admit relationship, and at marriages in either family would be much hurt if they were not invited, or *mānpān* was not given them, or the spot of *kunku* was not put on their foreheads. At Bālāpur it would appear that some of the Muhammadans were formerly Rājputs, because the old women still wear the Rājput *lahenga*, petticoat, instead of the Muhammadan *paijāma*, trousers, and at Akhāji those families observe the Hindu custom of sowing *dhān*, grain, in a basket. A Brāhman family near Bālāpūr gives up one member in every generation to become nominally a Muhammadan in order to secure the inheritance of a certain estate; the victim eats flesh like a Muhammadan on one day but lives the rest of his life as a Brāhman. Parties of Phās Pārdhis still travel with thousands of snares for buck, besides smaller snares; they callously keep, alive but untended, captured animals with broken limbs.

SOCIAL LIFE AND CUSTOMS.

Composition of villages.

106. The total population of the District is nearly 755,000. Of this total about 125,000 people are divided among 11 towns, with an average population of 11,000, another 75,000 live in villages of nearly 2800 each, and the remaining 555,000 are scattered among over 1400 villages with an average of just under 400 inhabitants—places of 80 houses each. Occasional villages are notable for having an unusual proportion of some particular caste, Mārwāris, Wānis, Wanjāris, Kolis, and so on, but the local division of castes is not very pronounced. The more aboriginal castes are more common in hilly parts, and Muhammadans are especially numerous in places of ancient importance. Within a village, again, the distinction of locality is scarcely applied except in regard to the lowest castes; Mahārs and Māngs almost always occupy quarters on the outskirts, distinct both from the general population and from each other. Banjāras, who are common in the south, also live separately; their quarters are called *tāndas* and used to be at some distance from the village-site; but Banjāras have a bad reputation and are now generally compelled to live close to the other houses so that they may be more readily kept under supervision. Sometimes, but rarely, a quarter within the village is practically given up to some other caste, to Muhammadans for instance. Even when Muhammadans are scattered among all parts of a large village they divide the area for their own purposes into separate *muhallās*; each of these has its hereditary *jamadār*, its *bangalā* or common house, and perhaps its separate procession in Muharram. Similarly a very slight degree

of localisation has developed in regard to occupation. In a large village one or two definite streets are known as the daily bazar, both permanent shops and stalls for vegetables being chiefly gathered there; the ancient crafts of turban and carpet-making have been located in definite parts of Bālāpur; the recent metalled roads have busy cartwrights' shops beside them; and cotton factories, just outside the village, often grow up side by side.

Private houses.

107. The houses of an old village are crowded together, and open on narrow winding lanes. People like to have a sacred *tulsi* plant growing in their little *āwār*, yard, and a parrot may be hung up in a metal cage; the main door of a house must not face the south. The larger houses have within one enclosure a dwelling-house, with separate places for cooking and for bathing, a yard, and buildings for cattle, agricultural implements, and perhaps grain. Berār is practically a land of peasant proprietors, though on the one hand there are a few large landholders and on the other there is a technical limitation which makes the tenure of land not strictly proprietary. Each petty cultivator needs something in the way of a farmyard but makes the little walled space within and about his dwelling-house answer the purpose. All the manure of the establishment used to be collected in a large pit in the midst, and this may still occur, but the practice is now commonly understood to be illegal; people say little about the sanitary considerations involved but complain of the present waste of their manure. In villages with a good water-supply houses have often their own wells within the same enclosure. The walls are commonly built of *māti*, earth, clay, or of a mixture of stones and *māti*; but brick walls are by no means uncommon, and dressed stone is used sometimes. Weal-

thy people often have attractive wood-carving on the fronts of their houses, Telhāra in Akot tāluk being especially distinguished in this way; Mārwāris and Cutchis perhaps most frequently use this means of ornament. Strongly-built houses are owned by men of the poorest castes as well as by people of wealthier communi ties, though sometimes a poor man's house is made of a kind of basket-work daubed with *māti*. Large metal sheets are often made of kerosine oil tins flattened out and soldered together; these are commonly used to shade the fronts of shops (which are always open) but sometimes for other kinds of roofing or even for the whole of a small building—such as the solitary, ill-situated hut occupied by the sweeper of a village. Houses occasionally have a flat top of *māti*, called *dhāba*, but more frequently they have sloping roofs of tiles, corrugated iron —called *tin*—or grass thatch; red chillies are spread out on these to dry. It is only the poorest, generally living at the sides of a village, who use thatch, because it causes great danger of fire. Tiles are more common in the north of the District and tin in the south; a little village in Bāsim or Mangrul tāluk, especially if close to a main road, may appear almost wholly roofed with tin. Tin is said to have the advantages of being easy to apply and seldom needing repair; it has the defects of being expensive, cold in winter, hot in summer, and noisy in the rains, along with a possibility of blowing off and hurting someone; a ceiling is rarely added to reduce the heat. Old men say that 60 years ago houses were almost alway scovered with thatch and were frequently huts of çotton stalks. The village-site, *gaothān*, is sometimes called *pāndhari*, white, because the ground within it approximates to that colour with the accumulations of long habitation. The depth of this soil would give some indication of the age of the village.

108. In practically every village stands one comparatively enormous structure, the village fort; usually it is called *gadhi* and belongs to the patel's family, but sometimes it is known as *kilā* and belongs to Government. It is often 30 feet high, and so large that the whole population with their cattle could find refuge within it. The walls are generally of *māti*, earth, but of such firmness as can not be equalled now-a-days; the old men say that even their grandfathers had no tradition about who built it, or about fighting in connection with it. The flag of Chāndkhān almost always flies above it, though very few know who he was; there are traditions of some unknown victim having been buried in the foundations; bones rarely come to light, but no one can say whether they are relics of that sacrifice or of some later fight. Very likely there was once a wall, *sapīli*, *gaokos*, round the village, with gates, *wes*; in some cases the remains are well preserved, but sometimes all traces have disappeared and are forgotten by most villagers. It is clear that these works, huge considering the capacity of the builders, would not have been undertaken in every village without some very pressing need of defence; they have a significance which is perhaps inadequately realised. Every village has at least a shrine of Hanumān, generally under the name of Māroti, who seems to be regarded as a kindly god of prosperity, and of Devi, or Mariāi, who holds disease and disaster in her hand; Mahādeo's temples are also common, Mārwāris worship Bālāji, and religion is closely connected with very much of the social life of the village. Every village has a building which might be described as the headman's office, where that official himself, the *jāglyā*, watchman—with blue coat trimmed with yellow and a leather belt and brass badge—and one or two

Public buildings.

Mahārs are generally to be found. The building is generally called *chāwadi*, especially when it is maintained at Government expense, but sometimes *madhi* and by Wanjāris *sopi*. Villages of any size have a school, built in the heavy style characteristic of Government architecture, and in some cases a police station, pound, *dharmshāla* (*sarai*, or rest-house for natives), and platforms for a weekly market. When the latter are uncovered they are called *chabutrā*, but when a roof has been erected, which does not seem to add in the least degree to their popularity, the name *mārket* is given them. A market-village used always to be distinguished by a large white flag, which is still prominent in some places. This weekly bazar is usually the most prominent sign of business life, but in most villages one finds a carpenter who both makes agricultural implements and builds carts, and perhaps a Kumbhār with rows of pots set out to harden. Other petty industries are carried on but are less prominent. Pedlars are frequent and often have a little crowd about them. Some are Mārwāri Brāhmans with bundles of sacred books packed on ponies, some have piles of brass pots and pans set out under an awning, sometimes a Muhammadan cloth merchant displays a great variety of brightly coloured cloths in the shelter of a *bangalā*, or another produces gaudy strings for *kardodās* from a couple of baskets, or perhaps an ingenious Baniā on his way home from a large weekly market spends the next forenoon at an intermediate village to sell a little additional grain and groceries there. Wandering Panchāls often pitch a solitary and battered tent, *pāl*, in some wide open space for a few days and do such smith's work as has accumulated.

Social life and character.

109. A close community of feeling is generally realised between the middle castes of Hindus, such as Kunbis and

Mālis, but their attitude toward Brāhmans is qualified by something approaching reverence, and they have nothing to do socially with the low castes. Muhammadans move largely in a separate social world and seem to be regarded with respect tinged with uneasiness, though all share to some extent in most of the festivals of either side, and there is very little on the surface to suggest anything but amity. Hindus of the middle castes have usually a few recognised meeting-places, often an open building, commonly called *baithak*, belonging to some well-to-do man. Groups meet here nightly for company and discussion, men usually finding an affinity in a particular gathering and habitually going to the same. Muhammadans very rarely belong to such groups, even in a small village, because, no doubt, of the real deep divisions between the two faiths. Hindus say that the quiet and timid Kunbi regards the Muhammadan as quarrelsome and feels doubtful about his principles in regard to women or is even fearful of the evil eye, while each of course transgresses one of the deepest religious principles of the other. The barber holds a very low position, so that his name and trade are terms of abuse, but he is a valuable gossip. The ordinary villager only calls him in once a fortnight but, except on unlucky days, he generally has some customer with whom to squat at the roadside. The men must attend to their cattle, but find time to dawdle about the village for some hours both morning and evening, while the women fetch water, gossiping at the wells, and cook the food. When people work in the fields before nine or ten o'clock it is often because the weekly market is held on that day and they want to do some work beforehand. In many parts the cattle that are to be driven out to graze must wait likewise on the bare earth for their herdsmen ; these are often boys, perhaps two of them to 50 head of cattle. The general life of such a village must be very quiet, but it has many petty relaxations in the way of weekly markets and small fairs and festivals—public and domestic—and is perhaps most suitable to the character of the people. They are admittedly very timid, but are also in most respects well-behaved. When plague appears in a village everyone lives outside for a month at a time, but a man will leave valuable jewellery in his empty house almost unprotected. Disputes occur especially among relatives and in regard to land ; when enmity is alleged in a criminal case and a cause is asked a man sometimes answers merely, 'He is my relative.' The parties dread the civil court, partly because the plaintiff by needing to prove his case is put at a disadvantage and partly because of the expense and uncertainty involved. So they assert their rights by force on a small scale, which results in petty criminal cases particularly full of false swearing and with most complicated questions of possession in the immediate background. Village life curiously combines beauty and crudeness: in the silence of early dawn there may pass, with no sound of footsteps on the dusty road, the voice of a devotee crying "Narayan! Narayan!"; or instead it may be the sound of someone moving slowly by and clearing his throat and mouth with painful efforts audible for a hundred yards.

Children and school-life.

110. The child-life of the District has of course some points of interest. A son is valued far more highly than a daughter, and perhaps female children are slightly neglected, but on the whole children of both sexes are regarded with great affection. Clothing is regarded more as a matter of ornament than a source of warmth, and small children are often left practically naked—

wearing perhaps only a silver bracelet and a string *kardodā* or *kargotā*—so that they must suffer from the damp and cold in the rains if at no other time. This *kardodā* is a thread, often a red string but sometimes made of silver, worn round the waist by boys and sometimes by girls. It is enjoined to be worn, under its Sanskrit name *katisūtra*, all their lives by males of the three upper castes. A girl after passing out of infancy and putting on the dress of a woman never wears it. A Brāhman boy after he puts on the *jānwa*, sacred thread, should continue to wear a *kardodā* of silk or *munja* grass, but should not wear one of silver; in fact he generally gives it up when he begins to wear a *dhotra* instead of a mere *langoti*. Hindus of Shūdra caste, such as Kunbis, have also taken to wearing the *kardodā* and often use silver all their lives. Even a Mahār who wants to tie together the legs of a buck which he is going to carry on his head, may suggest that his *kardodā* be cut and taken for the purpose. School fees are now exceedingly low, and a fair proportion of boys and a few girls attend school. The number of boys between 5 and 15 in the District is about 82,000, and the number of boys of all ages attending school is about 15,000. The children of the lowest castes are admitted into the ordinary schools but are by no means welcomed by the rest of the population, and their parents often value their small earnings too much to send them to school; a boy can help his mother appreciably at weeding or cotton-picking. Besides this, many small villages are practically out of reach of a school; fear is felt of harm happening sooner or later if children go more than two miles to school. These causes explain why, in spite of considerable keenness for education, more boys are not found in the schools. If other indications were not available a school could generally be discovered by the clatter of voices, not on account of habitual disorder but because a cheerful singsong seems, to the outsider, the recognised way of acquiring knowledge. Infant classes are to a considerable extent given instruction in a kindergarten style and sometimes thoroughly enjoy it. They sing with enthusiasm an action-song about colours, or one little boy recites a fable to the rest, who acknowledge every point with a strongly aspirated grunt of acquiescence, surprisingly deep and earnest. Singing or reciting—for the performance is not exactly described by either word—seems usually much liked by the younger boys. Physical drill, called *deshi kasrat*, has been regularly given for the last few years, and is sometimes said to have caused a distinct improvement in the health of the boys. Traces of school life are also seen in the streets. One is the occasional salute in military fashion with the open palm. Muhammadans have always taught their sons to *salām*, but Hindus used to consider that a boy showed most respect by not intruding himself in any way. Among all castes it is considered somewhat impolite to show the palm of the hand or the sole of the foot, but a detail of drill has had the unintended effect of largely breaking through these ancient but rather vague ideas. Boys, sometimes led by their parents, pass through the streets with slates and bundles of school-books; very rarely a little boy may have his body warmly covered, scarlet socks—but no shoes—on his feet, and his head wrapped up against the cold in a scarlet scarf; children of the wealthiest Hindu families go to the ordinary schools. The most extraordinary school the writer has seen in Berār is that at Keli Weli on the Pūrna river, where Mr. Sūryabhān Jānji, a Koli headmaster, has brought numerous institutions into the school and maintained them for 25 years. The boys themselves take a very large part in the details of management; thus they keep the books of a boarding-house which usually has 50 inmates at a monthly cost of about Rs. 2-8 a head; they fetch water from the river a mile away for their garden, and have in it little artistic columns, tiny tanks with large cotton ducks, a cataract, and a volcano—all certainly crude but, taken as details in a large scheme, very significant. The master received a certificate from the King-Emperor in 1903. Originality or sound independent thought seems rare among local school-masters but this is certainly an exception to the rule. Girls' schools are usually in charge of old men, because disengaged women of the attainments and character required are rare. Discipline in boys' schools is not rigid—occasionally the master sits with his feet drawn up on the seat of his chair, while a class gathers round with elbows set comfortably on his table—but it is slacker again among girls. If a girls' school is not open at eight in the morning when the proper time is half-past seven the cold is considered quite a sufficient reason; so the scholars are represented perhaps by two little girls sitting on the steps and crooning over sewing work of uncertain utility but brilliant hue.

Effects of education.

111. It is difficult to say what are the consequences of this education. People commonly declare that a boy who has been attending school for some years thinks himself superior to field work, wants better clothes than his father, and possibly finds exertion in the sun rather trying; but the great majority of such boys as pass through only the elementary classes must depend on agriculture when they leave school, and it is to be hoped that the tendency is not a serious one. Boys who proceed to the high school at Akola take their work very seriously. In the hostel attached they are supposed to sleep from 10 to 5, to do two hours of home work in the

evening and two more in the morning, and to be in school for six hours, of which one hour is given up to physical drill. A list compiled for the Keli Weli school shows what has become of every boy who has passed through the sixth standard there in the last 20 years, and is probably typical of the fortunes of the best educated boys of vernacular schools. Out of 157 boys 21 have died, 14 have as yet found no occupation, and five are not clearly classified, leaving 117 divided between different employments. Of that number 62 have used their acquirements to get employment under Government (41 as patels or patwāris and 19 as schoolmasters); 26 make direct profit of them in other ways, chiefly as agents of *sāhukārs* and shopkeepers; 25 look after their own fields; and six are engaged in petty occupations for which little knowledge is required. Three-quarters of the boys are thus making their living largely through the comparatively good education they received, and two-thirds of these have found employment in one way or another under Government. The prospects offered by Government appear to be the chief incentive to education, especially in its higher stages. It is difficult to estimate the degree of education attained. Boys who have passed the fourth standard, the highest in many of the village schools, should read and write with a certain degree of ease, but must be in great danger of forgetting their acquirements. The larger schools have a sixth standard; boys who have passed this should find reading a pleasure. It is sometimes claimed that a boy who has been through the high school can read and write ordinary English intelligently, but in fact both his knowledge of English and his general thinking power are very limited; the standard of education throughout the community is still low, and even the more fortunate boys must suffer in consequence.

Children's games.

112. In *Atya Pātya* or *Lonpāt* two equal sides are formed and a large oblong is marked out on the ground, perhaps by water being poured on the dry dust or sand. An additional line is made lengthways along the middle of the oblong, and cross-lines are also drawn. There must be, including the lines at the end of the oblong, exactly as many of these cross-lines as there are players on a side. The main idea is for the attacking party to try to run the length of the oblong without being touched, while the defending party tries to touch every one of them. Each of the defenders is placed on one of the cross-lines, his position being determined by the captain in such a way that the whole party may offer the best defence possible. All the attackers gather outside one end of the oblong. Their captain and the leader of the defenders, who is called *mridangyā*, touch hands, and the raid begins. The attackers are safe when between the cross-lines, and as each of these has only one boy to watch it there is a large chance in favour of most of them getting across any single line in safety; but as the attackers get fewer and more scattered their difficulties increase. Those that get through the oblong safely in one direction should then return. The chances of the parties clearly vary greatly according to the size of the ground marked out and their own organization—which is generally very slight. For *Kho Kho* two sides are formed, and all the boys of one side, except a single member, squat down in a row on the ground, the even numbers facing one way and odd numbers the other. The other side runs around these, and the single boy who is standing up tries to overtake and touch them, anyone caught in this way having to fall out. When this pursuer is tired he changes places with one of the boys who are sitting down, saying from behind

him, *Kho Kho*, get up, and the second boy takes up the chase. Sooner or later the whole side is caught, when they become pursuers in turn. In *Chīlīpāt* or *Chīlpāt* two sides are formed and stand opposite each other at a little more than arm's length. The game begins by representatives of each side striking hands with each other. Then the one party, remaining still, tries to pull some one from the other side across a line, real or imaginary, drawn between them. The sign that the opponent is captured—*melā*, dead—is that after being dragged across his leg is touched by one of the other side. When a single boy has thus been captured the sides change places. *Witidāndu* is a game played with a long stick, *dāndu*, and a short one, *witi*, between two equal parties. A small, narrow, trench is dug and the *witi* is placed across it. The striking party gather around it and the other party stand at a little distance. One boy places the end of the *dāndu* under the *witi* and jerks the latter as far as he can. If it is caught by the other side he is 'dead' and another of his party takes his place. If it is not caught he sets the *dāndu* upright in the trench and the other side throw the *witi* at it, 'killing' him if they hit. If they miss he balances the *witi* on the hand in which he holds the *dāndu*, jerks it up into the air, and hits it as far as he can. If it is not caught it must be again thrown in, and this time it is only necessary that it should lie within a *dāndu's* length of the trench. If it is further off than this the next step depends upon the exact distance between. If this is less than two lengths of the *dāndu* it is called *wakhat*, and the boy balances the *witi* on his instep and kicks it up in order to strike it again. If the distance exceeds two *dāndus* but is less than three, it is called *rend* or *lend*, and the *witi* is taken by the end with the fingers of the left hand, and struck thence. If another *dāndu's* length is measured out the distance is called *mund*, and the *witi* is balanced across the left fist and must be struck near the projecting end. Another *dāndu* makes a *nāl*, when the *witi* must be placed across the base of the extended first and fourth finger of the left hand; the *awid* sets it across the left elbow, or between the thumb and forearm, the *āru* across the right eye, and then the *tekya* or *jhaku* comes, in which the *witi* is again laid against the *dāndu* on the right fist. The various terms correspond with the cardinal numbers of the Dravidian languages, an indication of the origin of the game.

Marriage customs.

113. Infant marriage is almost universal, but there is a slight tendency among educated people to raise the age of marriage. No complete description of the ceremony is given, but a few miscellaneous customs are noted. Among Brāhmans and Kunbis the bride and bridegroom spit on each other when bathing on the second day after the marriage. Among Agarwāla Baniās the bridegroom is seated first on an ass—an animal regarded by Hindus with contempt—and then on a horse, or he at least touches an ass with his foot. Among Kunbis when the bride and bridegroom go to bow before the family deities they walk on brass plates turned up-side down. Kunbis and similar castes have a ceremony called *ghod sawāsin*, in which the bridegroom pretends to be angry and refuses to go to the bride's house. A small boy is dressed in woman's clothes and takes in his hand a pestle, *mūsal*, with *ghogar*, small bells, tied to it and dances around the bridegroom to pacify him. A Banjāra bride hides herself after the ceremony, and the bridegroom, accompanied by music, visits several houses in search of her. Rangāris have a ceremony called *jhumandal*, in which the women parade the roads with lamps of *sarki*, cotton seed, singing as they go. Rangāris,

Ghātodi Chamārs, Dhobis and Dohors, put the bride and bridegroom, wearing black blankets, to sit on a bullock and take them in that fashion to the temple of Māroti for worship. Rangāris, Bāris, and Dhangars practise the *ghōda nāchnā*, by which a man riding a wooden horse dances in front of the married pair when they go out at night for the *bīdh* procession. Well-to-do Muhammadans have the marriage ceremony performed according to strict Muhammadan ritual, but others adopt some Hindu practices. They often call in a Brāhman to fix an auspicious day, or they may perform the *fālnāma*, taking an omen from the first words seen on opening a book. They erect a marriage booth and cover it with either white cloth or green leaves according to their means. When the marriage procession goes to the bride's village it is always accompanied by the women of the party. It stops outside the village and members of the bride's family bring the *rukhmat kā gharā*, a pot filled with water, into which the bridegroom drops either a rupee or an eight-anna piece, then covering the pot with a new cloth. The bridegroom's father provides a feast on the second day, and the *kāzi* performs the ceremony on the third. For this purpose the pair are seated on a bedstead with a copy of the Korān and with a curtain held between them, the latter being presently withdrawn. The Berār Census Report of 1881, written by Mr. E. J. Kitts, which has numerous descriptions of curious practices, gives on pp. 50-51 several indications of wife-capture. Gonds and Kolāms still had a mock fight before marriage. (They performed the ceremony on the village dunghill. Marātha and Telangi Kalāls worshipped the dunghill immediately before the marriage.) 'Among the Lajjhars not only do 'the bridegroom's party erect the *mandap* (or shed) at the 'bride's house, instead of its being erected for them, but '. . .with the bridegroom is an assistant known as the '*lāndgā* or wolf. The bridegroom betrays no sign of 'his intention: the wolf brings the *sāri*, the yellow cloth, 'and the brass bangle. He dances for two hours before 'the bride's house; and, suspicion being thus lulled, 'seizes his opportunity to rush inside followed by his 'principal. They find the bride seated in a bamboo basket. 'The bridegroom, catching her by the right hand, makes 'her stand up and slips the bangle on her right wrist, 'gives her the yellow cloth, and propitiates her mother 'with the *sāri*. Then follows the Hinduized part of the 'ceremony. Among the Bhois, a caste which still permits 'adult marriages, the bride's maternal uncle ties a thread 'of sheep's wool with a brass ring and five betel leaves to 'the bridegroom's right hand. When the marriage is 'complete the bride's parents sometimes hide her in a 'neighbouring house, and the bridegroom is required 'personally to find her and bring her forth. Among 'the Telis, Kumbhārs, Bhois, Tāmbolis, Mahārs, Māngs, 'and Chambhārs . . . when the bridegroom approaches 'to snap the *toran* (the string which separates the 'women's apartment from the rest of the house) the 'bride's brother, armed with a pestle, asks him for some 'money. The bridegroom says that he has already paid, 'and refuses, whereupon he is saluted with a shower of 'cowdung and water.'

Dress.

114. The ordinary dress of a small cultivator or a labourer consists of a white *dhotra* with a narrow coloured border wound about his loins, a short jacket, a turban, a pair of shoes, and a kind of scarf called *uparna*. In cold weather he often wears also a blanket over his head, but on occasion he goes without the jacket and shoes. The cost of all these articles would be about Rs. 8. People almost always buy *dhotras* in pairs, a fact which sometimes facilitates identification in criminal cases. The

turban is generally red but sometimes white. Well-to-do people wear longer coats, fasten their *dhotras* in looser folds, and have all their garments of finer quality. The turban of a Brāhman or a deshmukh generally costs Rs. 5 but is sometimes much more expensive; it lasts about two years. People who come much into contact with Europeans introduce modifications accordingly, substituting (or adding) trousers, and perhaps wearing collars, with or without ties. The first garment changed, both fashion and comfort—though not convenience—being served, is the shoe; one may see a hospital assistant wearing 'Europe' shoes tied with the red and white laces issued by Government for fastening papers. Clerks and some others when working alone like to wear a round cap, *topi*. Women commonly wear a *lugdā*, or *sāri*, and a *choli*. The former is a piece of cloth about 24 feet long and 4 feet wide which is first wrapped round the waist and then brought over the shoulder, carried back between the legs, and tucked in at the back. The head may be left free or a fold may easily be raised to cover it; such a garment does not set off the figure but sometimes its free lines are graceful. The *choli* is a small and tight bodice. These garments may be of almost any colour, but dark reds and greens are much the most common; light and gaudy colours would in most castes not be respectable, and white and black are very unusual. Women may wear *wāhnā*, sandals, for field-work but otherwise leave their feet bare. Colour has only to a very slight extent been adopted as a mark of caste. Among Muhammadans the men generally wear *paijāma*, trousers, and a long coat, but not always; they sometimes wear a *dhotra*, H. *dhoti*, in a coloured check pattern, sometimes a plain white one. Their women also generally wear trousers, together with a *choli* and a scarf which is tied round the waist and brought over the head. Numerous differences used to be commonly recognised in the dress and ornaments of different castes, but though these are still often observed by individuals they are more frequently disregarded by people in general. With the enormous increase in travelling, bringing far more outsiders into Berār, people see a greater variety of fashions and largely adopt whatever pleases them. As a head-dress the simple *patkā* is largely superseding the turban, and though it may be tied in many different ways it often obliterates very characteristic differences. Perhaps old fashions survive, in India, among the women more than the men, though some changes have taken place in their attire also. Caste is most strongly marked in the case of Banjārā women, in this District commonly called Labhānis; they wear short but voluminous petticoats and are loaded with ornaments. The *choli* of a Bāri woman has sleeves which reach almost to her wrists. Rājput women sometimes keep to their old *lahengā*, petticoat, but have partly adopted the local *sāri*; when going out of doors they wear a white veil; Mārwāris also wear a *lahengā*. Among the Erandi Telis a woman should give up her *choli* after a child has been born to her. The end of the *sāri* is brought up in front over the right shoulder, behind the head, and then down over the left shoulder by women of Beldār, Mochi, Pinjāra, and Pardeshi Kumbhār castes and by Gujarātis, but other women wind it upwards over the left shoulder and then downwards over the right. Bāri and Phul Māli women draw horizontal lines of *kunku* on their foreheads, but most other castes apply round spots, which may not be worn by a widow. In most castes it is thought unlucky to wear gold below the waist, and so a well-to-do woman may have gold on her forehead and hair, in her nose and ears, round her neck, and on her wrists, but her armlets, anklets, and toe-rings are mostly of silver. Some have a tooth filled with gold to ensure that they shall be in contact with that metal at death. Women of the poorest castes other than wandering tribes generally have glass bangles and some heavy silver ornaments. The Kunbi is fond of smoking and of chewing *pān*, betel-leaves, and generally carries with him a *chanchi*, a cloth bag with three compartments, the lowest for tobacco, the next for *khānd*, a piece of betel-nut, and the top one for *kāth*, catechu; he places a few betel-leaves and a small tin of *nalkānde*, lime, upon this and folds them all together. His wife carries at her waist a little bag called *pishwi* in which are *supāri* and a few pice for herself and a *dabbi*, small tin or brass case, of opium for her infant child.

Food.

115. The everyday food of the agricultural and labouring classes consists chiefly of jawāri meal, pulse, onions, chillies, oil, salt, and a considerable variety of green vegetables and spices. One delicacy, called *kadhi*, is made of the meal of gram pulse mixed with sour milk, *dahi*, and served with spices. On days of festival particular dishes are served, especially among the well-to-do; such dishes are *puranāchipoli*, *kshīr*, *lādu*, *wade* and *bhaje*. On some festivals, again, further special rules apply. On Nāgpanchmi one may take fried cakes but not baked ones, because the serpent god would be burnt by an iron pan being put on the fire. On Mahālakshmi one should eat *āmbil phal* and vegetables of as many kinds as possible; and on Pola *chombadā* (jawāri boiled in water) and cucumber. Nothing *talalele*, fried, should be eaten during the prevalence of an epidemic. One should not eat *khichadi* on Monday or *besan* on Thursday because that would bring poverty. It is lucky to eat parched gram on Friday but not on Thursday or Saturday.

During a period of mourning most people abstain from sugar, milk, fried food, and turmeric. People who know *mantras* for the cure of snake-bite should never eat *padolā* or *shewāi*, a snake-like confectionery, or the *dodka*, *turai*, vegetable, apparently because their form resembles that of a snake. Most of the middle castes, represented by the Kunbis, eat the flesh of goats and fowls but refuse that of cows and pigs, though Mālis are said to eat both the wild and the domestic pig. They may smoke tobacco and drink *dāru*, the liquor made from the mahuā tree, but may not smoke *gānja* or drink *sindi* or *tādi*, liquors made from species of palm. Kunbis however insist on a Muhammadan *fakīr* pronouncing the *halāl* when the animal is killed. Rājputs generally eat the flesh of male animals only, and some of the higher castes are strict vegetarians and abstain from all intoxicating liquor. Among the very low castes some, like the Mahārs, refuse to touch the pig, but some, like Māngs and sweepers, eat it. These people have no objection to taking *gānja* or *sindi*. Castes with hunting associations, such as Pārdhis, eat the wild but not the domestic pig. Muhammadans will not touch the pig, and the men of understanding among them often observe the prohibition of intoxicating liquor, but others both visit the shops and take liquor contracts. Hindus are said to be trying to start a temperance movement, but the principles and prospects of the scheme are not yet clear.

Furniture.

116. Furnishing is much simplified to the ordinary cultivator because he prefers to squat, crouching and balancing himself on his feet, rather than actually to sit down, even if his seat is a rail or parapet; thus he needs no chairs or tables. The climate again makes it easy to live largely out of doors, and perhaps this reduces the

demand for comfortable furniture. The standard of comfort has been steadily rising for the last sixty years and perhaps will continue to rise. However the household furniture which contents the ordinary cultivator at present consists chiefly of a fairly long list of simple articles. These comprise—a *jāte*, H. *chakki*, stone hand-mill for his wife to grind flour (costing about R. 1-8), *patā* and *warawanta*, the slab and muller with which spices and so on are ground; *mundal*, earthen vessel for storing water (As. 6); *dauri* and *sarposh*, basket and lid for keeping bread (As. 3); *kāthot*, wooden tray for kneading flour (As. 8); *tāmbya*, or *thālya*, brass or copper pots for carrying and keeping drinking water (Rs. 2-8); *tadhāwa*, sleeping mat or carpet (Rs. 2 or Rs. 2-8); *ghonghdya*, blankets (at R. 1 or R. 1-8); *bāj* or *khāt*, a four-legged string bed; *wakal*, or *rajai*, a quilt made of old clothes; and *diwa*, a lamp. In families in a higher position there are more articles, and those of better quality; the wealthiest class has European furniture for at least ceremonial occasions. All classes need a variety of agricultural implements and a certain number of boxes for storing articles of value; grain is commonly kept in a *peo*, pit. It is given as a general rule that Hindus prefer brass utensils and Muhammadans copper.

LEADING FAMILIES.

Leading families.

117. Akola District, like most of Berār, is for all practical purposes a land of peasant proprietors; very few individuals are of much prominence. Every pargana, of which there are 43 in the District, has its own deshmukhs and deshpāndyas, but the office is now of little importance. *Jāgīr* villages number 55, but they are generally small and of little value; they have often been given to support a temple. The District contains 33 *darbāris*, including seven holders

of titles conferred by the British Government and 16 Bench Magistrates. They are men respected alike by Government officers and by their neighbours; they belong to the leading families in their own neighbourhood; but, owing perhaps to the good position taken by a large number of lesser men, they are not so distinguished from these as are the leaders in other parts of India. The Deshpândes of Bâlâpur say their rights are derived from a military ancestor who served under Aurangzeb. He was outcasted, retaliated by massacring his near relatives, but, repenting, adopted a child who had accidentally survived. Maulvi Muhammad Muntâjiuddîn, of Bâlâpur, is *khatîb* of Bâlâpur and *asl-kâzi* of Akola, though he acts through a *naib*, and is considered a Mufti by some Muhammadans. His father, Maulvi Muassan Sâhib, Khân Bahâdur, was formally recognised as Mufti and was immensely respected in Berâr. Saiyid Muhammad, son of Saiyid Ahmad Sâhib, holds *jâgîr* villages in Khâmgaon tâluk. The Deshpânde family of Adgaon have long been distinguished in Akot tâluk; Lakshuman Gopâl Deshpânde is an Extra Assistant Commissioner and Shrikrishna Amrit is a Bench Magistrate. A *jâgîr* of 1400 acres was conferred in 1846 on Nârâyandâs Pandit of Adgaon on account of his astrological knowledge; his son Gadâdhar now holds the *jâgîr*. The late Khushâlrao of Akot is said to have maintained a force of a few hundred Râjputs; his son Gopâl was a pleader at Akola but has retired, and his grandson is a pleader at Amraoti. In Murtizâpur tâluk Muhammad Hâtim, son of Muhammad Burhân, Bench Magistrate and retired Police Inspector, lives at Kâranja; *inâm* lands assessed at Rs. 92 have been given to him personally on account of the devotion shown by his uncle in assisting the escape of some English ladies during the Mutiny. The late Râmji

Naik Kannawa built at Kāranja one of the finest houses in the District; the family is represented by a boy adopted by the deceased but in the guardianship of his own father, Lakshmanrao Rāgho, Bench Magistrate, and is largely engaged in cotton trading. Prāgji Lilādhar is the third Bench Magistrate of the town. The Kāmargaon estate of 16 villages, producing a total revenue of Rs. 18,000, of which the estate holder receives Rs. 7,000 net, is in the hands of Mīr Yāwar Ali, son of Mīr Akbar Ali; it was given to the heirs of Mīr Imām Ali Khān, Risāldar, on account of services rendered by him during the Mutiny. Bājirao Akāji Deshmukh of the same village is a member of the District Board. Gopālrao Kāshirao, a Brāhman minor 10 years of age living at Mālegaon Jāgīr, represents one of the leading families in Bāsim tāluk; the title Rājā, along with a *jāgīr* of 52 villages in different parts, was conferred by the Emperor Jahāngir on an ancestor called Udājirām or Udhaorao, who is said to have left Berār and entered the imperial service on account of family disputes; the title Rājā is not recognised by the British Government, but the family holds rights of *deshmukhi* acquired under Aurangzeb. Uttamrao and Rustamrao, sons of Yeshwantrao, Wanjāris, of Rājura, represent the leading family of their caste in that part of Bāsim tāluk; the title *naik* is applied to them, and they have a kind of headship over 16 villages which are in the hands of Wanjāri patels. Their chief ancestor was Bibājirao, who was given the title of Rai Yeshwant by the Emperor Shāh Jahān. In Mangrul tāluk Jagadīsh Vishvāsrao, *jāgirdār* of Wāra, is commonly known as Rāja Udayrām and has an income as *jāgirdār* and deshmukh of nearly Rs. 3,000. The family attained and secured its position by services rendered in three generations by Udāji, Jagajīwanrao and Bāburao directly in the imperial service and also when in charge of 21 parganas in this part of India. The title of Rao Bahādur has been conferred on two pleaders at Akola, Dattātreya Vishnu Bhāgwat, and Deorao Vināyak ; the former has taken a prominent part in local government and has a steam oil-mill ; the latter has started a ginning, pressing, and spinning mill. That of Rao Sāhib is enjoyed by Dhondji Kondji, retired Police Inspector of Akola, a Bedar by caste and a man of distinguished service ; Khushālrao Ganpatrao Deshmukh of Andura in Bālāpur tāluk ; and Keshava Govind Dāmle, the Public Prosecutor of West Berār. Mirza Abbāsbeg, son of Mirza Husainbeg, *khatīb* and *naib-kāzi* of Akola, and Khān Jalāluddin Khān, son of Aimuddinkhān, *jāgirdār* of Māhān in the same tāluk, are other Muhammadans of influence. Rāmchandra Vishnu Mahājani, of Akola, is a pleader of long standing, has done much public service, and has recently been thanked by the Chief Commissioner for his interest in education. Pargana and village officers generally are greatly respected; patels and patwāris form, with certain inevitable qualifications, an admirable body of men. In every village a few castes have each their own hereditary headman called Chaudhari, Naik, Mahājan, Mehtar, Rājotya, and by other titles ; the other castes also contain groups respected for their wisdom, character, and experience ; *mukaddams* soon take the lead in new settlements of *hamāls* and other town labourers. Though the District contains very few individuals of conspicuous eminence it has a great many men of influence, hereditary and otherwise, in their own circles ; perhaps these, in turn, are more numerous and prominent through the absence of people overwhelmingly great.

CHAPTER IV.

AGRICULTURE.

SOILS.

Soils.

118. According to the technicalities of the Berār settlement system all land is brought under the main classes of black, red, and white soil, and is then put into a subdivision according to the presence or absence of certain specified advantages or defects. The classification is permanent and has the one net effect of making any particular field always liable to pay a definite proportion of any maximum rate of revenue which may be fixed for the village in which it lies. Records of all the details are kept but even at the making of a fresh settlement are not reconsidered. The classification, therefore, in spite of its constant importance, does not come into any prominence. Ordinary classifications naturally follow different lines. Thus, the two main questions about soil in Berār are whether it is black and whether it is hilly; in the latter case it will almost certainly be also light, probably with a *muram* subsoil, and largely mixed with small pieces of limestone. Black soil is *kāli*; hilly *bardi*; light *halki*; muramy *murami* or *murmād*; very light *khāri*; rocky and very light *khadkāl*; mixed with large pieces of limestone *bharki* or *kharpan*; with small *chunkhadi*; stony *gotāli*; red *lāl* or *tāmbadi*; white or yellowish *pāndhari*, *bhutādi*, or *bhurki*; sandy *retādi*; flooded *mali*; very wet *panthāl*; cut up by streams *wāhuri*; and lowlying *lawan*; waste land is *padīt*; an irrigated field used for ordinary crops *mala*; one for fruit and vegetables *bāgait*. For revenue purposes land irrigated by a bucket from a well is called

motasthal and that by a channel from a tank or river *pātasthal*. Most of the District consists of flat black soil, generally free from stones. One great tract of this takes in the north of Bālāpur, Akola, and Murtizāpur tāluks and the greater part of Akot; that is, it extends from the railway northwards to within a few miles of the Melghāt hills. The centre of Bāsim and the north-west of Mangrul have also good black soil, while smaller areas of it are scattered all over the District. On the other hand the south of Bālāpur and Akola, most of the border of Bāsim, the south of Mangrul, and the east and north-east of Murtizāpur are hilly, light, and stony, though valleys provide good soil in places. Ranges of hills are very distinct along the junction of Bāsim with Bālāpur and Akola, and again in the middle and south-east of Mangrul; they form in places *ghāts* which are almost precipitous. Such land is not only very light but is largely given up to forest, *bandi*, *jangal*.

STATISTICS OF CULTIVATION.

Progress of cultivation.

119. Old men all over the District say that since the Assignment of 1853 the area of cultivation has greatly extended; but owing to mistakes in the old records and to changes in the early boundaries trustworthy figures for the first 15 years are not available. In old days there was always a great deal of waste land owing to lack of cultivators; now there is scarcely any. A correct survey was finished and a settlement of the modern kind made in the four northern tāluks, Akot, Bālāpur, Akola, and Murtizāpur, in 1867–1868, and in the two southern tāluks, Bāsim and Mangrul, in 1872–1873. Revision Settlement Reports were made towards the close of the 30 years' period, giving the latest information obtainable at that time. They apply only to the

khālsa villages, but these include practically the whole District, and are in any case quite representative. Cultivation had extended in Akot tāluk by 1 per cent., in Murtizāpur by 3, in Akola by 5, in Mangrul by 8, and in Bāsim by 14 per cent.; no figures for Bālāpur are available, but there is no reason to suppose that its development was very different from that of the other tāluks. Cultivation extended everywhere, slightly in the tāluks which are most easy of access and much more considerably elsewhere, the difference being certainly caused by the fact that almost all the available land had been taken up in the former during the 13 years which had already elapsed since the Assignment. A considerable change has also occurred in the proportionate cultivation of different crops, *rabi* having much decreased and *kharīf* increased. In all parts of the District people say that *rabi* used to be very much more grown but that it does not answer now because of a great decrease in the rainfall. Figures on the point are only given in the first Settlement Reports for Bāsim tāluk, which show that in 1870 the chief crops there were jawāri with 29 per cent. of the whole, cotton with 18½, and wheat with 25. The next report shows that the average of the five years from 1895 to 1899 was—jawāri 27 per cent., cotton 21, and wheat 18. The average of the five years ending in 1908 gives jawāri 32 per cent., cotton 44, and wheat 4. In the middle of Akot tāluk a patel of 50 years' service says that wheat was the main crop, though people could seldom afford to taste it, little jawāri was eaten because little was grown, and cotton was not much cultivated; now almost every field has a *kharīf* crop. In the north of Akola tāluk people say that they used to sow 12 annas *rabi* and 4 annas *kharīf*; now there are not 2 annas of *rabi*, though *rabi*, in spite of the greater cost of its cultivation, would still pay with an ample rainfall. On the Pūrna one may hear that people sometimes had to eat their valuable wheat because they had not grown enough jawāri and other grains. It is necessary to refer to tradition in the matter, though with the greatest caution, because of the lack of early statistics. Fairly dependable figures are, however, available since 1877-1878. The bulk of the present Akola District then, and till 1905, formed the bulk of the old Akola and Bāsim Districts. Figures for the exact area of the present District cannot be given, but those for the two old Districts combined will give a reliable idea of the agricultural history of this part for 23 years. To avoid accidental variations statistics are given, not for single years, but for the average of five-year periods.

Kharif or autumn crops.	Average acreage, 1877-1882.	Average acreage, 1900-1905.	Total increase or decrease per cent.
Jawāri	868,500	964,000	+ 11
Cotton	761,000	996,000	+ 31
Tūr	42,000	42,000	..
Til	25,000	22,000	− 12

Rabi or spring crops.	Average acreage, 1877-1882.	Average acreage, 1900-1905.	Total increase or decrease per cent.
Wheat	257,000	84,500	− 67
Linseed	79,000	36,000	− 54½
Gram	83,000	50,000	− 39

Present state of cultivation.

120. Further figures are given to illustrate the present state of cultivation. The total area of the District in the last year reported, 1907—1908, when the yield was under 50 per cent. of the normal outturn, was 2,620,000 acres. The area cropped was 1,950,000 acres, that occupied but useless, *potkharāb*, 45,000, and that occupied but not cropped 219,000 acres. Of forest there were 101,000 acres given up to timber and fuel reserves, 13,000 to grass reserves, and 102,000 to pasture lands. Besides this there were 70,000 acres devoted to village sites and other village purposes, 97,000 to grazing outside the forests, and 12,000 unculturable but not included in any of the classes mentioned. The land available for cultivation but not actually occupied amounted to 10,600 acres, that is, about $\frac{2}{5}$ per cent. of the total area, or a little less than $\frac{1}{2}$ per cent. of the total on which cultivation is permitted. The normal area for the different crops was then officially reported as cotton 914,000 acres, jawāri 760,000, wheat 88,000, linseed 29,000, and til 10,000. Other food crops were estimated to cover 133,000 acres and non-food crops 12,000 acres. Irrigated land amounted to 14,600 acres, practically all of it worked by means of wells.

CROPS.

Kharif cultivation.

121. The main *kharīf* crops are jawāri and cotton, but tūr and til also occupy a considerable area. The ordinary rotation is merely between cotton and jawāri, but in some parts *rabi* is added, and individuals everywhere sow cotton two or three years in succession. The last practice is generally held to impoverish the soil, but sometimes people say that if manure is used cotton can be sown for any number of years in good land, though perhaps

manure must be applied every year and the land be really well worked; in parts of Bāsim they used to sow *rabi* repeatedly, and even without using manure. In preparing the soil the old stalks—*padhātyā* of cotton, *turātya* of tūr, or *phās* of jawāri—are first removed, generally by hand, a process called *upatne*. Some land is very liable to be choked with grass; in parts of Bāsim one hears that all kinds of weeds grow in land adjoining hilly forest, because the seeds are brought thence by the wind. To remove this grass it is generally necessary to use the *nāgar*, a heavy plough, and in such land *nāgarne* is done perhaps every year, or else once in two or three years. In land of good quality and not liable to weeds the *nāgar* is used much more rarely, sometimes not being applied once in ten years. Sometimes it is sufficient to use a heavy kind of *wakhar*—the smaller plough—with perhaps two pairs of bullocks and the driver standing on the plough to make it cut deeply. In other cases the ordinary *wakhar*, with one pair of bullocks, is alone used. Such *wakharne* is done late in the cold weather once along the length of the field and once across its breadth, and the soil is turned up again at the time of sowing, at the commencement of the rains.

Cotton.

122. The chief cotton formerly sown was *bani*, which produced a comparatively long-stapled plant, but this has for many years been giving way to cotton inferior in quality but stronger and more productive. People now generally sow a mixture of *kāthel*, *vilāyati*, *jari* and *bani*, the importance of the different species being according to the order in which they are mentioned. An expert can easily tell the species from seeing a single *bondh*, boll. The seed of *kāthel* has a *kāta*, thorn, and when fresh is *hirwat*, greenish, in colour but becomes *malkat*, dark, with keeping; that of *vilāyati* is black from the first,

and comes out from the boll free from cotton fluff. Seed is selected to a certain extent, but not very carefully. In the factories inferior *sarki* is sold for fodder and only the better samples are offered for seed, as people would be more likely to buy from a good stock. A few well-to-do cultivators gin their own seed, or buy hand-ginned seed; this would be chosen with some care. Almost everyone however sows *sarki* from the factories, though the seed is much less dependable than that from hand-gins, *hāt reche*. The Government experimental farm at Akola sows and sells seed of its own ginning in which 95 per cent. germinates, but good seed is twice as dear as factory seed and few people think it worth while to buy the former; to some extent they make up for the difference by sowing one-quarter more of the less reliable kind. It is the ordinary practice everywhere to sow cotton earlier than jawāri but not before the rains have actually broken, that is, generally in Mrig *nakshatra* (in the beginning of June). It would be useless to sow before rain came in the deep rich soil of much of the northern parts because such large cracks form that what was sown would be likely to be lost in them. In much of the shallow, stony, soil of the south cracks do not come, and people with inferior cattle sometimes sow in Rohini *nakshatra* before rain falls to escape the labour of turning up the saturated soil. In some other parts only the well-to-do sow before the rains break, because they get a bigger and quicker crop if rain comes favourably but will have to sow again if it does not; the seed is sown deep with a *dhussa* and a *wakhar* follows. This would answer perfectly if rain came at just the right time and in the proper quantity, but if only a little rain falls and a break follows the seeds will sprout but quickly wither up. Cotton seed is generally sown through a bamboo tube, *sartā*, trailed behind a *wakhar*, while another *wakhar* follows to turn the seeds into the soil; in some parts leaves of the *palās* plant are tied to the back of the *wakhar*, under the name *lāndgā*, wolf, to brush earth over the seed. Cotton is very commonly sown alone, but sometimes rows of tūr, or occasionally a little jawāri, is mixed with it to secure some early grain; such scattered jawāri is said generally to ripen safely; other seeds are more rarely mixed with cotton.

Weeding and picking.

123. Cotton needs to be weeded repeatedly, the number of times varying with the soil, the season, and the means of the cultivator. It is done partly with the *daura* or *dhussa*, a bullock-hoe—and at a later stage with a larger hoe called *dhunda*—and partly by hand. People often consider that the *daura* should be applied two or three times, and hand-weeding, *nindan*, done five or six times. Operations almost always begin by the *daura* being put over the field, but this is usually not done till the plants show four leaves, lest they should be themselves destroyed; a field generally needs at least one day of dry weather to make it fit for the bullocks. Sometimes, as in 1908 in some parts of the District, rain is so continuous that grass has grown high and strong before a break occurs. The *daura* might then merely slide over the grass, and it may be necessary to do hand-weeding at once, though at greatly increased expense. When breaks for weeding are very rare the hire of labourers rises so much that poor cultivators occasionally have to sacrifice their crops entirely. After that the Hasta rain, which should come at about the end of September, may perhaps fail altogether, as happened in 1908, and the whole crop in some fields would be worth little more than the cost of weeding. The *daura* not only removes the weeds but also protects the cotton plants by heaping earth around their stalks, and closes the capillary tubes through which the fallen rain might in

part evaporate. Government experiments show that healthy plants in good ground, well manured, are best thinned out so as to be about one foot apart for every foot of height; cultivators in general do not use much manure; where the land is good they sow the *tās*, lines, of cotton about 18 inches apart and thin the plants out, *iralne*, so as to be a span apart; in light land they leave them at just the intervals marked by the four fingers of a man's hand slightly opened, that is, at intervals of about an inch, or say that they dare not take up any plants because of the danger of the rest also dying in a poor season. Cotton picking, *wechne*, H. *chunna*, lasts from Diwāli, early in November, to the end of January. Some people think that the bolls, *bondh*, open better if women walk through the field; others are anxious to get a little money as soon as possible; cotton-picking is therefore begun as early as possible. Usually five pickings are done, at intervals of about a week, the second and third being most productive. In light soil there are fewer pickings, while in occasional villages even more are made, possibly through fear of wild animals or thieves. Payment in some localities is made in kind, the day's picking of each worker being divided into a number of parts, *unde*, previously agreed upon; the woman, for picking is done almost entirely by women (helped by a few children), then chooses whichever part she likes. In others a money payment is given at a fixed rate according to the amount picked. The second method is the more recent, and has been adopted with the definite object of making it easy to discover anyone who steals cotton, but seems to have extended over almost half the District. In some villages shares, *unde*, are made in the last picking only, the picker then receiving half, while very rarely both systems are to be found in the same village; labourers consider that they get less on the money system.

A fresh green appearance which the plants sometimes get during the picking season is said to be due to a lot of little hairs being produced by a touch of unusually cold weather.

Jawāri.

124. On the average of the last five years jawāri has occupied an area of 604,000 acres, or 32 per cent. of the cultivated area. People largely sow cotton for sale and jawāri for their own consumption; the grain is the staple food and the stalks, *kadbi*, are the chief fodder of the District; a considerable amount of jawāri and *kadbi* is however sold. Land is prepared for both crops in the same way, but jawāri is sown in Ardrā and Punarvasu *nakshatras*, a little later than cotton. It is invariably a *kharīf* crop. A great number of kinds are known, and the seed is always selected with care, not only as being good in itself but as suitable for the particular land to be sown. Thus the best kind for deep black soil is said to be *dhāmna*, though *lahi*, which has round pods, is most grown in some parts; the best for light and hilly soil is *nathora* or perhaps *jhagdan*. Jawāri is usually sown with a *tiphan*—though with a light soil or rainfall it may be necessary to sow it deep, when a *wakhar* would be used. Two *wakhars* are driven behind, or branches are tied to the back of the *tiphan*, to cover the seed, the process being called *rāsni* in the former case and *phasāti* in the latter; but some people have *phasāti* done by an additional pair of bullocks behind the two *wakhars*, the object then being to smooth the soil. Less weeding has to be done than is necessary for cotton because the high plant soon overshadows and kills any young weeds. Both jawāri and cotton need watching, *rakhwāli*, for about four months to keep off wild animals and birds. The harvest lasts from the beginning of November to the middle of January. Most Hindus begin it, as they do all agricultural opera-

tions, by 'taking the name of God,' some saying, 'If there are two *khandies* I will make it fly away (in charity).' The crop is often as high as a man, and sometimes much higher, each stalk bearing a single heavy head, *kanīs*, H. *bhutta*. The field is often divided for harvest operations into *pāt* of nine rows each. The jawāri is cut a few inches from the ground by men with sickles, *khurpā*, the process being called *kāpne* or *songni*. Then two men and two women undertake the work of each *pāt*. After the jawāri has been lying on the ground to dry for eight or ten days, according to its size, *khudan* is done, when the women cut off the heads and the men bind the stalks into bundles or sheaves, *pendya*. A *khalā*, threshing-floor, is made, either in the field or in the *khalwādi* close to the village, and the heads are taken there. Threshing, *tudawan*, *khurad*, is usually done by five, six, or seven bullocks being harnessed in a row and made to walk round and round upon the grain, an operation called *pāth*. Within the last ten years, however, it has become very common in the north of the District to drive a cart or two with single yokes of oxen round and round on the grain; this is said to bring the grain out more quickly and with less labour. People in the south know of the practice but say they do not get enough grain for it to be required; only those among them who have a large outturn follow it, one objection being that it does not clean the grain properly. It is said that six bullocks would take three days to tread out three *khandis*, 1600 pounds, of grain. Winnowing, *upanna*, may then be done at once.

Keeping of jawāri.

125. The stalks of jawāri are stacked and kept for fodder. In some of the Famine Reports it is said that people used at the break of the rains to burn what remained of last year's fodder, but this is generally denied in the District.

The cattle leave the lower end of the *kadbi* given them, and this is burnt for fuel for certain purposes—though in some villages much of it is eaten by the hungry cows and she-buffaloes of the poor; the stumps ploughed up in the fields are also burnt; but untouched *kadbi* has always been kept till consumed in the ordinary way. A stack of *kadbi* is often called *gud* if the stalks are placed upright, and *kathād* if they are laid horizontally. It is thatched with *padhātya* or *turātya*, cotton or tur stalks, and would keep for two years. The jawāri grain is in the northern parts of the District stored in pits, *peo*, but this requires a particular kind of subsoil, *piwala*, *man*. A *peo* is sunk first through a few feet of *pāndhari*, the white accumulation of the village site, then through a few more of black soil, and then enters the required substratum. Here a circular chamber is dug out and the jawāri is dropped into it and covered with layers of timber, grass, and black earth. In a good *peo* jawāri keeps for 20 years, though a top layer may be discoloured. If the pit is kept full one may enter it at any time, but otherwise poisonous gases may be generated and a lamp is lowered to test the air. A saying is current in some parts that one should have five years' supply in the *peo*, but only a few well-to-do cultivators actually keep any more than they expect to use. In many villages of the southern parts it is impossible to make *peos*, generally because the subsoil is too damp but sometimes because solid rock is met just below the surface. Different kinds of receptacles are then used; for instance, a second high wall may be built about a yard inside that of the compound and jawāri poured into the high, narrow, chamber, *barad*, thus formed; or bins, *khānga*, of cotton-stalks plastered with *māti*, earth, may be used; people with small stocks place them in sacks. A danger of fire exists in regard to some of these receptacles, but if necessary a watch can be kept, and in any case roofs of tin and tiles are so numerous that fire is likely to be confined to the house in which it started. The practice of taking the grain into the fields for safety in the hot weather seems almost unknown in Berār.

Miscellaneous *kharif* crops.

126. The *kharīf* crops third and fourth in importance are tūr and tīl, with an average acreage of 47,500 and 9,500 respectively, but these are trifling in comparison with the areas under cotton and jawāri. Tūr is sometimes sown along with cotton, but the latter is more commonly grown alone. Jawāri is very seldom sown alone, partly because mixing is thought good for the grains and partly with the idea that while the jawāri flourishes high in the air a smaller plant may grow on the same ground at its foot. Thus mung, urad, tūr, *barbati*, and *ambādi* are often sown with jawāri. Mung and *ambādi*, hemp, are most popular for sowing in good land, the former being a useful food-grain and the latter providing fibres for tying cattle. Urad is very liable to disease. Sometimes eight seers of urad are sown in the same land as four seers of jawāri, but that amount of jawāri would require four acres even if sown alone, while the urad would grow in about half an acre. The other seeds are sown in a very much smaller proportion, being mixed perhaps with twelve times their own weight of jawāri.

Rabi crops.

127. The chief *rabi* crops are wheat, gram, and linseed, with an average area for the last five years of 77,000, 26,000, and 20,000 acres respectively. Where the land is good people always say that far more *rabi* used to be grown, the traditional area in some parts being one-third and in some three-quarters of the whole extent of cultiva-

tion ; the decrease, often to the verge of disappearance, is said to be chiefly due to the deficiency and uncertainty of the rain of the last fifteen years. This may be true, but tradition is always untrustworthy, especially when it gives an account of causes ; it is significant that people seem never to have trusted to *rabi* crops for their staple food. The decrease over the whole District, taking the good land with the bad, is great but not as sensational as is represented ; in the period 1877—1882, when the rainfall was good, wheat occupied less than one-third of the area of either jawāri or cotton ; now it occupies less than one-eleventh. *Rabi* is most plentiful in Bāsim tāluk, where it occupies 99,000 acres, or 17 per cent. of the cultivated area ; it is least plentiful in Mangrul, where it has only 2,600 acres, or less than 1 per cent. It is almost always grown as a dry crop, but occasionally, as at Rājura in the north of Bāsim tāluk, in a *mala*, irrigated field. The land is prepared in much the same way as for *kharīf* crops but is cleaned more thoroughly. The stalks of jawāri and cotton are removed, often in the hot weather, and then the *wakhar*, or *wahi*, is put over the land three or four times a month from Akhādi to Diwāli, that is from July to October, when all weeds should have disappeared. The sowing is done with a *tiphan*, while a *wakhar* follows to cover the seed. The *tiphan* often requires three pairs of bullocks and even then only covers as much land in three days as the *wakhar*, used with two bullocks to clean the field, does in one day. Linseed, gram, and *lākh* are sown in Hastā *nakshatra* (September—October) and wheat in Chitrā Swāti (October). A few people give to a field of wheat a border of some other crop, such as linseed, which cattle do not eat. The crops begin to show seven or eight days after being sown. They always benefit by rain coming soon after the sowing, but in some parts such rain is hardly expected. *Rabi* is cut at about Holi, *Dāndipunawa* (February—March). It has to be watched day and night—though at night some cultivators content themselves with making occasional visits to the field—for the intervening five months. Circumstances may cause harmful deviations from the ordinary rules about sowing, but in any case the prospects of the crop are not assured till it is nearly ripe. Thus in some parts a west wind in the cold weather is said to make the ears large, while other winds may cause a lot of straw with little ear. Cultivators say that *ombi*, the ear, should only appear in Paush (January—February); if it appears earlier the crop is likely to be deficient.

Outturn.

128. No normal outturn has been officially recorded for the crops of the District, and it is most difficult to get satisfactory figures; even statements made in good faith are liable to be absolutely wrong, because cultivators have fixed their minds on a traditional but apparently ideal standard. Erroneous statistics are so very misleading that it is probably better to give no estimate of outturn.

Diseases and insect pests.

129. The first danger after the seeds are sown is that of *khurpadi*, that birds may dig them up. Diseases are caused by lack of rain, excessive rain, and other accidents, generally through the agency of insects. Cultivators sometimes observe the presence of these insects and even despair of giving a complete list of the varieties, but sometimes recognise the effect without knowing the cause. *Moā* or *molā* is caused by delay in the latter rain; in *mūr* the stalk *sadte*, rots, insects attacking it when it is half grown; in *chiktāra* a sticky substance comes which makes the leaves roll up and stick together; *morā* attacks the *phul*, flower, of urad, mūng, *barbati*, and some other crops, a substance

being formed on which insects like mosquitoes gather; *unni* may attack crops in either a wet or a dry season, insects referred to as *ali* or *khide* attacking the roots soon after they have sprouted; *lenda*, rust, makes the plant wither after the leaves have grown and just when the ear should be forming. In *daha* white spots appear on the leaves, in *tidka* red ones, without insects being observed. Jawāri is liable to *kānhi*, in which the ear becomes black, and old men have a tradition that this is due to bullocks crossing the drill when they are being yoked for sowing. *Udhali*, white ants, come when anything has been lying long on the ground, though it is said that some diseases are wrongly explained in this way; locusts are rare. *Dau*, dew, may be accompanied by cold which injures the plants; every few years hail may fall, perhaps almost ruining a good cotton crop in the beginning of the season by stripping off both leaves and bolls; extraordinary accounts are given of the size of the hailstones. In many villages a Gārpagāri lives whose chief business is to *gārā walwine*, avert hail; the writer was told at one village in the end of 1908 that a few days previously the Gārpagāri had *shankh phunkle*, blown a conch shell, in the village itself, and only small and harmless hail had fallen there, but on the border the fall had been very heavy and destructive. The Gārpagāri in other parts goes to the boundary of the village and follows a longer procedure. He has some of the blood of the he-buffalo killed at Dasahra, does *pūja* naked, offering the blood, and cuts his finger. Traditions exist of much more stringent measures in former days, when the Gārpagāri was more generally respected.

Fruit trees.

120. Fruit-growing is very unimportant in the District. Most of the larger villages have a few pieces of *bāgait*, garden, or irrigated land, but little fruit is grown there,

and it is seldom of very good quality; the kinds chiefly found are plain bananas, limes, oranges, mangoes, and guavas. Besides this there are a good many scattered mango groves, especially perhaps in the north of Akot tāluk. The fruit is of a stringy coarse kind, and people say they have not technical knowledge enough to grow anything better, even if the soil should prove suitable.

Agricultural implements. *Nāgar.*

131. Carts have changed greatly in build during the last generation and are now made in many varieties, but agricultural implements seem to have been the same for many years. The chief implements are the ***nāgar***, *wakhar*, *tiphan*, *mogda*, *daura*, and *dhunda*. The ***nāgar*** is a plough for deep ploughing. It consists of a heavy block of wood from 6 to 8 inches square in its broadest part and three or four feet in length, the bottom of which, when the implement stands upright, projects downwards and forwards to an ironshod point, the whole being fixed on a pole which takes a yoke for oxen. The body is called *akodā*, the upright part being perhaps 32 inches in length, and the lower part, which points forwards at an angle of about 135 degrees, 27 inches; the whole is made from a single piece of wood, and separate names seem not to be given to the upper and lower halves. The *nāgar* from its shape cannot stand upright unless it is held, while other implements do so. The pole for the bullocks is called *hāīs* or *halîs* in the case of the *nāgar*; it is fitted into a hole in the *akodā* and secured by a wooden pin, *khidi*, at the back of it. The bullocks are harnessed by means of a yoke, *juā*, tied to the pole; the yoke is fastened round their necks with a broad belting of cord, *beldi*, *beldya*. The ploughman supports and guides the *nāgar* by means of a piece of wood called *hadao* projecting backwards at right angles near the top. The actual share, *khusha*, is a long, pointed piece of

iron which projects a foot or more below the toe of the *akodā*, and is bound to it by means of an iron ring called *kalāsi* ; the body of the share lies against the front of the lower part of the *akodā*, and the butt of it is sunk into the body of the *akodā* just below the pole. The *nāgar* is drawn by either two or three pairs of bullocks, according to the strength of the animals and the nature of the ground. The driver needs to be both strong and skilful, because the plough progresses slowly and with great jerks, almost stopped sometimes by a root and then the point of the share jumping to the surface; an additional boy or man may walk by each pair of bullocks.

Wakhar.

132. The *wakhar* or *wahi* consists of a heavy cross-piece fixed to the pole and having beneath it two projecting pins connected at their points by a blade of iron. It is made in a large and a small size, the former for turning over the soil immediately after *nāgar*-ploughing, or sometimes as a substitute for that operation, and the latter for ordinary ploughing. The cross-piece is called *khod* and is about 3 feet long and of a width and depth varying in different specimens, the width again being greater near the ends than in the middle. The pole is called *dāndi* and should be 5 hands, 7½ feet, in length, but it is sometimes made yet longer so that if it breaks it may still be used. The two projecting pegs, *jānkhod*, are about 12 inches long, while the iron cross-blade, *phās*, between them is about 40 inches long, 3 deep, and ¼ or ½ an inch thick ; when the *wakhar* is in action this blade is drawn through the soil, slanting backwards from its (dull) lower edge ; it is fastened at each end to the peg by an iron ring, *yidi*. The pole is not inserted in the middle of the cross-piece but about 3 inches to the left, while it slants very slightly to the right ; about the same distance on the other side of the middle there is inserted a stick, *topan*,

about 18 inches long, the other end of which touches the pole but is not fastened to it; the *dhan*, ropes for harnessing the bullocks, are fastened to this stick, and its presence causes the animals to walk at equal distances on either side of the middle of the plough. The *wakhar* is guided by means of a stick, *rumna*, about 2½ feet in length, which is fixed in the upper part of the cross-piece and has its higher end bent backwards, forming about half a right angle with the perpendicular. A man lifts this *wakhar* without much difficulty, but the large kind would make a heavy weight to carry; the top of the cross-piece with the latter is made broad enough for a man to stand upon it, so that it may go deep. For sowing cotton a bamboo tube, *sarta*, is tied to the cross-piece with a string about 3 or 4 feet long, and seed is dropped through it by a woman who carries the *sarta* behind the *wakhar*.

Tiphan, etc.

133. In all the other implements the pole for the bullock is called *dāndi* and the cross-piece *khod*, as with the *wakhar*, and in every case the *rumna* for guiding the plough or hoe can be easily taken out from one machine and fitted into another. The *tiphan* is a treble drill used for sowing jawāri. The pole is split for about 3 feet from the cross-piece and the two parts are fitted into holes at equal distances from the middle of the latter, so as to aid the drill to go straight. To prevent the pole splitting yet further an iron ring, *lokhandi ban*, is fastened around the base of the split. The wooden pegs, *dātā*, are about 18 inches in length and are toed with pointed iron sheaths, *phail*. A kind of bamboo tripod is fitted on to it for sowing, three hollow tubes, *nalyā*, fixed into and communicating with holes in the front of the pegs, while at the top they are crowned with a round wooden basin, *chāla*; this would not hold more than a

quarter of a pint of seed and must be constantly fed, the seed running through three holes into the *nalyā* and thence down through the *dāta* and out behind the *phail*.

The *mogdā* is like a *tiphan* but heavier, so that it needs two pairs of bullocks, and is used for sowing *rabi* crops. It has often *kuchlya*, iron shares or spikes sharper than the *phail* of the *tiphan* and dropping the seed more deeply. The *dhunda* is practically a small, and the *daura* a very small, *wakhar*. The *phās*, cross-blade, is about 18 inches long for the *dhunda* and 14 for the *daura*.

A very few individuals have iron implements of foreign make. One such cultivator said that his iron *nāgar* cost Rs. 42 while a wooden one cost from Rs. 3 to Rs. 5, and the former needed more repairs and an extra pair of bullocks; but on the other hand it had done as much land in one week as the old *nāgar* would do in six, and was in fact so successful that after only a year's experience he had bought another. Clearly, however, expense as well as conservatism would stand in the way of the small cultivator buying the foreign implement.

Manure.

134. People recognise the advantage of manure but find it impossible to use much. One difficulty is also felt about it that if the rainfall happens to be poor the manure actually injures the crop for that year, causing it to wither. Jawāri may be ruined in this way and cotton suffers to a less extent. In any case the full benefit of the manure is not felt till the second or third year after it is applied. Almost the only manure used is the dung of cattle, and only the wealthier cultivators are generally able to get enough of this. It is said that a score or two of large cattle are needed to provide dung enough for one *tiphan*, four acres, and a poor man often has not enough cattle

to supply him with fuel and leave a surplus worth storing. In much of the rains *gaurya* firm enough to be stacked and used as fuel can not be made; some small cultivators make little heaps of manure then. Those who can collect manure store it in a pit from three to five feet deep in one of their fields and clear out the pit every hot weather. It would, they say, be possible to keep it for perhaps three years, but after that it would lose its properties. Only the most valuable crops are manured, and cotton is given the preference to jawāri. Good land rather than light is again given the benefit, so that in hilly country it is sometimes only the hollows that are manured. In some parts tobacco, *baru* (hemp), til, and *harbhara* are occasionally sown in poor land to benefit the soil, as they make it for one succeeding season as productive as ordinary good land. The urine and excretion of goats, *mûtra*, is considered peculiarly valuable, and on this account an occasional Dhangar pens his goats at night on his own fields, or people make petty bargains with wandering Bhangi Dhangars, who pass across the District every few years, for their goats to be penned similarly.

Experimental Farm.

135. A Government Experimental Farm has been maintained at various times at Akola. A farm of 271 acres was taken over in 1906 three miles from Akola on the Bāsim road and put in charge of a trained superintendent; excellent buildings have been put up, Mālwa cattle and patent implements provided, and roads, drains, and fences made. All the night-soil of the town is to be taken to the farm. Careful experiments are being made in regard to seeds, manure, and other important points; implements are shown and sold. The enterprise may clearly be of the greatest utility, but it has not yet had time to establish its value.

IRRIGATION.

136. *Irrigation.* Irrigation is comparatively unimportant in the District, as only 14,500 acres, or $\frac{3}{5}$ per cent. of the cultivated land, is irrigated. While the rainfall is fairly plentiful the standing sources of supply are scanty. Indeed people with land at one village sometimes have to live at another through lack of water in the first. Digging a well is then both an important and an expensive matter, Rs. 100 a year being perhaps spent for some time on it. Someone may be called in beforehand who will both indicate a good spot and tell at what depth water will be found. To do this he sometimes burns camphor and does *pūja*, sometimes listens intently with his ear close to ground, sits staring fixedly downwards, or adopts other methods. The settlement rules in force are intended to encourage irrigation, but there seems to be actually little scope for it. Two methods are however followed to a slight extent, *motasthal bāgait* being garden land irrigated from a well by means of a *mot*, leather bucket, and *pātasthal* that to which water is brought by a *pāt*, channel, from a river or tank. All the tāluks except Akot have also a little irrigated rice land for which a combined rate of Rs. 6 an acre is levied. Bāsim has over 21,000 acres, an area which had doubled in the last settlement period, but the total area under rice in the whole District is only 25,000, or 1 per cent. of the cultivated land. Irrigated land is used chiefly for the growth of sugarcane, brinjals, onions, garlic, sweet potatoes, oranges, plantains, guavas, and various kinds of Indian green vegetables.

CATTLE.

137. *Bullocks.* Different breeds of cattle are recognised to a varying extent and named according to the countries from which

they come, but much thought is not as a rule given to questions of breeding. Old men say that cattle used to be much larger than they are now, and that they were carefully bred and well fed; for instance a cow used to be surrounded with walls of a certain colour to secure the same colour in her calf. Banjāra bullocks come from the Melghāt; they are small and not fast enough for travelling, but strong and good for field work; their distinguishing feature is their very large horns. Mālwā bullocks are long in the body, big, well adapted for field work, and marked by very large ears and hoofs. Shingāji bullocks, coming from beyond Khāndesh—but sometimes identified with Khandwa animals—somewhat resemble them. Those from the Digras and Umarda direction are sometimes considered fitted chiefly for work at the *mot* of a well or for hauling loaded carts along a road, and are often driven without *wesan*, nose-strings, but they are sometimes identified with the true Berār breed. In this the size varies, but the bullock is generally fairly large and both fast and powerful. Some consider the Hinganghāt animal larger again; while others speak of a Konkani breed, with very large ears and very small horns, as the biggest of all. A very good bullock would probably be white or red; its tail should be thin, its hoofs well rounded and straight, its back flat, and its *mānechā sar*, neck, thick and strong. If it has fine hair, or is *kājra*—having black just under its eye—it will be fast and spirited. If possible it should be *deoman*, having two perpendicular lines of hair of about the length of a finger, one on each side of its chest; it will then be both trustworthy about its work and lucky to its owner. If it is *gom*, having a line of reversed hair on its back, people will probably consider it unlucky and refuse to buy it. There are however, very naturally, a complicated science and vocabulary about bullocks.

The price of cattle has risen so much that in *Muglai* times the whole village would go to see a pair of bullocks which cost Rs. 50, but now a Rs. 200 pair is hardly thought worth looking at. A pair of ordinary bullocks for field work costs Rs. 100, though poor people buy old animals for perhaps Rs. 20 each. In a village of some little wealth there would be a few pairs worth from Rs. 250 to Rs. 400 a pair. Thoroughly good animals would do 50 miles or more between sunrise and sunset. It is a common thing to drive in the morning from Palsoda to Akola in time for the opening of the kacheri and to return again in the evening, 18 miles each way, or to go in one day the 34 miles from Adgaon to Akola. A bullock is castrated at about three years of age; people think that it would not grow big if the operation was done earlier. They begin to work a bullock at three-and-a-half or four years, and it takes from two to four months to break in; special trainers are not employed. First they put the *khadhon*, a kind of yoke, of a *wakhar* on its neck, then yoke it with an old animal to a pair of timbers or a *wakhar*, and presently harness the two to a light cart on a road. A bullock reaches its full strength and highest value in its fifth year, and retains its power for five or seven years. After that it generally goes to a poor man and presently reaches the butcher. In the south of the District one sees all varieties of bridle. There may be only a cord round the forehead at the base of the horns, or there may be fittings all about the head, with perhaps a muzzle. Nose-strings are common. In Bāsim tāluk people say nose strings should be used when a pair from a village goes on a main road, but that for ordinary work they may or may not be needed according to the animal's temperament, and that this does not depend noticeably upon the breed The amount of land which one pair is supposed to be able to cultivate varies according firstly to the nature of the fields, whether they are flat or hilly; and secondly to the crops, because if these are divided between *kharīf* and *rabi* one pair is sufficient for more land. One pair is often considered necessary for every 24 acres; neighbours would lend each other their animals for heavy work, an arrangement called *sāyad*; but the larger the holding the fewer comparatively are the bullocks needed by the cultivator, because he can arrange the work conveniently for them. In some countries it has been the custom to sing to bullocks at work; here occasional drivers sing, especially perhaps when working the *mot* of a well, but abuse is more common; sometimes at hard work in the fields hoarse encouraging ejaculations are used, with cries of "*O bahāduryā*, O champions," and the like.

Other animals.

138. According to the official returns the District contains 181,000 bulls and bullocks, 105,000 cows, 7000 male buffaloes, 51,000 cow-buffaloes, 86,000 calves and young buffaloes, 113,000 goats, 30,000 sheep, 6000 horses, 6000 donkeys, 3 mules, 200 camels, 20,000 ploughs, and 48,000 carts; but these figures, perhaps more than other agricultural statistics, are open to some doubt. No other animal approaches the bullock in importance. A cow's milk is generally devoted entirely to her calf, but well-to-do people use it to some extent for themselves and their children. They would then give her *sarki* and *dhep*, cotton-seed and oil-cake, and a good cow ought to yield 2 or 2½ seers, four or five pounds weight, of milk twice a day; but if people did not give this special food the yield would not be more than half as much. If one had to buy all the food given to a cow kept for family use it would cost about Rs. 8 a month. The price of a cow varies from Rs. 25 to Rs. 50. People of the middle and upper castes

when they do not use cow's milk take that of the buffalo, not goat's milk, though of the two they would give the latter only to their children. A she-buffalo costs from Rs. 35 to Rs. 125. If her price is as much as Rs. 100 she should give from 12 to 15 seers a day, the two milkings together. A male buffalo (or a barren female) is very occasionally yoked in a cart, sometimes along with a bullock, but is generally regarded as useless and allowed to die of starvation and neglect. The ponies native to the District are small and poor-looking animals and cost from Rs. 15 to Rs. 50. An animal at the latter price, if carefully fed and looked after, should be able to cover 30 or 40 miles in a day, even for two days in succession Ponies are not much used except in the rains, though travelling merchants often rely on them. A pedlar making Akola his base might take in one-half of Akot tāluk; he would travel always at a walk but cover from 10 to 20 miles a day. Ponies are most numerous in Akola and Mangrul tāluks and least numerous in Bāsim and Bālāpur. A small number of animals of a better class are scattered over the District, some of them sturdy ponies brought perhaps from the fair at Deulgaon Rājā in Buldāna District, and some of them Kathiawāris and the like brought by caravans of horse-dealers. Many subordinate officials need fairly good horses for their work, and these animals have occasionally a great attraction for them. Horses are never castrated.

CHAPTER V.

LOANS, PRICES, WAGES, MANUFACTURES, TRADE, AND COMMUNICATIONS.

LOANS.

Government loans.

139. Money was very occasionally advanced to cultivators by Government before the Assignment, when it was very difficult to get enough land occupied to secure a good revenue ; it is now issued either for permanent improvements or for temporary purposes. The general name applied to all these loans is *takāvi* or *takai* ; they are made under the Land Improvement Loans Act or the Agriculturists' Loans Act according to the permanence or otherwise of their object. Owing to the changes which have occurred in the composition of the District it is impossible to get complete figures about the matter. In the famine of 1896-1897 Rs. 29,000 under the Improvement and Rs. 6000 under the Agriculturists' Act were advanced in five tāluks, but the advances in Akola tāluk are not known. Bāsim tāluk received the largest sum under the former Act and more than half of the total under the latter. In the great famine of 1899-1900 it would appear that in the same five tāluks about Rs. 75,000 were issued under the one and Rs. 30,000 under the other, Bāsim again having the largest total ; but the figures preserved are very incomplete. Since the famines the figures have been about Rs. 1000 a year for each tāluk under the more important Act, except that Akot takes less than half that amount, and mere trifles under the Agriculturists' Loans Act, except again that Bāsim takes an average of Rs. 2000

a year. The rate of interest is only 6 per cent. per annum, whereas from 12 to 24 per cent. is commonly charged by money-lenders, but *takāvi* advances are clearly not popular; the reason seems to be summed up in the word rigidity. Applicants find themselves faced with numerous formalities and officials and by considerable delay; perhaps also there is sufficient positive outlay, in travelling and otherwise, appreciably to reduce the cheapness of the loan. To some extent these difficulties are inevitable, but they may perhaps be reduced. During the last few years Co-operative Credit Societies have been introduced; they are described in a later paragraph.

Private loans.

140. *Sāhukārs* in all parts of the District have lower rates of interest among themselves than for the public in general. The rate within their own community at Akola depends upon the bank rate and varies immensely at different seasons; elsewhere it is often 8 or 10 annas a month, that is 6 or 7½ per cent. per annum; but it might be as little as As. 6 or as much as As. 12. The rate for other people depends chiefly on the security they can offer but largely also on their position and character and on the season. Legal processes are slow and expensive, and a *sāhukār* requires more interest from a man who may compel him to resort to them than from one in whom he has confidence. When crops are good the rate of interest falls, owing to the decreased demand for loans, but two or three bad seasons make it rise considerably. In a few parts of the District, owing to three successive bad seasons, it is said just now that the *sāhukārs* have lent all their capital, or that they are afraid to lend any more on land, and that therefore loans are not to be had at all, but this is very rare. The standard rate for loans on land seems to be from As. 12 to R. 1 a month for a perfectly safe cultivator, and

R. 1-8 or Rs. 2 for one of ordinary or poor standing; Rs. 2, sometimes called *dohotra*, is quite a common rate. In a few places it is said that these rates have been constant ever since the famine of 1899-1900, but generally one hears of a slight rise through the poor harvests of the last few years. On the other hand rates run a little lower than this in an occasional village where there happen to be a number of capitalists. Deductions are occasionally, but rarely, made in the name of a *gorakshan*, home for cows, and at least one large firm makes other deductions on petty loans. Another system, *sawai*, is often followed for small loans to poor people, especially for loans made in the sowing season which are to be repaid at harvest. According to the *sawai* agreement the borrower must repay five-fourths of what he borrowed, and as the period for repayment in these cases is only four or six months the rate comes to 50 or 66 per cent. per annum. Loans to be repaid in kind are now very rare, but in a few villages a man might borrow a maund of cotton seed and return a maund of cotton in the boll. *Sāhukārs* complain, truly or otherwise, that people's trustworthiness, *imān*, has greatly declined during the last generation or two. They say that formerly when a loan was made it was common merely to make a rough memorandum on a scrap of paper and to utter the formula *Sāksha Parameshwar*, God being witness, but now debtors resort to all kinds of fraud, pledging their land, for instance, over and over again to different *sāhukārs*; a few add that the law favours debtors. Borrowers on the other hand complain that a *sāhukār* finds it very easy to get the law on his side in order to enforce unreasonable demands; the rule of *dāmdupat* prevents a Hindu from suing for more than twice the original sum lent, however long interest may have been accumulating, but when he comes under this limitation he gets a fresh deed drawn up with the original capital and interest thrown together as its base; again, he may insert in the deed provisions in his own favour which the ignorant borrower wholly fails to understand and a venal sub-registrar omits to explain, for sub-registrars are considered to have wide opportunities for petty exactions and corruption; a third course is said to be easy with the rough account books in use, especially perhaps with the very irregular *pathāni-wahi*—the Indian ink of the entry is rubbed out with a moistened thumb and a fresh entry is inserted. A man in whom a *sāhukār* feels full confidence can still borrow without pledging any property as security, but it is said that the practice of demanding security is growing. The amount required is as much as will ensure both the return of the original loan and the payment of overdue interest, which at 24 per cent. per annum soon amounts to a large sum. On land or houses *sāhukārs* seldom lend more than one-half or one-third of the value of the property, but if gold or silver is left with them in pledge they will lend three-quarters of its value.

Co-operative Credit Societies.

141. The interest demanded seems needlessly and oppressively high, and Co-operative Credit Societies have recently been started to provide money at lower rates. The principle seems to have been first put into operation six or seven years ago by the Industrial Association of Akola, under the leadership of Rao Bahādur Deorao Vināyak. Grain banks were instituted by this agency at three villages in Akola tāluk; those at Bhorad and Morgaon still survive and it is proposed to register them under the Co-operative Credit Societies Act. After several months of careful enquiry throughout the District 13 Societies were started by Government in 1906, Mangrul tāluk having three and each of the other tāluks

two. Mr. Krishnarao Purushottam Bhat, Extra Assistant Commissioner, has been in charge from the beginning. He says that the scheme was everywhere received with much appreciation. The local organisation consists in each case of a secretary, treasurer, and banker guided by a committee of five, six, or seven villagers and controlled by a central committee of three, including the Tahsildār; both the last-named and the Subdivisional Officer audit the accounts. Two systems have been followed, that of share-capital and that of deposit. The former has been applied only at Keli Weli and Palsoda in Akot tāluk; members must buy one or more shares at Rs. 10 each, and that sum, together with as much as can be borrowed at a low rate from capitalists, forms the loanable capital of the Society. The total capital at Keli Weli is Rs. 2710 and that at Palsoda Rs. 2100, over a half in each case consisting of share money. The Society at the former village has been working admirably; half the members have loans of about Rs. 100 each at unusually low rates, while all are getting over 12 per cent. interest on petty sums which would otherwise have been uninvested; the members number over 50 and more are eager to join. The deposit system was alone applied in the other Societies; a considerable sum of money is borrowed at 4½ per cent. for a term of five or more years and forms the bulk of the loanable capital; members are invited to invest small sums at 4½ or 6 per cent. but are required to pay only an entrance fee of eight annas. This has the great advantage of imposing only a very light burden on poor cultivators, but the disadvantages of depending altogether on loans made from mainly charitable, not economic, motives and of giving little opening for small investments by members. Only one of the deposit Societies has a capital of more than Rs. 1000, and most of them have from Rs. 300 to Rs. 500. The rate of interest charged has in all cases been R. 1 a month, 12 per cent. per annum, and various regulations provide for reserve funds being built up and other measures of security being taken. Two Societies advance small sums for trading purposes, but otherwise the only objects recognised are agricultural. The scope of operations is in some places confined to a single village and in some to a circle of about 4 miles radius. Loans are sometimes advanced without any security, sometimes on the personal security of one or two well-to-do villagers. One of the smaller Societies has failed to take any action, in some others the money has been allowed to lie idle for months, and sometimes interest has not been promptly repaid, but the system has been at work for so short a time and in such bad years that the progress made cannot be considered unsatisfactory; it is too soon to form any more positive conclusion. It is under consideration to start a central bank at Akola, but this has not yet been carried into effect. Village *sāhukārs* have not shown any hostility to the system and have often been ready to help, but they might possibly regard its extension with apprehension. Villagers generally are of course conservative, but they hear of the scheme with interest and agree that it may prove very valuable.

Former economic position of cultivators.

142. It is very difficult to get a convincing view of the extent to which cultivators as a class are now or were formerly indebted. General statements, whether made by prominent residents of the towns or by the villagers themselves, are helpful but inadequate, because the standard of comparison employed is uncertain; and indeed very few individuals combine the wide outlook and detailed knowledge required. Cultivators willingly construct a typical balance sheet showing the items of income and expenditure, but they are so cautious that the first result is generally a large annual

deficit; they admit that this is wrong, and perhaps suggest such alterations as would balance the account, but corrections made solely with that object are clearly untrustworthy. Some points however stand out with greater or less clearness. It is universally said that there was little *karja-bājāri*, indebtedness, in Muglai times; this is very partially true and requires large qualifications. Firstly, land had scarcely any value, and the cultivator had no rights in it; fear of both thieves and the Government prevented him from possessing either ornaments or other forms of wealth; he could, and did, borrow upon his crops and personal security, but had very little else to offer. The total debt may have been small, but it was apparently as much as the cultivator could bear. This is proved by written records and supported by traditions. The earliest Revenue and Settlement Reports speak of debt as having been a very heavy burden but one rapidly decreasing. Thus Major P. A. Elphinstone wrote in the Jalgaon Settlement Report of 1865: 'There will be little chance of the 'sowcar ever again obtaining the absolute power he had 'previously exercised for centuries past over the ryot.' The Berār Gazetteer of 1870, p. 226, says, 'Even until 'within the last few years the cultivator of this part of 'India was a somewhat miserable and depressed creature. 'He was deeply in debt.' Universal tradition relates that cultivators frequently gave up their land and ran away to avoid paying the land revenue, but they were brought back and made, by a mixture of force and conciliation, to cultivate again. When revenue became due a *jhapti sipāhi* was sent to a village and prevented any goods leaving it till payment was assured; security was given by *sāhukārs* who apparently recouped themselves by getting rights over the growing crops. One hears of barbarous means being employed by the money-lenders of the time to compel payment. Clearly therefore the tradition of light indebtedness is misleading. It may be in part due to the tendency, common perhaps in all ages and all countries, to magnify the good and minimise the evil of the past. It is partly true in that people were far less able to borrow then than now, because their wealth was much less. Perhaps also a distinction should be made between the different classes in a village; relatives of the pargana and village officers must have had a firmer position than the other cultivators, who are still called *asāmi's*, tenants, clients; but it is impossible to work out the details of this at present. Tradition says again that common food-grains were not only cheap but easily obtainable; a man might give up his land at any time and turn labourer in another village confident of finding employment and support. Whatever may have been the case in a good year it is hard to see how this could have occurred when the harvest was generally poor. Another explanation would be that in such years people regarded suffering as a matter of course and therefore gave it no prominence in tradition.

Present economic position.

143. Unfortunately no records of the general material condition of the cultivator for the first few years after 1853 are available at Akola. It is said, however, in all parts of the District that both cultivators and labourers now have houses, food, and clothes much better, as well as more expensive, than they had 50 or 60 years ago; they give entertainments on a far larger scale, and they feel no necessity to work for long hours. The subject is certainly very complicated, but these indications appear unmistakeable; it is difficult to doubt that the general economic position of the cultivator has immensely improved. At the same time

his condition is not wholly satisfactory; cultivators themselves feel the burden of debt keenly. Two prominent considerations apply to this. The first is that 24 per cent. per annum is a common rate of interest for long loans and 50 per cent. for a small loan made for sowing or weeding. Such high rates on the one hand make even a small debt serious and on the other ensure that a man shall keep his total debt within fair limits or be speedily ruined; if he can pay so much interest in poor seasons he will be able easily to repay the capital in good years. The second is that, though cultivators are in most respects frugal, yet social events, especially weddings, are made the occasions of great extravagance; for instance, a man of 55 says he can remember when a wedding in his family cost Rs. 100, but now it costs Rs. 1000. People say as a matter of course that they must copy any fresh extravagance of their *soyarās*, the set with whom they intermarry, and that this involves them seriously. Extraordinary economic changes have occurred within the memory of men still living: the Muglāi condition, 60 years ago, was one of very plain living and scanty wealth, except in a few official circles; high-priced cotton and low-priced land, under greatly improved political conditions, brought for many years a new and ready prosperity and constantly supported fresh expense, but now more economy is becoming necessary; thus villagers will point to a field which was sold 20 years ago for Rs. 150 and has just been sold again for Rs. 2000. It may be that these changes have not yet worked themselves out, and in particular that the new system of economic freedom has not become adjusted to the endless grades of the caste system. There is clearly room for mixed results from changes so considerable.

144. An illustration given to the writer personally

in apparent good faith by the leading men of a village, and corroborated by enquiries in villages in all the six tāluks, will show how these considerations apply. A man whose land is worth Rs. 1800, his pair of bullocks Rs. 100, his house Rs. 200, and his ornaments Rs. 100—a total of something under Rs. 2500—would spend from Rs. 200 to Rs. 300 or even Rs. 400 to marry a son, and half as much for a daughter; if he wanted an adult wife for himself he would spend perhaps Rs. 1000 to marry a widow, though again he might be able to make the same amount by re-marrying a widowed daughter (his own expense then being perhaps Rs. 25). He could run into debt up to Rs. 400, paying Rs. 100 a year interest and getting small loans at higher rates every year for temporary purposes; but if his debt increased much more he would be ruined by the interest; his land revenue would be Rs. 30. In a hilly village in the south of Bālāpur it was said that the holder of 20 acres, worth from Rs. 300 to Rs. 400 and assessed at Rs. 10, might be Rs. 200 or more in debt, paying Rs. 50 as interest. The term *sādhāran*, common, is generally applied to men who have 70 or 80 acres of land and three pairs of bullocks, but this is misleading; in the village first quoted it was estimated that about 12 men had holdings of this size, 40 or 50 had over 24 acres but less than 80, and about 75 had less than 24 acres (which is generally considered just as much as one pair of bullocks can cultivate). Land is often held on a rather smaller scale, but these proportions are not uncommon; only a small minority of cultivators would be called *sādhāran*. Land is generally cultivated by the actual holder, but in every village some fields are held on the payment of either a fixed rent or (by *batāi*) a share in the crops. The ratio between assessment and value varies so much that people commonly say there is no

Illustration.

connection; that is probably an exaggeration, but in fact the actual condition and value of a field are dependent on many other causes besides its permanent factors of fertility. Perhaps the first cultivator quoted is rather favourably situated in regard to assessment; he has a larger capital than the average; but the figures given for him appear fairly typical.

Indebtedness in general.

145. It is difficult, again, to say how much debt he would be likely to incur. Probably half the cultivators are as deeply in debt as they can endure with any comfort, but the debt is not large in comparison with the interest they manage to pay. Large land-holders who can borrow at about 12 per cent. are often as seriously involved as the poorer classes. Absolute freedom from debt on the one hand and bankruptcy or hopeless debt on the other both appear uncommon. Indebtedness has been in existence for very many years; it is said to have increased distinctly during the famine of 1899—1900 (not merely because of the revenue demand but because people often sacrificed a field in order to postpone application for relief), and in a few parts where the seasons were especially unfavourable it has increased during the last two or three years. The land revenue assessment is of course a serious item of expense but is not burdensome; the main cause of debt is the undue expenditure on ceremonies; people recognise this, and Mārwāris have made a deliberate and apparently successful attempt to reduce the expense, but most castes feel helpless in the matter. On the other hand the burden of debt is seldom overwhelming; a really good season has not come for six years, and people hope to be greatly relieved by one or two good harvests. The cultivating classes are, with many limitations, shrewd and intelligent men; the more fixed features in their

economical position are favourable, and there is no reason to think that the long period of their prosperity has come to an end.

PRICES.

Price of jawāri.

146. It is impossible to give a satisfactory history of prices in the District because different authorities are so very inconsistent; an illustration will show this clearly. Two official accounts are published of the price of jawāri in the old Bāsim District as a whole, O'Conor's 'Prices and Wages in India,' and the Revenue Administration Reports; prices in the Mangrul tāluk of that District are also given separately in two accounts, both printed in the Revision Settlement Report—the one supplied by the Tahsildār and the other compiled by the Price Current Inspector from the books of local merchants; the prices of jawāri according to these four accounts for the ten years from 1873 to 1882 are shown in the following table :—

Quantities sold for a rupee in sers of 80 tolas.

Year.	Bāsim District.		Mangrul Tāluk.	
	'Prices and Wages'	Rev. Admin. Report.	Tahsildār.	Grain Merchant.
1873	24	..	30	42
1874	52	..	25	42
1875	57	..	22	52
1876	49	..	26	26
1877	19	24	20	21
1878	17	15	13	21
1879	10	14	13	21
1880	17	30	44	46
1881	44	48	45	46
1882	34	32	30	38

Thus the two accounts for Mangrul have an average annual difference of 40 per cent. and the two for Bāsim District one of over 25 per cent.; there seems to be no means of reconciling the different statements. According to the Settlement Officer the figures got from the grain merchants are more likely to be right than those of the Tahsildār, but all official returns are based upon reports made by the latter. Similar variations occur between the returns for different tāluks; so much inaccuracy makes the figures most untrustworthy; it is impossible to draw useful conclusions from statistics in which an error of 40 per cent. is common. Most, but not all, of the Settlement Reports however agree that there was a very considerable rise in the price of jawāri in the last 30 years of the nineteenth century; the rise is in some cases estimated at between 30 and 40 per cent. and in some at greater and less amounts. It is possible that the returns for more recent years are more reliable; according to them the average price of jawāri from 1901 to 1906 was 19 seers, or 38 pounds, to the rupee; in 1907 it rose to 15 seers. It is clear that there were formerly great variations in the price both from year to year and from tāluk to tāluk; these variations, more especially the latter, have now been immensely reduced.

Other prices.

147. The price of cotton during the settlement period is admittedly most uncertain; this is probably due in a large measure to the employment of different tables of weight. The Settlement Officers of almost every tāluk remark on the absence of reliable records, but it appears on the whole that the price fell; meanwhile the kind of cotton grown was changed, so that cultivators got a much larger crop at the same expense as formerly; the cultivation of cotton thus remained very profitable. From

1901 to 1906 the rate apparently varied between Rs. 147 and Rs. 223 a *khandī* of 784 pounds ; but the quality of cotton varies so very much that considerable technical explanation would be needed to make even these figures clear. The same uncertainty applies to other prices. According to 'Prices and Wages in India' wheat became distinctly cheaper during the period 1867 to 1897, but according to the Settlement Reports it either remained fairly constant or rose 25 or 30 per cent. During the years 1901 to 1907 it has been on an average 9½ seers to the rupee. During the same seven years gram has been 13 seers, and linseed has varied between 5 and 11 seers (with a tendency to rise), and rice between 7 and 10 seers ; salt is said to have varied from 7 to 12 seers between 1861 and 1874, to have had an average price of 11 seers during the rest of the century, the variations tending strongly to diminish, and to have varied between 11 and 15 seers between 1901 and 1907 ; its price has been affected by changes in the charges levied by Government.

Present rates.

148. Reports made by the Tahsīldārs during the cold weather of 1908-1909 give a fairly trustworthy account of present prices. Salt is generally 16 seers to the rupee, European sugar from 2½ to 5 seers according to its quality, *gur*, Indian raw sugar, from 4 to 5, butter 1¼, *ghī* just under 1, buffalo's milk 8, mutton 4½, potatoes 8, onions 8, mūng 7, masūr 5½, *bhusā*, chaff, 11, edible oils 2, and cotton seed 1; full-grown fowls are As. 8 each, and eggs As. 4½ a dozen ; kerosine oil is sold at 8 bottles for a rupee, and firewood is 80 seers in Akola and 96 in Akot. The prices are usually fairly constant in all six tāluks, but occasionally there is considerable variation ; thus in Bālāpur eggs are As. 3 a dozen and fowls As. 5 each, but in Akola eggs are As. 6 a dozen and fowls As. 12 each ; prices are generally higher in Akola than elsewhere.

WAGES.

Village servants.

149. Every village has a certain number of hereditary servants who work for the whole community and are not paid by the piece but receive annually *haks*, dues, paid chiefly in grain, from the cultivators. The list of servants and the rate of payment vary greatly from place to place, and apparently the system is less complete than it used to be. The rights of one class alone, the Mahārs, are protected by a special summary procedure in the revenue courts, and in fact part of their ordinary remuneration is not secured by any legal remedy. A few educated men argue that Mahārs are now servants of Government, not of the village, but this view appears to be both unusual and mistaken. Certain families of the Mahār caste share the *watan* of public service in their village, and representatives of those families are always in office accordingly. They generally divide themselves into *kāmdār* and *bigāri* Mahārs, the former doing watch and ward and all kinds of menial work for the community within the village and the latter carrying letters and so on to other villages. Very rarely a division into *kāmdār*, *eshkar* and *nāthkar* Mahārs is made; the word *eshkar* seems to be connected with *wes*, gate, and the men so named do work in regard to the fields; *nāthkar* may be derived from *nāth*, lord or master, and refers to the men who work for officers in camp. These distinctions however are not officially recognised. The number of Mahārs on duty varies in most villages between 2 and 15, but in the largest places more are found. These men are supposed to devote themselves entirely to their public duties while other Mahārs generally work as labourers. If however for any particular piece of work more men are needed than those in office, for instance to pitch large tents or to help in the transport of camp

baggage at night past a small village, other members of the *watan* families usually help. The chief payment received consists of *haks* of grain, usually at the rate of so many seers of jawāri an acre but sometimes according to the vaguer system of *kādi pendya*, when basketsful of grain in the ear are given. Payment by the acre generally applies only to land bearing edible crops but sometimes to all cultivated land; the rate is generally 2 seers an acre but varies in different villages from 1 to 3 seers. Government reserves the right of altering the number of seers and of extending the liability from edible crops to all crops when the total *haks* have diminished from any cause. Besides this, Mahārs are almost always considered entitled to the skins of animals which die in the village unless the animals belonged to the village officers or their *bhaoband*, agnatic relatives; the claim however has never been enforced by the revenue courts and appears now to be rejected by the civil courts. In a very few villages no right to the skins is recognised, probably because the Mahārs were at one time suspected of poisoning animals; still more rarely the right is in the hands of a deshmukh, who holds perhaps the *watans* of *deshmukhi*, *patelki*, *patwāripana*, and *mahārki*. In fact aged animals are generally sold to butchers, and thus the Mahārs neither have the duty of removing the carcass nor get the hide. In some cases further trifling gifts of grain are also made. The remuneration received in these ways varies greatly from village to village. The main ingredient can usually be roughly estimated by calculating that jawāri is worth one anna a seer, but sometimes people give an inferior grade of grain which is worth a little less. The total of the grain *haks* sometimes gives each Mahār little more than Rs. 30 a year and seldom gives as much as Rs. 70; perhaps the ordinary rates are between Rs. 50 and Rs. 60. This is considerably less than would be given to a private servant, but the work is generally light, there are trifling perquisites, and the position is in fact generally much prized. Practically every village has also from one to five *jāgliās* or *chaukidārs*, but they are paid in cash by Government and, whatever their early history, can hardly be classed exactly with the ordinary village servants. These, however, include as a rule two other important menials, the barber and washerman. Two more have artisan's duties, the blacksmith and carpenter; they do repairs in consideration of their annual *haks* and make new implements at fixed additional rates. Sometimes permanent cultivators pay them grain while men who have taken a field in the village for a single year pay money; blacksmiths and carpenters apparently prefer money-payment. The rates vary greatly in different villages but in fact amount to just enough to support the different individuals according to their grade. Occasionally a Gārpagāri is also in office, with the duty of *wālwine*, turning away, hail that threatens the village. A Chambhār, leather-worker, may receive *haks* from people who have irrigation wells with leather buckets. The *joshi*, family priest—as distinguished from the priest of a particular temple—also receives *haks* but of course occupies a much more distinguished position.

Agricultural servants.

150. Wages for agricultural work vary greatly in different parts of the District, being much less in remote parts than elsewhere. Servants engaged by the year are generally paid wholly in cash, but if it happens to be more convenient they may take their food with the employer and receive correspondingly less cash. In the cheaper parts a servant paid wholly in cash gets from Rs. 50 to Rs. 84 a year, in the dearer parts from Rs. 80 to Rs. 100. The pay depends largely upon the individual, a young or old man

not getting as much as one in the prime of life; it is generally paid wholly in advance, but in Murtizāpur tāluk wages paid in advance are often reduced from the rate of Rs. 7 a month to the total of Rs. 70 or Rs. 75 a year. Sometimes a turban or other article of clothing is included in the agreement. The pay of the casual labourer has been high in the weeding seasons of the last three years, 1905—1908, owing to the irregular rainfall, and often puts him in a better position than the yearly servant; in fact the latter is in some places commonly driven to accept service by the need of a large sum of money for a marriage or other social purpose; the labourer has moreover days of idleness, provided for by small savings, but work can always be found for a yearly servant. In some parts they say that the old rate for *nindan*, weeding, was As. 1 for a woman and As. 1½ for a man, and complain seriously because it has now risen to As. 1½ or As. 1¾ for a woman and As. 2½ for a man; in other parts it used to be As. 2 or As. 3 but has risen lately to As. 5, 6, or 7, and in rare cases to As. 10; however, when very high pay is given for weeding it shows that there has been a long interval of rain during which no labour has been engaged. During harvest all operations connected with jawāri are paid in kind, generally with heads of jawāri; people can earn several days' food-supply with one day's work. Cotton picking is paid in kind in some villages, the picker selling her week's cotton on the bāzār day; equally commonly it is paid in cash, the picker receiving so much a *man* for what she has gathered. A woman would in most parts of the District not go to work till the middle of the forenoon and would leave before sunset, her earnings varying from A. 1 to As. 3 according to her skill and the rate of payment; in the north of Murtizāpur tāluk, however, a woman working for cash would be in the field all day and might earn as much as As. 6 The system of payment in cash is of recent extension and is especially intended to facilitate the detection of people who steal cotton from the fields; a labourer with stolen cotton in his house can no longer pretend that it was received in payment for field-work. Very rarely the earliest picking is paid in kind because the cultivator has no spare money; more often the last picking, when danger of theft has almost ceased, is shared equally between cultivator and picker. The labourer probably earns a little more under the system of payment in kind. Labour on other crops, such as tūr, til, linseed, and wheat, is generally paid in cash. A great deal of miscellaneous employment arises, the payment for which varies locally but is fairly constant from year to year. The uprooting, *upatne*, of cotton stalks, *padhātya*, or other stalks, *kopdya*, is in some villages done by contract; a party of ten or twelve people agree to clear a field at perhaps Rs. 3 or 4 a *tiphan* of four acres. In other parts people say it would be scamped if done on this system and so must be paid by the day. Individuals are engaged in the rains as watchmen in the fields; sometimes their pay rises with the growth of the crops, varying from Rs. 1 to 3 a month for a field of 25 acres—a fortunate watchman being engaged for three or four adjoining fields. In some cases a watchman is engaged only by day and the cultivator merely visits the field at night himself; in others he is engaged only by night, in others for the 24 hours. In some villages *rabi* crops are alone watched at night, the object being to keep off antelope; in others people trust to scarecrows and say they are very effective, but occasionally one sees the antelope waiting very significantly on the hills above a field at nightfall; in others *kharīf* crops are watched at night against thieves. Wages vary according to all these differences, but probably watchmen generally get in one way or another from Rs. 6 to Rs. 9 a month. During the rains again most cultivators need an additional helper for every pair of bullocks, to be paid probably at the local rates for a day-labourer, perhaps from As. 3 to As. 5 in the more expensive parts. No restrictions prevent the engagement of low-caste men for any particular work in the fields except that in some cases men of particular castes will not work at the same implement with them.

Urban wages.

151. The rates of urban wages are best represented by the pay given in cotton factories, though no single employment is completely typical. The different classes of employees at Akola during the season of 1908-1909 have been getting —a woman feeding cotton gins As. 3½ a day, an unskilled male labourer on a cotton press As. 6 to As. 10, a *hamāl* (porter) As. 12 to As. 14, a watchman Rs. 8 a month, an oilman Rs. 9 or Rs. 10, and a fitter Rs. 40 to Rs. 50. Thus Rs. 8 a month is the lowest pay quoted for a man; a strong *hamāl* might well make over Rs. 20. However in March 1909 a contractor removing cotton stalks from a field close to Akolā was paying his men only As. 2½ a day; they worked from sunrise till noon. Artisans, such as carpenters, find plenty of employment and would often require more than Rs. 20 a month, but pay varies very largely according to the season and the individual. The hire of a cart is nominally Rs. 30 a month but sometimes rises to Rs. 2 a day. Meanwhile an engineer with a second class certificate would get Rs. 65 a month and a first class engineer Rs. 140, along with lodging, light, and fuel. The pay in trading firms of employees of high caste, able to read and write, is comparatively low; it often starts at Rs. 8 or Rs. 10 a month and very seldom rises beyond two or three times that amount, though there are exceptional cases. The pay of Government clerks varies from Rs. 20 or Rs. 25 for a copyist to Rs. 200 for the principal clerks in a District office, with a few posts

even more highly paid elsewhere and a pension to follow. However the employee of a private firm has often less exacting work and may be given small presents at festivals, an advance which is in fact a present for his marriage, and other miscellaneous advantages.

MANUFACTURES.

Petty manufactures.

152. The manufactures of Akolā District have long been more important than those of some parts of Berār, but are yet very scanty. Gold and silver workers almost all belong to the Sonār caste, which numbers about 8000; even coolies in the factories often wear gold earrings, partly perhaps as a means of saving money, while heavy silver ornaments are common among women of all castes. Early in 1909 a Kunbī boy herding cattle in Bāsim tāluk was murdered for the sake of Rs. 70 worth of ornaments which he wore. The customer always supplies the metal and watches the Sonār carefully while he is at work, for the profession has a bad reputation for making dishonest profit out of its work. Blacksmiths are needed everywhere, but the work is often done by Panchāls, who wander in single families from village to village under a vow to settle nowhere till their ancient city of Chitor is restored. Carpenters are more numerous, but statistics are not available; their chief work is the making and repair of carts and agricultural implements, which contain far more wood than iron. The business of transport along the great metalled roads has been partly specialised, and the making and repair of carts gives occupation to a large number of workshops there. Ornamental work in masonry is often done by workmen especially imported for the purpose; the fronts of large houses are sometimes ornamented with carved woodwork, which is frequently done by Mārwāris who have settled

in the District. A number of oil-presses worked by bullocks survive, but no recent statistics are available; the bullocks working a press walk round and round for hours in a dark room hardly large enough for the press to turn. At Akolā two steam presses for extracting oil have recently been started and seem to answer well; most of the oil-cake is exported to Europe. A few Mahārs in all parts have looms for making coarse blankets, and a few Koshtis make rough cotton cloths, but the industries are already trifling, and seem steadily to decline. At Akot and Bālāpur carpets, some with stamped patterns and some ornamented by hand, are made by Muhammadan *satranji-wālās*; the fabric is rough but strong and not without interest. Bālāpur has also a colony of Muhammadan Momins, who make turbans of mixed cotton and silk, such as well-to-do men wear in the villages, but their trade is also dying out; the maker sits with his feet in a hole in the ground and the material of the turban stretched forward and backward the whole length of the house. It is said that they used to make for Nawāb Salābat Khān at Ellichpur *mhonda* cloth so strong that Rs. 50 worth of copper could be lifted without the cloth tearing. *Kāgazi* Muhammadans at Bālāpur, who alone intermarry with the Momins, used to make paper by hand; the manufacture has only stopped during the last five or ten years. The material of manufacture was *san*, hemp; this was cut into pieces of about two inches in length, which were soaked in water for three days and then dipped in lime, *sajjīkhār*, and left for the same length of time. The mixture was spread on a large stone, well beaten under water in a cistern, washed at the river, and again cleaned with a kind of soap, *khārīchā*, containing oil, lime, and other ingredients, and the process was repeated for eight days. Finally a *tatti*, screen, of *kaus* grass was placed on the surface of the cistern, and sheets of paper formed upon it. They were taken out one by one and dried ; *chikki*, paste made of the flour of wheat or rice, was applied ; and the paper was rubbed with a smooth stone to give it a gloss. The paper thus made is of poor colour and somewhat ready to tear, but is yet quite a serviceable article. A few dyers are scattered over the District.

Steam factories.

153. At Akola a new step has just been taken in the opening of two steam mills for making cotton cloth, the Native Ginning and Spinning and the Akola and Mid-India Mill. The latter employs 900 hands; it is only now beginning work (early in 1909) but should give Akola a claim to be considered a manufacturing town. Factories for ginning and pressing cotton number 92 (ginning 67 and pressing 25), and employ about 8000 hands; they have a capital of scores of lākhs, but the total cannot be ascertained. The rate for pressing is kept up by a ring. Most of the towns have on one side a belt of factories, each in its own compound, giving the place a pronounced industrial air. The number of factories has been steadily growing for several years, though alterations in the legal definition of a factory affect the statistics. Many of the larger and some of the smaller villages have single factories, but these do not seem to pay in remote places; it is true that labour is cheap, cotton can be got at a lower rate, and a large area may be brought under contribution, but on the other hand the promoters are liable to try to take too much advantage of these points, and again there is a difficulty in disposing of the ginned cotton. Cultivators are willing to go long distances to secure higher rates and fairer weights for their cotton, so that carts come to Akola from Pusad tāluk and the Nizām's Dominions. Work is seldom kept up through the night, children are

nominally seldom employed, the machinery is not very complicated, and few accidents have to be reported. Some factories burn wood and some coal, the latter to an increasing extent; a very few are lit by their own electricity.

Weights and measures at Akola.

154. The following weights and measures are in use at Akola. Jawāri and other food grains are generally sold by measure with the table—80 tolas make 1 seer, 4 seers 1 *paili*, 12 *pailis* 1 *man* (maund), 20 *mans* 1 *khandi*. Other terms used in such tables are—10 tolas make 1 *ardhāpāoser*, 20 tolas 1 *pāoser*, 40 tolas 1 *aster* or *ādser*. Vegetables, chillies, sugar, *gur*, betel-nut, turmeric, and so on are generally sold by weight with the table—5 tolas make 1 *chhatāk*, 10 tolas 1 *atpāo*, 20 tolas 1 *pāo*, 40 tolas 1 *aster*, 80 tolas 1 seer; 25 tolas make a *kachchā sawāser*, but 100 tolas 1 *pakkā sawāser*, also called 1 *pāsri*; 8 *pāsris* or 10 seers make 1 *man* for retail trade, but 10½ seers 1 *man* for wholesale trade; 20 *mans* make 1 *khandi*. Cotton seed is sold by weight, 100 tolas making 1 *pāsri*, 2 *pāsris* 1 *dhadā*, 4 *dhadās* 1 *man*, and 20 *mans* 1 *khandi*. Cotton, whether cleaned or uncleaned, is sold by weight; 39 tolas make 1 *rattal*, 7 *rattals* 1 *dhadā*, 4 *dhadas* 1 *man*, 5 *mans* 1 *dokdā*, 2 *dokdās* 1 *bojā*. Oil is sold by measure, and both *kachchā* and *pakkā* tables are recognised. The *kachcha* scale is—2½ tolas make 1 *nawatka*, 5 tolas 1 *pāoser*, 10 tolas 1 *aster*, 20 tolas 1 seer, 18 seers 1 *dhadi*. The *pakka* scale is—2½ tolas make 1 *nawatka*, 5 tolas 1 *chhatāk*, 10 tolas 1 *atpāo*, 20 tolas 1 *pāo*, 40 tolas 1 *aster*, 80 tolas 1 seer, 4½ seers 1 *dhadi*, 4 *dhadis* 1 *man*, and 20 *mans* 1 *khandi*. Butter is sold by weight, and only by a table called *kachcha*—8¾ tolas make 1 *pāoser*, 17½ tolas 1 *aster*, 35 tolas 1 seer. For *ghī* the table is—5 tolas make 1 *chhatāk*, 10 tolas 1 *atpāo*, 20 tolas 1 *pāo*

40 tolas 1 *aster*, 80 tolas 1 seer, 210 tolas, that is 2½ seers plus 1 *atpāo*, 1 *dhadi*, 4 *dhadis* or 10½ seers 1 *man*, and 20 *mans* 1 *khandi*. Milk is nominally sold by weight, but measures seem to be generally recognised as corresponding with the different weights; the ordinary terms are *atpāo*, *pāoser*, *aster*, and a seer of 80 tolas. For gold and silver the scale is—2 jawāri grains equal 1 grain of wheat, 2 grains of wheat 1 *gunj*, 2 *gunj* 1 *wāl*, 4 *wāls* 1 *māsa*, 12 *māsās* 1 tola, 26⅔ tolas 1 *chip* (a term used by one of the banks), and 80 tolas or 3 *chip* 1 ser. A tola is of the weight of a rupee. In measures of length 1 *bot* or *girhā* is the length of the middle finger on the inside, 2 *bots* make 1 *wīt*, span, 2 *wīts* 1 *hāt*; a *hāt*, hand, is the distance of the tip of the middle finger from the inner bone of the elbow, and is considered to be 18 inches; if the hand is clenched the space between the knuckles and the elbow, inside, is a *munda*; and two *hāts*, or 1 yard, is called *wār* in the case of cloth, and *gaj* in other cases. A *kawatal* is the space a man can reach with his arms outstretched, and a *purush*, man, in measures of depth is generally the height a man can reach by raising his hands above his head, though some say that except when measuring water the hands should not be so raised. An acre contains 40 *gunthas*; a *tiphan* 4 acres in level and 3 in hilly parts. A *barās* is 100 cubic feet of clay or the like.

Tables in the villages.

155. The weights and measures of a large village, especially if a weekly market is held there, always prevail to some extent in its neighbourhood, but there are endless variations between different bazar-areas, if not between individual villages within the sphere of a single market. A few of these differences are noted. Usually 80 tolas make a seer, but it is sometimes 78, 120, 150, or 160 tolas. The number of seers in a *paili* may be 2, 4,

4½, 7½, or 8, causing corresponding variations in the larger measures. Generally 12 *pailis* make a *man* and 20 *mans* a *khandi*, but the *man* has sometimes 16 *pailis*; or 8 *pailis* make a *kudawa* and 20 *kudawas* a *khandi*. The *pāoser* and *aster* vary with the seer, being ¼ seer and ½ seer respectively; a *chawatka* and *nawatka* are sometimes formed of 10 and of 20 tolas, sometimes in a more complicated way, and sometimes unknown. The terms in the measures of weight used for vegetables and so on are usually those of Akola, but differences are by no means rare; thus a *pakkā sawāser* may be 105 tolas instead of 100, and a *kachchā sawāser* 26¼ tolas instead of 25; 84 tolas sometimes go to a ser, or 16 sers to a *man*; fresh terms, such as 50 tolas 1 *adsadi*, may be introduced; the distinction between *kachcha* and *pakkā* is used to a varying extent; the larger terms in the table sometimes vary for different articles, so that 12 seers may make a *man* of gur, chillies, or turmeric, but 10½ seers a *man* of sugar and other groceries. Cotton measures vary hopelessly; thus the *pāsri* for the seed may be 560 or 720 tolas instead of 100; the terms *rattal* and *dhada* for the cotton itself are often not known; in the measure for uncleaned cotton a *sawāser*, 1¼ seers, varies from 40 to 50 tolas, while for cotton cleaned in a hand gin a *sawāser* sometimes means 55 tolas. For oil a *kachchā* seer is sometimes 10 tolas and a *pakkā* seer 40 tolas. For butter a seer may contain 42, 44, or 80 tolas, and *kachcha* and *pakka* tables may be distinguished. The seer of 80 tolas is very common for *ghī*, but that of milk is sometimes 40 tolas; sometimes 9 *tāk* of milk equal 10 tolas. The table for precious metals again seems fairly constant, though sometimes 28 tolas make a seer, but goldsmiths have a reputation for cheating in every possible way. Metal pots are sold by a table in which 80 tolas make a seer and 13½ seers a *man*.

Varying tables and fraudulent weights.

156. Thus the chief grains and oil seem always to be sold by measure, most other articles by weight, and milk practically by measure, though nominally by weight. Articles are classified all over the District in much the same way for the application of tables, and the same terms are generally used for the table of the same article in different villages, but the meaning of the terms varies repeatedly from place to place and can only be ascertained by minute enquiry. The classification into *pakkā* and *kachchā* is a common cause of difference, but further variations occur in each division. Sometimes there seems to be a definite purpose of favouring the large buyer, for instance by making the *man* especially large for wholesale trade or by making a large term a shade more than the even multiple of a small one; other irregularities look as if the buyer had in different ways insisted on having full weight; but the general result is certainly very irregular. As far as trade is confined to a small local circle no great harm is perhaps caused, but the variations must now cause unnecessary difficulty to all traders from a distance and so cause loss both to them and to the local public. A further difficulty springs from the fact that the weights and measures used, whether for small or for large transactions, are very often false. Cultivators selling cotton used to be cheated to an extraordinary extent in this way, so that fortunes are said to have been made by the fraud; the evil in cotton dealing has apparently decreased but is still sufficient to affect considerably the popularity of a particular market; cultivators on the other hand sometimes water their cotton—though this injures the cotton seed—or put in it stones which not only add to the weight but may smash machinery in the factory. Some firms with pressing-factories also cheat the pur-

chaser in Bombay; sometimes they press a quantity of poor cotton in the middle of a bale with cotton of better quality at both ends; sometimes they water most of the bales before pressing; a private arrangement with the purchaser's *mukaddam* in Bombay prevents detection. When the cotton of a certain neighbourhood has a good reputation other cotton is sent considerable distances to be forwarded from a railway station in that part. Firms setting up factories are themselves cheated over the weight of the metal work supplied them; they have no scales large enough to test the consignments, and they say that the consignor would cause weighment at the railway stations to be manipulated in his favour. Weights casually taken up in village shops vary again, the bystanders explaining that one is used for buying and the other for selling. The fraud is at present very difficult to check, but much harm must result from the continuance of these complications and irregularities.

Markets.

157. The Berār Gazetteer of 1870, p. 234, says in reference to Akola District: 'The 'weekly markets have tided over 'heavy tolls and duties, to which the traders were liable 'at every village on their line of route, in default of a 'certain protection by the patel of the market village to 'which they happened to be bound. In order to start a 'weekly market the patel of the village had to make 'valuable presents to the traders who attended the 'inaugurative gathering. The annual fairs (*jātras*), as 'they intervene, attract all the traders within wide circles, 'and are visited by crowds from long distances. Fairs 'usually have a religious origin. Both the markets and 'fairs suffered from the dangers attending transport of 'goods before British rule; since then they have re'covered, and far exceed what they ever were before,

'even according to local tradition.' Small weekly gatherings which are markets in their nature are held in many villages; no official account is taken of them unless the right of collecting dues (at certain fixed rates) can be sold for Rs. 100 or more; if the bazar reaches this degree of importance the right of collection is sold by public auction, and one of the local bodies, receiving the sale-price, makes various provisions for the bazar—building stalls, digging a well, planting trees, or attaching a sweeper to the village as occasion requires. The weekly markets of the four municipal towns are in the hands of the local municipalities and are all of some importance. Including these and the bazars at the *jāgīr* villages of Mālegaon in Bāsim tāluk and Umarda in Murtizāpur, the total number of weekly markets in the District is 75, of which Mangrul tāluk contains 9 and Murtizāpur 10, and all the other tāluks have 13 or 14 apiece. The selling price of the Akola market for the present year, 1909, was Rs. 2900. Among the village bazars there were 9 which sold for over Rs. 1000 each, Rājanda and Borgaon in Akola tāluk, Mundgaon (Rs. 4755), Mālegaon (Rs. 4000), Asegaon, and Akoli Jāgīr in Akot, Bālāpur (Rs. 2275) and Murtizāpur (Rs. 3150) in the tāluks to which they give their names, and Shelu bazar in Mangrul. (The exact price has been given whenever it exceeded Rs. 2000). Thus Akot tāluk, which has many wealthy villages remote from the railway, has by far the most important bazars, its revenue from this source, Rs. 15,500 (excluding municipal bazars), being more than double that of any other tāluk; Bāsim in fact only provides Rs. 3000 and Mangrul Rs. 4000. Bāsim appears to be outside the busier circles of bazar trade, while the north of Mangrul, where Shelu bazar fetched Rs. 1500, barely falls within them. Every village in the flatter parts is within reach of a different bazar for almost every day of the week, though of all these a single one would be preferred above the remainder. A number of traders make their living by visiting six or seven important bazars every week, carrying their goods in carts or on ponies. Almost anywhere within six or eight miles of a bazar like Mālegaon in Akot tāluk on the morning after bazar day such traders keep passing singly or in little strings, while on the day itself the chief roads close to the village are hidden in clouds of dust. A bazar village used to be marked by a high white flag, but this is not always noticeable now. A large bazar is a busy sight, but it is very difficult to get reliable figures of the attendance or sales. The chief articles sold are firstly, all kinds of grain; secondly, such groceries as salt, oil, and Indian and other sugar; thirdly, various articles of clothing; fourthly, cattle; and fifthly, a large number of miscellaneous articles such as pots and pans, cotton-seed, vegetables, betel-leaves, and timber. People who have received payment in kind may exchange their cotton or jawāri for other goods. Money-changers attend almost all bazars. Bi-weekly markets are held only at Akot, Bāsim, and Borgaon; the bazar at Umarda alone lasts for two days.

Fairs.

158. Fairs vary from a little gathering hardly known outside its own village to a concourse numbering some thousands and including representatives from distant parts of India. It is impossible to give correct statistics, both because general estimates of number are very unreliable and because the popularity of a fair may change considerably in a few years; Government gets no revenue from fairs. The largest fair in the District is said to be that at Sindkhed in Akola tāluk; it is held in honour of Shri Moreshwar Mahādeo, and lasts for five days in the hot weather; the attendance has at times

been officially estimated at 50,000; Pinjar in the same tāluk is said to have 25,000 people in the rains on account of Withoba Rukhmai. Donad and Kothali both attract 5000 visitors; so that Akola seems to have far more important fairs than any other tāluk. A fair in November at the temple of Narsingboa at Akot is in the same class with these. In Bāsim tāluk 10,000 people are said to attend fairs lasting a month in the cold weather at Pārdi Asra in honour of the Asrās, and at Nāgardās both in the hot weather and the beginning of the cold weather in the name of Bhawāni or Devi. Bāsim itself has 5000 people at the temple of Mahādeo in October, and Sirpur attracts 2000 Jains a little later. Mangrul has a fair of some size at the tomb of Hayāt Kalandar; Umri and Gibba Majra Dongarkhed in the same tāluk are said to have an attendance of 4000 and 3000 respectively; Pātur in Bālāpur tāluk was formerly the scene of a great gathering in honour of Nāna Sāhib, but its importance has almost vanished. Petty fairs are very numerous. Some of these meetings used to be distinguished by hook-swinging, the hook-dance, and other barbarous acts of devotion, a painless representation of which is still given at some places. Malsud in Bālāpur tāluk, which is said to get 1600 visitors, has fire-walking and the penance of vicarious and symbolic castigation. Alegaon is visited in April by 1000 Mānbhaus.

TRADE.

General development.

159. Practically the whole trade of the District is carried by the Nāgpur branch of the Great Indian Peninsula Railway. The chief stations are Akola and Murtizāpur, where metalled roads running for considerable distances north and south meet the line. A certain amount of traffic belonging to Akola District

passes through stations a little beyond its borders, especially Shegaon on the west and Badnera and Amraoti on the east, but on the other hand a considerable fraction of the trade of Akola and Murtizāpur stations passes through the District to places in the Nizām's Dominions and Pusad and Daryāpur tāluks. Upon the whole the statistics for these two stations give a fair though perhaps somewhat exaggerated idea of the trade of the District as a whole. Comparing the figures for the year 1868-1869 with those of 1907 it appears that in the former year Akola station had only half as much export trade as Murtizāpur, though its import trade was 50 per cent. more; in the latter year Akola had in both respects more than twice the trade of Murtizāpur. Again, the total exports of the earlier year weighed 330,000 maunds and were worth Rs. 45,55,000; the imports weighed 240,000 maunds and were worth Rs. 42,50,000. In 1907 the exports weighed 1,830,000 maunds and were valued at Rs. 2,78,00,000; the imports weighed 2,330,000 maunds and were worth Rs. 1,73,00,000. The transport of cotton by the railway was very dilatory between 1865 and 1867 but rapid by 1870; traffic by road may have been of comparatively greater importance in 1868-1869 than in 1907, but in both years it must have been very slight in comparison with railborne trade. Thus in 39 years exports increased about sixfold in both weight and value; imports increased nearly ten times in weight but only four times in value. The volume of trade, which is probably best indicated by weight, appears therefore to have increased from six to ten times; the nominal value of the exports has kept pace with this. Imports judged by any standard have greatly increased, but the value of one maund of them has fallen from Rs. 17 to Rs. 7; it is impossible to examine the matter thoroughly, but it seems clear that present imports are purchased at far less cost per unit than past imports.

Relation of exports and imports.

160. During the six years from 1902 to 1907 the value of the exports has varied between 206 lākhs and 349 lākhs, the average being 279 lākhs; that of imports meanwhile has risen steadily from 122 lākhs to 173 lākhs, the average being 149 lākhs; thus there has been an average excess of 130 lākhs of exports over imports. Various points in this connection are interesting; thus the land revenue of the District is only 25 lākhs, less than one-tenth of the average exports and accounting for less than one-fifth of the difference between exports and imports; while the staple food, jawāri, is grown within the District. The excess of exports is 87 per cent. of the total imports; natives of Berār do not invest much money outside the Province; on the other hand most of the trade and finance of Berār is in the hands of people, such as Mārwāris and Cutchis, from other parts of India. Economic questions are exceedingly complicated, but it is possible that part of the large excess of exports represents the payment or profit received by these immigrants for exploiting the District. The value of the imports has risen by curiously regular gradations 42 per cent. in six years; that of exports—which depends very largely upon the accidents of the season—has meanwhile shown an uncertain tendency to rise, but nothing more; this may indicate, though the facts are too scanty to warrant the least confidence, that the capitalists who are developing the District are to an increasing extent coming to be residents of it. The number of factories for ginning and pressing cotton has been growing considerably, while mills have been opened for weaving cloth and expressing oil; this is reflected in the trade returns by the fact that imports of iron,

'wrought and manufactured,' have risen fairly regularly in the six years from a value of 8 lākhs to over 18 lākhs; imports of 'metals' have risen similarly from 11 to 21 lākhs; these articles formed 9 per cent. in value of the total imports in 1902 and 12 per cent. in 1907. It is evident that the inauguration of a number of new companies with expensive plant and premises, and with capital subscribed partly within and partly without the District, must complicate the normal relations of export and import.

Chief exports.

161. Raw cotton is by far the most important article of export; in the six years from 1902 to 1907 its average weight was about 1,125,000 maunds (52 per cent. of the whole) and its average value was Rs. 2,03, 50,000 (over 2 crores, 73 per cent. of the whole). The total value of the cotton was within 7 per cent. of this average in four of the years, but in 1902 it was 30 per cent. below it and in 1905 it was 26 per cent. above. Cotton-seed is the article of export coming next in weight, with 557,000 maunds (26 per cent. of the whole); its average value was Rs. 7,50,000 (7½ lākhs.) The export of jawāri varied between 3000 maunds in 1903 and 1904 and 231,000 in 1906; its average on the six years was about 100,000 maunds, valued at a little over 2 lākhs. The distillery at Akola exports country liquor weighing 52,000 maunds and valued at 49 lākhs. Oilseeds (other than cotton seed and linseed) were valued at 13 lākhs in 1902 but have never since reached 1 lākh; oil-cake has risen meanwhile from Rs 13,000 to a little over 1 lākh; it is largely produced in two steam mills lately started at Akola. Raw hides and skins have on an average weighed 11,000 maunds and been worth 2½ lākhs; the price has risen in years in which the weight did not rise, though on the whole both tend to increase.

Linseed has varied between 1½ and 5 lākhs, with an average of 2¾; it was most largely exported in 1905. Twist yarn, with its best year in 1904, has an average value of Rs. 54,000; bones amount to Rs. 8000, and hay, straw, and grass to Rs. 6000. This list leaves less than 8 lākhs of miscellaneous small exports, besides some articles of unknown weight and value.

Chief imports.

162. The imports of the greatest total weight in the last six years have been coal and coke (for factories) with an average of 187,000 maunds, wheat (171,000), salt (144,000), and rice, unrefined sugar, gram and pulse, and wrought iron (123,000 maunds); no other article is reported as exceeding 100,000 maunds. The articles of greatest value were European piece-goods with an average of 21 lākhs, wrought iron (10 lākhs), miscellaneous provisions, refined sugar, and unrefined sugar (8 lākhs each), spices and Indian piece-goods (7 lākhs each), rice (6 lākhs), wheat and betel-nuts (a little over and a little under 5 lākhs respectively), manufactured iron (over 4 lākhs), kerosine oil and salt (4 lākhs each), cocoanuts (nearly 4 lākhs), gunny bags (3½ lākhs), gram and pulse (3½ lākhs), oils other than kerosine (3 lākhs), twist yarns (2½ lākhs, of which two-thirds were European yarns), wood (nearly 2½ lākhs), tobacco (2 lākhs), and dried fruits and nuts (1½ lākhs); in both 1906 and 1907 chillies were imported to the value of 1½ lākhs, but the figures of the earlier four years had varied from Rs. 13,000 to Rs. 95,000. The greatest variations took place in the import of wheat, which amounted to nearly 400,000 maunds in 1902, was only 5000 in 1905, but rose to nearly 200,000 in 1907; people apparently imported just the amount necessary to supplement the home-grown supply. Slighter variations occur similarly in the case of other supplementary importations and illustrate the influence

of foreign trade in steadying supplies and prices. Salt rose from 128,000 maunds in 1902 to 154,000 in 1907, partly no doubt because the duty on it was reduced in 1903, 1905, and 1907. Other imports were fairly constant but with a tendency to a rise in both quantity and value. It is perhaps a sign of prosperity that the imports of sugar should be about 16 lākhs, betel-nuts 5, and cocoanuts 4 lākhs.

COMMUNICATIONS.

Railway and main roads.

163. Akola District has comparatively good communications. In the first place the Nāgpur branch of the Great Indian Peninsula Railway runs from west to east across it. The line passes through the northern parts of Bālāpur, Akola, and Murtizāpur tāluks, a total distance of 57 miles, within which are ten stations. Geographically it is considerably north of the middle of the District, but in view of the balance of wealth it is fairly central. The town of Akola is on the line, as is that of Murtizāpur. Bālāpur is connected with Pāras station by a District Board road six miles in length, but the river Bhuikund comes between; the crossing is always rough, and in the rains is sometimes blocked by a flood for two or three days at a time. The project of building a bridge, to cost Rs. 36,000, is under consideration, but the expense forms a serious difficulty. Akot in the north is connected with Akola by a metalled road, partially bridged and drained, 28 miles in length, and Bāsim in the south by a similar road of 51 miles. This southern road is a part of a road to Hingoli, important when British troops were stationed there, and 's continued within the District ten miles south of Bāsim to the Penganga river. Mangrul, the headquarters of the remaining tāluk, lies on a road partly metalled and partly otherwise surfaced

which runs north-east from Bāsim to Kāranja, an important town in the south of Murtizāpur tāluk, and thence north to Murtizāpur. It is 25 miles from Bāsim to Mangrul, 17 more to Kāranja, and 20 from Kāranja to Murtizāpur. Besides the roads connecting the headquarters of the various tāluks there are several others *made* in one way or another and passable throughout the year. From Akot a road runs north through Khathāli to Sālu in the Melghāt, having nine miles within the District, and enables timber to be brought from the forests. Another runs south-west across Akot and Bālāpur tāluks to Shegaon, on the railway in Khāmgaon tāluk, having 25 miles within the District; it branches off from the Akola-Akot road ten miles south of the latter town. A further branch, running almost due north from Adsul, connects this with Telhāra, ten miles away; but parts of these roads get into bad condition in the rains. A road two-thirds metalled and one-third surfaced with *muram* runs from Khāmgaon, on a branch line in Buldāna District, south-east through Bālāpur to Pātur, on the Akola-Bāsim road, and has a total length of 23 miles within the District. A road runs south-east from Bāsim to Pusad and Umarkhed, having 17 miles within the tāluk; another runs nine miles north from Murtizāpur towards Daryāpur in Amraoti tāluk; and another connects Kāranja with Dārwhā, to the south-east in Yeotmāl District, having seven miles in the tāluk. These roads are under the Public Works Department, except that from Pāras to Bālāpur, and belong technically to Classes I, I—B, or II (*a*), 2—B; all are either metalled or surfaced with *muram* or similar material; none are bridged and drained throughout but all are partially bridged and drained. That is, they are almost all passable throughout the year except where a stream is in temporary flood, and, though rough in places, they are fit for a motor-car or bicycle. The cost of maintenance varies with the different roads but is usually from Rs. 300 to Rs. 400 a mile; only Rs. 150 a mile is allotted to the Adsul-Telhāra branch, from Rs. 250 to Rs. 290 to a few other stretches, and from Rs. 480 to Rs. 534 to most of the Akola-Akot, Shegaon-Akot, and Murtizāpur-Daryāpur roads. Road of the 'first class' measures 172 miles, and that of the 'second' 75, the former costing a total of Rs. 70,000 a year, and the latter Rs. 20,000. The Jālna-Nāgpur dāk line runs across the south-east of the District, passing from Mehkar in Buldāna District across the north of Bāsim and Mangrul tāluks, through Kāranja; thence one branch runs north-east through Dhanaj to Amraoti and another runs due east into Chāndur tāluk. It is in charge of the Public Works Department but cannot be classed with the roads previously mentioned because only Rs. 45 a mile is allotted for it.

Lesser roads.

164. The District Board has 28 miles of 'Class I, 43 of 'Class II,' and 450 of 'Class III' roads. Either Rs. 100 or Rs. 200 a mile is allotted to all these, the total cost being over Rs. 50,000. Most of the roads in Class I and Class II are very short but very useful pieces connecting important villages with the nearest railway station or main road, while those in Class III form a loose network of important routes throughout the District. The standard is much lower than that of the roads under the Public Works Department, but it provides, at least for heavy traffic, a great improvement on the untouched country road; in particular the effort is made to build a stone causeway for every awkward nullah. The causeway—*pharshi*, Irish bridge—was first introduced into Berār by Colonel K. J. L. Mackenzie when he was Deputy Commissioner at Bāsim; it was then made of *muram* instead of stone, but was considered a most valuable

idea, so that the name of 'Mackenzie Bridge' was proposed for it. The great bulk of villages are however situated on roads where money is never spent on improvement, though faggots and earth may be thrown into the bottom of a muddy nullah to provide firm crossing, or other slight improvements may be made by the agency of Mahārs. Where the soil is free from stones and the route unbroken by bad nullahs such roads are admirably fitted by the middle of the cold weather for ordinary country traffic, though sometimes cracks appear or ruts are formed which are awkward for a horse. Rocky and stony ground means rough roads, but roads good for ordinary traffic are to be found throughout most of the District.

Characteristics of certain roads.

165. The great metalled roads are generally marked by their straightness; they bend to secure an alignment along a watershed and to pass near a large village, but scarcely for any other reason; they are purposely laid out so as not actually to pass through ordinary villages on account of the expense and difficulty involved in maintaining a road there. They are shaded in part, and schemes are in course of execution which will very gradually give them fairly continuous shade. Every road has characteristic features of its own. That from Akola to Bāsim, after crossing a slight ridge in the 15th and 16th miles, climbs a steep and lofty *ghāt* in the 24th and 25th; its course in the plain below is marked by a long cloud of dust winding in and out along the foot of the hills. Halfway up are a large stone and flag dedicated to Mhasoba or Arkeshwar, described in books as a river-god with the head of a buffalo. He was formerly located in a lonely place in the plain below but has been set here for some years to protect wayfarers. Cart-drivers throw him a scrap of cotton as they pass toward Akola and offer a cocoanut as they return; any chance passer

picks up the cotton. Peacock may be seen at the foot of the *ghāt*; above it, east of the 25th milestone, is a valley much frequented by *nīlgāi*. Camels carry the mail from Bāsim to Pusad. The road from Bāsim to Kāranja passes, as it approaches Mangrul town, along the very backbone of the country with wide though not very interesting views on each side. At Dastgaon a number of Pandharpur immigrants have settled; a small tank was made for them by damming the head of a valley; they have set up a god called Vetāl, in a form simple but seldom seen in Berār—four or five stones first whitened, then reddened, and set up in an open circle of white-washed stones; Vetāl is said to be a vampire king of the *bhūts*. When the road to Akot was first opened people were found driving by the side of it because they thought it was to be reserved for the Sāhib-log; they had no doubt been forbidden to use it while it was under construction. The Pūrna river is forded in the tenth mile; this causes some inconvenience, but far less than might be expected from so large a river; it would be very expensive to build a bridge. Some of the country roads in the north of Akot tāluk are lined with both trees and flowers, but the former are gradually being cut down and there is no grass except in river courses. Traffic is far greater in the cold weather than at any other time. Cotton provides the greatest part and leaves its traces in patches of white caught in the trees. Men on foot and in carts, and women in long files, go to and from their work in the fields. On market days comes a faster passing of travelling merchants and countryfolk. A thin sprinkling of religious wanderers is always to be found, sometimes *fakīrs* or *sādhus* from distant parts of India, sometimes cartloads of women and children with a few menfolk going for *darshan*, the sight of a sacred place, to some shrine locally famous. Late in the cold weather marriage processions pass, with drums and gay trappings.

CHAPTER VI.

FORESTS AND MINERALS.

FORESTS.

Government forest.

166. The forest of the District amounts to 340 square miles, less than 9 per cent. of the total area; it is all Government land; of the three main divisions A Class occupies 160 square miles, B Class 20, and C Class 160. The chief tract lies along the hilly land which runs from east to west across the middle of the District, extending into the south of Murtizāpur, Akola, and Bālāpur tāluks, and the north of Mangrul and Bāsim tāluks. Narnāla fortress in the extreme north stands in a tract of A Class forest dating from 1894 and now covering 7 square miles. Several other isolated tracts are dotted about throughout the District; they are mostly babul *bans*, but some contain a variety of trees and some are reserved chiefly for the supply of grass. The stretches of forest along the central hills are all much of one type—thin jungle growing on rough stony ground which developes in places into actual *ghāts*. They contain little good timber; the total revenue from this source has not risen above Rs. 18,000. Firewood, sold chiefly in Akola but largely also in Kāranja and to a less degree in other markets, produces from Rs. 20,000 to Rs. 24,000. In the two years 1906-1907 and 1907-1908 grass was taken away to the extent of 17,000 and 32,000 tons respectively, giving a revenue of Rs. 20,000 and Rs. 35,000. The chief source of income is grazing, which yields from Rs. 53,000 to Rs. 64,000. Minor produce is unimportant, yielding less than Rs. 5000; the most prominent article in it is *mahuā*, which is collected chiefly

for the manufacture of country liquor, but slightly also for local food-supplies ; bamboos yield sometimes a few score and sometimes a few hundred rupees. Forests of A Class are fuel and fodder reserves, and those of B Class, *ramnas*, are purely fodder reserves; both are fire-protected ; C Class forests are primarily pasture-land and are not fire-protected. Goats and sheep have been excluded from A Class forest since 1886 ; in the year 1908-1909 the number of other animals admitted was limited to one head to every 1½ acres. Complaints are often made of the inadequacy of grazing, but this restriction was necessary to prevent the reserves being over-grazed and ruined. People living in villages largely given up to forest are on the other hand commonly anxious to have more land given out for cultivation ; the adjustment of the forest area involves difficult questions. There are no forest villages. It is impossible to show the development of the forest system in the District because the area upon which statistics are based was entirely altered in 1905; the old Akola District was a part of the Buldāna Forest Division ; Murtizāpur, Bāsim, and Mangrul tāluks were divided between two other Forest Divisions. In 1907-1908, however, the area was 219,135 acres, the revenue Rs. 1,32,000, and the expenditure Rs. 40,000. The charges made for passes are As. 6 for a cartload, and As. ½ for a headload, of grass or wood ; As. 3 a year for a cow, As. 1½ for a goat, and As. 1 for a sheep in C Class forest; and As. 6 for cattle in A Class forest.

Roadside avenues.

167. The Public Works Department has charge of eight roads with an aggregate length of 233 miles; avenues, in every case incomplete, have been established along 66 miles. More than one-third of the Akola-Bāsim-Hingoli road has been planted in this partial fashion, less than one-quarter, on an average, of each of the other roads.

To provide trees for a road a nursery is established for every 12 miles, maintained till that space is covered, and then abandoned; the trees chiefly planted are *nīm*, mango, *jāmun*, and *shīsham*, and they are watered for three years. The expenditure in the year 1906-1907 was Rs. 1000 for planting and maintaining trees, and Rs. 1200 for the upkeep of nurseries. The District Board has already planted trees along 6 miles of road, on the station-roads at Kuram and Māna and the drive at Akola. It has now taken up an arboricultural scheme, to cover the years 1908 to 1918, which is to cost Rs. 17,000 altogether and will be wholly confined to planting the 18½ miles of road from Akola to Māhān. The Board has in its care 52 miles of metalled or *murramed* roads, and 450 miles of fair-weather roads; the completion of this scheme will mean that nearly one-half of the present system of made roads in its care has been provided with continuous shade

MINERALS.

Minerals.

168. The District is not known to have any mineral wealth, except unworked iron ore in the hills in the south of Murtizāpur tāluk, but salt-wells in the valley of the Pūrna were of value as late as 1870. The salt was of inferior quality and bitter, and the industry has now long ceased; but in 1855-1856 there were 400 of these wells, yielding to Government a revenue of Rs. 24,000. A subterranean lake about 50 miles in length and 10 in breadth seems to lie in the valley of the Pūrna, its centre being at about Dahihanda in the south-east corner of Akot tāluk, and unlimited quantities of brine were obtainable from it. Wells of three or four feet in diameter, the sides protected by a kind of basket-work, used to be sunk into this, water being found at a depth

of from 90 to 120 feet. The operation of tapping was thus described by Mr. Bymonji Jamasji in the Berār Gazetteer of 1870, p. 22: 'The men go digging and 'building these wells till they think that water might be 'below a foot or a foot and a half. They then stop dig-'ging and complete the whole work. Afterwards an ex-'pert man descends into the well, seated in a cradle, and 'some four or five sharp men stand on the top of it hold-'ing the ropes of the cradle with great caution. The 'man who descends digs the ground very slowly, and 'when he finds that there is water below half a foot, he 'warns the men on the top to be watchful, and then 'strikes a final blow with a hoe very strongly. The water 'then shoots up like a spout, and fills the well at once for 'fifteen or twenty feet up. When the man strikes the 'final blow the men on the top pull him up, for it might 'perhaps happen that he would be drowned; but such 'instances occur rarely, if at all.' The water was then poured into shallow drains and left for a few days to evaporate, work continuing all the year except in the rains. Caravans of Banjāras with pack bullocks used to come and carry the salt away into the Central Provinces and elsewhere. People at Dahihanda and Kutāsa say that the wells used to be let out on contract to parties of four men, the price never exceeding Rs. 500, and the output used to be worth Rs. 1000 or more. This was the *hundebandi* system, but wells not so taken up were worked on *rawibandi* by men who received *takāvi* advances and other payments from Government and gave up all the proceeds; Kshatriya Kolis were chiefly employed. The wells have now all fallen in.

CHAPTER VII.

FAMINE.

Akola District in 1896-1897.

169. The Berār Districts very rarely suffer from famine; in 1871 a deficient monsoon resulted in some distress, and in 1877 a long break in July caused a great though temporary rise in prices; actual famine has however only occurred twice since the Assignment, in the years 1896-1897 and 1899-1900. The tāluks which now form Akola District were then divided between the three old Districts of Akola, Bāsim, and Amraoti. Akola District contained the five tāluks of Akola, Akot, Bālāpur, Khāmgaon, and Jalgaon; Bāsim District contained Bāsim, Mangrul, and Pusad; Murtizāpur tāluk belonged to Amraoti District. The present chapter describes separately the famines as they occurred in the old Akola and Bāsim Districts; Murtizāpur tāluk is dealt with in the Amraoti volume.

During the rains of 1896 Akola District received only 26 inches instead of an average, calculated on the preceding ten years, of 35 inches. Heavy rain fell in the early part of August but there was practically none later; most of the other Districts in Berār received useful rain in November. Cotton reached an average of eight annas all over the District, that is more than half a normal crop; jawāri was estimated at eight annas north of the railway line and four annas to the south; *rabi* crops completely failed. These conditions would have caused little more than a shortage of employment but that the monsoon failed throughout India, causing a great rise in price; on the 28th of September the price of jawāri in Akola rose suddenly from 20 to 13 seers per rupee and that of wheat from 12 to 9½ seers. Apparently the rise was immediately caused by large purchases for export but was much intensified by speculation; *satta* dealings, for forward delivery, were very common in Akola and Khāmgaon and kept prices there 15 per cent. or more above the level of other places in Berār. At Khāmgaon Mārwāris who wanted prices to run high were said to buy up the first cartloads of grain at rates higher than the owners asked. The sudden rise in prices caused a popular panic for a few days; people closed their grain stores to prevent export, and the difficulty of getting grain caused a danger of rioting. The famine was more severe in Akola than in any other part of Berār, except the Melghāt, but caused no permanent harm; people now speak of it as the 'six-anna crop dearness' or in similar phrases.

Public health, crime, food-supplies.

170. Public health was better than normal from September 1896 to April 1897, but worse from May to the following October. In ordinary years the death-rate per thousand is from 2½ to 3½ between May and July and from 4 to 5 between August and October; in 1897 it was from 4 to 4½ in the former period and rose to 11 in August. The chief causes were dysentery and diarrhœa, but cholera also prevailed; people were very unwilling to go any considerable distance in search of relief, and suffered by living at home on poor and insufficient food. Scarcely any deaths were caused by starvation; the few victims were chiefly wanderers from other provinces. Crime increased considerably, the object being generally to get grain; it was not committed by organised bands, but by lazy people who preferred crime to labour on relief works. The increase began

in September with house trespass and petty riots in bazars, and developed in October into robberies and dacoities. In August and September 1897 a great deal of crime occurred; people had returned to their villages but received wages very low in view of the high prices still prevailing. It is very difficult to estimate the supply of jawāri, the staple food-grain; it is chiefly stored in grain pits and people are very unwilling to say how much they have. Little seems, however, to have been imported into the District, and though there was considerable anxiety in 1897 lest the famine should continue it is almost certain that there were a few months supply in hand. The average price of jawāri in the different months during the decade in which the famines occurred varied from 20 to 22 seers a rupee; from October to December 1896 it varied between 12 and 10; it remained at the latter rate till May 1897, rose to nine in June and July and eight in August, but then fell steadily till it returned to normal in the beginning of 1898. Water-supply caused great anxiety, especially in Khāmgaon and Jalgaon tāluks. Cattle suffered, but less severely than in some of the other Berār Districts. Land-revenue collections caused little difficulty; only Rs. 23,000 were suspended and no remissions were given, but in the whole of Berār no single defaulter had to be imprisoned, and only 43 fields were sold. This was due partly to the general prosperity, partly to the low rates of assessment, and partly to the fact that good prices had been realised for the crops of 1897 before the demand for that year became due

Relief measures.

171. Relief operations began with petty works opened by local boards at rates between ordinary and famine wages, and were continued by different agencies. The Public Works Department spent Rs. 68,000 on diverting the

Shāhānur river in Akot tāluk, to avoid the flooding of land on its lower course and the obstruction of the Akot road; the Department also constructed a tank at Eranda in Akola tāluk (Rs. 22,000), and roads from Telhāra in Akot tāluk to Adsul and Jhiri (Rs. 19,000). Khāmgaon municipality spent Rs. 20,000 on improving the Januna tank, which supplies the town with water. A total of Rs. 44,000 was spent by the different authorities in collecting broken stone metal; several tanks were repaired and small pieces of road made. The total cost of these works was Rs. 1,92,000; their estimated value was Rs. 1,44,000; the number of persons employed, calculated 'for one day' and including dependents, was 1,384,000, a little over 2 per cent. of the population. Ellichpur District, which contained the Melghāt, spent Rs. 77,000; the other four Districts spent from Rs. 46,000 to Rs. 53,000 each; Akola had more than twice as many people on relief as any other District. Government loans to agriculturists were somewhat hampered by a difficulty in applying to Berār a circular letter of the Government of India, but they amounted to Rs. 35,000, many times more than the total of ordinary years. The figures given do not sufficiently represent the intensity of the famine; private charity was very generously exercised, both reducing the numbers in need of Government relief and dealing with distress beyond the scope of Government operations. The District subscribed over Rs. 15,000 to the Charitable Relief Fund, from which it received over Rs. 35,000; in the large towns a daily distribution of food was made to all poor wanderers; patels and factory managers, Mārwāris and Brāhmans, vied with each other in providing shelter and cooked food; Government officials, missionaries, and other private persons subscribed most liberally for poor-houses and charitable relief.

Bāsim District in 1896-1897.

172. The famine of 1896-1897 was felt severely in the old Bāsim District, though less than in Akola. The rainfall was only 24 inches instead of an average of 44, but nearly 2 inches fell in November. Cultivators used commonly to keep only enough grain to last till the next harvest, surplus stocks being largely in the hands of *sāhukārs*; these demanded ruinous terms when the famine harvest failed. The number of leases and deeds of sale and mortgage almost doubled during the year, and ornaments were sold at rates from 25 to 30 per cent. below the ordinary prices. Many cultivators must therefore have become deeply involved, but no permanent ill effects were caused. Public health was good till June 1897, but the death-rate from July to October varied between 5½ and 8 per thousand; the maximum rate had been surpassed in epidemics of cholera, but the ordinary rate of those months was only three or four. The roads were patrolled to rescue starving wanderers and only 32 deaths from starvation occurred. Crime increased considerably, but no additional police had to be engaged. At first some petty grain riots occurred, apparently with the partial object of securing free board and lodging in gaol; this was checked by whipping being inflicted. During the ten months from January to October 1897 there were less than 20 dacoities and less than 20 robberies; but housebreakings numbered 230 instead of the average of 70, and thefts 350 instead of 150. Some dacoities were the work of organised gangs; the large transport of grain offered many opportunities to bad characters; some individuals felt driven to crime by want; but on the whole the increase of crime was slight enough to form clear proof of the law-abiding disposition of the people.

173. The local supply of food grains would have

sufficed for the District, but it was largely reduced by exports to Akola and Murtizāpur; fortunately there was a bumper crop of *dādri* jawāri, a *rabi* crop, just across the Nizām's border; large quantities were imported, except during an interval in which the Nizām's officers stopped the traffic. The water-supply in ordinary years is ample in Bāsim tāluk but inclined to scantiness in parts of Mangrul and Pusad; in February 1897 difficulty was felt in the jungles to which a large number of cattle had been driven; in villages both man and beast suffered through May and June, and in parts of Pusad throughout July. Both grass and *kadbi* were also scanty on account of the poor rainfall. The reserved forests were opened to the extent of 72,000 acres at rates reduced by either two-thirds or five-sixths, but, perhaps on account of the distance of the forests from villages, only 14,000 cattle were brought to graze. Cattle suffered severely from the lack of fodder and water; Banjāras and other owners of large herds lost very heavily; buffalo flesh was sometimes cheaper than grain, even on relief works. The plough bullocks were however saved and cultivation in the next year was not retarded by lack of cattle. No pressure was exerted to bring in the land revenue except when enquiry revealed ability to pay; less than Rs. 7000 out of a total of Rs. 672,000 was suspended, while 33 per cent. of the *rabi* instalment, or 8 per cent. of the whole, was actually paid in advance. Cultivators from long tradition regard the land revenue demand as inexorable and some must have satisfied it by borrowing, but it can have caused no great distress. In the less fertile parts of Mangrul and Pusad tāluks some land used every year to be taken up by people who meant to abscond after harvest without paying the land revenue

Food, water, fodder, cattle.

a certain number of fields were sold there to realise the demand, but this happened every year.

174. Practically the whole District was affected by the famine; relief measures had to be taken up in all parts in February 1897, when field labour became scanty. The number of persons relieved, calculated for one day, was altogether 618,000, the great majority on large works but 30,000 in poorhouses and 13,000 in their own homes. On the average of the months from February to October 1897 nearly 6 per thousand of the population was in receipt of relief, but relief on a large scale was taken only during the months of April, May, and June, when the ratio per thousand was—for April 7, May 28, and June 7. Gratuitous relief was given from provincial and municipal revenues on only a small scale. Poorhouses were opened at the tāluk headquarters on these resources and at Risod and Sirpur in Bāsim tāluk on a small fund of private donations. A Relief Committee also opened a cheap grain shop at Bāsim, affording relief to the extent of Rs. 4,000. These agencies were all more or less under Government auspices. Relief labour was utilised to deepen four tanks, and Rs. 8,000 were issued in loans for improving wells. Many well-to-do agriculturists took advantage of the cheapness of labour to improve their wells, and charitable Mārwāris deepened the tank at Mop in Bāsim tāluk. Private charity was fairly active throughout the District. Subscriptions to the Charitable Relief Fund amounted to Rs. 8,000, and expenditure from it to Rs. 10,000. No famine allowances were made to public servants. Loans to agriculturists amounted altogether to Rs. 15,000. The chief relief works were the improvement of the Nāgpur dāk line, especially important in view of the opening of the Godāvari Valley Railway at Jālna, and the making of a road from Mangrul to Shelu. The

Relief measures.

former work cost Rs. 17,000 and the latter Rs. 9,000 The country in Mangrul and Pusad tāluks is very rough, and much valuable work was done in improving *ghāt* roads. The total amount expended was Rs. 50,000; the value of the work done was estimated at Rs. 36,000 only, but there was great doubt about the estimate because many of the works were not valued till the rains had set in and made judgment difficult. Other relief measures included the free use of the *mahuā* crop, which must have saved many lives in the jungly tracts; and payment of *takāvi* instalments was suspended. It was noted that though the condition of the cultivators had much improved since the period of high prices in 1876-1877 it was not clear that their power of resisting bad seasons had increased. The habits of the Kunbi had formerly been very simple, and owing to the low value of his land he had slight facilities for borrowing money. He now found it easy to borrow and had got into a habit of squandering money on very slight pretexts, thus largely sacrificing his prosperity. However the crops immediately after the famine were excellent and there was every prospect that with a few more good seasons the cultivators would wholly recover their former position.

Akola District in 1899—1900.

175. In Akola in the two years which succeeded the famine of 1896—1897 the rainfall was deficient but came at the right times to secure good *kharīf* crops. There were thus good harvests of cotton and jawāri, and stocks of the chief food grain were replenished, though prices were low. *Rabi* crops had been poor for three years before the first famine and were even worse in these two years. They occupied only 7 per cent. of the whole cropped area, but the loss was considerable, especially as the people were unaccustomed to poor crops. The rains of 1899 commenced in

the second week of June, but for the whole period of the monsoon gave only scattered showers. The average rainfall of the District for the preceding 10 years had been 5 inches in June, 10 in July, 6 in August, and 6 in September. In 1899 there were only 3 inches in June, 2 in July, 1½ in August, and 1 in September; and the local distribution of even this scanty fall was most irregular. There were constantly promising clouds, and cultivators remained hopeful right into September. As many as three sowings were often made, and people looked forward to good *rabi* crops when it was too late to sow jawāri, but the rain never came. There were in a few villages close under the hills a little stunted jawāri and a cotton crop estimated at something between half an anna and one anna in the rupee, but with this trifling exception the crops were a total failure. The loss to the whole District entailed by this failure of all unirrigated crops was estimated at Rs. 1,13,45,310. The irrigated area, though the largest on record, was under 10,000 acres, or less than $\frac{1}{10}$ per cent. of the whole cultivated area of the District. It was believed, though certainty was impossible, that there was less jawāri in hand at the beginning of the second famine than in 1896. At any rate the greatly increased demand in the rigorous and widespread famine of 1899 caused prices to rise more quickly than in the earlier year. The average price of jawāri during the period just before the famine had varied only between 19 and 22 seers at different times of the year. In September 1899 it was 14 seers, from October to May 1900 it was 10, from June to August 9, in September and October 10, then 12 in November, 16 in December, and presently a normal price again. Even though local crops had completely failed it was at first thought that the stocks in the District were sufficient to allow of export, which continued briskly from August to November, the jawāri going chiefly to Bombay; and a considerable quantity was lost by repeated sowings. Prices reached a famine level by September. From December till the end of the famine cheap rice from Burma and pulse and various other kinds of grain from northern India poured into the District, and this kept the price of jawāri fairly steady in most places—though in some villages remote from the main roads it rose to 7 seers a rupee. Competition was too active, and in most parts communications were too good, for any ring to be formed to keep up prices. Famine conditions were prolonged owing to the cotton crop of 1900—1901 being backward. The monsoon burst late, and cultivators found a difficulty in getting seed and bullocks, and in paying for labour. Thus the labourers who had come to relief works found agricultural labour scarce till the harvest began, and they suffered more acutely during the months from July to October 1900 than at any other time. The population of the District was 575,000, of whom 35 per cent. were petty cultivators and 31 per cent. agricultural labourers.

Relief measures.

176. Preparations for a very severe famine were begun in August and the District Board was asked to be ready to start test works at a week's notice. The Board responded promptly and admirably, and proved able unaided to meet the great rushes of panic-stricken labourers that ensued. Four test works were opened in September and their number was increased to ten in October. In the middle of September they contained 1700 workers, at the end of the month 6000, and by the middle of October 13,600. Eight of them were then converted into large relief works under the Public Works Department, and more similar works were added till they numbered 23 in

June 1900. The chief relief works were devoted to the repair of the great roads and of certain tanks and to the earthwork of the proposed Khandwa-Akola-Bāsim and Khāmgaon-Jālna railways, but very numerous minor works were also carried out. The number of labourers on these works rose from 30,000, or 5 per cent. of the population, at the end of November to 60,000, or 10 per cent., in December and to 83,000, or 14½ per cent., toward the end of June. In the middle of November kitchens were attached to works for the relief of dependents, the number of whom gradually rose to nearly 13,000 in May. At first many of the better class of workers supported their families out of their earnings and reserves, but this gradually became impossible. Gratuitous relief by private charity was organised in August and preparations for the distribution of Government doles were completed in November, though distribution was not commenced till January. The number in receipt of these doles rose in June and July to nearly 6000. As the private grain funds in villages became exhausted, which happened in the hot weather, names were transferred from their lists to Government lists. An order to open village kitchens was received from the Resident in April and was carried into effect in May. They were meant chiefly for the relief of poor children and proved most effective. Their number was increased when the breaking of the monsoon caused people to return to their villages, and as the system was more economical than that of relief by doles incapable adults were transferred from the doles list to the kitchen list. In August the number of kitchens at work was 146, the total number of inhabited villages in the District being 966, and on a date toward the close of September the number of persons relieved by them was 25,000, or over 4 per cent. of the population. Poorhouses were opened early in December 1899. They were established at the five tāluk headquarters and at Shegāon in Khāmgaon tāluk and Telhāra in Akot tāluk. They were periodically cleared out, incapable wanderers being alone retained and others being sent either to their villages for gratuitous relief or to relief works. During the four months from April to July over 15 per cent. of the population was in receipt of relief, and this proportion rose in June to 19 per cent. Apparently about 25 per cent. of the labourers on receipt works in the hot season were cultivators, but almost all of these returned to their villages when sowing commenced. Cultivators needed their little savings for the preservation of their cattle, a far more expensive matter than the preservation of human life; they could only have obtained credit on ruinous terms, but were able to maintain their position fairly well by coming to the relief works. The proof of this is that no land was relinquished; the normal area was brought under cultivation in the next year, showing the resisting power of the cultivating class. District officers remarked the small proportion of Muhammadans on the works and considered that a distaste for manual labour was one of the causes. The cost of supporting an adult during the 14 months of the famine was estimated at Rs. 52, and that of every head of cattle saved at Rs. 100 or more. Well-to-do cultivators freely took advantage of cheap labour to improve their property, and great private charity was exercised by all classes. The Indian Charitable Relief Fund received subscriptions of Rs. 35,000 from the District and allotted Rs. 1,83,000 to it. Labourers on relief works were often reported to be lazy, and their work was finally valued at only a quarter of what it cost, but Kunbis showed both considerable independence and great gratitude for the help of the fund.

177. In the year 1895-1896, which was a normal

year, there were registered 3,390 mortgages of land with a value of Rs. 10,77,000, and 4,160 sales of land with a value of Rs. 11,00,000; in 1899-1900 the mortgages numbered 4,550 and were valued at Rs. 10,38,000, and the sales numbered 4,050 at a value of Rs. 10,30,000. Thus the mortgages increased in number by 35 per cent., though the increase in value was by no means proportionate, and the sales decreased in both number and value. Compared with the famine of 1896-1897 the mortgages of the second famine increased by 24 per cent. and the sales decreased by 2 per cent. Many cultivators again would be unwilling to mortgage their land and would obtain loans on simple bonds or on stamped acknowledgments. Yet even if the figures are regarded in the most unfavourable light it is clear that the cultivating class survived the disaster of a second and very rigorous famine far better than might have been feared. Weavers were expected to go to the ordinary relief works if they were capable of doing ordinary work; relief was given in their own villages to others from March 1900, the total number so assisted being 13,000. There are few weavers in the District, and most of these live in Akola, Akot, and Bālāpur. It was calculated that nearly Rs. 7,00,000 worth of gold and silver ornaments and utensils were sold during the famine, but it was impossible to get exact statistics. The selling rate in these cases involved a loss of about 36 per cent.; brass and copper utensils sold at a loss of 50 per cent. Far more of these articles were sold than in the former famine; gold and silver idols were openly offered in the market. The total value mentioned would come to R. 1-4 per head of the population. A little emigration into the Nizām's Dominions occurred at the very beginning of the famine owing to false reports of good crops and of the generosity of some Rājā there,

Economic effects.

but most of the wanderers soon came back. Some of the smaller villages were wholly or partially deserted while the people were away at the relief works, but by the end of the famine the inhabitants had returned and there were few visible traces of their wanderings except occasional ruined houses. Indebtedness must have increased considerably and there was a great loss of cattle, the better class of cultivators suffering even more than the poorer, but considering that this was the severest famine on record and that it closely followed another famine extraordinarily little permanent harm was done. This must be attributed to the general previous prosperity of the District and the very liberal assistance given by Government. In both famines the labouring class, once the immediate stress had passed, was left very little the worse.

Public health; children.

178. Public health was poor before the beginning of the famine, possibly through an unusual cycle of deficient monsoons. The death rate in the hot weather immediately before the famine, when there was nothing to suggest conditions dangerous to health, was almost as high as during the corresponding quarter in the famine year. It fell in July, was normal by September, and remained above the normal for the rest of the famine. It was between 4 and 6 per thousand in the cold weather months, when it is usually between 2 and 3; was 6 in May and June, 9 in July, and 11 in August (which in that decade usually ranked as the most unhealthy month in virtue of a death rate of 5), after which it gradually sank to a normal 3 in December. There was a good deal of cholera through most of the famine year, more than was shown by the village statistics; because the headmen found more than usual difficulty in making the special daily reports required when cholera has been declared.

When the rain came, in July, all conditions became temporarily more unhealthy still. The poorer classes usually ate *tarota bhāji* during the rains, but in the famine they ate also *tarota* and tamarind leaves and seed, grass seed, *gullar* or wild figs, *umra*, *kātsewari* flowers, *ubātya* beans, *gokhar*, and other plants, and mixed with their jawāri some of the oil-cake given to cattle. The labourers on relief works had generally been in good condition and it does not appear that they had been weakened by getting insufficient pay. A curious point rises in connection with the question of age mortality. Throughout the famine about 75 per cent. of the deaths were among children under 5 or adults over 50; there was a general impression that these classes, the very young and the old, were especially badly hit by it. In fact however during the five prosperous years ending in 1895 the proportions were just the same, or rather the children suffered less in the famine year than in those years. This seems to suggest that the relief measures were very successful, though it brings out the fact clearly that in ordinary years nearly one-quarter of the deaths are among children under one year of age, another quarter among children of from one to five years, and about a quarter more among people of over 50 years. Privation is apparently inevitable in times of severe famine, but only 13 cases of starvation were reported and only two of these proved on investigation to be genuine. The victims were in both cases wanderers from outside the District; no one in the District died from not being within reach of food or from the inadequacy of relief arrangements. Hardly any cases of children being abandoned by their parents were observed. A list of 1200 orphans was made out during the famine and it was expected that an orphanage would have to be started for them, but all were suitably provided for by local charity. The birth rate, which is usually 40 per mille per annum, fell during the famine by less than half a point.

Crime, food-supply, etc.

179. Crime naturally increased. The number of murders and attempts to murder was double the normal. Most offences against property increased in the same proportion, and dacoities increased twelve times. However most of these crimes were only technically serious; there was, for instance, no system of organised dacoity. Additional police were enrolled to watch treasure at famine camps, but for no other purpose. There was considerable ill-feeling at first at the sight of *sāhukārs* making large profits by exporting grain when others could hardly afford to buy enough for their own needs, but under the circumstances the people were very quiet and law-abiding. The food grains exported by railway from September to November 1900 amounted to 275,000 maunds, and those imported by the same means to close upon 2,000,000 maunds. Probably one-half of this went through the District to Bāsim or Buldāna. It was calculated afterwards that there must have been nearly 2,000,000 maunds more stored in the District, that is, at half a maund or 45 pounds per head per month, nearly seven months' supply. The imports were largest during December and January; they were left to uncontrolled private enterprise, which answered quite satisfactorily. Cheap grain shops to the number of 31 were established by private charity and managed by committees under official supervision. At Akola Rs. 38,000 were raised for this purpose by a very trifling rate on all sales made by tradesmen, a system to which people willingly agreed. Admission to the shops was restricted to the needy and so no competition with ordinary shops resulted. Water was so scanty that people at many villages and most

relief works had to depend on shallow wells sunk in the dry beds of streams. Shegaon suffered more severely than any other municipality. Cattle are largely fed on jawāri stalks for eight months of the year; when jawāri failed completely and grass almost entirely it is clear that very great difficulty was caused. Many cattle were taken far into the Melghāt hills in search of fodder and water but were unable to stand the change to hill life. There was tremendous mortality among the cattle in the District, so that animals were sold in the markets for two or three rupees. An annual census of cattle is taken by village officials but the results are not very reliable. A special census taken in this one District in July 1900 showed that 46 per cent. of cows and 36 per cent. of bullocks had died, but it is quite possible that the figures should be 50 per cent.; this correction is borne out by the figures about export of hides given by the railway company. Village officials at first pressed cultivators for the payment of land revenue, not only in the supposed interests of Government but also because their own emoluments are payable after 90 per cent. of the revenue has been collected. Enquiry was made to find out who were in a position to pay and who were not, but it was found that the lists made by village officials required further scrutiny on behalf of the cultivators. Every patel was warned that no one was to be reported as able to pay unless he could do so without borrowing. By the end of July 1900, five months after the proper date, 66 per cent. of the demand had been paid, by February 1901 only 7 per cent. remained, and thanks to good prices almost the whole of this was rapidly paid up.

Bāsim District in 1899-1900.

180. **Bāsim** District also was severely affected by the famine of 1899-1900. Relief measures were begun in the middle of November in the former year and

continued till nearly the middle of December in the latter. The District contained a population of close upon 400,000, of whom about 70 per cent. were either agriculturists or agricultural labourers; 5 or 6 per cent. more were unskilled labourers and would suffer equally severely from a general failure of employment. Distress was more widespread than was anticipated in the report submitted in October 1899, partly because it was impossible at that time to foresee how complete would be the failure of crops and partly because of an extraordinary influx of people from the Nizām's Dominions. The famine was very acute everywhere but was most severe in Pusad taluk and in the south-west of Bāsim tāluk around Risod. Much of the land in Pusad tāluk is poor and very many of the cultivators were Andhs and Banjāras, people averse to steady labour and in the habit even in good years of living from hand to mouth. In Risod pargana there was usually a great deal of *rabi* cultivation, which this year failed entirely, and the land was to an unusual extent in the hands of *sāhukārs*. The rains of 1899 set in favourably and though they were much below the average there were occasional falls till the middle of September; but by the beginning of November most of the jāwāri had withered so much that the cultivators cut it merely for fodder; its estimated outturn was only a fraction per cent. of the normal. Scarcely any *rabi* was sown and practically none survived; irrigation is always negligibly small. Good harvests in the two years following the famine of 1896-1890 had brought the price of jawāri to a normal rate; this was maintained till September 1899, but a great deal of grain was exported in that month and the following, and prices then rose at a much more rapid rate than in the previous famine; jawāri was selling at 10 or 11 seers per rupee till January of the previous famine, but it rose to 8 or 9 by October of this one. The unpromising opening of the rains of 1900 caused prices to remain high for a long time. Cultivators in Berār do not work as hard as they do in some places; owing to the prospect of discipline and fairly hard work in the camps they did not as a rule seek relief till their resources were really exhausted; the minimum wage was rather low, but many people preferred to remain upon it rather than do a fair amount of work. When the rains broke labourers sometimes lived largely on jungle produce in order to save something out of their wages, and their health suffered in consequence. Wages were reduced in July and replaced by cooked food in November, when the number of labourers fell greatly. Adult dependents and non-working children on relief works were from the beginning given cooked food, the cooks being generally Kunbīs; this answered well on the whole, suiting all the lower castes except Bhois. Sheds were erected that children might be kept in the shade. During the dry months labour was concentrated on large works, generally road-making; people were usually reluctant to go far from their homes; in June small works were opened so that they might obtain relief near their own villages. Such Mahārs as were left in the villages for public work were given gratuitous relief and also made some profit by selling the hides of dead animals, the flesh of which they ate. Offences against property increased from 460 in the previous year to 1440 in the famine year, the largest proportionate increase in Berār. The District contained a large number of Chāran Banjāras who found regular work very distasteful; they wandered a great deal, suffered severely, and were responsible for much of the crime committed. Immigrants from the Nizām's Dominions also wandered aimlessly, especially if any attempt was made to send them back to their homes—from which they had just made a long and painful journey;

residents of the District as a rule moved little and with deliberation.

Economic aspects and relief measures

181. The average value of mortgages of land had been Rs. 311 in a normal year; in the first famine it was Rs. 273, in the second Rs. 211. The number of mortgages of land in the year 1895—1896 was 250,000, in 1896—1897 it was 420,000, and in 1899—1900 it rose to 470,000; the sales of land in the same three years were 170,000, 260,000, and 280,000; the number of both transactions thus rose a great deal in both famines, but was especially high in the second. The Deputy Commissioner made careful enquiries and concluded that the object was very seldom to pay the revenue, because cultivators knew it would readily be postponed or remitted; people would sacrifice a field, perhaps already mortgaged, in order to remain at their homes as long as possible. The District contained only 6000 artizans; no special relief was given to them, but many found employment at their own trades at the relief works; the Charitable Relief Fund allotted nearly Rs. 1,70,000 to the District, and Rs. 10,000 of this was spent in buying cloth from weavers. People commonly make investments by buying silver and gold ornaments; these and utensils of other metals were extensively sold by families who wished to postpone application at the relief works. It was clear that the District would take some years to recover from the effects of the famine; the revision settlements of Bāsim and Mangrul tāluks, which were due in 1902, were postponed till 1904, but no further relief was thought necessary; that of Pusad was postponed six years. The daily average number of persons on relief was 60,000, or nearly 15 per cent. of the population; the average throughout Berār was 9 per cent.; the maximum was reached

in May, when 35 per cent. of the population, the highest percentage recorded in Berār, was in receipt of relief. Mortality was below the normal till November 1899, but above it from that month till December 1900; for six months, April to September, the rate was above 9 per mille, rising in July to 19. These were by far the worst figures recorded in Berār, but they are in fact misleading because a large number of the deaths were among immigrants from the Nizām's Dominions; these wanderers also greatly aided the spread of cholera. Statistics to show their numbers cannot be given because they commonly gave a false account of their origin to avoid being sent back, but they were to be found in every relief institution, and more than half the applicants at poorhouses on the border sometimes admitted themselves to be from the 'Muglai.' The loss of fodder was not as serious as that of food grain; a fair outturn of *kadbi* was obtained in most parts of the District, so that large quantities were exported to Amraoti and Akola Districts; however the price of *kadbi*, which was usually Rs. 2 per hundred pullies at Bāsim in the hot weather, rose in the famine to Rs. 10. Stacks of fodder are not generally kept, the District being dependent on the yearly supply. Cattle on the whole suffered very heavily, especially in Pusad tāluk, though there was more grass there than elsewhere; reliable statistics could not be obtained, but it appeared that about one-third of the total number of cows and buffaloes died, and one-fifth of the plough oxen. Just under 89 per cent. of the revenue demand was collected in the year 1899—1900, whereas in 1896—1897 there had been 99 per cent. collected; no permanent remissions were required. The relief works included Rs. 9,00,000 spent on road work, Rs. 1,30,000 on the proposed Khandwa-Akola-Bāsim railway, and Rs. 300,000 on tanks. Various useful *ghāt* roads in Mangrul and Pusad tāluks date from the famine; but during the monsoon work of little economic value had often to be undertaken in order to provide employment near the homes of the workers. The expenditure on the relief of dependents at kitchens in large works amounted to Rs. 1,80,000, that on doles in villages to Rs. 2,60,000, that on kitchens in villages in the rains to Rs. 2,00,000, and that on poorhouses to Rs. 70,000. In most of these cases the total spent in Bāsim was larger than that of any other Berār District and the incidence of cost per head in such a remote District was also naturally high. Loans to agriculturists under the Land Improvement Loans Act and the Agriculturists' Loans Act combined for the two years 1899—1900 amounted to Rs. 96,000. Missionaries spent Rs. 15,000. The total expenditure on the famine came to more than Rs. 30,00,000, while that in Akola was Rs. 28,00,000.

CHAPTER VIII.

LAND REVENUE ADMINISTRATION.

Early administration.

182. For some time before the Assignment of 1853 the important divisions for the purposes of land revenue were the pargana and the village. It is impossible to say when these were first established or which of them is the older. Clear traditions about the old system cannot now be obtained; contradictory statements are made in different parts. Apparently each pargana was for most purposes in charge of a Naib appointed by the Nizām's Government, while parganas were grouped, with greater or less fixity, into tāluks under higher officers. For land revenue collection contracts were taken by *maktedārs*, who secured payment largely with the help of the deshmukhs and deshpāndyas, the hereditary officers of the pargana; but apparently the influence of the different officers varied greatly in different parts. Local *sāhukārs* were called in to give security for payment and to transfer the revenue, by means of *hundīs* and other negotiable instruments, to Hyderābād. Within the village it was frequently a question of inducing unwilling cultivators to accept land, either by a show of force or by a promise of light assessments, or, very rarely, by *takāvi* advances. In all parts of the District the difficulty was felt that cultivators were very liable to give up their land and thereby endanger the revenue; so that people sometimes say deshmukhs had to keep armed followers, Rājputs and Rohillas or other Muhammadans, simply to compel runaway cultivators to return. Security of tenure was an unknown idea, whether or not it had always been so, and no one

cultivated his fields with very great care, but there was always plenty of land to be had. Definite traditions exist of representatives of the Bhonsla Rājās of Nāgpur being stationed in certain villages and taking a greater or less share of the whole revenue.

District boundaries.

183. Under the organisation in force since 1853 the pargana has not been taken into account (though its limits are still remembered), but villages have been grouped into larger areas with the name of tāluk, and tāluks have been formed into Districts. Berār was at first divided into two Districts, later into four, and by 1870 into six, but in 1905 it was again reduced to four. Akola seems to have been the headquarters of a District from the first, but the limits of the area subject to it have greatly varied. In 1870 it consisted of the tāluks of Akola, Akot, Bālāpur, and Jalgaon, but in the same year Khāmgaon tāluk was created—largely by shifting eastward the boundaries of Bālāpur—and was included in Akola District. Bāsim similarly had at first only the two tāluks of Bāsim and Pusad, but in 1875 Mangrul tāluk was added, its villages being taken chiefly from Bāsim tāluk but largely also from the Dārwhā tāluk of the Wūn District of the time. In 1905 Bāsim District was abolished; Akola District retained three of its own old tāluks, Akola, Bālāpur, and Akot, and received three fresh ones, Murtizāpur from Amraoti District, and Bāsim and Mangrul; Buldāna District took Jalgaon and Khāmgaon, and Yeotmāl District received Pusad.

Tāluk boundaries.

184. Tāluk boundaries have also varied considerably. In 1853 Akola tāluk contained 142 villages; in 1857 it received 12 from Bālāpur and gave one to Kāranja (now Murtizāpur); in 1858 it gained 259 villages taken from Bāsim; in 1865 it received three more from Bālāpur and ten from East Berār

but gave 25 to Kāranja; in 1870 it lost 55, given to Bālāpur; in 1875 one went to Mangrul, and at some time it has received four more villages from Bālāpur and five from Murtizāpur; it has now 354 villages. Akot tāluk in 1853 contained 85 villages, in 1859 the Dahihanda pargana of 57 villages was added, in 1862 came Panaj and two other parganas with 74 villages which were only then made over by the Nizām, in 1865 Adgaon and Panchagawhān parganas with 110 villages, in 1866 seven villages from Jalgaon and Anjangaon (now Daryāpur), and later five more from Jalgaon, while one village has been given to Jalgaon and 71 have been transferred to Daryāpur; Akot has now 266 villages. Bālāpur had 304 villages in 1865; in 1866 three were transferred to Malkāpur and four to Akola, in 1870 when Khāmgaon tāluk was formed Bālāpur gave it 148 villages but received 55 from Akola, so that it now contains 204 villages. Bāsim tāluk consisted in 1873 of 502 villages, but 156 villages were taken in 1875 to help in the formation of Mangrul tāluk, 50 have been given to and 21 received from the Nizām's Dominions to simplify the Berār boundary, and 11 have gone into Pusad and 33 been received from it; so that the present total is 338 villages. Murtizāpur tāluk consisted in 1869 of 337 villages, but transfers have been made of two villages to Chāndur tāluk, two to Amraoti, one to Bāsim, and 16 to Akola, while two have been received from Daryāpur; the total now being 318. Mangrul tāluk was formed in 1875 by the transfer of 156 villages from Bāsim tāluk, ten from Pusad, 86 from Dārwhā, and one from Akola, but in 1905 one (Dewalgawhān) was given to Pusad; the total now being 252. This account is incomplete, partly because the details of a complicated series of transfers are differently stated in different accounts, but is substantially right. It shows that numerous changes were made in the first 25 years after the Assignment, firstly to build up tāluks and secondly to reduce them to manageable proportions, but that tāluk boundaries have been almost constant for the last 30 or 40 years.

Early British administration.

185. When the British took over Berār the rates of assessment were high and uneven, especially as they had been raised in the last year or two, but exact statistics cannot be given. All the early accounts emphasize the untrustworthiness of the only available figures. Thus the Akot Settlement report of 1867 says, 'The nominal area under cultivation of the 228 villages 'under the Native Government amounted to nearly '210,000 acres, but on it being roughly measured in '1854—55 the actual area was ascertained to be about '154,000 acres, the assessment on the same being 'Rs. 2,82,000, and the collections Rs. 2,63,000.' The average rate in North Berār was Rs. 3 As. 12 per *bīgha*, but in certain cases this ran up to Rs. 5 or Rs. 6, while for *bāgait* land, irrigated merely by means of wells, it was sometimes Rs. 25. The Berār Gazetteer of 1870, p. 258, quotes, 'The large tāluk of Argāon used to be covered 'with gardens, and the hedges are still perfect, but the 'whole has become field (dry) cultivation; much of the 'arable land has fallen to jungle.' Mr. Bullock, whose name is still remembered in the District, reported in 1854 that *jāgīr* villages were the most prosperous and best cultivated, mainly because the tenants were well treated, though again the *jāgirdārs* had picked out the best villages. In 1854 land was divided into three classes and fixed rates of Rs. 2 As. 4, R. 1 As. 14, and R. 1 As. 8 per *bīgha* were introduced. At first one or two bad seasons occurred, but cultivation and revenue steadily and in most cases very rapidly expanded. Between 1853 and 1855 110 families settled

in Sirpur pargana, which contained 60 villages, and in Ansing pargana eight deserted villages were reinhabited. The Gazetteer of 1870, p. 259, shows that in Bālāpur tāluk the occupied area of 299 villages in the 8 years 1855—1863 was returned as increasing from 228,000 acres to 292,000, while the revenue rose from Rs. 2,84,000 to Rs. 3,65,000; in Akola, for 395 villages, the area in the years 1858—1868 rose from 175,000 acres to 241,000 and the revenue from Rs. 1,88,000 to Rs. 2,76,000; in Murtizāpur, for 333 villages between 1861 and 1869, the occupied area increased from 202,000 acres to 241,000 and the revenue from Rs. 1,64,000 to Rs. 2,00,000. Again, when a proper survey was made it was found that in all tāluks the occupied area had been much understated by village officers submitting false returns; so that the 242,000 acres reported for Akola tāluk should really have been 340,000, and in Akot 280,000 acres were reported, but in fact there were 365,000. Cases of mis-statement in individual villages were very striking. Thus in Akola tāluk the village officers of Borgaon had returned 5500 acres when there were really 8150, those of Donad Bujruk returned 240 instead of 770, and those of Jāmbrun 76 instead of 446. There had been great inequalities in the demand on account of the imperfect returns, so that in villages classed together under the new settlement the old rates had varied from As. 6 P. 6 to R. 1 As. 13 P. 7.

The ryotwāri system.

186. The great change made by the British was that uncertainty and inequality were replaced by definiteness and moderation; a tenure both fixed and equable was established, and the rights and liabilities of the cultivator were minutely defined. The great bulk of the District is *khālsa* land held on *rayatwādi*, ryotwāri, tenure. According to this system Government deals, not with the head of the

village, but with the individual holders of separate fields. The cultivator is given the right, firstly, to occupy his land permanently. Secondly, he may dispose of it in any way he likes; he may either cultivate it or leave it waste, keep, surrender, sell, or mortgage it; but no land newly given out by Government for cultivation after 1905 can be encumbered or alienated without the consent of the Deputy Commissioner. Thirdly, the assessment of a field will never be raised on account of improvements made by the cultivator, though the assessment of a village or group of villages may be raised at the end of a settlement period for general reasons. The great liability is simply that of paying the land revenue at which the field is assessed; the amount is absolutely definite and is only altered at intervals of 30 years; cesses however have also been imposed for special purposes. The only other important limitations are that—as the land is given only for cultivation—the tenant has no right to minerals and may not without special permission diminish its agricultural value by quarrying or building houses. For the fixing of the assessment all the land is divided permanently into fields of from 20 to 25 acres each. These are marked off from each other by a strip at the side, called *dhura*, being left uncultivated; the *dhura* is 4½ feet in width and is liable to assessment. Further, mounds of earth, *warali*, 10 feet in length and 5 in breadth, and stones, *gota*, *patthar*, 2½ feet in length, are placed according to a definite system at angles in the boundary. Certain tests are made to discover the depth and kind of soil and the presence or absence of important specified defects, and the field is permanently valued at so many annas (compared with standard land of 16 annas free from all defects). When a settlement is made a certain rate is fixed for the standard land of the village; the holder of each separate field pays an amount which holds the same proportion to the general rate as his land holds to land of standard quality. (The use of the word 'standard' in this connection is somewhat technical; land altogether free from defects is so rare that a field classed at 12 annas would be considered good in any part of Berār.) The name of a single *khātedār*, registered occupant, is entered against each separate field in the revenue records, except in cases in which there happened to be more than one co-sharer when the original settlement was made. The *khātedār* is primarily responsible for the payment of the land revenue, but when he sells his field it is not necessary to get the name changed on the records; the actual occupant of the field would be responsible in the second resort, and in fact actually pays the assessment, but very frequently sees no reason to get the name of the *khātedār* changed. The settlement is revised every 30 years; all indications of improvement or decline in the economic position of the cultivating classes are taken into consideration; and the rates are raised or lowered accordingly.

The survey settlement.

187. The first settlement of this kind was made in the different tāluks between 1864 and 1872, taking effect first in Bālāpur, and then in Akola, Akot, Murtizāpur, Bāsim, and Mangrul. Major P. A. Elphinstone and Mr. R. R. Beynon shared the work, holding the post of Settlement Officer in turn but relying largely on each other's work. The rates imposed on land of standard quality varied in Bāsim and Mangrul tāluks from As. 14 to R. 1-8, in Murtizāpur from R. 1-4 to Rs. 2, in Bālāpur from R. 1-6 to Rs. 2, in Akola from R. 1-6 to Rs. 2-4, and in Akot from R. 1-12 to Rs. 2-4. Again, the commonest rates were, in Bāsim and Mangrul R. 1-1,

in Murtizāpur R. 1-10, in Bālāpur R. 1-13, in Akola Rs. 2, and in Akot Rs. 2-4. The rate for land irrigated by means of wells was usually from Rs. 3 to Rs. 4, but was in Akot tāluk from Rs. 4 to Rs. 6. Land irrigated by channels from tanks was assessed at a maximum of Rs. 6, and rice land paid the same. Special rates applied to the very few villages under exceptional tenures. Land in much of the District falls so far short of the technical 'standard' quality that the rate actually levied was commonly from one-third to one-half of the maximum stated above.

The settlement period.

188. It is very difficult to get convincing figures about prices during the settlement period, as contradictory accounts come from equally authoritative sources. Many facts of economic importance are however clear. The prosperity of the District depends mainly upon cotton, and though the price obtained for this seems to have fallen yet through a more dependable and prolific kind being increasingly grown throughout the period the crop has constantly been very profitable. Communications have been greatly improved in every tāluk, giving easier access to the railway and the great markets. Population increased considerably, the rise up to 1891 being 15 per cent. in Bālāpur tāluk, from 21 to 25 in Akola, Akot, and Murtizāpur, 34 in Mangrul, and 109 in Bāsim; though it fell again by a small fraction per cent. through famine in the decade 1891-1901. Wealth greatly accumulated; houses were better built and everywhere increased considerably in number, though the percentage of increase exceeded that of population in Bālāpur and Akola only—in Bāsim it was less than half as much but still 48 per cent. The number of plough bullocks, according to the imperfect returns available, increased only 4 per cent. in Akot tāluk, where there had been little room for exten-

sion of cultivation, 11 in Bālāpur, 82 in Murtizāpur, and from 32 to 57 elsewhere; though again the full effects of the famines were not known when the Settlement Reports were written. Cows and buffaloes increased from 36 to 109 per cent. everywhere except in Murtizāpur tāluk, where a decrease of 33 per cent. occurred; no convincing explanation of this fall is given, but perhaps it is connected with the unusual increase reported for plough bullocks; sheep and goats increased everywhere. Any increase in stock is noteworthy because grazing land, whether permanently set aside for the purpose or temporarily fallow, had considerably diminished. The number of horses and ponies fell off everywhere except in Akot and Akola, but this was probably through people being able to use carts more than before. Carts increased 17 per cent. in Akot, from 59 to 90 per cent. in Murtizāpur, Bālāpur, and Akola, 149 per cent. in Mangrul, and 205 per cent. in Bāsim. Wells increased from 29 to 76 per cent. Cultivation in acres increased 1 per cent. in Akot, 3 in Murtizāpur, 5 in Akola, 8 in Mangrul, and 14 in Bāsim. The smallness of the rise in the former tāluks is due to the fact that there was scarcely any land to be taken up; thus only 100 acres were left in the whole of Akot (which contained nearly 300,000 acres altogether), and only 300 in Murtizāpur, while Bāsim had less than 2000 left, and Mangrul less than 5000 (together with 5000 more from a resumed *izāra* village which, though technically available for cultivation, was in fact to be made forest as soon as necessary formalities could be completed); almost invariably again the land left unoccupied is very light soil, which might hardly repay the labour spent on it except in good seasons; thus the average assessment of the unoccupied land in Mangrul was As. 4½ only, the lowest standard assessment being As. 14. Cultivation had extended till there was no valuable land left available. Again, the past revenue had been collected with ease and regularity. In the three years immediately preceding the reports for Bālāpur and Akot tāluks not a single case of distraint for non-payment of land revenue had occurred, while in Akola there had been an average of only six cases a year. For Murtizāpur, Bāsim, and Mangrul, for which figures for six years are given, there had been an average of one case a year. No remissions had been made. The value of land had risen immensely, for at the beginning of the period it was in many parts valueless while at the end it was everywhere in demand and fetched a corresponding price. Thus there was good reason for an increase in the land revenue.

The revision settlement.

189. The question of the rate of increase had been to some extent cleared beforehand, for a revision settlement had just been made in various tāluks of Buldāna District which closely corresponded with those now forming Akola District; a considerable discussion had taken place with regard to Malkāpur tāluk. Major R. V. Garrett conducted revision settlement operations in Akola and Akot tāluks and Mr. F. W. Francis conducted them in the other four tāluks. The new rates came into force in the year 1896-1897 in Bālāpur tāluk, the next year in Akola, the next in Akot, and the next (1900-1901) in Murtizāpur; they were applied in Bāsim and Mangrul in the spring of 1904. The new maximum dry crop rate, the rate on land of standard quality, varied in Bāsim and Mangrul from R. 1-2 to R. 1-12; in Bālāpur, Akola, and Murtizāpur from R. 1-14 to Rs. 2-10; and in Akot from R. 1-14 to Rs. 2-12. The rates for land irrigated by means of wells are determined by different principles according to whether the well was dug before or after the first settlement. In the former case the land is

assessed at the maximum dry crop rate fixed for the village; in the latter at the rate which would have been fixed if there had been no well. The land revenue in the present year, 1908—1909, amounts to—*khālsa* villages, Rs. 24,79,189; *jāgīr* villages, Rs. 17,052; the Kāmargaon Estate, Rs. 11,101; *izāra* villages, Rs. 6291; and a *pālampat* village Rs. 1645; total Rs. 25,15,278. The occupied area, exclusive of *pot kharāb*, unculturable, land in the last year reported, 1907—1908, was 2,169,167 acres; on combining this with the total of the land revenue it appears that the average assessment per acre is in fact R. 1-2½.

Kinds of tenure.

190. All over Berār the ryotwāri tenure which prevails in *khālsa* villages is the most common, but there are also a few *jāgīr*, *izāra*, *pālampat*, and *inām* villages (or fields in the last case); Akola District has *inām* fields but no *inām* villages; it contains however the Kāmargaon estate held on a tenure different from any other in the Province. The following table gives the number of villages held by each form of tenure:—

Tāluk.	Khālsa.	Jāgīr.	Izāra.	Estate.	Pālampat.	Total.
Akola ..	336	18	..	..	..	354
Bāsim ..	321	16	..	..	1	338
Murtizāpur ..	296	6	..	16	..	318
Akot ..	264	2	..	..	..	266
Mangrul ..	227	5	20	..	..	252
Bālāpur ..	193	9	..	..	..	202
Total ..	1637	56	20	16	1	1730

Jāgīr tenure.

191. The District contains 56 *jāgīr* (Marāthi *jāhāgir*) villages; their total assessment is Rs. 77,405, of which Government receives Rs. 16,232 and the *jāgirdārs* get Rs. 61,173. A *jāgirdār* holds a whole village, sometimes making no payment whatever to Government, sometimes paying a fixed quit-rent, and sometimes a certain proportion (generally 40, 50, or 60 per cent.) of the ordinary assessment. The original survey of a *jāgīr* village is never revised except either at the request and cost of the *jāgirdār* or for special reasons; the quit-rent or the proportion of revenue payable is also fixed permanently. The nominal assessment of all *jāgīr* villages is however revised every 30 years along with that of *khālsa* villages; the object is to fix the amount of cesses payable in *jāgīrs* held free or on a quit-rent and that of land revenue in the others. The *jāgirdār* makes whatever arrangements he likes with his tenants, except that certain land in the possession of individual cultivators at the time the *jāgīr* was given has sometimes remained *khālsa* from the beginning. The history of the tenure is given in the Berār Gazetteer of 1870, pp. 101-102. A *jāgīr* could apparently only be created by the sovereign power; thus almost all the *jāgīrs* in Berār were given by either the Delhi Emperor or the Nizām; the Bhonslas gave none. *Jāgīrs* seem at first to have been given only for military service and for the maintenance of order in special neighbourhoods. They were given for life but might be continued from father to son; in a few cases they became practically hereditary, but even then carried an obligation of service and were theoretically liable to be resumed. The system gradually broke down, partly because the *jāgirdār* often ceased to maintain any real force and partly because the Marāthas took 60 per cent. of all revenue assigned to *jāgirdārs* within the areas under their control; in 1853 such purely

military *jāgīrs* as remained were surrendered to Government. In course of time, however, other *jāgīrs* than purely military grants had been made. Revenues were assigned to civil officers for the maintenance of due state and dignity or were acquired by court influence without any substantial reason. They were not originally hereditary, but the grant was in fact sometimes continued to the heirs of the first holder; in this way many *jāgīrs* became practically hereditary without any condition remaining attached to them. These were all confirmed by the British Government. Some *jāgīrs* were also given to pious or venerable persons, *saiyids*, *fakīrs*, *pirzādas*, and others, and were made hereditary in the original *sanads* or patents; these also were confirmed. In fact the great majority of *jāgīrs* in the District are grants of no very great value for the support of temples and tombs. The organisation of *jāgīr* villages has been assimilated to that of *khālsa* villages but, provided the work is properly done, appointments are made by the *jāgirdār* instead of Government.

Izārā tenure.

192. *Izāra* villages number 20, all in Mangrul tāluk; their total assessment is Rs. 12,582, of which Government receives one-half. They are held under the 'Waste Land Rules of 1865'; these formed a system according to which whole villages were leased out to individuals at a low rental for a period of 30 years or less, at the end of which time the lessee was given the option, provided he had brought one-third of the land under cultivation, of keeping the whole village in perpetuity on payment of one-half of a fair assessment. The object was to encourage cultivation, but in fact such liberal terms were unnecessary; the option of permanent possession was taken away in 1871. An *izārdār* is for most purposes in almost exactly the same position as a *jāgirdār*.

The Kāmargaon Estate.

193. The Kāmargaon Estate consists of 16 villages which formerly constituted the Kāmargaon pargana. In 1859 the collection of the land revenue was leased out for ten years to a tālukdār, according to the Hyderābād system. This was Mīr Imām Ali Khān, a Risāldār in the Second Regiment of the Hyderābād Contingent Cavalry; he was a little later appointed an Extra Assistant Commissioner in the Hyderābād Commission. Meanwhile his regiment was ordered on service against the rebels in Central India and he chose to accompany it at the risk of losing his civil appointment. He was the first man to reach the rebels' battery at the battle of Banda, but was killed in the fight. As a reward to his family it was decided to continue the grant of the pargana on more favourable terms than had at first been granted. Mīr Akbar Ali Khān, uterine brother of the Risāldār, was therefore given the pargana for ten years, subject to full protection of the rights of the cultivators, at a rate which was expected to give him a net profit of Rs. 1200 a year; and a permanent right of engaging for the revenue of the pargana was also granted. During the ten years the yield of the Estate doubled. In the settlement of 1871 the lease was renewed at an annual payment of Rs. 6000, but the assessment rates of cultivators were fixed; it was estimated that this would give the holder a net income of over Rs. 4000. At the end of the settlement period the rates of assessment were raised again, part of the difference to take effect immediately and part at the end of 15 years; the result would be a total increase from Rs. 13,600 to Rs. 18,700. It was ordered that the holder should pay to Government Rs. 9000 from 1903 and Rs. 9500 from 1915, besides the former allowances to pargana officials and the emoluments always paid in

khālsa villages to village officers. In dealing with either village officers or cultivators he has almost exactly the rights which Government permits itself in the Patel and Patwāri Law and the Berār Land Revenue Code. Thus he has a right to the produce of unoccupied land and to land left unclaimed but he is debarred from any arbitrary interference with existing rights; the Revenue Courts do not assist him in recovering rent from tenants.

Pālampat tenure.

194. Kāta, in Bāsim tāluk, is the only *pālampat* village in the District; its total assessment is Rs. 3200, of which Government receives Rs. 1645. This village was the subject of various interesting proceedings in which the holder repeatedly profited by long accidental delay and by mistranslation. The word *pālampat* is said to mean a lease for protection or development. Kāta was granted in 1837 by a lease signed by Rāja Chandulāl upon a fixed payment; the purpose of populating the village was recorded. Under the British Government careful calculations were made of the holder's profits, which included dues on produce, oil-presses, and marriages; these dues were abolished and it was ordered that after certain allowances had been made for village expenses and other matters Government should receive 60 per cent. and the *pālampatdār* 40 per cent. of the ordinary assessment.

Inām tenure.

195. A large number of *inām* grants have been made in the District by different Governments; the holding usually consists of a very few fields and the purpose is generally to secure the maintenance of a temple or tomb. An *inām* is sometimes held free of assessment and sometimes on the payment of a fraction of the ordinary assessment. Muhammad Burhān, Bench Magistrate of Kāranja, holds *inām* lands assessed at Rs. 92 given some

years ago in recognition of services rendered by a relative during the Mutiny. The *inām* lands of the District amount altogether to 21,000 acres with an assessment of Rs. 31,000; the *ināmdārs* get Rs. 26,000 of this and Government gets Rs. 5000. Thus about 1 per cent. of the culturable land of the District has been given on *inām*; more than one-third of the whole is in Akot tāluk, which has had an extraordinary number of well-known saints.

Cesses.

196. Nominally three cesses are levied throughout Berār, the *jāglia* and local cess, the school or education cess, and the road cess; in fact the first two are paid by cultivators in addition to their land revenue while the last is set aside by Government out of its receipts. The primary object of the *jāglia* and local cess is to provide *jāglias*, village watchmen; the surplus is made over to the District Board for employment on general local purposes; the names of the other cesses fully indicate their objects. In *khālsa* villages the cultivator pays one anna in the rupee for *jāglia* and local cess and a further quarter-anna for the school cess; Government pays 1 per cent. of the land revenue for the road cess. In *jāgīr*, *izāra*, and *pālampat* villages the holder may make his own arrangements, subject to the supervision of the Deputy Commissioner, for the provision of village watchmen, but must pay both school and road cess; the rate of payment is 1 per cent. for each cess.

Amount of cesses.

197. These cesses are all of more than 40 years' standing, but only reached their present form in 1885. In the year 1907-1908 the *jāglia* and local cess realized Rs. 1,62,000, of which Rs. 87,000 were spent on the *jāglia* force and Rs. 75,000 transferred to the District Board. The school cess came to Rs. 42,000, a further Rs. 26,000 was

contributed from Provincial funds, and altogether Rs. 83,000 were spent on education. The road cess amounted to Rs. 25,000 from Government and Rs. 1000 from alienated villages; the District Board spent Rs. 33,000 on roads. Further expenditure is made and controlled by the Provincial Government.

CHAPTER IX.

GENERAL ADMINISTRATION.

District organization.

198. The Deputy Commissioner, who is also District Magistrate, is at the head of the District. Ordinarily he is assisted by two Assistant Commissioners and two Extra-Assistant Commissioners, of whom one is Treasury Officer and one District Registrar. Occasionally an Assistant Commissioner in training is attached to the District. The District is divided into three Subdivisions in charge of Assistants who are termed Subdivisional Officers, and these are subdivided into six tāluks under Tahsīldārs assisted by Naib Tahsīldārs. The Akola Subdivision consists of the Akola and Murtizāpur tāluks; the Akot Subdivision of the Akot and Bālāpur tāluks; and the Bāsim Subdivision of the Bāsim and Mangrul tāluks. Each tāluk contains from 200 to 360 villages, about one-seventh of which are uninhabited. An Extra-Assistant Commissioner is in charge of excise work as District Excise Officer. The District forms a division for forest purposes, and is at present worked by an officer of the Provincial Service.

Akola is the headquarters of the Sessions Judge of the West Berār Division, whose staff consists of an Additional District and Sessions Judge, two Subordinate Judges, and three Munsiffs, of whom one Subordinate Judge and one Munsiff sit at Bāsim. A District Superintendent of Police is stationed at Akola and is ordinarily assisted by an Assistant Superintendent of Police and a Deputy Superintendent. Education is supervised under the direct control of the Deputy Commissioner by a

Deputy Inspector with two Joint Sub-Deputy Inspectors. The Civil Surgeon, who is also the Superintendent of the Jail, is assisted by two Assistant Surgeons, of whom one is at Bāsim and one at Akola. The Public Works Department is represented by an Executive Engineer with two Subdivisional Officers stationed at Akola and Bāsim respectively. The Land Record Staff consists of a Superintendent of Land Records, an Assistant Superintendent, and 22 Revenue Inspectors. Each of the latter has on an average 80 villages and 30 patwāris in his circle.

Village organization.

199. All the land within certain boundaries belongs to and forms a particular village. The average population of a village, including places which have each a population of over 5000 people, is 425, and the average area is 678 acres. The village officers and servants from the administrative point of view are firstly, patels and patwāris; secondly, jāglias or chaukidārs; and thirdly, *kāmdār* Mahārs. The patel and patwāri are the headman and accountant of the village, respectively. Every village has a resident patel, and sometimes the duties of the office are divided, the revenue or *mulki* patel performing some and the police patel being responsible for the rest. Sometimes also there is rotation, one man officiating for ten years, then the other succeeding him. The office of patel is hereditary, provided that the heir reaches a prescribed standard of moral, mental, and physical eligibility. The patel has a long list of duties to perform. He collects land revenue and pays it in at the tāluk headquarters; inspects crops and boundary marks; reports the commission of offences and encroachments on public lands; controls the other village officers and servants; supervises the sanitation of the village; assists in the service of summonses, collects vital

statistics, and is responsible for many other important functions. Patels are paid by receiving a certain percentage on the land revenue of their villages, and in some instances the remuneration is very small. The village cattle pound is often in charge of a patel, and he receives an allowance on account of it. The position of patel is universally recognised as the most honourable one in the village, and it usually carries a right of precedence, *mānpān*, at festivals and ceremonies. Patels are on the whole an excellent body of men. A patwāri may have only one or several villages in his circle. The office is hereditary, but an educational standard higher than that required from patels is now insisted on. In a large number of villages the duties of patwāris are performed by substitutes. These duties are largely summed up in co-operation with the patel and carrying on all the writing work connected with the village. This involves the keeping of accounts connected with land revenue collection on every field, and the writing of registers and reports on a great variety of matters concerning Government rights and the health, protection and prosperity of the village. The patwāri receives a slightly larger percentage on each village than the patel, because of his special expenses for writing, and as he generally holds three or more villages and the patel only one his total remuneration is considerably bigger. In this District it amounts on an average to Rs. 216 a year, while the patel's average is only Rs. 63.

Jāglias.

200. The jāglia or chaukidār works under the patel and patwāri in the performance of their duties. He is also employed as a village watchman, and is frequently used to carry reports to the tahsīls and police stations. No hereditary right and no caste restriction is attached to the office, but usually men of the very lowest castes

are not appointed. Most villages have at least one jāglia, whose pay varies according to the size of the village and the amount of land revenue. The pay is usually Rs. 4 or Rs. 5 a month. The jāglia receives a coat and a turban every year, and has a belt and badge. The pay is so small that considerable difficulty is often experienced in obtaining suitable men for the post. In villages held under special tenures the holders are permitted to make their own arrangements, provided these are found to be satisfactory.

Mahārs.

201. *Kāmdār* Mahārs are under the control of patels, and, as with jāglias, their principal duties consist of patrolling the village at night and carrying reports. They are also responsible for the conservancy and sanitation of the village. The right to act as ***kāmdār*** Mahār runs in rotation among the *watandār* families and is strictly hereditary, though it may be forfeited by conviction in a Criminal Court. Remuneration is received in the form of dues, *haks*, in grain, which are fixed by custom but may now be modified by Subdivisional Officers. The rates in fact differ from village to village, for in some places they are calculated on all cultivated land, and in some on edible crops only; in addition to these dues the *kāmdār* Mahār receives the skins of the dead animals he removes. This claim cannot be enforced by the Revenue Courts and has been disregarded in the Civil Courts. In addition to the above small presents are also made at the time of festivals and ceremonies.

Crime.

202. Criminal justice in the District is largely in the hands of the Subdivisional Officers, sitting as Subdivisional Magistrates, the six Tahsīldārs, sitting as Magistrates of the second and third class, and a certain number of Naib

tahsīldārs who are invested with third class magisterial powers. The Extra-Assistant Commissioners who do not hold charge of Subdivisions also dispose of a certain amount of criminal work, and there are four Benches of Honorary Magistrates, at Risod, Telhāra, Akot, and Kāranja. The District Magistrate supervises the whole and at times takes original cases himself. The total number of criminal cases disposed of in the District during the year 1908 was 2801, of which 637 were cognizable. During the five years ending 1908 the average number of persons convicted of offences affecting human life was 15, of robbery and dacoity 10, of grievous hurt 7, of house-breaking 52, and of theft 105. Crime is usually most common in the neighbourhood of the railway line, and criminals from other Provinces are fond of exploiting the District.

Civil justice.

203. Suits in which the property involved is of a less value than Rs. 500 are decided by Munsiffs. The institutions in 1908 in the courts of the Sub-Judges, who decide suits from Rs. 501 to Rs. 5000, were 798. The chief classes of suits in the lowest courts are for money. The payment of loans is generally to be made in the cotton season, *i.e.*, from November to February. Mortgages by conditional sales are common, and suits to enforce a right of pre-emption possessed under the Berär Land Revenue Code by a co-sharer in a field are also to be met with. The rule of *dāmdupat* is recognised and followed by the courts. Defendants always allege repayments without written receipts but can seldom prove their case. Suits for foreclosure of mortgage, sale of immovable property, and redemption, are numerous.

Registration.

204. The office of District Registrar is held by an Extra-Assistant Commissioner. The District contains 16 sub-

registrars' offices, of which six are held by rural registrars, who are paid on commission, and ten by salaried sub-registrars. The working of the department during the last three years is given below :—

Year.	No. of documents registered.	Receipts.
1906	9,707	Rs. 30,524
1907	10,408	,, 32,778
1908	12,172	,, 36,040

205. The receipts under the chief heads of revenue are given firstly for the different periods prior to the reduction in the number of Berār Districts which took place in September 1905, in order to illustrate general development; and secondly for the District as it is now constituted so as to show present conditions. The figures for the three years 1880-81, 1890-91 and 1900-01 were :—

Statistics of revenue.

	1880-81	1890-91	1900-01
Land Revenue and Cesses.	17,72,034	18,77,254	23,28,965
Stamps ..	1,67,776	1,92,899	1,73,964
Excise ..	2,95,588	3,44,155	2,76,300
Forest ..	Not available	42,975	42,541
Registration ..	16,148	17,625	19,654

The revenue year of 1900-01 was affected by the famine which ended in that year. The receipts for 1907-08 were:—

	Rs.
Ordinary Land Revenue and cesses	26,99,626
Miscellaneous Land Revenue ..	65,260
Stamps	2,92,689
Excise	7,50,168
Forest	1,32,034
Registration	36,040
Income tax	67,126

Income tax has been levied since 1904. Some similar tax called '*pāndhri*' appears to have been previously levied, and from 1862 to 1904 the town fund tax was collected.

Excise.

206. Excise revenue is derived from European liquor, country spirits (*dāru*), opium, *gānja*, and *tādi*. Country spirits of 25 under proof and 60 under proof are made from the mahuā flower and sold under the contract-distillery or Madras system. Revenue is derived from a duty on the spirit and from the sale of the right of private vend. The Local Administration has the option of applying in the District different rates of duty; the present rates are Rs. 3-2 per proof gallon for the Akola, Akot, Murtizāpur, and Bālāpur tāluks, and R. 1-14 for the Bāsim and Mangrul tāluks. The liquor is manufactured at the Government Distillery at Akola by Messrs. Umrigar and Co. of Bombay. A warehouse has been built, or is under construction, at each tāluk headquarters, except in the case of Bāsim, where the old tahsīl building is being adapted for the purpose. At each warehouse a Government Sub-Inspector and an Agent of the firm are stationed, who watch and record every stage

in the preparation of the liquor. In the warehouse the liquor is diluted by water and brought to a strength at which issue is sanctioned; that is, it must be either 25 under proof (*rāshi*) or 60 under proof (*bewada*). Retail vendors purchase on a pass from the sub-treasury, where the wholesale price together with the duty is paid. The right of retail vend is auctioned annually. Usually this right is sold separately for each village containing a shop and payment is made by monthly instalments. Occasionally owing to the proximity of two or more shops a group composed of these shops is auctioned. The District in 1907-08 contained 193 shops, or one to every 21 square miles. The average value of a shop in the same financial year was Rs. 1400. Since May 1908 the consumption of liquor has fallen very considerably owing to indifferent crops and a temperance agitation connected with politics. Toddy, *tādi*, is procured from the *sindi* tree, which is scarce; and the revenue from the liquor is consequently small. Opium is imported by Government from the Ghazipur Factory and is issued to retail vendors at Rs. 23-8 a seer. The privilege of retail vend is sold by auction; and the proceeds for 1907-08 were Rs. 61,047. Opium is smoked and given to infants, invalids, and old people of all castes. The manufacture of *gānja* in the District is prohibited. It is imported from the Government store house at Khandwa in packages of one seer, and a duty of Rs. 5 per seer is paid by the wholesale vendors. The District contains seven licensees, to whom licenses are issued free. As in the case of country liquor and opium the right of retail vend is put to auction. In 1907-08 the sale proceeds amounted to Rs. 13,355. Owing to the comparatively low price of the drug in His Highness the Nizām's Dominions considerable quantities of *gānja* are smuggled over the border into the District, and the revenue therefore is small. Some five or six licenses for the sale of European liquors are issued. A demand exists among certain castes for cheap and inferior European spirit, but it is not the policy of Government to facilitate drinking in opposition to caste rules.

District and Tāluk Boards.

207. The District Board came into existence in 1889. It consists of 44 members, of whom 36 are chosen by a process of double election and the others nominated. The primary electors are cultivators who pay not less than Rs. 100 land revenue, all male adults who formerly paid a certain amount of town-fund assessment, and all patels and patwāris. They elect twelve representatives who form, together with six nominated members, Tāluk Boards, and these bodies each elect six of their number to sit on the District Board. The total income of the District Board as estimated in the budget for 1906-1907 was Rs. 2,58,730, and that for 1907-08 was Rs. 2,72,716. It is almost entirely drawn from cesses levied along with land revenue, cattle pound receipts, weekly market receipts, and contributions from Provincial revenues. Until recently fees for education were also received by the Board, but these are now taken by the school committees. In 1907-08 the estimated amounts from each of the above sources were:—

	Rs.
Cesses	1,40,711
Cattle Pound Receipts	11,895
Weekly Bazar Receipts	39,715
Provincial Contributions	53,800

Of the last item Rs. 25,600 were given for education, Rs. 16,800 for civil works, and Rs. 11,400 for general purposes. On the 1st of April 1909 the District Board had a balance in hand of Rs. 3,64,854. In 1907-08 the following amounts were provided for the various main objects:—

	Rs.
Establishment	8,522
Pension Fund	10,910
Education	64,405
Medical	26,246
Civil Works	1,40,887

The District Board and Tāluk Boards are responsible for the upkeep of roads not maintained by the Public Works Department, primary schools, public wells and tanks, cattle pounds, and local works or measures likely to promote the health, comfort, or convenience of the public, besides being partially responsible for relief works in times of famine or scarcity. In the important towns and villages which have no Municipal Committees conservancy establishments are maintained out of the Board's funds, and a scheme of arboricultural operations to be carried out by the Board is also now in force. This scheme provides for the planting and maintenance of avenues along the main roads not belonging to the Public Works Department.

Municipalities.

208. The four municipal towns in the District are Akola, Bāsim, Akot, and Kāranja. The Akola Municipality was first constituted in 1868, and the number of members on the Committee is 24, of whom six are nominated and 18 are elected; the Deputy Commissioner has always been the Chairman. The income in 1907-08 was Rs. 60,180 and the expenditure was Rs. 71,110. The town requires extending, and a proper system of drainage and an improved water-supply are the most urgent wants. The Bāsim Municipality started life in 1869 and has three nominated members and nine elected members on the Committee; the town has fallen in importance since the

abolition of the Bāsim District. In 1907-08 the municipal income was Rs. 22,677 and the expenditure Rs. 22,028. Akot became a municipal area in 1884. Of the members of the Committee three are nominated and nine elected. In 1907-08 the income and expenditure were Rs. 16,062 and Rs. 19,533 respectively. Like Akot, Kāranja is a small municipal town, and the benefits of the municipal rule were extended to it in 1895. The number of the members of the Committee is twelve, and the electoral system will be brought into force in April 1909. All the Municipalities depend for their income on taxes imposed on houses and lands, trades and professions, animals and vehicles, bales of cotton ginned and pressed, scavenging tax, pound receipts, surplus cotton market receipts, and slaughter-house fees. No octroi is in force, but the Akola Municipal Committee have recently imposed a toll tax on vehicles and animals coming into municipal limits. The main heads of expenditure are: establishments, lighting, water-supply, drainage, conservancy, education, and medical.

Village sanitation.

209. No Village Sanitation Act is in force, but in a few of the larger villages sanitary Committees supervise the conservancy with pecuniary assistance from the District Board. Villages are as a rule dirty and insanitary, and considerable difficulty is experienced in persuading the people to adopt cleanly habits.

Public Works.

210. For purposes of the Public Works Department Murtizāpur tāluk is in the East Berār Division and the remaining five taluks are in the West Berār Division. Executive Engineers are stationed at Amraoti and Akola, and Subdivisional Officers at Akola and Bāsim. The District contains 156 miles of metalled road. Among the principal buildings are the district courts and offices and the jail,

at Akola. Other buildings include the tahsīls, hospitals and dispensaries, inspection bungalows, and police stations.

Police.

211. The sanctioned strength of the police force is 704 officers and men. These comprise one District Superintendent of Police, one Assistant Superintendent of Police, one Deputy Superintendent of Police, one Reserve Inspector, one Prosecuting Inspector, one City Inspector, five Circle Inspectors, one Sergeant, 25 Sub-Inspectors, 106 head constables, 560 constables, and three camel sowārs. The Muhammadan members of the force number about 200, and a large number of men, known as Pardeshis, from Upper India are enlisted. The District contained 28 station-houses, five outposts, and four road-posts in the year 1908. The station circles are now being re-arranged, and the five outposts will be replaced by stations.

Jail.

212. The District jail was formerly one of the two central jails of Berār, and has accommodation for 465 convicts and 30 undertrial prisoners. The average daily number of prisoners in the last three years has been 163, and that of undertrial prisoners 23. The convicts are chiefly employed on stone-breaking, corn-grinding, and labour in the large garden attached to the jail.

Education.

213. A Government high school and a training school and Anglo-vernacular school are maintained at Akola together with 5 municipal schools. Anglo-vernacular schools are to be found at all tahsil headquarters. The District Board is responsible for primary schools in non-municipal towns and villages. Girls' schools were formerly maintained by the local bodies but they have now been taken over by Government. Low caste boys pay no fees. A

technical school was opened a few years ago at Bāsim, but its progress has not been entirely satisfactory. The American Alliance Mission maintains a small industrial school at Akola where carpentry and kindred trades are taught. A scheme to develop and enlarge this school is now under consideration. The total number of schools in the District is at present 240. Education is popular and most schools lack sufficient accommodation. Vernacular weekly papers number four, all published in Akola town; one sometimes contains English articles.

Medical relief.

214. The District contains 12 hospitals and dispensaries with a certain amount of accommodation for indoor patients. The daily average of indoor patients during the last three years has been 23 and that of outdoor patients 559; while the annual number of operations was 2419. The salaries of the staff are paid by Government, and the local bodies give fixed annual contributions towards the upkeep of the dispensaries. Private subscriptions are also collected and the fee system is in force. No leper or lunatic asylum is maintained in the District. Vaccination is compulsory only in municipal towns, but it is carried on throughout the District. The special vaccination staff consists of one Superintendent, one Assistant, and eleven vaccinators. The annual cost of carrying on vaccination is Rs. 32,501, and the annual proportion of successful operations for the last three years has been 35 per mille of the population. During epidemics of plague inoculation has been resorted to, and the people are becoming less opposed to this form of prevention.

APPENDIX.

GAZETTEER OF TALUKS, TOWNS, IMPORTANT VILLAGES, RIVERS, AND HILLS.

APPENDIX.

GAZETTEER OF TALUKS, TOWNS, IMPORTANT VILLAGES, RIVERS, AND HILLS.

Adgaon.—Adgaon is a village in Akot tāluk nine miles west of Akot. It was the head of a pargana when the Ain-i-Akbari was compiled, and it has an earthen *kila*, fort, in which a *naib* was stationed under the Nizām; the pargana was only included in Akot tāluk in 1865, and a petty Civil Judge held his court here for some time after that; the population was 3437 in 1867 and 3131 in 1909. Adgaon is therefore a place of some slight importance, but it contains little of interest. The river Nandini flows close by and holds water throughout the hot season; there are also numerous wells, as is indicated by the name. A broad strip of land near the village, uncultivated for the last ten years, marks the route of the proposed Bāsim-Akola-Khandwa Railway. A number of temples exist, but none are large or striking; that of Dwārkeshwar, built outside the village in 1080 F. (A.D. 1671) by a Gaoli called Dwārki who was an officer of the Bhonslas, has two elephants fairly well carved over the doorway; the shrine of Dattātreya, built recently by Mānu Mānbhau, is known for the relief of people possessed by evil spirits. The great battle of Argaum was fought on 29th November 1803 near Sirsoli, three miles south of Adgaon, and brought to an end the authority of the Nāgpur Rājā in Berār. Sirsoli is a village of 1889 inhabitants; old men still repeat what their fathers saw of the battle. According to their account the chief fighting took place on some waste ground, now covered with *bābul* trees but then open, immediately to the west of the village, and the marks of two cannon-balls are shown on the wall of a small temple near by. Fighting was however spread over a large area. The grave of Major Bullock, a name well known in Berār, lies a mile north of the village, and another English officer is said to have been killed to the south of it. A watercourse of some size runs roughly north and south, but the ground is mostly flat. The Gazetteer of 1870 says, 'A deep ravine or watercourse 'is still shown which lay across the rear of the broken 'army and checked their confused retreat until they had 'been sufficiently sabred by cavalry and pounded by guns.' Old men say that Sirsoli had then stronger fortifications than most villages and the people of other places came for shelter, neither man nor beast going outside for seven days; no harm was done to the village and no soldier from either side entered it. The people add however that the battle lasted for the whole seven days and that the gates were too strong for either army to force. They relate also that Benising, a defeated general of the Bhonsla's, fleeing toward Narnāla killed first his children and then himself.

Akola Tāluk.—Akola tāluk lies between latitudes 20° 53′ N. and 20° 23′ S. and longitudes 77° 25′ E. and 76° 54′ W; it is a block with an average length of about 30 miles from north to south and a breadth of about 25 miles from east to west; its area is 739 square miles. The tāluk is an old one and contained 401 villages at the original settlement in 1867, but several of these were transferred to Bālāpur in the changes connected with the formation of Khāmgaon tāluk in 1870, and the total is now 354 villages, of which 339 are *khālsa* and 19 *jāgīr*. It has Bālāpur tāluk on the west, Akot and Daryāpur on the north, across the Pūrna river, Murtizāpur on the east, and Mangrul and Bāsim on the south, so that it occupies the very middle of the District. The north, east, and centre of the tāluk consist of fertile plain with rich black soil, but some miles in the extreme south are hilly, with shallow and inferior soil, and this poor soil runs halfway up the eastern border; however rice is grown in the east. The greatest height recorded is 1442 feet at Saukhed in the south; next come Rudrama hill in Rajankhed village, Haldoli, and Pimpalgaon in the south with 1384, 1367, and 1347; while all other heights recorded, including Māhān (1206), are between 1200 and 1300; higher land occurs across the southern borders. The drainage of the tāluk is from south to north. The Morna on the west and Kāte-purna toward the east, with several tributaries of the latter, hold water all the year round; the Lonār, in the middle of the northern part, has water through most of the cold weather, but there are no other streams of any importance. Wells number on an average eleven to a village, but there is often a scarcity of good water, especially in the salt tract in the north. The chief tanks are at Ghusar and Akhatwāda in the north, but they are apt to fail in the hot weather. The total area is 473,000 acres, of which 50,000 are forest, 400,000 occupied for cultivation, and 361,000 actually cropped; only 900 acres of cultivable land are left unoccupied. Between 1900 and 1906 jawāri varied between 120,000 and 170,000 acres, with a tendency to decrease, while cotton varied from 165,000 to 190,000 acres, inclining to increase, so that it constantly exceeded jawāri. Other crops are comparatively unimportant; wheat, gram, and linseed each varied from 5000 or 6000 to 14,000 or 16,000 acres, one gaining what another lost, but for the last three years wheat had the largest area; in most of the six years til covered less than 4000 acres; there was no irrigation. The Nāgpur branch of the Great Indian Peninsula Railway passes from west to east for 22 miles across the northern part of the tāluk, with stations at Akola, Yāwalkhed, Borgaon, and Kātepurna; the line here is still single. A metalled road runs north from Akola to Akot, having a length of 11 miles within the tāluk, and another runs south to Bāsim and Pusad, having 15 miles within the tāluk, so that traffic centres in Akola. Country roads are numerous and are mostly very good for bullock carts throughout the busy season, that is in the cold weather, and some of them have been much improved by the District Board. Weekly markets are held at fourteen places, that at Akola being the chief. Sāngwi in the north is also important, partly because it is conveniently situated for travelling merchants on their way to the big markets of Akot tāluk; Borgaon, where a bi-weekly market is held, is also of considerable size. Large fairs are held at Pinjar in Ashādh and Kārtik (both during the rains) and at Sindkhed, on the Morna river, in April, but a weekly market which used to be held at the latter village has been almost ruined by the opening of a new one at Rājanda, two miles to the south. Factories for ginning cotton number 25 and those for pressing it 13 ; Akola town has a distillery, two cloth mills, and two steam oil mills. Hand manufactures are dying out here as elsewhere. The population of the 335 *khālsa* villages increased by 25 per cent. between 1867 and 1891; that of the old tāluk was 110,000 in 1867, and that of the present tāluk 139,000 in 1881, 138,000 in 1891, and 150,000 in 1901, when the density was 204 persons to the square mile. During the famine decade no other tāluk in Berār had as large an absolute increase of population as Akola, and only Mangrul had as much proportionate increase. The tāluk in 1901 contained seven towns or villages with a population exceeding 2000, Akola, Bārsi-Tākli, Borgaon, Pinjar, Ugwa, Kurankhed, and Māhān. No description of Ugwa is given elsewhere because it is a commonplace village; it has a fairly good position near the Akot metalled road; its population was 2655 in 1891 and 2473 in 1901. Māhān, on the Kātepurna river in the south, is of more ancient importance, as it was the head-quarters of a small pargana. Its population in 1891 was 1802 and in 1901 it was 2239. It stands on level ground with fairly good soil close to the southern hills and is specially distinguished from a distance by a large white house built some years ago by a Muhammadan trader. A case of *sati* occurred in 1908 at Deodari, a few miles south of Māhān; the mourners said they left the spot while the body was still burning and the widow threw herself upon the pyre and was killed; the couple were of the Gaoli caste. The widow is said to have been a childless woman of about 30 and her husband had been 40. Kurankhed is situated on the Kātepurna river in the east of the tāluk within two miles of the railway. It was also the head of a pargana, and had a population of 2560 in 1891 and 2316 in 1901. During the settlement period, according to the Settlement Report of 1896, cultivation in the tāluk increased by five per cent., leaving only 320 acres unoccupied out of an available total of 370,000 acres, so that practically all the land was taken up; the numbers of wells, plough cattle, other cattle, houses, and population all increased from 32 to 57 per cent., horses by 14 and carts by 90 per cent., and there was great general prosperity; this was somewhat checked by the famine of 1899-1900. The first settlement was introduced in 1867, when the maximum rates varied from R. 1 As. 4 to Rs. 2 As.4 and were generally Rs. 2 or a few annas less. A revision settlement was introduced in the year 1897-1898, when the maximum rates varied from R. 1 As. 14 to Rs. 2 As. 10; the higher rate was applied to more than half of the tāluk. The total land revenue in the year 1907-1908 was Rs. 5,71,263 (apart from cesses). Police stations are situated at Akola, Bārsi Tākli, Borgaon, and Pinjar, and there are two hospitals at Akola. Government schools in 1908 numbered 52, besides a training college with 67 pupils. Among the schools were 42 Marāthi schools for boys and three for girls, four Hindustāni schools for boys and two for girls, and one high school; the average attendance was reported as 57. Private schools are rare and of little importance.

Akola Town.—Akola town, the headquarters of the District, stands in latitude 20° 43′ N. and longitude 77° 04′ E. at an elevation of 925 feet above sea-level. The Morna river, a tributary of the Pūrna, flows through it. The part on the west bank, enclosed by a wall, is known as *shahar*, while Tājnāpeth, on the east bank, contains the Government buildings and the civil station; most of the population now live in Tājnāpeth. Floods used to form a great barrier, so that the Muhammadans had a *jamā masjid* on each side of the river, but at one time a floating bridge was in use, traces of which still remain, and traffic now passes over a good stone bridge opened in 1873. The Nāgpur line of the Great Indian Peninsula Railway passes within municipal limits at one point, though only a few quarters recently inhabited lie to the north of it. All trains stop at Akola, and the station has a fine platform, but the entrance is across a lofty and very inconvenient bridge over a siding. The embankment of the proposed Khandwa-Akola-Bāsim Railway lies to the east of the town. The municipality has an area of 1674 acres and contains the whole of eight revenue villages and parts of three others; the land is all *khālsa* and, according to Berār custom, no rent accrues to either Government or the municipality except for 66 acres bought by the latter. The population was 12,236 in 1867, 16,614 in 1881, 21,470 in 1891, and 29,289 in 1901, so that Akola is the second largest town in Berār. At the last census Hindus numbered 21,000, Muhammadans 7500, Christians 360, Jains 230, Animistics 90, Pārsis 83, and Sikhs 3. The revenue and expenditure of the municipality are about Rs. 70,000; no octroi is levied, but in 1908 a toll was instituted on animals and carts entering the town. The water-supply is obtained chiefly from wells at Majhoda, ten miles to the south, but this is insufficient and people also use wells; the Morna river is dammed in two places near the town, comparatively small barriers holding up the water for a distance of three miles or more, and this probably helps to maintain the level of water in the wells. Masonry drains have been made for the *shahar* and part of the *peth*, and large intercepting drains are being built along the banks of the river to prevent the sullage water polluting it within the town. Few gardens exist at Akola, owing to lack of water, but one is maintained by Government. In the *peth* are the usual offices connected with the headquarters of a District, including a jail with accommodation for 560 prisoners, a sessions court, Anglican and Roman Catholic places of worship, buildings belonging to the Alliance Mission, a small European club, a native club, a library known by the name of Bābuji Deshmukh, a rest-house called Pestonji *sarai* or Bymonji *sarai* after its builder and its restorer, a large town hall and municipal office, a hospital, a high school, a block of buildings connected with the name Rām or Shrirām, and other buildings of a public nature. The Shrirām temple and theatre are built side by side, the latter having been constructed by the temple authorities out of funds given on trust by Bachulāl Gondulāl, while the front has been occupied with good shops. The whole scheme has been admirably carried out and has provided Akola with some valuable buildings. The buildings of the *shahar* are not as a rule striking, but among the more interesting are the temples of Lakshmi Nārāyaṇ and Ganpati and a new Jain temple; the Muhammadans have several mosques and a great number of tombs; there are several Government schools of different grades, and a so-called national school is just being started by voluntary effort. Beside the Shiwani road are a Pārsi tower of silence and the farm settlement, Santa Barbara, of the Alliance Mission; a rifle-range has been laid out near the station and a race-course near the Malkāpur road; and there is a Government experimental farm on the Bāsim road 3 miles south of Akola. The town stands in a good position for trade; the Akot road brings it most of the traffic of a very wealthy tract on the north, and the Bāsim road is the main outlet of an extensive area on the south; practically the whole trade of Bāsim tāluk, much from Pusad, and some from the Nizām's Dominions follows this road to Akola. Cotton is the chief article of commerce, and the principal dealers are Mārwāris who operate largely by means of money advanced by the different banks. Part of their transactions, connected with the forward delivery of different articles, is known as *satta* and forms a branch of speculation bordering closely on gambling, but it has decreased of recent years. Factories for ginning and pressing cotton number 21 and 12 respectively. The Native Ginning Pressing and Spinning Company started a weaving mill a few years ago, and the Akola and Mid-India Mill, occupying a large structure, began work toward the end of 1908; it was rumoured in some villages that a child was to be buried under its boilers Two firms of recent origin express by steam the oil of linseed and til-seed, exporting the oil chiefly to the

Central Provinces and the oil-cake to England. A distillery provides *dāru*, the liquor made from the mahuā plant, for a large area. A large number of carters and cartwrights live in the town and various petty industries are carried on; the workshop of the Alliance Mission, under the direction of Mr. R. M. Stanley, helps to set a good standard. Shops are fairly well-stocked and occasionally have a customers' chair outside; the weekly market attracts large numbers on Sundays. Labour, rent, and farm produce are dear. The civil station is simply but neatly laid out; a large open space where cricket and football are played separates it from the town. The surrounding country, though fertile, is flat and unpicturesque; Akola is very hot, but the heat is dry and relieved by cool nights. Jānu, a wealthy Mahār of Pāras in Bālāpur tāluk, caused a boarding-house to be opened a few years ago so that Mahār boys from the country might attend the Akola schools. More recently a night-school, now attended by 32 adult Mahārs, has been started; the funds were chiefly provided by natives of higher caste, and the scheme owes a great deal to Mr. Vishnu Moreshwar Mahājani. The town contains the ruins of a fortress and a wall; some of the gateways are still in good condition, but there are no buildings with striking associations. A Hindustāni school called *hawā-khāna*, taking the air, is held in a building in the highest part of the fort, and an old gun near by is fired at midday; a small tower on the north-west has a spike apparently meant for a gun to turn on. An inscription on the Dahihanda gate gives its date as 1114 Hijri, A.D. 1697, 'during the reign of the Emperor Aurangzeb Alamgir when Nawāb Asadkhān was minister *Jāgirdār* in the time of Khwāja Abdul Latīf.' Another on the Fatehburuj bastion near by has no exact date, but mentions the same Khwājā; the Emperor however is Shāh Alam and the minister Asaf-ud-daula. One on the *idgāh*, place of prayer, contains texts and a statement that the building was finished by Khwāja Abdul Latīf in 1116 Hijri. A Marāthi inscription on the gate called Agarwes says that it was built by Govind Appāji in, apparently, A.D. 1843. According to the Berār Gazetteer of 1870, p. 160, 'Akola 'may have got promoted above the ordinary rank of sub-'stantial villages about the beginning of the 18th century. 'It had for a long time been the headquarters of a sub-'district before the British took charge of this country. 'There was one fight here (date uncertain) between the 'Nizām's forces and the Marāthas; and in 1790 the Pindāri 'Ghāzi Khān got worsted before the town by the Bhonslā's 'commander. General Wellesley encamped at this place 'for a day in 1803 (going hence through Andura to 'Adgaon or Argaum). The people now (1870) say that the 'prosperity of the place was severely damaged some 30 or '40 years ago by the uncommonly bad administration of a 'tālukdār, who robbed inordinately himself and did not 'keep off other robbers; so there was a great emigration 'to Amraoti.' An exhibition was held at Akola in 1868; the town is said to have been at that time almost in ruins, but Government cleared some of these away, built shops along newly planned streets, and sold the shops. A large square tomb stands on the north of the Shiwani road about a mile and a half from the town; it is said to mark the grave of a single military officer; several smaller European tombs lie near the town. The present *kila*, fortress, was built, according to tradition, by a *naib* called Sāle Muhammad Khān who held the *tankhwāh* from the Nizām; it was dismantled by Government in about 1870. In 1842 or 1843 a great fight between Muhammadans and Rājputs seemed imminent at Akola. One cause of quarrel was that the Rājputs began to build a stone house on a platform near the east end of the bridge, still called *Rājputonki gadhi*; the *khatīb* had given them the platform but said they had no right to do this. Presently the Rājputs killed a Muhammadan Momin, turban-maker, on the road to Bārsi Tākli, and then great forces of Muhammadans and Rājputs gathered from all parts of Berār. Troops belonging to the Contingent Force were brought from Ellichpur, and Khān Bahādur Muassan Sāhib, Maulvi of Bālāpur, used his influence with the Muhammadans, and in the end the danger was averted. Muhammadans used to get a great deal of semi-military employment; thus until 1853 there was a guard of perhaps 15 men at every gate, and the English at first gave somewhat similar employment to *daroga's*. Formerly when a new Naib came he would call in a local Muhammadan with a few men as orderlies, and these would get the attendant perquisites till another Naib came and engaged someone else. For more serious work a force of about 50 Arabs used to be kept. In those days no Muhammadan went outside his house without being fully armed, nor did a Rājput, but practically no other Hindu carried any weapon. Brawls and fights used constantly to occur between Muhammadans of different *muhallas*, and between Muhammadans and Hindus at festivals, but the Rājputs, who were comparatively a small body, never fought among themselves. General Doveton was here for some months before he took Nāgpur in 1817; the force was camped on the ground now occupied by the Deputy Commissioner's *kacheri* and the jail; it left behind such thousands of *sharāb* bottles that the boys of two generations found the supply endless for stone throwing. A great flood happened in about 1833 and another, not quite as large, in about 1885. The *kāzi* (Mirza Abbās Beg, *khatīb* and *naib-kāzi*), whose reminiscences have been largely used in this section, has seen the rent of certain fields rise from R. 1 to Rs. 100 an acre, the wages of an agricultural servant rise from Rs. 2 to Rs. 8 a month, and the price of jawāri and *ghī* increase 75 per cent. According to tradition Akola was founded by Akolsing, a Rājput of Kānheri, a village six miles away, and took its name from him. The site of the town was covered with thick jungle and the only building was a temple of Mahādeo. Akolsing's wife used to visit the temple alone to worship the god, but her husband became suspicious of her motives and finally followed her with a drawn sword. When she found him at the door she prayed to the god to give her an eternal place of refuge; whereon the head of the image opened and she disappeared within it. Her husband was in time to grasp her *sāri*, and the only trace left of her was a piece of the cloth which for years protruded from the head of the image. Akolsing mourned for his wife and made a settlement on the spot where he had last seen her. He moreover built an earthen *gadhi*, village-fort, on the place where the present *kilā* stands; the spot was indicated to him by the prodigy of a hare pursuing a dog across it.

Akot Tāluk.—Akot tāluk lies between 21° 16′ N. and 20° 51′ S. and between 77° 12′ E. and 76° 46′ W. It was first settled in 1868, when it contained 331 villages, but 71 villages were transferred to Daryāpur tāluk on the formation of the latter, and one village has been given to, and five villages have been received from, Jalgaon tāluk. It now contains 264 *khālsa* and two *jāgīr* villages and has an area of 517 square miles, so that it is the smallest—though perhaps the richest—in the District. It is a compact tract roughly square in shape and with an average length from north to south of 26 miles and a breadth of 20 miles. On the north lies the Melghāt tāluk of Amraoti District, the boundary being marked by a line of fine *ghāts*; a narrow tongue runs up in one place to the fortress of Narnāla. The southern boundary is the Pūrna river, with Bālāpur and Akola tāluks beyond it. On the east is the Daryāpur ṭāluk of Amraoti District and on the west the Jalgaon tāluk of Buldāna District. Akot tāluk is almost entirely plain, though in the south a few nullahs running from east to west cause considerable depressions and the extreme north includes some of the rough ground at the foot of the Sātpurā ranges. The soil is deep, black, and free from stones through the greater part of the tāluk, but a belt of six or eight miles in width along the north is stony and much lighter, falling in parts under the description of 'white' soil. The only large river is the Pūrna on the southern border, but a large number of small ones, dry for the greater part of the year, join it from the north. The Shāhānur, which formerly flowed for some miles past Dahihanda and Kadholi, was diverted in the famine of 1896-1897 from the former village to join the Pūrna two miles away, and has from that time ceased to have a continuous current. Many of the small streams hold water for months near the hills, where the ground is much cut up by nullahs, but disappear in their lower courses. The Pathāl, which is an example of this, also illustrates other characteristics of these rivers. It has changed its course in the last five years so much near Warur that 4 acres of good land have been washed out of two fields, survey numbers 26 and 27, and 8 acres have been left dry in the old bed. In one field a dam was built 17 or 18 years ago to hold up the water to supply cattle, but the stream has merely eaten away the soil on both sides and carried off about an acre of valuable land. Such large variations are however unusual. Many villages in the southern half of the tāluk suffer severely from lack of water, complicated by the fact that throughout a large area water when found is likely to be too brackish to drink. In some cases drinking water is generally obtained only from shallow *jhiras* sunk in watercourses, and has during the hot weather to be fetched from a village two miles away, while cattle have to be sent even a greater distance. Occasional wells have been sunk both by the local boards and by pious individuals, but the difficulty is far from being removed. In the north of the tāluk mango groves are frequent and country roads are sometimes lined strikingly with trees and flowers, but old men say that waste land, water, and trees have immensely decreased in the last 50 or 60 years. People at Panchagawhān point to one or two solitary trees as the sole survivors of a jungle between the village and the river which as children they feared to pass through, and similar reminiscences are given elsewhere. The tāluk has been fully cultivated for many years, though irrigation is scarcely practised at all. Statistics for the last 6 years show that he area of the tāluk is 331,000 acres, of which on an average 310,900 have been occupied for cultivation and 302,000 have been cropped. Jawāri has 100,500 acres, cotton 178,000, and the *rabi* crops have 126,000 acres. Communications are distinctly good without being quite satisfactory. A good made road runs 28 miles south from Akot to the railway at Akola, 17 miles lying within the tāluk. A made branch road, passing about two miles south-east of Panchagawhān and fording the Pūrna at Andura, connects this with Shegaon, with a length of 18 miles within the tāluk. A third road runs north from Akot to Khatkāli in the Melghāt and bears a large timber traffic. A fourth, less carefully maintained, runs 10 miles north from Adsul to Telhāra. The country roads of the tāluk are generally excellent during the dry months, the soil being so fine over large areas that constant traffic fails even to cause awkward ruts, though there is apt to be a very great deal of dust. The tāluk has an unusual number of large and wealthy villages; places with a population of more than 2000 number 38 in the whole District, but Akot tāluk alone has 12—Akot, Hiwarkhed, Telhāra, Mundgaon, Adgaon, Dahihanda, Belkhed, Akolkhed, Pāthardi, Dānāpur, Mālegaon, and Akoli Jāgīr. Most of these are described separately in the Appendix, but some are of little interest. Akolkhed (2525), Akoli (2089), and Panaj (1298) are two miles apart in the north-east of the tāluk, and from 5 to 7 miles distant from Akot. Large villages have to a curious extent formed at short intervals across the north of the tāluk; immigrants from the Central Provinces, known as Jhādiwālas, now help to continue the process; they are mostly labourers and petty artisans, but a few take fields on *batai*; their houses have a slightly different look from those of true Berāris. At Panaj the Muhammadans are said to be increasing in numbers and prosperity; they were not formerly important in the village. Akolkhed has about 200 families of Mālis, 150 of Jhādiwālas (of different castes), and 120 of Kunbis; Akoli has about 100 families each of Kunbis, Mālis, and Mahārs, besides less numerous castes. Akoli is a *jāgīr* of Shri Sitārām Mahārāj, whose *sasthān*, sacred place, is at Hyderābād, but no temple in his name stands in the village. Pāthardi (2402) is 7 miles south-west of Akot. Manufactures are of little importance, but there are 21 factories for ginning and 5 for pressing cotton; and rough carpets are well made at Akot town. Weekly markets number 14 and, without being unusually numerous, are far more important here than in any other tāluk. The largest are those at Akot, Mundgaon, and Mālegaon, the contracts for collecting dues in each of these selling for Rs. 4000 or more, but those at Asegaon (Rs. 1275), and Akoli Jāgīr (Rs. 1150) are also far larger than the average bazar of the District. The tāluk has an extraordinary number of tombs and temples dedicated to saints, and most of these are the sites of annual fairs; the largest is that at Narsingboa's temple in Akot in Kārtik (October-November). The original settlement came into force in the year 1868-1869, when most villages in the north were rated at Rs. 2-4 and most in the south at Rs. 2, but a few were rated at R. 1-12. A revision settlement came into force in 1898-1899; the new rates varied from Re. 1-14 to Rs. 2-12, but the most common was Rs. 2-10; the land revenue in the year 1907-1908 was Rs. 612,344, which is more than is yielded by any other tāluk in the District. Police stations are to be situated at Akot, Hiwarkhed, Telhāra, and Dahihanda. Government schools in 1908 numbered 51, with a combined average attendance of 2300.

Akot Town.—The town of Akot is the headquarters of the tāluk of the same name and is situated 28 miles north of Akola. A first-class road under the Public Works Department joins the two. It crosses a few considerable undulations in the south of Akot tāluk, but none of these is sufficient to cause much difficulty to traffic. The ford of and ascent from the Pūrna river, in the tenth mile from Akola, cause more inconvenience, but are not a serious difficulty during the greater part of the year. The population of Akot was 14,006 in 1867, 16,137 in 1881, 15,995 in 1891, and 18,252 in 1901. Besides other institutions the town has a dispensary, an Anglo-vernacular school with a ninth standard, a new boarding-house which cost Rs. 13,000, and bazars on Wednesdays and Sundays, the latter having sales estimated at Rs. 30,000. A municipality was founded in 1884; its income and expenditure amount to Rs. 16,000 or Rs. 17,000. The town contains a cotton market and ten ginning and four pressing factories;

the value of the cotton bales exported from them is said to be Rs. 5,00,000. *Sāhukāri*, moneylending and investment, is carried on largely, and there is a considerable trade in timber from the Melghāt. Good carpets of a plain make are manufactured, the daily bazars are fairly large and busy, and petty industries, such as a primitive kind of rope-making, are carried on. Approaching from Akola one passes first through a belt of factories which give a large idea of the business of the town; the shopping centres have a characteristic mark of city life in a tea vendor with a *chūla*, a kind of tin urn, and a charcoal stove. The town consists of three revenue villages, Jogaban, Chinchkhed, and Kamlāpur, and is fairly compact, though a part on the south-east, called Somwārpeth, is separated from the rest by the Khai nullah. The houses used to be mostly thatched but are now generally tiled, the walls being usually of mud but sometimes of brick; almost every house has its own well. Akot has long been of some little importance; it had a mud wall and six gates which have now disappeared; the tahsīli stands in what used to be the fortress, *kilā*, and has a lofty brick gate as an entrance; a considerable proportion of the people are Muhammadans. The most striking buildings are some old private houses, the residences of former officials, which have fine wood-carving on a large scale. The best is perhaps Diwākar Bhau's *diwānkhāna*, but the *havelis* of Sardārsing, who is said to have been in command of Narnāla fortress, and of the Fadnavīs, who is said to have been in financial charge of the tāluk on behalf of the Bhonslas (with the duty, for instance, of paying the Pindāri bands), are also good. The latter building has large and strong cellars which were possibly meant for defensive purposes. The *sardeshmukh*, or chief deshmukh, says that a long underground passage leads from his house to a distant garden. A small hill, called after the tomb of Pīr Shāh Darya Sāhib and having a mosque upon it, was the scene of an attack by the local Rājputs upon the Muhammadans. It happened that a Muhammadan upon the hill jested with a Rājput woman on the roof of a house close by. That night a band of Rājputs came to the gateway in the wall that surrounded the hill, declared that they were Muhammadans, and asked to be admitted. When the door was opened they made a sudden rush and killed a number of the Muhammadans. A less credible story says that an underground passage used to lead from a well, now fallen in, upon the top of the hill to Narnāla, 11 miles away, and that this was proved by the sole survivor of a score of sheep turned loose at Narnāla appearing at the bottom of the well. Akot has also some buildings of religious interest. Close to the Akola road on one side is the domed tomb of Gada Nārāyan, which is very much like the *ghumat* at Dharud, while on the other is the smaller tomb of Mīr Najar Karoda with a resident *fakīr*. Both of these, and the *jama masjid*, which is not striking, have Persian inscriptions. Gada Nārāyan was considered a saint by both Muhammadans and Hindus, so that the two religions have joined in giving him a double name, but his personality is now forgotten and his tomb neglected. A descendant of Mīr Najar Karoda has an *inām* for the second tomb and maintains a small *urus*, sacred gathering, but again nothing is known about the saint. The tomb of Gaibi Pīr close by has a reputation for removing colds and fevers, for which people vow bread and vegetables to the *pīr*. Hindu temples are fairly numerous and of some size, but not very fine. That of Nandi Bāg has a bull carved in black stone with a fresh garland round its neck; there is a large but plain step-well close by. A temple to Nāna Sāhib of Pātur is covered with pictures. Other temples are dedicated to Bālāji and to Keshaorāja. The most important however is that of Narsingboa, about whom the Gazetteer of 1870 says, p. 192, 'The holy man now in the flesh at Akot 'has only taken over the business, as it were, from a 'Muhammadan *fakīr*, whose disciple he was during life; 'and now that the *fakīr* is dead Narsingboa presides over 'the annual veneration of his slippers'—a veneration which still continues. The saint died in 1887 and the building, which was erected by Māroti Ganesh Asalkār at a cost of perhaps Rs. 25,000, was begun before his death. A festival, said to be attended by 20,000 or 25,000 people, is held in Kārtik (October-November) and the presence of a Kitson light shows that it is managed with enterprise. Land measuring 120 acres has been made over for the support of the temple, and some income is also derived from a *haveli*, large private building, given by Māroti for use as a theatre. A printed life of Narsingboa gives an authoritative account of him. He was a Kunbi, but his mind had so marked a religious bent that in boyhood he used to be seen worshipping stones as gods. However he was married and had three children. He went daily to a Muhammadan saint, Kuwatali Shāh of Umra, and learnt from him. The Muhammadan explained that the only difference between religions was that they named God differently, upon which the Kunbi became his disciple, standing before him as a sign of devotion for 21 days without taking food. Narsingboa's family had taken refuge in the strong village of Sirsoli, 5 miles from Umra, on account of the Pindāris, and one day news reached him that his mother was dead. Kuwatali Shāh divined this and told him to go to her; upon his arrival and amid his lamentations life returned to the corpse and it comforted him and then expired again. Kuwatali Shāh then sent him to live at Akot, where he used to spend the day in the jungle playing with the god Vishnu and in the evening would take a little food and smoke a *chilam*, earthen pipe. An atheist, *nāstik*, once tried to destroy the image of Withoba at Pandharpur by a blow with a cannon-ball, and struck it upon the foot, which straightway began to bleed. Narsingboa, wearing only a turban of rags and a *langoti*, took the lead among the horrified worshippers. He applied medicine to the wound and prayed the image to heal itself, which it did, whereon faith was re-established and the atheist died. Gopāla, a follower of Narsingboa, had in his cellar a treasure guarded by a spirit, but Narsingboa destroyed the spirit and brought forth the treasure. He offered it first to his faithful disciple, the *sāhukār* Ganesh or Ganoba Naik, but the latter replied that the company of the saint was worth more than any treasure, so they left it with Gopāla. An incurably vicious cow was once offered to Narsingboa; he declined the gift but reproved the cow for conduct unbecoming in a goddess; whereon she became quiet and gave no further trouble. Once he bade the wife of Ganoba Naik to die, saying she had already enjoyed all that was good in life and further existence was unnecessary; either she or one of her sons must expire; and upon the day he fixed the pious woman breathed her last. Later he saved her granddaughter from dying during her marriage ceremony, ordering a cocoanut to be tied to her stomach till she recovered. Narsingboa took upon himself both a skin disease and an ear disease to save men who were suffering from them and came to him for relief. When Ganoba died his son Māroti went to Benāres to perform funeral ceremonies, and Narsingboa gave him a brass ring with injunctions never to part with it. Māroti went to bathe in the river Yamuna and gave the ring to his sister to hold meanwhile, but she lost it. Māroti addressed the river saying he would drown himself if he could not recover the ring, whereupon the Yamuna appeared to him in the form of a woman and told him who had taken it and where it would be found. Narsingboa knew all this before Māroti returned. The saint finally died on a day he had foretold, and was buried, at his own command, in a pit just dug for the building of his temple. The body of a Phul Māli saint called Khida is buried near that of Narsingboa. It was only at the bidding of the latter that the corpse of Khida closed its eyes, and, again at the word of the greater saint, four years after burial it was still whole and ate a morsel of bread. The management of the temple funds is still in the hands of Māroti Ganesh.

Alegaon.—Alegaon is a village on the river Nirguna in the south of Bālāpur tāluk and 17 miles from Bālāpur. It had a population of 2707 in 1891 and 2848 in 1901. A considerable traffic in timber passes through it, so that timber is lying in open spaces everywhere; a weekly market is held on Sundays. Alegaon is a place of pilgrimage for Mānbhāus, and especially, it appears, for the Bhoyars among them, the adherents who have not wholly separated themselves from worldly life or donned black garments. Fairs are held on Chaitra Pūrnima (April-May) and Kārtik Pūrnima (October-November), when pilgrims come from places 50 or 100 miles distant and sometimes even from Nāgpur. The objects of reverence are two temples, one of Wālkeshwar Mahārāj on the bank of the Nirguna and one of Uttareshwar in the *gāokos*, within the old village wall. It is said that an incarnation of Krishna passed through the village on his way from Iswi in Mehkar tāluk, ate some *wālka* fruit by the river-side, and left on the north (*utar*).

Ansing.—Ansing is about 15 miles south-east of

Bāsim; the Pusad road passes about half a mile from it and a metalled road branches off to the village. Ansing was the head of a pargana, and a large road formerly passed through it. The population was 1965 in 1891 and 2087 in 1901. The name is derived from that of the *rishi* Shringa, to whom a temple on a deserted *gāothān* half a mile away is dedicated. The building was apparently of a plain Hemādpanthi style originally but has gone through a rather nondescript restoration. The villagers have within recent years bought six fields for its support, the total income being however only Rs. 75 or Rs. 80. Water can always be got in a large plain step-well close by or in a nālâ adjoining. A *satīchā hāt*, *sati's* forearm, is carved on the side of the well, and a shrine dedicated to her stands near, but no particulars about her are known. The reason for carving only an arm in memory of a *sati* is not generally known but is said by some to be that the arm, protected by bangles, is not consumed; the body of the original Sati, who killed herself on account of a quarrel between her father Daksha and her husband Shiva, was torn limb from limb by the latter and fell in 51 different *pitha-sthānas*, and this may have some significance. Land in the neighbourhood is very light, often consisting of a span of earth with *khadak*, rock, beneath, so that much of it is assessed at only As. 8, though some rises to R. 1-8. The Dangrāla tank, which was cleaned in the famine of 1899-1900, holds water throughout the year and three others hold water for some months, but the supply is insufficient. The village has a police station, a school with four standards, and a weekly market. A short history of it was compiled by the village officers in about 1854, but the record states merely that from 1810 to 1837 it was in the hands of nine successive *maktedārs*, revenue contractors, each of whom 'populated the village by means of *jamādārs*', that is, sent out men to compel unwilling cultivators to come and live there. From 1838 to 1844 it was held by Messrs. Pestonji and Company, who seem to have leased out land on favourable terms, and though a different contractor appears for almost every year till the Assignment of 1853 it is merely recorded that they 'recovered rental.'

Bālāpur Tāluk.—Bālāpur tāluk lies between 20°55′ N. and 20°17′ S. and between 77°2′ E. and 67°38′ W. Bālāpur town was an important centre under the Nizām's administration and a Bālāpur tāluk has been in existence ever since the Assignment of 1853. At the time of the first of the modern settlements, which was spread over the years 1864-1868, the tāluk contained 300 *khālsa* and 4 *jāgīr* villages. In 1866 three villages were transferred to Malkāpur tāluk and four to Akola. In 1870 Khāmgaon tāluk came into existence and received 144 *khālsa* and 4 *jāgīr* villages from Bālāpur, which however itself received 46 *khālsa* and 9 *jāgīr* villages from Akola tāluk. It now contains 193 *khālsa* and 9 *jāgīr* villages, one of the former consisting of the town of Bālāpur to which no lands are technically attached. The tāluk has an area of 569 square miles and is thus next to the smallest in the District. Its shape is roughly that of a crescent extending from north to south with the hollow side on the west. Its extreme length from north to south is 40 miles and its average width is only 12 miles, except in the south, where it broadens to 30 miles. The greater part of its western border is formed by the Khāmgaon tāluk of Buldāna District, the Chikhli and Mehkar tāluks of the same District continuing the border on the south-west and the Jalgaon tāluk touching it on the north-west. Most of the northern boundary is that of Akot tāluk, the Pūrna river marking the division, and Akola tāluk lies on the east and Bāsim on the south-east. The northern half of Bālāpur tāluk is practically flat but has in many parts very broad and gentle undulations. The soil here, and throughout three-quarters of the tāluk, is black and rich. The rivers pass through the soft soil in deep and broad channels and the surface of the fields is often sharply cut by the action of water. The southern and south-eastern parts are hilly, the ranges being frequently very strongly marked, and the soil is mostly stony and light. The drainage of the country is from south to north, flowing into the Pūrna. Two streams, the Nirguna, called in its lower course Bhuikund, and the Man, are of considerable size and contain water for most of their course throughout the year. They flow the whole length of the tāluk near its western side and unite three miles north of Bālāpur town. Irrigation is very little practised. The tāluk has long been fully cultivated. Statistics for 7 years show that its area is 361,000 acres, of which 279,000 have been occupied for cultivation and 250,000 are annually cropped; no land available for cultivation is left unoccupied. Jawāri has an average of 101,000 acres, cotton 121,500, and all the *rabi* crops together have only 12,000 acres. Communications within the tāluk are fairly good though not altogether satisfactory. The railway runs from east to west across the northern half, a distance of 14 miles, with stations at Pāras, Jaigaon and Dāpki. Made roads connect Bālāpur town with Pāras, Pātur (through Wādegaon), and Khāmgaon; the road from Akola to Bāsim passes for 10 miles across the south-east of the tāluk, through Pātur, and that from Shegaon to Akot traverses 10 miles of the north-west part. Unfortunately the Bhuikund river flows between Bālāpur town and its railway station at Pāras and forms a most serious obstacle to traffic in the rains. A bridge to cost Rs. 36,000 is under consideration. Country roads across the tracts of level black soil are very good in the dry season. Manufactures are unimportant, but there are four factories for ginning and pressing cotton and some oil-mills turned by bullocks; turbans and rough carpets are made by the Momins and *satranjiwālās* of Bālāpur town, and there are a few weavers of coarse fabrics. The tāluk has 13 weekly markets, but only that at Bālāpur town sells for more than Rs. 1000; small fairs are held in February at Pātur and Malsud. Schools number 37, with an average attendance of 1800 male and 180 female scholars. The original settlement came into force in the years 1864-1868, the rates varying from R. 1-6 to Rs. 2 but with more than half the villages rated at R. 1-13. The revision settlement came into force in 1897-1898, the rates varying from R. 1-14 to Rs. 2-10, and the land revenue of the tāluk in the last six years has been on an average Rs. 3,62,000. Police stations exist at Bālāpur, Pātur, Chānni and Andura. The population of the tāluk was 107,200 in 1881 and 104,495 in 1901, when the density was 184 to the square mile.

Bālāpur Town.—Bālāpur town is the headquarters of the tāluk of the same name. It is situated at the junction of the rivers Man and Mhais, six miles south-west of the railway station of Pāras. No revenue-village of Bālāpur exists, but the town is formed by the houses of five separate villages—Kāsarkhed, Kalbai, Bābulkhed, Gājipur, and Mudhāpur (deserted)—in close proximity; the name is taken from a temple of Bālā Devi situated between the rivers close to their junction. Bālāpur is mentioned in the Ain-i-Akbari as one of the richest parganas in the Sūbah of Berār. The town therefore probably existed long before the Mughal invasion. Under the Mughals it was the chief military station of Berār after Ellichpur. Azim Shāh, son of Aurangzeb, is said to have lived here and to have built a mud fort. In 1721 a bloody battle was fought between the Nizām-ul-Mulk and the imperial troops 6 or 8 miles west of the town. The present fort of Bālāpur was finished, according to an inscription on the outer gate, in 1757 by Ismail Khān, first Nawāb of Ellichpur. It is massively built of brick and is the largest and probably the strongest fort in Berār, the hill forts of the Melghāt excepted. It crowns a small hill at the junction of the Man and Mhais and during the rains is actually surrounded by water except at one point, where a very recent causeway generally keeps a road dry. The fort has three gateways, one within the other. The middle one has doors studded in their upper parts with long spikes to resist elephants. The innermost one has elephants and a horse, besides some flowers, cut in the stone beside it; it is a common thing in important Muhammadan buildings in different parts of Berār for some such small ornaments to be carved; the idea is said to be not so much to provide adornment as to give the visitor some special characteristic to carry in his memory. Inside the fort are one mosque and three wells. The highest and innermost walls are ten feet thick and their ramparts are pierced with numerous slits at three different angles for the discharge of missiles. It is a curious point that a stone stand for a flagstaff, to carry a Muhammadan ensign, has been made a flower-stand for a *tulsi*, basil, plant, such as is grown for religious motives in almost every Hindu house; but on the other hand a tomb and flag dedicated to the Muhammadan saint Chāndkhān are very prominent both here and in Hindu forts. A path has been trodden through the vegetation all around the ramparts, a testimony to the interest which the fort excites in country cousins who come to Bālāpur for weddings and other festivities or who have to visit the *tahsīli* in the fort. A veterinary dispensary has been established in the outer gateway, an elementary Urdu school in the first enclosure, and the *tahsīli* in the heart of the fort. Whether or not this is altogether desirable the *tahsīli* has a very striking situation; it also contains some fine carved woodwork which is said by some to have been brought from Wyāla when the fort there was dismantled; it is proposed to rebuild the present *tahsīli*. The temple of Bālā Devi already mentioned lies just under the fort on the southern side. It was much extended, and steps leading from it to the river Man were built, about 15 years ago by Rukhmābai, the childless widow of Withoba, a Rangāri, but it still looks small and unimposing beside the fort. The *jāma masjid* on the west of the river was built, according to an inscription, in 1622; it is a fine building, 90 feet long, and has very graceful arches. The town also contains a fine *haveli*, built in 1703 by a local saint, Saiyid Amjad, and a mosque of 1737 in Kāsarpura known as Kānkhān Masgul, which contains the remains of another saint, Maulvi Māsun Shāh; both buildings have inscriptions. A very pretty *chhatri*, umbrella-shaped pavilion, 25 feet square and 33 feet in height, stands on the river bank on the south of the town. It is supposed to have been built by Sawai Jaising Rāja, who came with Alamgir to the Dakhan and was one of his best generals. Its foundations were much injured in a great flood called the *dhādya pūr* which occurred more than 50 years ago, but after some years the damage was repaired at a cost of Rs. 3000 sent from Jaipur. People are sufficiently educated to scrawl their names on all parts of the *chhatri*, and a stone in the middle has been coloured with the ubiquitous sacred red. The frivolous say that visitors to the *chhatri* must do three things. Firstly, they should note the *chār bot ki patthar*, four-fingers stone, which has been let in near the top of a pillar on the south; no one has 'done' the *chhatri* who has not seen this. Secondly, they should count the pillars, a confusing operation. Thirdly, they should try to throw a stone from the platform on which the *chhatri* stands to the far bank of the river, which requires some skill. Other relics of antiquity are fortified gates which protected some of the different parts of Bālāpur separately. The population of the town is 10,000, of whom about one-half are Muhammadans. The late *khatīb*, a resident of Bālāpur but *kāzi* of Akola, Maulvi Muassan Sāhib, Khān Bahādur, who died many years ago, was a most influential Muhammadan in the western half of Berār, and his son, Maulvi Muhammad Muntajiuddīn, is regarded by some as one of the only two Muftis in the Province. Saiyid Muhammad, son of Saiyid Ahmad Sāhib, says that he has two treasures of special interest. The one is a hair of the beard of Miran Mohiuddīn Saiyid Abdul Kādir Gilāni (of Bāghdād) which is solemnly displayed to a gathering of a few thousand Muhammadans on the 11th of Rabi Awwal (in March-April); one of his *jāgīrs* was granted for the expenses involved in this. The other treasure is a *Kurān* brought from Bāghdād by Saiyid Muhammad's ancestors more than 300 years ago. It is beautifully and most regularly written, but is so ingeniously arranged that every line begins with *alif* and every *sipāra*, of which there are 30, begins at the top of one page and ends exactly at the bottom of the opposite page. Both the families mentioned have numerous other ancient documents. Among the Muhammadans were skilful and prosperous handicraftsmen, including turban-makers, carpet-makers, and paper-makers. The first, Momins, intermarry with the last, but not with other Muhammadans. They used, it is said, to make *mhonda* cloth for Nawāb Salābat Khān of Ellichpur so strong that Rs. 50 worth of copper could be lifted in a single fold. They still make good turbans, but their trade is greatly declining, as is that of the carpet-makers, while no paper has been manufactured at Bālāpur for four years. The prosperity of the town has greatly declined, not only through the decrease in its official importance, but also because trade has been diverted to towns on the railway. Owing to the river Bhuikund intervening it has not been found possible to make any satisfactory road from Bālāpur to the railway, though a scheme involving the expenditure of Rs. 36,000 on a bridge is under consideration. Among the Hindus no single caste is predominant; there are perhaps 100 families of Mahārs but not more than 80 of any higher caste. Many fine old houses belong to Gujarātis who have long been settled in the town. Many of these are Jains of the Shwetambari sect; they are building a temple which has already cost Rs. 17,000 and will require Rs. 50,000 before it is finished. They give the name of a *jhati*, or *sādhu*, who was a great *jyotishi* or *shāstri* among them over a century ago, Sukhārak Bhāgchandji, but can tell no details about him. About 20 families of Digambari Jains also live at Bālāpur. Weaving used to be an important industry, but the Koshtis have suffered with other artisans. Cotton has lately provided increasing employment. Until about 1900 there were no factories at Bālāpur, but now there are three ginning factories and one pressing factory. This not only gives work to a number of hands, but causes a great deal of cotton to be bought and sold in the town which would otherwise go directly to some other place. During the forenoon one sees groups of *adatyās* surrounding every cart as it reaches their stand, snatching at the cotton and bargaining about it. One factory alone burns wood and has enormous stacks ready. The private institutions of Bālāpur include a library, near the temple of Bālā Devi, started within the last ten years, and a Muhammadan *anjuman* started toward the end of 1908. Among

Government institutions are a hospital and dispensary and schools for boys and girls, the highest being an Anglo-vernacular school for boys. A large bazar is held on Saturdays. The dāk bungalow is pleasantly situated on a hill within a few hundred yards of the *chhatri*. A pleasant though sunny walk can be had from the bungalow along the river beyond this building, when both duck and *chikāra* may be seen.

Bārsi Tākli.—Bārsi Tākli is a village in Akola tāluk 11 miles south-east of Akola. Tradition makes it an ancient place and various indications bear this out. The name of the original village is said to have been Tankāwati. The *peth* was founded later, and because it was begun on a *bāras* day, that is the day following *ekādeshi*, the name Bārsi was added, and the whole was called Bārsi Tākli. (Local accounts of derivation are naturally erratic.) The names firstly of a Muhammadan saint, Sulaimānkhān Wali, and secondly of a Hindu, Govind Mahārāja, were added later but have again been dropped. Bārsi Tākli was the headquarters of a pargana of fifty-two and a half villages, and has a *kāzi* whose *sanad* was given by the Emperor Alamgir. Its population under the Nizām's rule is said to have been at one time 22,000 but was greatly reduced by three calamities. Firstly there was a great Pindāri raid in which the town was looted for seven days; afterwards came a great fire, and finally a terrible famine, possibly that of 1803. At that time no supplies could be got from places outside the District, and a great many people permanently deserted the village. The population was 5377 in 1881, 5046 in 1891, and 6288 in 1901; a metalled road is now being made through Bārsi Tākli to Māhān and may cause increased prosperity. The village contains a police station, post-office, three schools, a large weekly market, and a ginning factory. Muhammadans form one-half of the population;

they are generally poor and sometimes inclined to pugnacity. The village site contains 127 acres, but this is much more than is now necessary, and land has been given out for cultivation in the midst of the village. Tradition points out on the north, near the present police station, the sites of the Nizām's old *mokāswāda* and the Bhonsla's *kacheri*, the headquarters of the two powers in the eighteenth century; it is said that 40 per cent. of the revenue used at that time to go to the Nizām and 60 per cent. to the Bhonsla. Bārsi Tākli contains, besides the town-gates, five ancient buildings of some interest. Two of these are Hemādpanthi temples. One is dedicated to Devi; it is of a highly developed style and in an excellent state of preservation, thanks partly to recent slight repairs effected by Government; it faces north, but two tiny windows on the east, each in the form of a cross, allow the first rays of the sun to fall on the head of the goddess. The other temple is that of Mahādeo and is surrounded by work of comparatively recent date; two *dipmāl*, fire-pillars, stand near it, and the site of a *sati* shrine is shown close by. The other three buildings of interest are a mosque, tomb, and well built by Sulaimānkhān, a *tālukdār* of not much more than 100 years ago, according to an inscription on the tomb. The well has steps leading down to the water, close to which two subterranean rooms are accessible in the hot weather. It is said that the well was once in a busy part of the town, but it is surrounded now by garden cultivation. Sulaimankhān left his mark on the place in other ways; in particular he stopped the practice of sacrificing a buffalo at Holi, and the prohibition is still observed; it is said that he also prevented the Muhammadans from killing cows, but this restriction has long been neglected and there is just now a slight difficulty about the site of the meat market.

Bāsim Tāluk.—Bāsim tāluk lies between latitudes 20° 27′ N. and 19° 51′ S. and longitudes 77° 23 E. and 76° 37′ W. and has an area of 1046 square miles At the original settlement, in 1872, it contained 502 villages, but, owing largely to the formation of Mangrul tāluk in 1875, the number now consists of only 338, of which 321 are *khālsa*, 16 *jāgīr*, and one *pālampat;* even so Bāsim is by far the largest tāluk in the District. In shape it is, roughly speaking, a full crescent with the hollow side toward the south. A straight line taken east and west to connect the horns of the crescent would be about 45 miles long, while one north and south through the depth of it would be 30 miles. The whole southern border is formed by the Nizām's Dominions ; on the north-west is the Mehkar tāluk of Buldāna District ; on the north come Bālāpur, Akola, and Mangrul tāluks ; and on the south-east is the Pusad tāluk of Yeotmāl District. In the western part of the centre of the tāluk are rich plains of black-soil, where *rabi* crops are largely grown. In the extreme north-east and north-west are very rough hills ; others less marked occupy the south-east and south-west corners ; while lesser hills, often very stony and having very light soil, form much of the rest. Most of the tāluk is a tableland, the *ghāts* lying just beyond its borders in the south of Bālāpur. The circuit-house to the north of Bāsim town stands on ground 1840 feet above sea-level ; the greatest height recorded, Jāmbrun (a little to the north), is 1877 feet; Jorgaon, Jāmbrun Mahāl, Pārdi, Bhera, Shelu, and Wālki all rise above 1800 feet ; and the least heights recorded, Wāri and Khedkhed, in the north, are 1560 and 1582 feet. The climate is generally cool and healthy, and a good water-supply is provided in most parts by wells. The only river of importance is the Penganga, which enters from Mehkar tāluk, flows south-east across the western half of Bāsim to Yeoti, and thence forms the southern boundary for the eastern half of the tāluk ; it contains water throughout the year in most of its course. The Nirguna, Morna, Kātepurna, and Adān rise in the northern half but do not become large streams till they have passed outside the tāluk ; however there is fine scenery in the hills through which the first three flow. Moreover those three flow north to the Pūrna and thence westward into the Indian Ocean, while the other rivers and their tributaries pass east and south into the Godāvari and at last into the Bay of Bengal, so that the high land of Bāsim forms a continental watershed. Large tanks exist at Bhar, Risod, and Wākad, and a certain amount of irrigation is done at Risod. At Bāsim itself and other places tanks are used chiefly for watering cattle ; each village has on an average 14 wells. The total area is 669,000 acres, of which in 1907-1908 there were 575,000 occupied for cultivation and 3300 available but unoccupied. During the years 1900-1905 jawāri occupied from about 160,000 to 200,000 acres, being near the lower limit for the last three years, and cotton varied irregularly between 145,000 and 160,000 acres, occupying in 1905-1906 exactly the same area as jawāri. Wheat varied from a little over 20,000 to 80,000 acres, rising fairly steadily during the six years and gaining at the expense of jawāri. Gram varied irregularly between 10,000 and 27,000, linseed between 2000 and 10,000, and tūr appears to have risen from 7000 to 12,000. No railway passes through the tāluk, though a line to lead from Akola through Bāsim to Hingoli has been under consideration for some years ; embankments were thrown up all along the route in the famine, and further formalities connected with Government taking possession of the land were completed in 1908. The chief outlet for trade is that provided by the metalled road which runs to Akola, about 28 miles from the northern boundary ;

this is continued south to Hingoli in the Nizām's Dominions and has a total length of 33 miles within the tāluk. Another metalled road runs north-east from Bāsim through Pārdi Tākmur to Mangrul and Kāranja, having 11 miles within the tāluk ; and a third connects Bāsim with Pusad and Umarkhed on the south-east, passing out of the tāluk near Shelu Bujruk, 15 miles from Bāsim. The part of the Akola road north of Bāsim was constructed before the settlement of 1872 but the rest have been made since then. The old Nāgpur dāk line also passes north-east through Mālegaon Jāgīr but is not kept in good repair and is now of no particular importance. A metalled road to Risod in the south-west is projected ; the tāluk is large and wealthy, and in addition to its own traffic lies on the route of considerable trade from Pusad and the Nizām's Dominions ; perhaps its present roads are inadequate. The country roads have in many cases the benefit of Irish bridges to cross difficult nullahs, that idea having been introduced into Bāsim tāluk by Colonel K. J. Mackenzie about 40 years ago when it was unknown elsewhere in Berār ; but in many parts these unmade roads are rough and stony. Weekly markets are held at 14 villages, the chief being those at Bāsim and Mālegaon Jāgīr, but Risod and Sirpur also have large markets ; Bāsim alone has two market-days in the week. Fairs with an attendance varying from 4000 to 10,000 are held at Nāgardās in the north-west, Pārdi Asra in the south, Bāsim, and Sirpur, and smaller fairs elsewhere. Factories for ginning cotton number eleven and those for pressing it three ; three-quarters of them are situated at Bāsim itself and only three are as much as 10 years old ; the scope of their operations varies greatly but satisfactory figures are not available. Owing to changes in the area of the tāluk simple comparative figures of its population cannot be given ; but in the 321 *khālsa* villages which were within its borders both in 1867 and 1891 the population increased during the 24 years by 109 per cent.; it fell off again in the famine decade of 1891 to 1901, the density of the whole tāluk falling from 169 to 147 the square mile, and the total was 153,320 at the last census. Houses then numbered 30,322, giving an average of five persons a house. The only places with a population of more than 2000 were Bāsim, Risod, Sirpur, Medsi, Rājura, and Ansing. Medsi stands on the Akola road in the north and owes its importance wholly to that thoroughfare; its population was 2286 in 1891 and 3615 in 1901; it contains nothing of particular interest. Rājura, which is three or four miles east of the road, was formerly the most important village in the north. Its patel is a Naik of the Wanjāris and holds a vague supremacy over 16 villages, all held by Wanjāri patels; his house is naturally the most important in the village and memorials in the form of tombs are built to members of his family, though the bodies are in fact burnt, but there are no buildings of particular interest; the present Naik is Uttamrao Yeshwantrao, Naib-Tahsīldār. A good deal of *rabi* in the neighbourhood is grown in *malas*, irrigated fields, but the soil is mostly light and stony. Mālegaon Jāgīr, on the main road 14 miles north of Bāsim, has a flourishing appearance. It is held by Gopālrao Kāshirao, a boy of about twelve, who is generally given the title of Rājā. The population of the village was 1499 in 1891 and 1964 in 1901. Busy cartwrights work by the side of the road, and the village contains several large new shops; some belonging to Cutchis have simple but pretty fronts of carved wood. An inspection bungalow stands at Amāni, two miles to the south. In the north-east of the tāluk stands another Mālegaon, sufficiently distinguished in Marāthi pronunciation by the fact that the *l* in it is guttural, but it is surrounded by rough country, largely forest, and its population is only 402 ; lack of water in the village causes half the cultivators to live elsewhere. The original settlement came into force in the tāluk in 1872-1873, when the rates varied from As. 14 to R. 1-8, half the villages being assessed at R. 1-1 (for standard land). The tāluk was very prosperous in the settlement period, nearly all the land available for cultivation being taken up and population and the appliances of cultivation increasing from four to eight times as fast as cultivation itself. A revision settlement was introduced in 1903-1904, the rates varying from R. 1-2 to R. 1-12 ; the land revenue in 1907-1908 amounted to Rs. 3,88,570. Police stations are placed under a scheme introduced in the beginning of 1909 at Bāsim, Sirpur, Risod, Jawalka, and Ansing ; and there are hospitals at the first three places. Schools number 37, with an average combined attendance of 1800 ; only three are girls' schools.

Bāsim Town.—Bāsim town, M. *Wāshim*, was the headquarters of a District from 1868 to 1905, but is now at the head only of a Subdivision and a tāluk, both named after it. It is situated 52 miles south of Akola and is connected with it by a good road which surmounts a considerable *ghāt* in the 24th and 25th miles. Bāsim stands in latitude 20° 6′ 45 N. and longitude 77° 11′ E. and is 1800 feet above sea-level. Its population was 8531 in 1867, 11,576 in 1881, 12,389 in 1891, and 13,823 in 1901. It is an ancient town and the head of a pargana ; it was looted by Pindhāris in about 1809. A municipality was started in 1869, the bulk of the members have been elected since 1889, and the revenue during 1907-1908 rose to Rs. 22,000. The municipal office is situated in what is called the Jubilee Town Hall, which cost nearly Rs. 6000 and was opened in 1889. A hospital and veterinary dispensary are maintained, the town and Camp have separate post-offices, and the ordinary schools include two for girls and an Anglo-vernacular school; besides which a technical school is kept up by the public. Bāsim has a few score of old looms operated by Koshtis and Dhangars, making *sāris* and blankets respectively, but the work is not profitable or largely carried on. Factories for ginning cotton number six and those for pressing it three. The town lies to the south of the Camp, or civil station, fields and the compounds of cotton factories intervening. It has a busy daily bazar and streets full of corners, indicating its antiquity; the houses are very largely roofed with *tin*, corrugated iron. The Camp is situated at the side of an uncultivated plain, the bungalows of former district officials stand in fairly large compounds, and roads have been laid out for pleasure as well as use. Both the Subdivisional Officer and the Tahsīldār are now accommodated in the old District *kacheri*. A garden maintained by the municipality is called the Temple Garden after Sir Richard Temple. The whole place is pleasantly situated, though much of the land in the neighbourhood is poor and stony. The great interest of Bāsim however is religious, the town being connected not merely with recent saints but with the classical deities. The most striking feature in the town is the Deo tank, flanked on one side by the temple of Vyenkateshwar Bālāji and on another by that of Rāmchandra. These all apparently date from the eighteenth century and are said together to have cost some lākhs of rupees, but the traditions connected with them are much older. Bāsim in its religious aspect is called Watsa Gulma Kshetra, the sacred place of the gathering of Watsa, and legends about it are given in a manuscript called Watsa Gulma Purān. In the *Tretāyuga*, the second age, this country was a part of the Dandakāvanya, or Dandak-jungle, and the *rishi* Watsa had his *āshram*, hermitage, here; his *tapobal*, merit acquired by austerities, was such that consternation covered the world; rivers ran dry and trees were withered, and even the gods feared. They came therefore in a body to Bāsim and took up a temporary residence at various places within a radius of 5 miles from the town. Shankar, or Siva, alone, whose devotee Watsa had proclaimed himself, went directly to the *rishi*, whom he found absorbed in *tap*, austerities. At the sight of his virtue Siva was so much overcome that he wept, and the tears filled a dry well at his feet and flowed forth as the river Karuna; then he promised to grant any request Watsa might make. The latter asked that Siva should remain for ever at the *rishi's* abode to save his worshippers from affliction. Siva granted this, and his *ātmalinga*, embodied essence, remained there in consequence. Then the other gods appeared in a single gathering, *gulma*, and promised to stay in their divine essence, *ansharūp*, at the various places at which they had halted; and so the neighbourhood is called Watsa Gulmāchi Pāch Koshi, the Five Kos of the Watsa Gathering, and is considered a *kshetra*, sacred area. In this *kshetra* there are said to be 108 *tīrthas*, holy places or sacred springs, associated with different gods and *rishis*; the chief are Padmatīrth created by Vishnu, Daridra Haran Tīrth by Datta, and Chandreshwar Tīrth by Chandra. From them flow six sacred rivers, the Chandrabhāga, Pusha (Pus), Karuna (Kātepurna), Wachara, Aruntuda (Adān), and Prānita (Penganga). Each of these has its own story, and the efficacy of the *kshetra* as a whole is extolled in the *purān* as equal to that of Benāres. The same authority explains the origin of the name Bāsim. A poor Brāhman orphan was protected by a learned member of the caste, but after some time stole a necklace belonging to his protector's wife. In the morning when she bewailed her loss he repented and sought to restore the necklace but could not find it. Meanwhile the woman laid on the unknown thief the curse that he should suffer from a loathsome disease and his body should be covered with insects, upon which the boy went to Prayāg Tīrth (Allahābād), did penance for the theft, and threw himself into the holy Ganges. On account of the *punya*, merit, thus gained, he was born again as a son of the king of Kankādripura in the Carnatic, when he was given the name Wāsuki. In course of time he both married and succeeded to the throne, but presently his wife Kanaklekha discovered that when he was asleep at night his body was infested with maggots. One day when shooting he washed his hands and face in a small and dirty pond, and that night so much of his flesh remained wholesome. He and his wife sought the pool again, here in Watsāranga, but could not find it. They went to Vasishta *rishi* and told him about it, whereon he related the story of the king's previous life and of the religious importance of Watsagulma Kshetra, and showed them the pool. This was the Padma Tīrth, and Wāsuki first bathed and was wholly cleansed and then took up his residence near the spot. The new town was called Wāsuki Nagar, but became corrupted into Wāshim, or Bāsim. The Padma Tīrth is a tank about half a mile north of the town, the sides are built up with cut stone, and people like to bathe there. According to the Settlement Report of 1871 it used to supply all the drinking water of the town, but people both washed clothes there and threw the ashes and bones of the dead into it; when the latter practice was stopped they complained that the water lost its purity of taste. The images in the temple of Vyenkateshwar Bālāji are said to have been buried during

Aurangzeb's reign to save them from destruction. All trace of them was lost, but in about 1760 a horseman happened casually to turn up a little earth with his stick and perceived a finger of an image. Images of Brahma, Mahādeo, Pārvati, Devi, Ganpati, and Nāg were taken out, but one image still remained and could by no means be moved. At that time Nawāb Hashmatjang, a relative of the Nizām, was in charge of Bāsim, and held *jāgīrs* there. A Hindu story says that Hashmatjang had in a former existence been a Brāhman and a worshipper of Vishnu. He used never to take food till he had worshipped the god; one day while he was bathing in the Padma Tīrth the image was stolen from the bank, but he vowed that he would still abstain from food and drink till it was found. Meanwhile he offered prayers to the image of Chandreshwar Mahādeo, but while so doing he happened to spit, whereupon the god laid on him the curse that in his next life he should be a Muhammadan called Hashmatjang. However Vishnu also appeared to him in a dream and said that as a reward for his constancy he should in that next life discover a large image of either Vishnu himself or Bālāji. While the Hindus were still unable to move the image in the ground it appeared in a dream to Nawāb Hashmatjang and bade him take it out himself, and when he put his hand to it the image in fact came out from the ground. At that time Bhawāni Kālu, who had been patwāri of the village Khadi Dhāmni in Mangrul tāluk but had become Diwān (or according to some accounts, a general) of the Bhonsla Rājās, was at Bāsim, and Hashmatjang handed the image over to him. He set up the present temple, a fine building standing in a large paved quadrangle, with a well-built verandah for pilgrims to stay, a *bhandāra* for Brāhmans to take food, and various offices. The work took 12 years, but was finished, according to an inscription on a pillar in front, in 1700 Shāke, A.D. 1779. The Deo or Bālāji Talao, a large square tank with stone-built sides, strongly and handsomely finished, and with a *jal kridāsthān*, resting-place for swimmers, in the middle, was made at the same time. The chief image is of black stone and sparkles with ornaments; a fine view of the town is to be obtained from the top of the temple gateway, though the staircase is rather abrupt. Large *jāgīrs* and *ināms* were given for the support of the temple, the present revenue being Rs. 11,000 from those sources and Rs. 3000 from *kāngi*, offerings. The management is in the hands of Bhāwanrao Vithal Kālu, a descendant of Bhawāni Kālu in the sixth generation. He accepts his own maintenance from the funds but has no fixed pay. A large staff is employed, including seven *kārkuns*, clerks, on pay varying from Rs. 5 to Rs. 20, 12 peons, from Rs. 5 to Rs. 8-8, 2 *pujāris*, worshippers, on Rs. 6, two *tīrthas* on Rs. 4 to give holy water to the public, two *haridās's* on Rs. 5-6 to tell mythological stories, two *purāniks* on Rs. 3-8 and Rs. 4 to recite the *purāns*, and four *chaughadwālas* on Rs. 4 as drummers. A festival lasting a fortnight is held during Ashwin Shudh (in October) at a cost of Rs. 5000, and lesser festivals cost Rs. 1200 a year. In Muharram a small present is given to the Muhammadans, and the man who represents Nāl Sāhib shows no sign of animation till it is received. On another side of the Deo Talao is a temple of Rāmchandra, a large enclosed building but not by any means as fine as the temple of Bālāji. It contains images of Lakshman, Sīta, Māroti, and Rādha-Krishna as well as that of Rāmchandra. It is said to have been built about 200 years ago by Bhagwandās Mahārāj Bairāgi, and its management is now in the hands of Rāmānujdās Bairāgi, whose *chelās* worship the images. A *jāgīr* producing Rs. 1100 is attached to the temple, out of which wandering Bairāgis must be entertained and given parting presents of Rs. 2, 3, or 4 as *dakshina*, from Rs. 20 to 50 is given to village and pargana officials, two festivals are celebrated in a small way, and repairs are done; no debt is incurred in either of these temples. Another temple of Bālāji, a small one, is in the hands of the Sangwai family, and has a *jāgir*. Numerous other temples are situated either in or near Bāsim. A story is told about that of Devi at Dewāla, a mile distant on the south, that a former member of the Diwākar patel family used to go daily to Māhur, 60 miles away, to worship the image, but when he got old it followed him home to save him the journey; however he looked back at Dewāla, against the goddess's command, and the image stopped there.

Belkhed.—Belkhed is situated in the west of Akot tāluk, 3 miles from Akot. Its population is 2698, a number which fully occupies the village-site, though people here, as in some other villages, have put up with the inconveniences involved for generations. One patel, Sakhārām Krishnāji, says he has been in office since the Assignment of 1853, the patwāri, Krishnāji Rāmkrishna, has done 33 years' service, and both are still active. Huts of grass or cotton stalks have gradually been giving place to houses with flat, *dhāba*, or tiled roofs, and there has been a corresponding development in the comfort of living in other ways. The *chāwadi*, largely erected by the present patel, is unusually good, and some temples and the mosque have been rebuilt; but the village has no striking buildings. The present stone mosque replaced a thatched one about 25 years ago. The population includes about 330 families of Mālis, nearly 100 of Kunbis, and 60 or 70 of Muhammadans. A bazar is held on Wednesdays. The *khalwādi*, ground set aside for threshing corn, is situated about a quarter of a mile away on a long-deserted village site.

Bordi.—Bordi is a village in Akot tāluk 4 miles north of Akot. Its population is only 1512, but short notes are given about it because it is a centre of some interest. A three days' fight is said to have taken place in 1851 between Daryāji Deshmukh of Dhārud, who lived at Bordi, and Sirājuddīn Munsif of Akot; the cause was an attempt by the Nizām to resume possession of the village, which had been held as a *jāgīr* by the Nawāb of Ellichpur. The deshmukh held the village with a small force while the Munsif attacked him with much greater numbers and with the garrison and stores of Narnāla in reserve, and the Hyderābād troops were victorious. The curious assertion is added that the deshmukh when in flight met an English lieutenant with two guns and 2000 men and returned with him to fight again at Surji Anjangaon and at Bordi itself; it is mentioned that the lieutenant's hands had been hurt by a gun bursting. The story appears impossible from the political conditions but is a curious instance of the growth of tradition. In the end the deshmukh came to terms with the Munsif but was suspected by the Nawāb and carried off to Ellichpur, where he remained till in 1853 Mr. Bullock released him. A settlement of immigrants from the Nāgpur direction has been growing here, as in many other villages in this neighbourhood, for the last 10 or 12 years. They are quiet people who have found their way on foot, mostly labourers but including a few craftsmen, and are marked off from the Berāris by slight differences in their dress and houses. Bordi has a temple dedicated to Nāgāswāmi, with a large car which is taken round the village on his festival. Nāgāswāmi was a Kanaujia Brāhman who first became a Gosain with the name of Rāmgir and then was known as Nāgāswāmi because he went naked. It is said that once when a man who kept a Mhāli mistress denied the fact before the saint and placed his hand to his eye in asseveration the eye came out in his hand, and when the *sādhu* cursed a man who constantly laughed at him the latter got black leprosy on his mouth. Nāgāboa finally had himself buried alive because Bakābāi, wife of Raghuji Bhonsla, was coming to him to entreat that she might have a son and he knew that this was not fated. At Dhārud, about two miles north-west of Bordi, there are the *ghumat* of Kasban and the tomb of Ambi Awalya. The former is situated in a field a few hundred yards from the site of Dhārud and is a rather striking building of cut stone with a dome, *ghumat*, of brick. The style is a combination of square and octagon, with pointed arches sunk deep into the wall, this being about 4½ feet thick within the arches and 13 feet between them. The base of the building is over 30 feet in breadth inside, and has two niches in the western wall and a staircase in the south-east corner leading up to the bottom of the dome. It is in just the same style as Bāg Sawār's tomb in Narnāla and the tomb of Gada Nārāyan at Akot, but the Dhārud *ghumat* is empty; there is a tomb just outside with the ruins of what is said to have been a *masjid* near by; the people of the neighbourhood seem to have no tradition about it. Dhārud was the head of a pargana but is now deserted and its mud fort is in ruins. The tombs of Ambi Awalya and some relatives occupy a large stone platform and are kept in good order, but are quite plain. The saint is said to have helped in conquering the Hindu demons who held Narnāla in early times. At Umra, 2 miles east of Bordi, is the tomb of a much more recent saint, Kuwatalishāh Miyāsāhib. He belonged to the Punjab but came to this part of India about 60 years ago. The first knowledge people had of him was that he used to pass certain houses at night with the cry, '*Hāzir huā to bhej*—Send while I am present,' but he was gone before anything could be brought him. Presently they learnt to be ready for him and discovered also that he was living in the lands of Jitāpur, a mile and a half from Umra, and caressing tigers and panthers. When people feared to approach him he said the animals were his dogs but sent them away. They persuaded the saint to come to live in Umra, where he spent his days in drawing water—throwing the earthen jar into the well miraculously from a distance—and filling little pits for birds to drink from. In the evening people brought him bread and he gave one pice for every loaf, no matter how many were offered, drawing the money from some unknown store. Raoji Thüte of Makrāmpur, 2 miles away, brought him a loaf daily for 12 years, and once when he was stopped by a flood in the river Lendi but was bidden by the saint to proceed without fear the water miraculously became shallow to let him pass. Kuwatalīshāh was 94 when he died, and Narsingboa, who was mentioned in the Berār Gazetteer of 1870 as still alive, was a disciple of his; so also was Eknāthboa, a Muhammadan who came to be considered a Brāhman. The tomb of the Miyāsāhib is regarded by Muhammadans as a *dargāh*, tomb, and by Hindus as a temple, and both worship there. The Hindus worship in the *bhajan* form every Thursday, and also do the *kākad ārati* ceremony there. An annual fair is held here, and another, rather more largely attended, at the *samādh* of Wākājiboa, a contemporary of Kuwatalīshāh, and his sons Sakhārām and Raising. The only point told about Wākājiboa is that he gave food to everyone who asked for it. At Shiupur, 2 miles from Bordi, is a shrine famous locally under the name of Chainuboa for the cure of snake-bite. About 35 years ago a man of the surname of Golambkār was cutting wood when he chopped off the tail of a snake. The reptile attacked him and he fled to the village with it in pursuit, but about two fields from his goal he glanced behind and saw the snake at that very moment stop and turn back. That night it appeared to him in a dream and told him to make an image of itself, promising that this should be a cure for snake-bite for all its worshippers. He therefore made a silver image a few inches in length, and it has been placed in a small shrine. When bitten one should apply earth to one's forehead in the name of the god, bring *ghī* to offer at the shrine, and bathe and pass water there, when the cure is complete. If the victim cannot walk to the shrine he may be carried, no restrictions limiting the mode. Intelligent people of the neighbourhood are convinced of the certainty of the cure, provided one has faith. One told of a relative who had been bitten by a 'cowrie' snake and turned green from his foot right up one side of his body. He came a week later in that condition, and in two minutes his flesh was wholesome again. Another man bitten just behind the ankle, usually considered a most dangerous place, was cured. In all 400 or 500 people are said to have come for the cure, of whom only one died. In that case while the boy was at the shrine a woman in a state of ceremonial impurity passed and her shadow fell on him, whereupon not only did he die but the upper half of the image turned black and to this day cannot be cleaned. The narrators of these points were men of intelligence and position, but their limitations are indicated by the fact that the most prominent believed all snakes to be poisonous. A pilgrimage of 1000 or 1200 people passes through this neighbourhood in Shrāwan (July-August). On Sunday they go to Irāniboa's temple at Kāsod, on Monday to Mahādeo's temple at Dhārgad in the Melghāt, thence to the tomb of Saiduliboa near Narnāla, to Budhānuddīn's tomb and to see the fort at Narnāla, and back through Shāhānur to Nāgāboa's temple at Bordi. It is an awkward journey in the rains and all do not follow it exactly, for in fact the great day at Nāgāboa's temple is a Tuesday, the 3rd in Shrāwan.

Borgaon.—Borgaon, often called Borgaon Manju, is a village in Akola tāluk 10 miles east of Akola. It is on the railway line and a station is named after it. The population was 3891 in 1891 and 3861 in 1901. Before the Assignment it formed a *taraf* of Akola pargana and had a wall and gates, all now fallen, and so was of some little importance. As often happens in such cases there is a large Muhammadan population, this now including about 200 families. Mahārs are equally numerous, but the largest caste of Hindus proper, the Māli caste, has only 150 families, and there are only about 50 Kunbi houses. The population is now increasing owing to the prosperity brought by the railway. Two ginning factories and one pressing factory have been established in the last six years, and most of the cotton of the neighbourhood is brought to them, though the price is slightly higher at Akola. The village has a police station, a post-office, a Marāthi boys' school, three *dharmshālās*, and a good bazar-site ; the weekly market is held on Tuesdays, and its dues are sold for Rs. 1000. The name Manju is taken from Manjumiya, a Muhammadan saint whose tomb, to which a small *inām* is attached, stands in the village. Manjanshāh Rahmatullah Ali was one of the Chaudah Sau Pālki, the fourteen hundred palanquin-borne champions mentioned in all parts of the District as having made a great crusade, if the term may be used, for Islām against idolatry ; a small fair is held in his honour, and people, especially Hindus, make vows to him ; but no detailed account of him has been handed down. On the right of Manjumiya's tomb is that of Tolambi, and on the right again that of Amānsāhib, brother of Manjumiya. Borgaon has three other Muhammadan saints, Asabwali, Māhmudsāhib, and Saidain-amma, whose husband's name is not known, but again no details are known. It is a remedy for cold and fever to prostrate oneself before the tomb of Māhmudsāhib in a garden here, a piece of jawāri bread and some vegetables being vowed to the saint. An old temple of Gopāl Krishna is of some interest, and there are others of Vithal Rukhmai and Mahādeo. Bājirao Anandrao, the deshmukh-patel, is building a temple of Rādha-Krishna at a cost of some thousands of rupees. The style is lighter and more open than one often sees. Bājābai, widow of Balwantrao Deshmukh, has also just built a temple of Mahādeo.

Dahihanda.—Dahihanda is a village in the south-east corner of Akot tāluk, 18 miles from Akot; its population is 2847. Muhammadans number about 200 families, Kolis about 150, and Kunbis only about 20. The patels however are Kunbis, and though the deshmukhs call themselves Marāthas, or even Rājputs, they can intermarry with patel families. Dahihanda has a police station, sub-registrar's office, sub-post office, boys' vernacular schools, pound, weekly market (on Saturdays), and a ginning factory, and some wealthy *sāhukārs* live here. It was formerly the head of a pargana of 82 villages and had a mud *kilā*, fort, and *sapīli*, wall. Both have long disappeared, but the patel has still part of the lofty gate of the *kilā* with elephant spikes in it. A Nawāb Sāhib, with 700 horses and an elephant, used to live here on behalf of the Nizām, had under him a Naib and Peshkar with their *kacheri*, and sent 60 per cent. of the revenue to Hyderābād. He held the *kilā*, while a Mokāsdār appointed by the Bhonslas lived in a *haveli*, large private house, now fallen, and sent 40 per cent. to Nāgpur. Dahihanda used to be interesting on account of its salt-wells, but work in them has long ceased and they have fallen in. They used to be from 90 to 120 feet in depth and three or four feet in diameter, and were lined with a kind of basket-work to keep the sides firm. The salt tract extended for many miles on both sides of the Purna, but Dahihanda was the most important centre and had 60 wells. Some of these were let out yearly at prices rising sometimes to Rs. 500 a well, and the salt was sold to Banjāras, who used to bring large quantities of goods into the town on their pack-animals; the salt was not of good quality. Kāzi Shujāuddīn Nizāmuddīn gives a little curious information, from old papers unfortunately destroyed, about the early days of the village. It was founded by Mirza Bulākhibeg, a Māmlatdār, who came from Rāmtīrth in the south of Daryāpur tāluk hunting. When following a deer he saw that a hare was also following it. The Māmlatdār shot the deer on the site of the present village, which pleased him so much that he brought people and made a settlement there. He gave it the name Dehinda, "giving" (Persian), of which the present name is a corruption. Dahihanda contains a *dargāh* of Saiyid Dāud, one of the Chaudah Sau Pālki, who fought under Abdul Rahmān Shāh Gāzi at the defeat of Rāja II of Ellichpur and then settled here. The tomb was built by Sawarkhān, a Hyderābād Naib, but became ruined and was rebuilt seven or eight years ago at a cost of Rs. 6000 by a Kasār *sāhukār* called Vithal Nāgoji. Vows are made to Saiyid Dāud, and a small urus is held in Rabilāwal (March—April). A tomb called *chilla* was built by Echakadshāh *fakīr* in honour of Mahbūb Subain, who died in Bagdād. The *jamā masjid* is said to have been built in the time of Mirza Bulākhibeg. The chief temples, none of which are impressive, are those of Bālāsāhib and Rupnāth. The former is maintained by a *jāgīr* of three villages; the latter was built by Rupnāth himself, and additions have recently been made by Vithal Nāgoji, the Kasār *sāhukār* already mentioned. Rupnāth at first settled in the jungle and lived naked on a *chabūtra*.

People asked him to come into the village and showed him a site on which they wished a temple built; he approved, but the workmen were presently taken on *bigār*, or commandeered, by the *mokāsdār* for his own purposes. The saint cursed him so that a temple and residence he had built were overthrown and his family died out. A tomb of Fattepuriboa is the scene of vows for the relief of cattle-diseases.

Dānāpur.—Dānāpur is situated 18 miles west of Akot on the river Wān, which here forms the boundary between Akot and Jalgaon tāluks. It had a wall, long fallen, and a very large tank which is not known to have held water for the last 200 years, and its population was 2126 in 1901. About 200 families are Kunbis, chiefly of the Dhākre and Wikre *adnao*, surname, and about 80 are Bāris. The tank is about half a mile north-east of the village and has at its shallow end a curious isolated hill called Rāsātek with a rough brick building on it known as *kasbīnīchā makān*, or the prostitute's house. The river has a broad and stony bed, but the water does not remain even through the cold weather; a good supply is however obtained from wells, and a fair amount of fruit is grown in irrigated land for local markets. The one striking feature of the village is the *dargāh* of Mastanshāhmiyā, which is both larger and more pleasing in design than such buildings often are. The saint came to Dānāpur from the Punjab about 100 years ago and at first used to beg his bread from door to door, but after a time he was attacked by a bull-buffalo and his back was so injured that he could no longer walk. A mad Wāghya, devotee of Khandoba, wounded him in several places with a sword, but the wounds miraculously healed in three or four days and the Wāghya upon eating a piece of bread given by Mastanshāh recovered his sanity and became one of the saint's followers. Mastanshāh similarly recovered from the bite of a snake. Though people built a hut for him he not only remained naked but would sleep with only his head inside the hut and his body outside. A Rājput called Bholāsingh wished to become his disciple, but Mastanshāh first sent him to visit the holy places of Hinduism. Bholāsingh returned after a complete tour, which took three years, with the same desire, and the saint gave him some bread and his name was changed thenceforth to Bholāshāh. A horse was dedicated to Mastanshāh, and when a thief took it both he and the animal were afflicted with blindness, which vanished only when they were brought before the saint, who let the thief go. A wall with four *buruj*, towers or bastions, round the *dargāh* was built by some *gānja* dealers who got a good crop after vowing to devote a large sum to the saint. Hasumiyā, Nawāb of Ellichpur, was summoned to Hyderābād to answer certain charges. On the way he came, seated on an elephant, to ask Mastanshāh's help. The latter asked how he would like to exchange his present mount for a donkey, and that degradation was in fact ordered by the Nizām. Shekh Dālla, a professional dacoit, was to some extent a disciple of Mastanshāh. The saint was himself a prophet, and even a parrot of his used to tell what visitors were coming when they were still a *kos*, two miles, away. Mastanshāh died in 1843 in his hundreth year. The present *dargāh* had previously been built by Bholāshāh, who died three years later. The *dargāh* and various out-buildings are well maintained, partly by a small *inām* but chiefly by voluntary subscriptions, and successive *ināmdārs* are nominated as boys with the condition that they remain celibate. They have sometimes belonged to Hindu deshmukh and patel families but become Muhammadans. The present *ināmdār* is a child of about eight wearing a large silver anklet.

Hiwarkhed.—Hiwarkhed, in the north-west of Akot tāluk and 14 miles from Akot, has a population of 6143 and is thus the second largest town in the tāluk—indeed the population is too large for the public lands. It has long been a large place, but comparatively little of interest attaches to it. A considerable proportion of the population are Muhammadans, so that four or five separate processions are formed in Muharram. They have practically rebuilt two mosques in the last ten years at a cost of some thousands of rupees, some of the stone work done by Mārwāri masons, being fairly good. An Urdu school which was formerly kept up was allowed to go out of existence after the famine of 1899-1900 and is only now being restarted. The Marāthi schools are well situated and have 180 boys, with a separate girls' school. A police station has just been opened (replacing that at Adgaon, five miles away), there is a branch post office, a weekly market is held on Mondays, the daily bazar is moderately large and busy, and a ginning factory is at work. None of the temples are striking, though one or two are of fair size. A tradition of a local battle is repeated, which is very unusual. It is said that Raghujī Bhonsla established a *thāna* with a small garrison in the *gadhi*, which is a good specimen of village forts. The deshmukhs to whom it belonged were not at the time well off, but Ruprao Deshmukh got help from his relatives at Jainābād, near Burhānpur, and attacked the garrison, who numbered 20 or 25 men. In the end Ruprao regained the *gadhi* and settled there with full rights of *deshmukhi* and *patīlkipana*, and the village is still known as Ruprao Hiwarkhed.

Kāmargaon.—Kāmargaon is a village in the centre of Murtizāpur tāluk, 13 miles south of Murtizāpur. Its population was 2857 in 1891 and 2346 in 1901. It is in most respects a very common-place village, a Wednesday market, a *dharmshāla*, and a school with four standards being among its chief institutions; but it is unique in the one point that it gives its name to the "Kāmargaon Estate." This is to all intents and purposes a *tāluk* of the Muglai period given permanently to the heirs of Mīr Imām Ali Khān, Risāldār. The Risāldār fell in action at Banda during the Mutiny just after being appointed an Extra Assistant Commissioner. He had recently contracted for the right of collecting revenue in the Kāmargaon pargana of 16 villages; this right was continued to his heirs on very favourable terms. The total land revenue, including cesses, comes to Rs. 18,000; of this total Rs. 2000 are devoted to the emoluments of pargana and village officers, Government receives Rs. 9000, and the Estate-holder, who is commonly called a *jāgirdār*, Rs. 7000. Kāmargaon also contains, besides some small temples, the tomb of Godarshāhwali, about whom some striking stories are told. He is said to have marked out, by pouring water on the ground, a certain space which he said should always be inhabited, and it thereupon received the name Amargaon, Everlasting Village, which has since been corrupted into Kāmargaon. Once the saint Hayāt Kalandar, or Badar-ud-dīn, of Mangrul passed through Kāmargaon on his way to visit a fellow-saint, Dulya Rahmān, at Ellichpur; Hayāt Kalandar was riding on a tiger, and his reins were formed of a living snake with a scorpion at each end. Godarshāhwali was squatting on a wall cleaning his teeth; he ordered the wall to move out of Hayāt Kalandar's way, which it did. The latter then dismounted and asked him to tie up his "horse"; upon which Godarshāhwali called his cow Jamna and she swallowed the tiger When it was wanted again he told the cow to fetch it, and she produced it from her mouth. The saint does not allow a dome to be built on the tomb, but has twice flung it far away when the attempt has been made. He rides in procession through the village sometimes on a Thursday night, dressed in white and carrying a lance in his hand. It is said that about 12 years ago a Muhammadan *jāglia* stole Rs. 17 or so which had been laid before the tomb; the saint denounced the *jāglia* by speaking from his tomb to a passing Pardeshi Thākur, telling him to inform the patel but promising to deal with the matter himself; and the *jāglia* and his three sons met with an accident and died.

Kāranja.—Kāranja is an important town in the south of Murtizāpur tāluk. It was the headquarters of a tāluk for several years after the Assignment and is now so important that it forms a municipality, while Murtizāpur does not. It stands on the old Jālna-Nāgpur *dāk* line, along which a great deal of traffic passed before the railway was opened. Its communications now depend chiefly on a metalled road running 21 miles north to the railway at Murtizāpur, another running 29 miles south-west through Mangrul to Bāsim, and another south-east to Dārwhā, 24 miles distant, besides a number of unmetalled roads. It is an ancient place, and four gateways and the remains of a wall show that it was enclosed in a large fortification; it had also a *kilā*, fort, formerly occupied by a Government officer. Its population was 11,750 in 1867, 10,923 in 1881, 14,436 in 1891, and 16,535 in 1901. It is now a busy trading town, with a cotton market open six days in the week and the same site occupied for a general market on Sundays. Factories for ginning or pressing cotton number 11, two of them lit by electric light. The manufacture of *sāris*, half cotton and half silk with a broad silk border, and of other fine articles of dress, used to be carried on largely but seems now on the point of disappearing. The municipality was established in 1895 and had in 1907-1908 an income and expenditure approaching Rs. 18,000; besides this a large balance has been accumulated for a drainage scheme. Kāranja stands on fairly level ground between low ranges of hills; much of the land in the neighbourhood is light and stony, but it fetches a good price on account of the nearness of the town. Population tends somewhat to move toward the north, because the great roads enter upon that side. One quarter here is given up to Gaolis, many of whom find employment as cartmen. The houses of Kāranja are generally roofed with either tiles or tin, the latter having the special advantage that monkeys do not easily remove it, but occasional thatched houses are to be found in all parts—sometimes indicating the decline of a family which was once wealthy—and are numerous in the poorer quarters on the outskirts. The large ancient houses which are frequent in the *shahar* (as distinguished from the more modern *peth*) often had very extensive cellars, divided into small rooms with intricate inter-communication and in one case at least connected by means of a long passage with the open country outside the walls; these houses have in many cases deteriorated into ruins most undesirable in a large town. The daily bazar is busy and the Cutchis have built a mosque along the top of some of their shops, but less thought seems to be taken here than in some places to have good-looking business houses. Kāranja however contains one private house which has very few equals in Berār, that built a few years ago by the late Rāmji Naik Kannawa; it is a handsome building, large and lofty, built in a modern style and well supplied with European furniture. Public buildings include a hospital, police station, Anglo-vernacular school, post and telegraph offices, and a large *sarai*; they are sometimes situated in the midst of ancient public works. The Bench Magistrates are Messrs.

Prāgji Lilādhar, Lakshmanrao Rāgho Dahihandekar, and Muhammad Hātim, son of Muhammad Burhān. A very pleasant dāk bungalow is situated beside the Mangrul road and near the chief tank. This tank, the Rishi Talao, is the most striking feature in the neighbourhood of Kāranja ; it has an area of several hundred acres made over to the Forest Department, and is perhaps two miles in length ; long bunds, across which cattle file morning and evening in strings of 50 or 100 at a time, were put up in the famine and divide the tank into three parts ; but the water shrinks very considerably in the hot weather. It is said that the tank was originally created by the goddess Amba in order to heal a disease which afflicted the *rishi* Kāranj, from whom the town takes its name. Some people invariably drink its water, which is supposed to prevent spleen disease, though well-water is commonly drunk. A small tank called Chandya or Lendi Talao lies to the east of the town ; it is said that at one time anyone who wanted to give a feast had only to pray beside the water, and all the food and utensils he required would be provided by it, but he was required to return the dishes again ; finally someone, securing gold dishes, kept them, and the miraculous supply ceased from that time ; its water is said to be good for curing itch. Another small tank, called Sārang Talao, seems to have no story attached to it, but the Bindu Tīrth in the middle of the town, a plain, square step-well, which is regarded as the source of the Bembalā river, has a double legend. A number of *rishis* wished to perform a sacrifice, but there was no water available ; each therefore poured out a pot of water which he had brought from some holy place, and from this accumulation sprang the river Bembalā. Meanwhile a Teli near by, ignorant of what was being done, stepped from his oil-press into the new pool and was drowned, and the river has since that time come from the oil-press itself. The town was once known as Kāranja Bībī, because it was part of the dowry of the daughter of the king of Ahmadnāgar, and her tomb still exists in a dilapidated condition. Later it was called Lādāncha Kāranja because of the number of Lāds who had settled there; associated with these are three Jain *mandirs*, temples, and a ruined *haveli*. The first temple, that of Kāsta Sangai, which contains an image of Pārasnāth, has very elaborate wood-carving; that of Shengan has a great deal of neat and pretty work done in the last decade of the nineteenth century at a cost of about Rs. 15,000; and the name Bālatkār is applied to the third. A Jain festival, not on a very large scale, is held in Bhadrapada (August—September). The story of the Kasturi Haveli is connected with a Lād called Lekur Sangai, who was in fact very wealthy but had been living in a miserly fashion. A merchant once arrived at Kāranja with 60 (or as some say 25) camels loaded with musk, *kastūri*; he had been searching India to find someone who would buy the whole at once and pay for it with 60 camel loads of rupees all stamped with the name of the same Emperor. Lekur Sangai offered to become the purchaser and told the merchant to choose any reign he liked for his rupees. The latter laughed at such an offer from a man who looked so poor, but Lekur Sangai showed him 12 cellars full of rupees and in fact paid him in coins of Akbar's reign. He was having a new house built at the time, and merely threw his costly purchase into the foundations. A strong scent lasted for years, and people used to come from a distance and carry off scented earth as a memento. Kāranja also contains a number of Hindu and Muhammadan temples and tombs. The temple of Siddheshwar Mahādeo, together with the smaller ones of Keshaorāja, Withal, and Bālāji, and a *haveli*, is said to have been built by a *mokāsdār* from Hyderābād who, when on an expedition toward Bengal, was terrified here by a tremendous storm. A temple of Rām was built, ornamented, and endowed in 1876 by Tukāram Bhagwān Kannawa at a total cost, it is said, of a lākh of rupees. The temples of Kāmākshi Devi, Ekākshi Devi, and Kholeshwar Mahādeo (on the Rishi Talao) are said to have been built by the god Rāmchandra, but are not striking. Aurangzeb is said to have torn down a Hemādpanthi temple and built a mosque with its materials. A printed account glorifies Sadārām Mahārāj, whose shrine is at Kāranja, in a somewhat unusual style. It is said that he shampooed his *guru* for 24 years under the water of a river, sat untouched in fire when drops of water from his *sandhya*, meditation accompanied by the sipping of water, burnt a rash visitor to ashes, had images at Pandharpur come to life and feast with him, and caused any twig to grow and bear flowers. Various saints prophesied the day of their own death; one foretold a slight accident to the Extra Assistant Commissioner who used to be stationed at Kāranja, whereon a punkah fell on his head; one had forsaken his business, money-lending, at the casual reproach of a woman who said that thought of it and forgetfulness of God had once made him fall asleep, in one case a Brāhman officiates at a Muhammadan tomb (that of Lāl Imām); and vows are made at various tombs.

Kātepurna River.—The Kātepurna river rises near Bāsim, winds northward and eastward into Akola tāluk, its course near the border being among steep hills covered with light forest, then passes north by Māhān, Donad, and Kurankhed, and across a corner of Murtizāpur tāluk into the Pūrna. Its course is mostly among rather rough country, where its bed is often rocky, but the last few miles are sandy. It contains numerous large pools or deep hollow reaches, the name Donad referring to one of these. Floods pass rapidly along it in the rains, while in the hot weather a trickle of water still runs from pool to pool.

Kuram.—Kuram is a village 14 miles east of Murtizāpur and three miles south-west of the station which bears its name, a good road connecting it with the railway. It was formerly the head of a pargana, and its population was 3368 in 1891 and 3293 in 1901; the *kilā*, a *māti* building, belongs to Government, and is entered by means of a long flight of steps. The most striking feature in the village is a *masjid* built a few years ago on a scale and after a pattern unusual in the District; the architect belonged to northern India. Irrigated land is extensive and is mostly held by Mārwāris. A few temples, old and new, are of moderate interest; a police station is to be built. On the railway line west of the station is the 'Dancing Bridge,' which is constantly shifting a little, for which reason trains cross it very slowly. A Muhammadan tomb stands close by and is popularly associated with the difficulty; passengers therefore throw out showers of pice as they pass, and the driver is said to do *pūja*. Some railway people say that the tomb is of quite recent construction and represents an ingenious but unprincipled investment.

Kutāsa.—Kutāsa is a village in the south-east of Akot, ten miles from Akot town. Its population according to the census reports was 2224 in 1891 and 1866 in 1901, but the people say that the last figures are misleading. It happened that on the night of the census two or three very large weddings were in progress at neighbouring villages, and some hundreds of the inhabitants had gone to attend them. Any marriages taking place in Kutāsa at the same time were altogether too small to counterbalance this. The difficulty might easily occur, as the census was taken in the height of the marriage season and some marriages are very largely attended. People will say, "There were a hundred carriages (in this connection *gāri* seems inadequately translated by *cart*) at So-and-So's wedding"; and everyone knows that one *gāri* can take a lot of people. The lamentable consequence has ensued that Kutāsa is not supplied with sweepers by the District Board, because its population just falls short of the necessary standard, 2000. The area of the village is just under 8000 acres and the land revenue is well over Rs. 18,000, Kutāsa in both respects exceeding every other village in the tāluk. There are five patels, one of whom is a police patel, all sharing in the *mālik patwāripana* but acting through a single substitute patwāri. No bazar is held here, but most of the other institutions of an important village exist. A large tank was put in order in 1874 and is said to have been very useful for 20 years, but now it has silted up; at one time officers put boats on it. Plague has happily never visited the place; people escaping from an infected town are kept outside the village. Kutāsa has a *shāstri*, a mark of distinction because these learned men are very seldom found outside the headquarters of a tāluk. It was formerly a *taraf* of Dahihanda pargana and had half the pargana under it; it is said to have had 40 salt-wells, each of which produced on an average salt of the value of Rs. 1000 annually. The five patels had five separate *gadhis*, village forts, which is unusual. People derive the name from Koteshwar (Mahādeo); a Hemādpanthi temple of his stands in the middle of the village and, further foundations having been discovered about three years ago, a great deal of new building has been put up; the whole work is expected to cost Rs. 10,000. The temple has a short inscription in Devanāgri on one of the pillars, but it has not yet been deciphered. Beneath the letters is the form of a woman with her head turned back and holding a sword in her hand. People have also given about 32 acres of land and subscribe Rs. 1000 a year for a festival on Chaitra Wadya 7 (April—May), all the arrangements being in the hands of a *panch* or small committee. An unusual story is told about the earlier fortunes of Kutāsa. It contained a population of 5000 when Shāhbuddinkhān was appointed Kamaishdār, with the duties of collecting land revenue and supervising the salt wells. He kept a Māng mistress and threatened to make the deshmukhs caress her children. While this quarrel was at its height the Kamaishdār became the worse for liquor and attacked Raoji, son of Withuji Deshmukh, with a sword. The deshmukh caused an illegitimate son of his, called Ghusha, to shoot the officer. In fear of the vengeance of the Government practically every soul left the village and went to live elsewhere, and it was long before any real recovery took place. The tomb of Malangshāhmiyā is situated on the *bāndh* of the tank and is kept in good order, though it is a very plain tomb. He was one of the Chaudah Sau Pālki, and in his time Kutāsa contained 18,000 people but suffered greatly from lack of water. The *awalya* proposed to produce springs of good water in the tank but was opposed by Gangāji Khānduji Deshmukh on the ground that increased prosperity would involve increased suffering from Government in matters of *sarbarai*—details of administration thus shown to form a very old difficulty. Malangshāhmiyā went to Hyderābād and got an order against the deshmukh, but the latter refused to heed it. The *awalya* became enraged and dashing his hands upon the ground laid on the deshmukh the curse that for ever the senior representative of his family should be mad—an entail of insanity. People now give details of six generations, covering the whole period from that time to this, in four of which the curse has come true, while in another the heir to it died young. It is said also that Malangshāhmiyā used sometimes to plant the twigs with which he had cleaned his teeth, and they struck root and grew. He had a disciple called Budhsingh who was a Tākankār by caste and who presently went to live at Panori four miles away. Malangshāhmiyā died there but was buried at Kutāsa, and vows are often made at his tomb. A temple of Dāda Mahārāj Brahmachāri is to be built, Pāndurang Atmārām, patwāri of Rel, having given Rs. 3000 toward the work. He lived chiefly at Benāres and Pandharpur, and nothing is generally known about him, except that he observed the ascetic habits of a *sādhu*.

Mālegaon Bāzār.—Mālegaon Bāzār is a village with a population of 2115 near the western border of Akot tāluk and 17 miles from Akot. It is chiefly remarkable for its large weekly bazar, held on Fridays; the dues are now leased out for Rs. 4000. Mālegaon had both a *kilā*, Government fort, situated where the *chāwadi* now stands, and a *gadhi*, village fort. It belonged to the pargana of Wadner in Daryāpur tāluk but was not a *taraf*, though it has long been a large village. The population includes 50 or 60 families of Mālis, 50 of Muhammadans, and 40 of Kunbi-patels, who consider their caste separate from that of four other families of plain Kunbis. Mālegaon is widely known as the resting-place of Khākishāhmiyā. He came from Northern India 100 or 125 years ago—though some people add that he was at the time one of the Chaudah Sau Pālki champions who according to general tradition marched from Roja-i-sharif (near Aurangābād) in all directions against Hindu shrines. He lived under a *bad* tree in a field called Bala Kilā (after a fortress built there by Anandrao Mādhava, a Bhonsla officer). It was soon observed that he swallowed nothing but merely touched food with the tip of his tongue, and that he confined this diet to bread and vegetables, whereby he was recognized as a saint. Various miracles are ascribed and vows are still paid to him. Once, despite his protests and prophecies, a Shimpi woman called Yamai washed him, and in the evening the village took fire. Jangumiyā, a Hyderābād officer from Ellichpur, set before him balls of sweetmeat in some of which jewels were hidden; the *awalya* took up only those of pure sweetmeat, saying that the rest contained poison. The officer was irritated and struck him with a whip, upon which he said only, *Bhalekā bhalā hojāe aur burekā burā hojāe*, May good result from good and ill from ill; Jangumiyā's men and horses fell ill and he could not travel till he had asked the saint's forgiveness. Khākishāhmiyā was once kidnapped by the people of Adgaon but rescued by those of Mālegaon. He lived naked and, as his name implies, never washed; an inscription says that he died in 1824 when he was 94. The *ināms* here and at Dānāpur are said to have been procured by Mír Alauddīn, Māmlatdār of Akot, who had recovered 15 cartloads of treasure—the price of grain stored by Government and sold in a famine—from a fraudulent agent called Appāji Asalkār; the Māmlatdār passed through the two villages as he was taking the treasure to Hyderābād.

Man River.—The river Man rises in the Chikhli tāluk of the Buldāna District and flows northward through the whole length of Bālāpur tāluk till it reaches the Pūrna. Its total length is about 80 miles, three-quarters of it being within Bālāpur tāluk, constantly near and occasionally upon the western boundary. A tributary called Vishwāmitri flows past Khetri to join it a mile further on. This stream rises at Iswi in Mehkar tāluk, and is named after a *rishi* who lived there. Bālāpur town is situated at the junction of the Man and the Mhais, a tributary of some little size which comes from Khāmgaon tāluk on the west. The Man here flows in a broad and deep channel, the sides of which are greatly cut and roughened by tributary nullahs. A low dam opposite the town holds up the water to some extent. About three miles further north the Bhuikund, called in its earlier course Nirguna, joins the Man on the eastern side. The railway crosses the combined stream, still called the Man, a little to the east of Nāgjhari station, and the course curves considerably to the west before the Pūrna is reached. Apart from Bālāpur one of the most interesting points on the river is in the lands of Sirpur, near Khetri, in the south-west of Bālāpur tāluk. The Man here forms the boundary between Bālāpur and Khāmgaon tāluks; it is already a broad and imposing stream, so that to cross it dry-shod one must follow a long series of rocks which form stepping-stones. On the left bank, at Shāhpur in Khāmgaon tāluk, are the ruins of a palace built about A.D. 1596 by Murād, son of Akbar; on the right, besides the remains of a garden belonging to the palace, is the tomb of Nipāniwalishāh, a Muhammadan *fakīr*. The two are said to have been contemporaries. Nipāniboa, as he is called by Hindus, never drank water and took very little food. He lived in great hardship on a little island in the stream, and whatever flood might come failed to rise above the level of his lips. He finally died through a savage trick of Murād's, who made him eat chillies in the vain attempt to force him to drink. Murād himself, according to the saint's prophecy, died with some of his people in the same torture as they had caused Nipāniboa. Others of the prince's following only saved themselves by flight from the place, and from that time till the present no Muhammadan has been able to live at Shāhpur. The palace included two separate buildings, one of which is still described as the *kacheri*; people have rumours about the precious woods used to adorn it and recount Murād's intention to turn the 12 miles which separate Bālāpur from Shāhpur into one huge city. The buildings show some signs of their former state but are now hopelessly dilapidated and entirely neglected. By a curious contrast the saint's tomb is kept in perfect order and ornamented with flags; both Muhammadans and Hindus make vows to him in case of disease.

Māna.—Māna is a village seven miles east of Murtizāpur and is situated on the left bank of the river Uma and three-quarters of a mile from a railway station, with which it is connected by a good road. It has long been a place of some importance; its population was 2385 in 1891 and 2172 in 1901. The situation appears healthy, as the houses are spread over the tops and sides of two very broad nullahs or small valleys, ensuring both good drainage and openness to any breeze. The village is largely roofed with tiles, though tin and thatch are also common; the buildings are mostly in good condition and the shops are comparatively well supplied, though there are no striking houses. The soil in the neighbourhood is good, the ordinary rates of assessment being R. 1-12 and Rs. 2, and manure is applied with some freedom. More *rabi* is grown than is common in many villages, though far less than was once the case. The Muhammadan population amounts to about 900. A Hindustāni school was first opened for them in 1907, and there are now 52 scholars, but an Arabic private school has been maintained for some years, ten or twelve boys now attending it and learning nothing but Arabic (and that only to a very limited extent). A Marāthi school, held in a pleasant building on high ground, has about 70 boys. Māna was formerly the head of a pargana and has a fort belonging to Government. A new *jamā masjid* is just being built and promises to be quite a fine building; the *kārigir*, architect, is from Kāthiawād. The site is littered with stones which must have come from a fine Hemādpanthi temple; but they belonged to the old *masjid* and will be included in the new one. An *inām* for it dates from the time of Alamgir (Aurangzeb). A number of small but well-finished Muhammadan tombs lie near the village. Legend says that the name Māna was derived from Mānkeshwar, who was the *guru* of Rājā Babruhan, from whom the place was taken by Hāji Rahmān Sāhib. This was an *awalya* who had visited Mecca seven times and was then directed by Muhammad to preach Islām in India. He came to Mānā with a following consisting of Shāh Lāl Sāhib and 17 horsemen. Rājā Babruhan was a demon ruling a population of demons, and Māna was so large that it was divided into 13 *mahāls*, parts; his army consisted of a lākh of horesmen besides other troops, and he was advised by the sage Mānkeshwar Mahārāj. Hāji Rahmān Sāhib challenged him either to accept Islām or to fight, and the *guru* warned him that he was in great danger. To secure his retreat he made an underground passage from Māna to Rājnāpur Khinkhini, seven miles away, so large that his chariot and horesmen could pass along it, but he went out with 70,000 men to fight the Hāji's 17. Some of the Hāji's men were lost and Shāh Lāl Sāhib was wounded, but Babruhan was soon killed and the Muhammadans were at last successful. Shāh Lāl was set on the throne, and such Hindus as did not accept Islām were imprisoned in the old town of Māna, which the Hāji presently flung down upon them.

Mangrul Tāluk.—Mangrul tāluk lies between latitudes 20° 28′ N. and 20° 1′ S. and longitudes 77° 42′ E. and 77° 9′ W.; is very compact in shape, with an average length and breadth of 25 miles; and has an area of 635 square miles. It contains 252 villages, of which 227 are *khālsa*, 21 *izāra*, and 4 *jāgīr*. It was formed in 1875 by the transfer of 156 villages from Bāsim tāluk, 86 from Dārwhā, ten from Pusad, and one from Akola, but in 1905 one was given again to Pusad. The tāluks bounding it are Bāsim on the west, Akola and Murtizāpur on the north, Dārwhā on the east, and Pusad on the south, the two last belonging to Yeotmāl District. The greatest elevations recorded are 1805 and 1807 feet at Pimpalgaon and Shendurjana, in the south; the least are 1409, 1417, and two of 1420, at Amgawhān, Wāi, Rui, and Tornāla, in the north-east; heights of 1600 and 1700 feet are common. The northern half of the tāluk consists of an undulating tableland containing black soil of a productive nature but very variable in depth; a sharp and well-defined drop leads to the Arnāwati valley, which opens out considerably as the eastern boundary is approached and contains deep black soil of a rich description; the southern portion is mountainous and rugged, soils being mostly poor and shallow and communications difficult; the scanty traffic with the south is confined to a few passes. The Adān river passes across the tāluk and the Arnāwati rises in it, but neither attains any size within its borders; plenty of water is however obtained from wells, of which each village has an average of 11. The total area is 403,000 acres, of which 304,000 are occupied for cultivation and 255,000 are cropped, while 58,000 acres, including three whole villages, are given up to forest; only 6000 acres available for cultivation are left unoccupied, and the average assessment of this land is As. 3½, showing that it is very poor soil. During the six years from 1900 to 1906 jawāri and cotton both varied as a rule between 100,000 and 126,000 acres, the former tending to fall and the latter to rise, but in the year 1902-1903 jawāri had only 50,000 and cotton nearly 180,000 acres. Til had generally from 2000 to 3000 acres, though in 1900-1901 it rose to 7000, wheat seldom reached 1500, gram was always below 1000, and linseed only once reached 500. The irrigated area varied from 500 to 800 acres. Thus jawāri and cotton were the only crops of importance, and were just about equal, but cotton threatened to become predominant. No railway passes through the tāluk, and the station most ready of access is Murtizāpur, about 25 miles by metalled road (made during the settlement period) from the border; however Kāranja, five miles along that road, offers a good market. The Nāgpur dāk line passes north-east through Shelu towards Kāranja, but is not metalled and so is not much better than ordinary country roads. A road was made in the famine of 1899-1900 from Kāranja to Dārwhā, 24 miles to the south-east, and assists the traffic of the eastern side of the tāluk. The weekly markets number nine, those at Mangrul and Shelu being the most important and Belkhed and Kothari coming next. A large annual fair is held at Mangrul and smaller ones are held at Sāwargaon, Pohora, Umri, Gimbha, and elsewhere, but reliable figures about them are not to be obtained. The total population cannot be given for 1867 because the tāluk did not then form a separate area, but during the period from 1867 to 1891 the population of the 225 cultivated *khālsa* villages increased by 34 per cent. and in the next decade the total population increased by 10 per cent. more. The population of the whole tāluk was 76,142 in 1881, 82,446 in 1891, and 91,062 in 1901, the increase in the famine decade being perhaps helped by immigration from Pusad and Dārwhā. Mangrul (5793) is the only place with as much as 2000 inhabitants. Banjāras come on pilgrimage to Pohora in the south-east of the tāluk. A curious story is told about the little village of Khed Ābai in the Arnāwati valley. It was customary in *Muglai* times to make a small offering to Government officers who visited a village, a pot of curds and a rupee being considered most suitable; but when an officer once came to this village, then called Khed only, there was the difficulty that not a single cow or she-buffalo could be obtained to provide milk. A woman called Abai, a Warthi (washerwoman) by caste, supplied the deficiency with milk from her own breast; and the officer on discovering this treated her with the respect due to his own mother and made her a grant of the village, which also received her name. The original settlement came into force chiefly in the years 1872 and 1873, when the majority of the villages belonged to Bāsim tāluk; the maximum rates varied from As. 14 to R. 1-8, the most common being R. 1-1. The settlement period was a time of great prosperity and general accumulation of wealth, and communications were much improved by Government. In 1903-1904 the new rates were introduced, varying from R. 1-2 to R. 1-12. The total land revenue in 1907-1908 was Rs. 1,69,376, giving an actual average of As. 9 an acre. Police stations are to be at Mangrul, Manora, and Asegaon; Mangrul town has the only hospital and the only ginning factory in the tāluk. In 1907-1908 Government schools numbered 29, of which 26 were Marāthi boys' schools; the average attendance of all the schools together was 1100.

Mangrul Town.—Mangrul town is the headquarters of a tāluk to which its name is given. It lies about 39 miles south-east of Akola, but there is no good direct road between the two. Mangrul depends for its communications chiefly on the metalled road running north-east from Bāsim to Kāranja and thence north to the railway at Murtizāpur; it is 25 miles from Mangrul to Bāsim, 17 from Mangrul to Kāranja, and 21 thence to Murtizāpur. The population was 5753 in 1867, 4900 in 1881, 5241 in 1891, and 5793 in 1901. The town has a pleasant open situation, though with water-courses on three sides. It has long been the head of a pargana, and was possibly at one time a Muhammadan settlement of some importance, but it has been rather insignificant now for many years and has no municipality. Sanitary arrangements for private houses are under the control of a Sanitary Board with an income of about Rs. 400, while streets are cleaned by sweepers under the Tāluk Board and the street rubbish is removed by potters, who are content with the fuel thus secured as remuneration. The place is remote and quiet, and has only one factory for ginning cotton; a few new houses of some size—though sometimes very plainly built—give a suggestion of prosperity. The only features of interest are the *dargāhs*, tombs, of Shāh Badar-ud-dīn and other Muhammadan saints, the former of which dominates Mangrul even more completely than the temple of Vyenkateshwar Bālāji does Bāsim; the town is often called Mangrul Pīr on account of these associations. The actual tomb is on the top of a small hill, on which are also other buildings connected with it, while below are two large courtyards containing rooms for the accommodation of pilgrims; the whole is surrounded by a massive stone wall with nine bastions and four gates, forming a large fortification. Local tradition relates that Shāh Badar-ud-dīn, also called Hayāt Kalandar, came from Tus in Arabia in one of the Fourteen Hundred Palanquins, 652 of which actually halted at Mangrul; it is added however that he may have come along with the Emperor Aurangzeb, and that the time may have been 700 years ago. At that time a demon called Manglya, from which the present name is derived, dwelt in a temple on the little hill, which was surrounded by jungle. He was very malicious and used to kill animals 12 miles off by his breath alone. He asked Badar-ud-dīn for food and water, and the *awalya* first gave them and then flung down both the demon and the temple in which he lived, built a tomb there for his own residence, and brought settlers to the place. Badar-ud-dīn told a disciple called Shāh Shermastān Sāhib to build a dome over the tomb, and the latter found a daily supply of money under the matting on which he sat. The *dargāh* is supported by *jāgīr* land yielding crops worth Rs. 1700 and by an annual contribution from the Nizām of Rs. 500 (in *hāli sikka* rupees worth As. 14 each). A three days' *urus* begins on the 21st of Jamādilākhar (July—August) every year and is said to be attended by 20,000 people. That the *dargāh* may have greater honour no other house in Mangrul is white-washed, and formerly the sale of *tādi*, toddy, was not allowed; on account of it prostitutes, *bhatyāri*, do not thrive here. Vows are made to the saint by both Muhammadans and Hindus, and one door is half covered with horse-shoes presented by people who have vowed to give one if they got a horse; bread and vegetables are offered if cholera breaks out; an iron chain on one of the doors is dipped in water which is given to women to facilitate a painful delivery. A man who stole a golden *pāras*, spike, from the top of the dome is said to have been punished with blindness. The *jāgīr* now stands in the name of Manwarmiyā Hamjāmiyā; he tells a story about an ancestor called Muhammad Rāfik who had been directed by the saint to live in a certain place. An officer called Fatehjang Nawāb wanted to dislodge him, but immediately fell ill with a grievous pain in his stomach. At midnight a Māng, whose work was to beat a drum for the tomb, saw Badar-ud-dīn himself pass with a procession of 25 *fakīrs* clad in white; the Nawāb died and the Māng was blessed by the saint and prospered. The *jamā masjid* stands just below the tomb; it is a large but not very striking building. Close to the town stands the *dargāh* of Hazrat Shāh Amānsāhib, with that of his *guru* Shāh Amānullah in the same enclosure. It has an inscription and is of some size, though not on the scale of Shāh Badar-ud-dīn's *dargāh.* Amānsāhib, who came from Sialkot, is of less antiquity than the other and was distinguished by adopting the penance of remaining constantly for 12 years seated on the ground. Finally the Emperor Shāh Jahān came to Mangrul, and on his forming the wish that the *fakīr* should rise Amānsāhib did so, but with such pain and difficulty that the blood poured from his crippled legs; Shāh Jahān then gave him two *jāgīr* villages and some *inām* land. A third *dargāh*, that of Diwān Hāji Shāh Muhammad, stands two miles west of Mangrul on a hill called Dhanbaldi, treasure-hill, beside the Bāsim road. This saint is said to have been a *jamādār* in the Nizām's service, having charge of 14 horses, but his date can not be more definitely fixed. He came from Nasirābād in Khāndesh and was greatly pleased with the tomb of Badar-ud-dīn, a voice from which presently bade him to relinquish all worldly interests and live at the tomb; he did so and the *awalya* continued to give him directions from time to time. Thus he went to Mecca and afterwards to Burhānpur, where a saint called Shāh Allah Baksh gave him a cup containing the juice of certain herbs, whereby he was purified and became himself an *awalya;* again he was directed to live 50 paces behind the *dargāh*, where he built a mosque and dug two wells, and later to go to the site of his present tomb. While he was building a mosque and *dargāh* there a Gosain passed and gave him a tin of powder whereby 52 tolas of copper might be turned into the same weight of gold, but Diwān Shāh put it one side. The Gosain passed again some years later and, seeing the various works completed, thought his magic had been utilised, but the saint first showed him the untouched tin and then caused the Gosain to see the hill composed entirely of gold and silver, whence the present name of Dhanbaldi. Another *dargāh* and several Hindu temples of no particular interest also stand in the town.

Morna River.—The Morna river rises in Bāsim tāluk and flows northward to join the Pūrna, its total length being about 70 miles. The most important part of its course lies in Akola tāluk, but both in its early stages and again toward the end it crosses a corner of Bālāpur tāluk. Like so many rivers in the District it flows to the west for some miles just before joining the Pūrna. Akola is situated on the Morna, a bridge 450 feet in length uniting the two parts of the town. Two dams at Akola hold up the river for about three miles. At Sindkhed on the Morna, about nine miles south of Akola, there is a Hemādpanthi temple of Moreshwar Mahādeo of some slight interest. It contains a stone image of a bull covered with copper some years ago by an artist from Murtizāpur. A large wall around the temple is said to have been built by the Bhonslas of Nāgpur, and Aurangzeb is also brought into its traditions. A large fair is held in Chaitra (April—May).

Mundgaon.—Mundgaon is a village six miles south-west of Akot. Its population is 3329, and it has a large weekly market (on Tuesdays), a *chāwadi*, Marāthi schools for boys and girls, a *dharmshāla*, and a pound—the ordinary administrative equipment of a large village.

It has no striking archæological relics, though it is curious that the *patelki* family have two separate forts. Temples are numerous but are mostly built of clay and wood with iron gratings or railings. Some of them are of fair size and some are quite new, but the older ones are very largely allowed to fall into disrepair. A large fraction of the population are Mālis, but no explanation of this is given. Mundgaon was the head of a *taraf* of 11 villages within Akot pargana and therefore had deshmukhs of its own, but no history attaches to it. The village thus strikes one as being very commonplace, but a partial glimpse of its religious life may perhaps be interesting. It contains nine Hindu shrines or temples and one Jain temple, besides two mosques and the low caste places of worship. Almost every temple has a paid *pujāri*, minister or worshipper, and an annual festival, the cost of the latter varying from Rs. 10 to Rs. 300. Nearly all the temples were built by individuals whose families still live in the village. Two were erected last year, the builder in each case devoting all his wealth to the temple and the actual cost being in one case Rs. 1000 and in the other Rs. 6000. The gods to whom the various shrines and temples are dedicated include Mahādeo and Māroti, Vithoba, Bālāsāhib, Rāmchandra (with his brother Lakshman and his wife Sīta), and Lakshmi Nārāyan; three are Gosain's *maths*, containing tombs but no image and frequented only by members of the caste; and in one case the god is a man still alive, Gajanan Mahārāj, a well-known *sādhu* of Shegaon in Khāmgaon tāluk.

Murtizāpur Tāluk.—Murtizāpur tāluk lies between latitudes 20° 53′ N. and 20° 25′ S. and longitudes 77° 44′ E. and 77° 13′ W., and has an area of 610 square miles. Kāranja was the headquarters before the railway was opened, but Murtizāpur has been the tāluk town since then. The tāluk belonged to Amraoti District from early times till 1905, when, on the reduction of the Districts, it was transferred to Akola. At the original settlement it contained 337 villages but owing to various trifling changes it now has only 218, of which 296 are *khālsa*, 16 are leased as the Kāmargaon Estate, and 6 are *jāgīr*. In shape it is an oblong with a length from north to south of 30 miles and a breadth from east to west of 20. The Akola tāluk bounds it on the west, the Daryāpur tāluk of Amraoti District, across the Pūrna river, on the north, Amraoti and Chāndur belonging to the same District on the east, and Mangrul on the south, while the Dārwhā tāluk of Yeotmāl District touches it on the south-east. The greater part of Murtizāpur tāluk is a plain of rich black soil, but the south is hilly and light and the soil on the eastern border and in the north-east is also stony and poor; on the whole the soil is perhaps equal to that of Akola tāluk but inferior to that of Akot or Daryāpur. The greatest height recorded is 1500 feet above sea-level at Kāmatwāda in the south-east; Girda, Pasurni and Tuljāpur, in the high land of the south, have elevations of 1449, 1440, and 1437 feet; while Bapori, Kuram, Hinganwādi, and Rājura, in the north-east, rise only to 1011, 1013, 1041, and 1098 feet; The tāluk seems to get a better rainfall than Akola and has many streams which contain water throughout the year. The Pūrna, which forms the northern boundary, is the chief; the Adān forms nearly half of the southern boundary; the Bembalā is considered to rise within the town of Kāranja and flows at first north, then north-east, and finally bending east between Amraoti and Chāndur tāluks finds its way to the Wardhā river; the Uma rises a little to the west of Kāranja and, flowing slightly to the north-east past Kāmargaon, Kinkhed and Māna, but with a final turn to the west, enters the Pūrna ; the Pedhi flows through a few villages in the north-east, and the Kātepurna through some in the north-west, of the tāluk. Kāranja has a tank of about 600 acres, and every village has on an average 15 wells. The total area of the tāluk is about 390,000 acres, of which 179,000 are forest, 345,000 are occupied for cultivation, about 315,000 are annually cropped, and only 27 remain available but unoccupied. The area under jawāri in the six years from 1901 to 1906 varied irregularly between about 110,000 and 160,000 acres, that under cotton between 150,000 and 170,000, wheat between 4000 and 14,000, linseed between 3000 and 10,000, and til between 1000 and 4000, while tūr was usually under 4000 but rose once to 15,000 and once to 21,000 ; from 1200 to 3200 acres were irrigated. Thus there are considerable variations from year to year, largely on account of the peculiarities of the seasons but partly through mistakes in recording, but cotton and jawāri were by far the most important crops, and cotton tended to increase ; wheat inclined to extend at the expense of other *rabi* crops. The Great Indian Peninsula Railway crosses the tāluk from west to east, with a total length within its borders of 16 miles and with stations at Murtizāpur, Māna, and Kuram, while the Tākli and Badnera stations in Amraoti District also serve Murtizāpur. Metalled roads run south from Murtizāpur to Kāranja (21 miles) and thence south-west through Mangrul to Bāsim and south-east to Dārwhā, and north from Murtizāpur to Daryāpur (with nine miles within the tāluk). Others connect the different stations with the villages from which their names are taken ; and Rs. 100 a mile is spent on the less thorough maintenance of several other roads. Country roads are numerous and are excellent for bullock-cart or saddle-horse through the dry months in the plain country, though they are stony in the hilly parts. A great deal of traffic goes to Amraoti, villagers thinking that they get both better prices and fairer weights for their cotton there than at Murtizāpur. Kāranja used to produce fine *sāris*, but manufactures now scarcely exist at all ; however there are twelve factories for ginning and eight for pressing cotton, situated mostly at Kāranja and Murtizāpur. Weekly markets (let out at Rs. 100 or more) are held at nine villages, that at Umarda lasting two days. Murtizāpur itself has the most important market, but Umarda is known for its bullocks and Kuram and Shelu are known for *ghī*. Small fairs are held at various villages annually, twice a year, or weekly, but there are no large ones. The original settlement came into force in 1870-1871, the rates varying from R. 1-4 to Rs. 2, with R. 1-10 most common. During the settlement period communications were much improved, there was a large increase in almost all forms of agricultural wealth, the revenue was collected without difficulty, and all available land except about 300 acres was occupied, though the famine of 1899-1900 caused a check to this prosperity. The revision settlement came into force in 1900, when the rates varied from R. 1-14 to Rs. 2-10 ; the total land revenue in the year 1907-1908 was Rs. 4,11,288. Population between 1867 and 1891 increased by 25 per cent. ; in 1881 it was 110,573, in 1891 121,657, and in 1901, after the famine decade, 118,022 ; the density was then 193 persons to the square mile, with an average of five persons to each house. Only two towns had a population of over 5000, Kāranja with 16,535 and Murtizāpur with 6156 ; villages with over 2000 were—Sirso 4503, Kuram 3293, Kāmargaon 2346, and Māna 2172. In fact however the boundaries of a revenue village sometimes fail to correspond with the actual limits of population in a particular neighbourhood, on account of which the population of Murtizāpur town should probably be considered 9200 and that of Sirso only 1500. At Khinkhini Rājnāpur (population 392) is a Hemādpanthi temple largely built over with brick but showing very elaborate carving upon the doorway and pillars ; a kind of porch has slabs of stone shaped like long seats with sloping backs ; the word *me* is cut in *Bālbodh* on the front ; while a carved stone about three feet high outside the enclosure represents *gadha Bhoiniwar chadhtāna*. At Kāwatha (population 254) near by a temple dedicated to Sopināthboa is famous for the cure of snake-bite. The victim at once places a stone on his head in the name of the saint and as soon as opportunity permits visits the temple, burns camphor, and offers *shirni*, sweetmeats, of the weight of the stone. A fair is held every Monday, besides special gatherings on Polā and Nāgpanchmi, and three or four people who have been bitten are said to come every week ; it is considered that the influence of the saint is felt immediately they cross the boundary of the village. At Lākhpuri, on the Pūrna, there is a group of old temples to which pilgrimage is made, especially on Somwati Awas (a Monday at the end of a dark fortnight). Nausāla in the north-east and Bhām in the south-east have small Hemādpanthi temples. Dhanaj, on the Nāgpur dāk line, has an unfurnished bungalow and a large *sarai*, originally intended for a school ; an unusual proportion of Mārwāris have settled in the village. The tāluk has perhaps no castes of extraordinary interest, but Tākankars, Pārdhis, Gopāls, and Muhammadan Gaolis—the two last of whom are found especially in the grazing neighbourhoods of the south—have criminal tendencies. Police stations are to be at Murtizāpur, Kāranja, Dhanaj, and Kuram, and there are hospitals at the first two places. Schools in 1908 numbered 35, with an average daily attendance together of 1700.

Murtizāpur Town.—Murtizāpur is the headquarters of the tāluk to which its name is given and is situated on the railway line 20 miles east of Akola. Its formation is somewhat anomalous. A village nearly a mile south-east of the railway station is alone known as Murtizāpur for revenue or census purposes; its population was 4887 in 1881, 4438 in 1891, and 6156 in 1901. A new settlement, Mubārakpur, has formed immediately south of the line, lying across the Murtizāpur road, and it now contains over 3000 people; but the land on which it is built belongs to the village of Sirso, two miles to the north on the Daryāpur road; and Mubārakpur is for revenue and census purposes treated as merely a part of Sirso. Thus that village was given a population in 1867 of 3897, in 1891 of 2942, and in 1901 of 4503; but the inhabitants of the *gaothān* of Sirso have for many years numbered only about 1500; the rest live in Mubārakpur and are most closely associated with Murtizāpur station and town. The Kāranja metalled road strikes directly south from the station; the Murtizāpur branch road leaves it almost immediately, a dāk bungalow standing at the junction. This branch road first passes a number of factories, next crosses a wide open space where a large market is held on Fridays, and then enters Murtizāpur proper. Such a distribution of the population has some sanitary advantages, and there are open spaces east of Murtizāpur again, but there are always difficulties about the sanitation of places of such a size; no municipality exists, but there is a Sanitary Committee. None of these places have buildings or other associations of much historical interest, though both Murtizāpur and Sirso were pargana villages and the former has the remains of a *kilā*, fort, belonging to Government; it is said that 200 Arabs were at one time stationed in the *kilā*. The temples of Murtizāpur are of moderate interest. Bansilāl Gafurchand, who is building a temple of Trimbakeshwar Mahādeo, says it is very difficult to get masons. A small *veda shāla*, Veda school, has been in existence for ten years. Murtizāpur and Mubārakpur are busy trading places, with plain but fairly well-supplied shops and with nine cotton factories between them. The importance of the traffic with Kāranja and Daryāpur, especially that with the former, is illustrated by scores of carts, including both pony-tongās and *sawāri*, passenger, bullock-carts, waiting unharnessed on a plot of ground just outside the station to take people to those places. Murtizāpur has one or two quarters given up to Muhammadans, who number 250 or 300 families. They are mostly very poor but include a small community of Cutchis who control much of the trade of the town and, while taking four months' holiday every year, have some wealth and help the general community. A mosque has just been very neatly rebuilt and well roofed with tiles from Bombay. A community of Kanaujia Brāhmans live in another quarter, numbering 20 or 25 families altogether, and engage largely in moneylending; they often bring their wives from Ujjain and Mālwā. It is said that the name Murtizāpur is derived from Murtiza Ali, a Naib of some centuries ago. Mubārakpur only began to be populated between 1870 and 1880 and is called after the Tahsīldār of the time, Mubārak Ali. Houses have hitherto been built only on three waste fields containing 17 acres retained by Government, but in the beginning of 1909 two cultivated fields containing 36 acres were bought by the District Board for Rs. 4600, and this land will also be sold or leased out for building. Hitherto the best sites have been sold, and an annual rental of

As. 1 or As. 2 for 100 square feet has been charged for other sites. A trading community of Mārwāris and Bhātias, numbering perhaps 70 houses, has grown up. The bulk of the inhabitants of Mubārakpur are either labourers employed in the factories or cart-drivers. Most of them are Dakhanis from Poona, Sātāra, Pandharpur, and other places, and these include a few Muhammadans, but there are also some Pardeshis from Northern India. The (acting) patel and patwāri of Sirso live in Mubārakpur and have a *chāwadi*, office, there, but an influential member of the *watan* family lives at Sirso and the village officers visit the place daily. The rights of *deshmukhi*, *patelki*, *patwāripana*, and *mahārki watan* are all in the hands of one family, now represented by a minor.

Narnāla.—Narnāla is an ancient fortress in the hills in the north of Akot tāluk at a point where a narrow tongue of Akola District runs a few miles into the Melghāt. A description of the points of archæological interest it contains is given in Chapter II, but a few other details may be added here. It is uninhabited but is in charge of a patel and patwāri; the latter, Nārāyan Dattātreya, has a fund of information about it. The fortress lies about 12 miles north of Akot, the road passing through Bordi and the deserted village of Shāhānur. The latter village lies within the first roll of the hills but just at the foot of the real ascent. Its lands were made forest two years ago and signs of cultivation are rapidly disappearing. It has a bungalow and *sarai*, though no caretaker, and carts can go only as far as this. The rest of the road is under the care of the District Board but is in parts exceedingly steep and stony; however camels mount it, and it is possible to ride a horse all the way. The road climbs a spur of the hills and then follows a ridge, the whole ascent from Shāhānur occupying less than an hour. About half way up it crosses first one and then another piece of level ground, each thickly sprinkled with Muhammadan tombs. These are called *Lahān* and *Mota Sati Maidān*; on the left side of the road in the upper plot is a small broken stone having carved on it an upraised hand, a sun, and crescent moon, which is described as *Satīcha hāt*, Sati's hand. Presently the lower range of fortifications comes into sight, a line of blackened walls crowning cliffs of black stone and lying dwarfed but massive along the folds of the hill-side. Accomplishing three-quarters of the ascent the road passes through the first gateway, crowned like the rest with an arch lofty enough for elephants to pass. A curtain projecting on the outer side of the gateway is called Sāha Gotyāchi Sapīli because its full height, about 30 feet, is made up of six great stones placed one on top of the other. Lions in different attitudes ornament both the outside and the inside of the gateway. The path passes two other strong gateways and one slighter one before entering the heart of the fort, and climbs meanwhile to the uppermost *ghāts*. Between the last two gateways are the domed tombs of Bāg Sawār Wali and Gaz Bādshāh Wali. The former not only rode a tiger in his life but even now a tiny white tiger may be seen at night going to and from his tomb. Passing the last gateway one comes almost at once before the Ambar Bangala, the *kacheri* of former days and the chief rest-house of the present. It is a lofty building looking on to a cemented courtyard which formerly contained a fountain and was roofed with wood. The *bangala* has a flat roof reached by a long and steep staircase, and walls around the roof give shade during the greater part of the day, while openings afford a wide view over both plain country and hills. Akot is generally visible, with the nearer villages, and in the clear air of the rains one can plainly see the flooded Pūrna 25 miles away. At an equal distance on the west the fortress of Pimpardol crowns one of the two highest hills in that part of the Sātpurās, a fairly large fortification but one so little known that its existence is sometimes denied by people living just below it and even by Mahārs who go on pilgrimage to one of its tanks. Just across the courtyard is the tomb of Burhānuddīn, sometimes called "the dogs' temple," and beyond it is the Shakkar Talao, a tank of some little size. The tomb is a commonplace stone platform with a few tombstones upon it and a dilapidated building beside it. It has long been known as a place where the bite of a mad dog, jackal, or rat may be cured, and its fame has been at its height for the last five or six years. People come from Shegaon, Bālāpur, Māhān, and even Bāsim, 90 miles away, to the number of 100 or 150 in a year. They offer *gur*, *channa*, *ūd*, and *phūl*—country sugar, parched gram, incense, and flowers—walk five times around the stone platform, place in their mouths five grains of gram and a very little of the other food offered, and walk away with their eyes fixed on the ground till they have passed the first gateway of the fort (a few hundred yards away). One of the *jāglias* of Narnāla directs the proceedings and adds to his income by the gifts of patients. Intelligent people of the neighbourhood are convinced that the cure is effective if performed before hydrophobia has appeared in the patient, and the *jāglia* says it even takes effect later, but every year there are one or two cases of visitors who die of hydrophobia either just before or just after visiting the tomb. The local experts hold the common belief that hydrophobia is very apt to remain latent during the dry seasons and manifest itself at the first fall of rain. The number of visitors to the tomb does not increase just at that time, but the difficulty of travelling would explain this; people vow to make the pilgrimage at a more convenient time. The Shakkar

Talao is connected with various legends. The cow called Kapila, pure white, and Kāmdhenu, the granter of desires, descends from heaven at midnight and passes through the water to a *pinda*, shrine, of Mahādeo beneath it, and there yields her milk. Unhappily this story was told long ago to an incredulous Deputy Commissioner, who at first made the retort that though all other liars might be dead the relater was one left alive, and then had the tank sounded and searched by a Bhoi diver. Nothing was found but mud, upon which the officer added, 'Is there nothing in the tank? Then take the patwāri (who had told the tale) and drown him there'; and though the order was not enforced this unsympathetic attitude has greatly discouraged the recounting of anecdotes. It is said also that a *pāras*, spike of a dome, lies in the tank with the power of turning everything it touches into gold, and that an elephant's shackles were once changed in this way when it entered the tank. The water dried up in the famine of 1899-1900 and nothing was found, but it is remarked that no one knows what is hidden in the mud. At the west end of the courtyard mentioned are a pretty mosque and handsome stables, while near the other end is a block of four large covered cisterns with broken but graceful arches rising above them. Some have thought them Jain water-cisterns, but they are locally called *telāche tupāche tāke* and said to have been used for storing oil and *ghī* for the large garrison. The fort covers 392 acres, and the walls, which only approximately keep at the same level, wind about so much in following the shape of the hill that people say the full circuit measures 24 miles. It would certainly take very many hours to trace out all the buildings, especially as the walls, though generally in excellent condition, have crumbled in places and the enclosure is much overgrown with long grass and bushes. It is said that there were 22 tanks, six of which still hold water all the year, 22 gates, and 360 *buruj*, towers or bastions. The first fortifications, according to tradition, were made by Nāryendrāpuri, a descendant of the Pāndavas and at the time Emperor of Hastināpur (Delhi). Later Muhammad Bahmani of Bījāpur got possession, and nearly all the present buildings seem to be of Muhammadan origin. The fort passed afterwards to the Marātha, Dakhani, followers of Sivāji and his descendants, then to the Peshwa, the Nizām, the Bhonslas, the Nizām again, and finally to the British, but people say that throughout all this history no great fight ever took place over it. At the same time they tell some warlike stories about it. Muhammadans say that when men of their religion first came to this part of India Narnāla and Gāwīlgarh were held by *deotas*, spirits, who seized and ate any of them who approached the forts. Presently the Fourteen Hundred Champions came with supernatural powers. Narnāla was in the hands of three great *deotas*, Rājā Il, Narnālswāmi, and Rājā Bairāt, and its conquest was undertaken by two great *awalyas*, Ambi Awalya and Dulāsh Rahmān. The former is buried at Dhārud, 4 miles away, and the latter seems to be the traditional conqueror of Ellichpur, the city of Rājā Il. The *deotas* were at first contemptuous of 'these atoms of men,' but were soon obliged to take refuge in some vaults in the fort and were there captured. They were asked what they would have done had they won, and replied that they would have skinned their opponents and hung the skins, filled with *bhusa*, chaff, at the gates. The *awalyas* then turned the *deotas* into stone, the figures of Rājā Il and Narnālswāmi being still shown above a precipice not far from the ordinary entrance-road. Ambi Awalya struck the former with his fist and split the stone in two. Rājā Bairāt asked that his fate might take place at Ellichpur and that Muhammadans might worship on one side of him and Hindus on the other, and this was granted. A legend also connects a hill a little to the south-west of the fort with its capture in the time of Aurangzeb. On the top of the hill is the *dargāh* of Saiduliboa or Saiduliwali; it is said that a gun was taken up there unknown to the Dakhanis and delivered by night so effective a fire that the garrison fled. Again the name Sati Maidān is sometimes applied to the whole sweep of hill-side between Shāhānur and the fort, and the explanation is given that a vast number of men were killed here in the time of Aurangzeb, the tombs of the Muhammadans alone remaining; the name would then have the general meaning of Plain of Death. The vaults, *bhuyar*, mentioned lie a short distance to the west of the Ambar Bangala; they are a series of small chambers connected by low archways and are sometimes called *zanān khāna* on the supposition that they were meant for the residence of *gosha* women, women who must not be seen in public. Their purpose is however not certain, and their extent is not known. An attempt to explore them, inspired by the hope of finding treasure, was defeated by great numbers of bats coming upon the intruders, who were also afraid of snakes. A late *jāglia* of Narnāla, Gafūr Ahmad, is said to have driven a score of sheep into the vaults to see where they would come out. One emerged at Gāwīlgarh, more than 20 miles away, but no trace was ever found of the others. A cross stands on a high point on the eastern side of the fort and marks the grave of a European officer who was left in charge and died here after the battle of Argaum, but no trace of his name is left. Among the buildings on the east side is a *nagār-khāna* where prisoners used to be kept in a pit, with a big stone over their heads, to await execution. A few hundred yards off is the *khūni buruj*, where a platform was built on the edge of a sheer precipice over which criminals were sometimes hurled. The *nau-gaj top*, nine-yard gun, lies between these two. A ball from it is said once to have carried off the golden spike set on the domed building at Dhārud in the plain below and to have continued its flight till it fell into the tank at Kutāsa, 20 miles away. (It is also said at Narnāla that the Hemādpanthi temple at Kutāsa contains enough buried treasure to restore the fort, the repeated mention of Kutāsa perhaps showing its former importance). Formerly there was a sister gun called *khadak bijli*, terrible lightning, but this somehow fell over the cliff into Chandan Khora, the valley of sandal wood, and mysteriously disappeared from sight. Two other guns lie near the Akot gate, to the south of the ordinary entrance, but the bulk of the military stores were removed in 1858. Tantia Topi and Mugutrao were then at Jalgaon, the headquarters of the tāluk on the west, and it was thought that they might seize these stores, though the fortress was in the hands of the Nizām. The guns were therefore taken off to Akot, the Tahsīldār gathering 1000 or 1200 people together for the task of bringing them down the hills, and the guns being hauled across the plain by long teams of oxen in one great confused procession. The powder and sulphur were brought out of the magazine and watered and burnt, but a spark got into the last cask before it was removed ; such an explosion followed that one still hears how people's ears rang, and men were knocked down by the hundred, while two rockets went sailing across the fort into the hills ; but the magazine, a strong building, withstood the shock and is still to be seen. The Dhobi Talao is a pretty tank which holds water all the year. It has a series of arches at one side, with summer houses, if one may use the word, consisting of two stone chambers one above the other and covered by a flat roof. Water was taken thence to a garden, and one stone is grooved in almost a score of places by the rope which ran on it. The garden is ascribed to the Bhonslas and is still marked by some *champa* trees, while two lofty stands for *tulsi*, basil, plants also reveal Hindu influences. Moreover a shrine of Mahātoba, or Mhātoba, on the south of the tank, is famed for the cure of snake-bite. The victim must utter the name of the god and place a stone or piece of earth on his head. Upon this he has invariably strength to reach the shrine, the power of the poison being checked. Arriving there he burns a little *ghī* in a lamp, or *rāl*, *ūd*, *gugul*, resin or incense, or something of the sort. Presently he shivers and sweats—or according to the report of some eye-witnesses the god sweats—and straightway the man is cured; cattle are also healed. A Mahār of Warud who was cured in this way comes on a yearly pilgrimage and puts the shrine in order. Now it consists simply of a rough reddened stone on a rough platform, and its importance must be diminished by the snake god at Shiupur below the *ghāt*, 5 miles distant. Quite close to the stone of Mhātoba is an image of Mahābīr or Bajrangkāli, holding its hand upraised and supported by a much smaller figure. The *dalbādal*, containing the old mint, is quite near, and a Muhammadan graveyard is at no great distance. It is said that the Bhonslas had 2000 or 2500 men here, and the number and variety of buildings show clearly that there must have been a large population, but now the place is generally empty save when Hindu pilgrims visit the tomb of Saiduliboa and Burhānuddīn in the rains, or Muhammadans come in Ramzān, or the dog-bitten come for healing. Evil spirits, *bhūts* and *shaitāns*, are said to haunt it; wherever the walls are broken are the tracks of wild beasts, morning and evening peacock come to the tanks, and at night sāmbar also come thither, following well-worn tracks through the ancient gateways.

Nirguna River.—The Nirguna river rises in Bāsim tāluk and flows north through the middle of Bālāpur tāluk till it presently curves to the west and joins the Man about 3 miles north of Bālāpur. Its total length is about 50 miles. In the third part of its course it is joined on the east by a much smaller stream, the Bhuikund (on which Pātur Shekh Bābu is situated), and is thenceforward called by that name. At Alegaon, in the south of Bālāpur tāluk, the Nirguna is already a large stream and flows in a shallow bed of loose stones extending in places to 100 yards in breadth. Toward the end of its course it is more confined, and its current in flood time is such that it causes Bālāpur to be seriously isolated, as it crosses the roads leading from Bālāpur to Akola and to Pāras, the nearest railway station.

Panchagawhān.—Panchagawhān is a village in Akot tāluk about 16 miles from Akot; its population is 2885. It consists of six villages with separate officers; according to tradition there were at one time only five villages, whence the name, but another was afterwārds added and called Ubārkhed, the village over. Panchagawhān was the headquarters of a pargana of 36 villages; under the Nizām a Naib lived in a *gadhi*, now ruined, belonging to Government. One-half of the population consists of Muhammadans, who are divided into six *muhallas*; the *jamā masjid* dates from the Emperor Shāh Jahān but has recently been simply and prettily rebuilt. Education is flourishing; there are 50 pupils in the Hindustāni girls' school. The village has a weekly market of some size and a ginning factory. Men of middle age remember when thick jungle separated it from the river, where there is now scarcely a tree. It is said that very wealthy *sāhukārs*, men with crores of money, used to live here. One of them, Naorangrai Nimbawāle, was a poor man till a son was born to him, but when he dug a pit to bury the caul a pot of money was found at the bottom. Seven pits were dug and seven pots found; finally the father addressed the infant as Lakshmikānta (husband of the goddess of wealth) and prayed him to grant an empty pit. Gold could be found later wherever the child's urine had fallen; Naorangrai demonstrated this to the Government to prove that he was not getting his wealth dishonestly; the boy died at five years of age. Other very rich men were Dina Bāba Ghan and Bālāji Ganesh, each of whom built a temple of Mahādeo and a well. A *sādhu* called Lakhmappa, a Jangam Wāni by caste, lived here for a time and a *samādh* has been built to him, though he died at Risod in Bāsim tāluk; during an annual fair in his honour the weekly market is held in front of the *samādh*. Two stories are told about him, the Emperor Aurangzeb, who made a great impression in this part of India, appearing in both. Aurangzeb knew the *karāmat* of 52 *bīr mantras*, which gave him formidable miraculous powers. He spread a *chaddar*, cloth, over the mouth of a well, put four lemons on the corners to keep it in place, and then knelt on the cloth and offered prayers to God; Lakhmappa in his turn removed the cloth and stood upright over the well. From that time the two were on familiar terms. A Delhi merchant was once in danger at sea and vowed the fourth part of his stock to Aurangzeb, as to a god, if he should be saved. At that moment the Emperor and the *sādhu* were sitting under a tamarind tree playing *chausar* (*chaupat* or *songtya*, a game resembling draughts). The saint alone became aware of the vow and thrust a piece of cloth into a hole in the tree, presently bringing it forth streaming with water;

Aurangzeb asked for an explanation but was told only to note the date. This was understood when the merchant appeared; the Emperor sent him to Risod to offer his goods to Lakhmappa, who distributed them to the poor. Rudranāthswāmi, a disciple of Nānā Sāhib of Pātur, has a holy place with four (formerly five) small shrines in it. He was going to Pātur in company with Ambujiboa of Wyāla when they learnt that the master was dead and his body was being burnt; however they proceeded and at Nāndkhed, 6 miles from Pātur, saw Nānā Sāhib. Rudranāth wished to be taught some *guru mantra*, such as are given in secret to a disciple, and when water was required produced it by striking an empty *tala*, cistern. Rudranāth begot a son, Bhikājiboa, by giving his wife a partly chewed roll of betel. The village contains the remnants of a *sati* temple and three new temples. That of Vithal was built by Nānakrām Gangārām and that of Rāmchandra by Someshwardās Brāmhachari, a *sādhu* from Gujarāt, who collected Rs. 3500 for the purpose. This temple and that of Appaswāmi were designed and erected by Sakhārām and Dagdu Jairām, Teli masons of the village. The Muhammadans have also the tomb of a saint, Neknām Sāhib. He and his four sons were military officers of about the end of the seventeenth century A.D., and three of them fell in battle; curiously exact details are given about them. Neknām Sāhib still rides in a green-clad procession to Ner, 4 miles to the south, thence to Adsul, and back to Panchagawhān. Many have heard the galloping of horses within the tomb, and a Bhoi once accompanied the procession, holding the tail of one of the horses. On the return *malīda*, a kind of cake, was distributed; the Bhoi was warned to secrecy but gave his share to his wife and, yielding to her persistence, told her the whole story, upon which his whole family soon perished. An epidemic of cholera once ceased when a stone fell from one of the tombs.

Pātur Shekh Bābu.—Pātur, or Pātur Shekh Bābu, is a village in the south-east corner of Bālāpur tāluk, 21 miles south of Akola on the main road to Bāsim; another metalled road runs north-west from Pātur to Bālāpur and Khāmgaon. The village is pleasantly situated on the river Bhuikund in a well-wooded valley between sharp ridges of hill. It has long been a town of some importance and was formerly the head of a pargana, but its population has been declining for some years; it was 7219 in 1881, 6156 in 1891, and 5990 in 1901. It contains a police station, hospital and dispensary, post and telegraph-offices, dāk bungalow and *dharmshāla*, and Marāthi and Urdu schools, and has a large Muhammadan population. It is of considerable archæological interest because of some ancient caves cut in the hill-side and the tombs of a Muhammadan saint called Shekh Bābu and a Hindu called Nānā Sāhib. They are all on the west bank of the river, the caves and Hindu tomb several hundred yards from the nearest houses. The caves are chambers carved out of the rock of the hill-side on the model of the less developed Hemādpanthi temples. It is said that they were neglected for a long time but were cleared out in about 1881 by Mr. Bymonji Jamasji, Assistant Commissioner. They have generally been ascribed to Buddhism, but one certainly contains an emblem of Mahādeo carved out of the solid rock. They are entirely neglected from a religious point of view and no local tradition seems to attach to them; it is remarked merely that they 'must have been dug out for some *sādhu*.' The name of the Muhammadan saint, Shekh Bābu, is commonly added to that of the town to distinguish it from other places called Pātur, but Hindus say that the original name was the *nagari*, town, of

Pārāshara, an ancient *rishi*. The relics of Shekh Bābu now shown comprise the *jamā masjid*, some marks in the rocks of the river-bed, and his *dargāh*, tomb. The mosque and tomb bear inscriptions giving their dates as 1142 and 791 H., or 1118 and 1725 A.D., respectively; the mosque is said to contain a beam miraculously suspended in the air. The marks on the rocks are by the eye of faith recognised as the footprints of men, horses, camels, and elephants; they are said to have been made when the saint, having caused an army to disappear into the earth, called it forth again unharmed. The *dargāh* consists of successive enclosures with a tomb in the last; the building is not very fine in itself but is a fairly well-known place of pilgrimage. Such *fakīrs* as come are divided into the two classes of Bānwa and Madāri; the former mutilate themselves, abstain from begging, and eat only at the very place of pilgrimage, while the others differ on all three points. The *ināmdārs* of the tomb are bound to provide pilgrims with food. A manuscript account of Shekh Bābu given by the *kāzi* relates that the saint came from Mecca and passed Dholāpur on the river Chambal; there he and his disciples flung into the river a demon who once a year demanded human sacrifices. The feet of the demon are said still to be visible in the water, and Hindus on pilgrimage worship first at a shrine built in memory of the deliverer and next beside the demon's feet. Gyāsuddīn Tughlak is said to have been at the time Emperor at Delhi, and to have been succeeded by Abu Bakr, who was again dethroned by Nasiruddīn Muhammad, all three of the same family. Both the last two shared in the building of the present tomb, but it was never quite finished. The temple of Nānā Sāhib, a fairly large series of buildings, is perhaps a mile from the town. A history of the saint, together with a partial account of Mārkināthboa of Mārki in

Amraoti tāluk, is contained in a manuscript *granth*, religious poem, said to have been written by Mukundrāj, son of Nānā Sāhib himself, and now in the possession of Devidās Amle of Pātur, also descended from him. Nānā Sāhib was the son of a *sāhukār*, a Yajurvedic Brāhman of Pātur, and was originally called Nārāyan Kānhoji Amle. Even in his youth he spent a great deal in making gifts to Brāhmans and to the poor, which caused ill-feeling between him and his uncle Bābujiboa; he therefore went to Mārki and became a disciple of Mārkināthboa. Presently his parents came and took him home, where he was married, but he returned again to Mārki. Mārkināthboa sent him away once more but was so much gratified at his devotion that he prophesied that he would himself be born again as Nānā Sāhib's son. The latter lived at Pātur from that time, making the pursuit of religion his sole object, going naked, and so far disregarding caste restrictions as to take food from all men except Muhammadans and such *antyaja*, low-born people, as Mahārs and Māngs. His relatives used at first to lock him up, but he was quickly seen outside the house, no one knowing how he had got free. The other Brāhmans put him and his family out of caste, but he declared that as long as he prayed to Rām he did nothing requiring penance. Gradually he came to be regarded as a saint to whom ordinary rules did not apply, and a number of miracles are ascribed to him. For instance he would sometimes go to a money-changer in the bazar and distribute copper to the bystanders by the handful, yet the *sarāf* always closed the day with two or three times as much copper as he had in the morning. A mendicant Brāhman once asked him for money, and was given a letter addressed to the god Sri Bālāji at Giri in Madras Presidency; upon this being presented at the temple the god appeared in a dream and bade the priest in charge pay the money. Once a failure of the rains was imminent and the people appealed to Nānā Sāhib; he went to the temple of Māroti outside the village, climbed to the head of the image, and passed water there; rain came that very day. When a man asked him for money he once passed water on the petitioner's *uparna*, shawl; the man through lack of faith wrung out part of the urine but the rest became gold. A Muhammadan officer once insisted that the saint should eat flesh with him and he protested in vain; but when the dish was brought and the cloth removed the flesh had become a heap of flowers, and the Mansabdār prostrated himself before the *sādhu*. Once Nānā Sāhib gave his wife a roll of betel leaves half chewed by himself, and she upon eating it conceived and bore a son; the saint called him Mukundrāj and declared that it was his *guru* Mārkināthboa come to life again. Nānā Sāhib is said to have arbitrated between Udoji and Mādhoji Bhonsla and to have awarded the throne of Nāgpur to the elder. As death approached he asked to be buried instead of being burnt; people disregarded this, but even while his body was burning he appeared in the flesh at Nāndkhed, 4 miles from Pātur, before a prostitute who was a disciple of his, told her the circumstances, said he was going to Mārki, and gave her a bunch of plantains as a *prasād*, religious gift. It was finally decided that he was an incarnation of Lakshman, brother of Rām. Some of the saint's dialectic power seems to have descended to one of his three sons, who refused to marry any woman because his mother had been a woman. A grandson of Nānā Sāhib is said to have brought to life the son of a man in very high position at the court of the Bhonsla, whereon the latter erected the present temple. A fair is held in Māgh Shuddh (January-February); it was formerly very largely attended and miracles of healing used to occur, but its importance has now greatly declined.

Penganga River.—The Penganga river rises in the Chikhli tāluk of Buldāna District, close to its western border, and flows south-east through Chikhli and Mehkar tāluks, and then across the western half of Bāsim; it forms the boundary between Berār and the Nizām's Dominions from that point to its junction with the Wardha; its total course is about 300 miles, of which 60 are within this District. It contains water all through the year in most of its course and, flowing through fairly soft soil, has a large bed even at Yeoti. After passing beyond Akola District the bed becomes rocky and some very holy places are passed. Yeoti, where the river first reaches the Nizām's border, is a village of 900 inhabitants; there are no wealthy *sāhukārs* but the cultivators are generally prosperous, so that the cotton carts of the village pass along the Akola road in strings of a score or more at a time. A small and dilapidated Hemādpanthi temple stands close to the village.

Pinjar.—Pinjar lies among low rough hills in the south-east of Akola tāluk, 22 miles from Akola. It is surrounded by the remains of a fairly strong wall and has a brick *kilā*, fort. It is chiefly remarkable for a Hemādpanthi temple of considerable size in a very good state of preservation, though some details strongly suggest a judicious rebuilding or restoration at an early date. A long inscription, apparently in Sanskrit, is carved on a stone in a shrine in the courtyard; it has not yet been deciphered, but a fairly good copy could probably be taken with proper materials. Near by is a large Hemādpanthi step-well known as Chaubāri Wihīr, the square well. Pinjar was the head of a pargana and is said once to have had 2000 houses but to have declined on account of a heavy tax levied by

Mudhoji Bhonsla in 1772 A.D.; it contained 700 houses in 1867; in 1901 there were 612 houses with 2565 people. A temple of Vithoba, of some size, was built several generations ago by an ancestor of Wāman Saoji, a *sāhukār* of the village who himself spent over Rs. 2000 in 1908 on its restoration. The builder had dreamt that if a temple was erected in the village worship there would be as effectual as at Pandharpur, and there would be no need to make a long pilgrimage to the latter place. A *dargāh*, Muhammadan tomb, is known by the name of Shamsuddīn Wali; his ghost is said at irregular intervals to appear at midnight, clad in green and riding a white horse in a procession; and it is held due to his favour that plague has never visited the village. In the Settlement Report of 1867 it was remarked that Māhān, 8 miles to the south-west, was curiously immune from cholera, and it is clear that remote villages are more likely than others to escape epidemic diseases. Shamsuddīn is said to prevent a dome being built over his tomb.

Pūrna River.—The Pūrna is the largest and most important river in the District. It rises in the Morsi tāluk of Amraoti District and flows to the west, passing through the northern half of Akola District, and finally joins the Tāpti in Khāndesh near Bhusāwal. Its total length is about 200 miles, of which over 60 miles belong, on one or both banks, to Akola District. The Pūrna forms the northern boundary of Murtizāpur, Akola, and Bālāpur tāluks and the southern boundary of Akot. It flows through the midst of the Pāyanghāt, the rich middle plain of Berār, and all the surplus moisture of that country, westward-bound, joins it. Though not navigable it maintains a good current throughout the year, and during the cold weather most of the fords are knee-deep or more, while the great channel through which the stream flows is often 200 yards in breadth and 100 feet in depth. A curious legend is related in a sacred *pothi*, religious poem, about its origin. Gaya Chakravarti, King of the World, who ruled at Hemavanti in the Himālayas, once gave a great feast to four gods with their families and servants, Indra, King of Heaven, Brahma, Creator of the Universe, Vishnu, its Protector, and Mahādeo, its Destroyer. They in return bade him ask a boon, and he craved that he and all his people might receive *mukti*, salvation, deliverance from the round of existence. Mahādeo sent him to Varāh Tīrth to supply the wants of the *rishis*, sages, there. Varāh Tīrth is said to be the present Wāri, a deserted village in the north-west of Akot tāluk, the river Wān, which flows close by, being apparently regarded in this connection as the Pūrna, of which it is in fact only a tributary. Here Gaya Chakravarti found seven crores of *rishis* practising *tapashcharya*, penance. He both joined in this and actually found food for all the *rishis*, with the consequence that their glory declined while his virtue grew. One of their number, Nārad, son of Brahma, perceived this and persuaded them in self-defence to set their rival a task in his hospitality which should overtax his powers. They therefore demanded that on the next day they should all receive their fill of hot milk. The king was in despair, but again the gods came to his aid and Mahādeo commanded the moon, which produces nectar, to see that his requirements were fulfilled. Thereupon Indukala, daughter of the moon, sprang from his side and showered upon the *rishis* hot milk far beyond their powers of consumption, so that it flowed away in a torrent. They pursued the wonderful maiden so as to secure such bounty for ever, and when she sank into the earth tried to dig her up. Finally Brahma commanded her to flow continually as a river of hot milk from the

Sātpurās and promised *mukti*, deliverance, to everyone who should bathe in the stream. Thus food was provided for the *rishis* and salvation bestowed on the king and all his people. The river was called at first Payoshni, which means hot milk, and its name has later become Pūrna; even now holy men at rare intervals see in the stream a trickle of milk and dip it up and drink it as a *prasād*, religious gift, of the river, while it is a valued privilege for all to bathe there. (On Tilsankrānt in 1909 the writer met on the high road a little band of Kunbis belonging to a village on the Morna river going a few miles to the Pūrna for that purpose). The chief tributary of the Pūrna on the northern bank is the Shāhānur, the old channel of which joins it midway in in its course across the District; but most of the water now comes in occasional floods along a channel close to the eastern border cut during the famine of 1896-1897 and greatly deepened since by the action of the current. On the southern bank there are the Pedhi, Uma, and Kātepurna meeting it in Murtizāpur tāluk, the Lonār in Akola, and the Morna and Man in Bālāpur. The banks of the Pūrna are everywhere merely earth, often rising sheer in red cliffs, but the great channel formed between them is very constant. At a few places however people can point to small changes, the disappearance of part of a field, a temple, or, as at Wāgholi in Akola tāluk, of an old village-site. Very large floods sometimes occur, so that people in places point out cliffs half a mile apart as the flood-banks, no land between them being cultivated; or they say, as at Keli Weli in Akot tāluk, that once in ten years a flood reaches a village a mile away from the ordinary channel. The land close to the banks is left waste in most places, partly on account of floods and partly because it is very much cut up by petty tributary streams. The actual current of the Pūrna through the greater part of the year flows with a breadth varying from 50 to 100 yards along the bottom of this deep and wide channel, winding from side to side and varying between rapid shallows and quiet deeper reaches. A number of petty industries, though no large ones, are dependent upon it. In some places the Bhois, fishermen, raise low walls of earth so as to cut off a stretch some hundreds of yards in length and breadth from the rest of the stream, leaving only a narrow opening, to be closed by a net, through which fish can enter or leave. Again the Bhois place a net right across the stream and lie on the bank till the catch is secured. Other shallows, with upright stakes along their sides, are fenced off for the preparation of *san*, hemp ; in other places stretches of sand are formed into ridges and furrows or lines of little heaps. Fifty years ago the country for some miles on both sides of the Pūrna was famous for the salt it produced, and the banks are now marked with long streaks of white stuff with a salt taste. Villages are mostly on high ground some hundreds of yards back from the river, but the bed opposite them is usually a busy scene. The cattle are gathered there for some hours of the day, with diligent herdsmen scrubbing the buffaloes in the evening ; strings of women with vessels on their heads, and occasionally men with bullocks carrying skins, come for water ; here and there people squat to bathe, clothes are being washed, and an occasional cart splashes across the ford. The river is naturally an obstacle to traffic : on the main roads approaches some hundreds of yards in length have been cut, but elsewhere it sometimes requires great care to take a cart up and down safely. At long intervals a big ferry-boat is moored against the bank for use in the rains. Some of the villages on the Pūrna are of a little interest. In Murtizāpur tāluk a group of old temples is situated at Lākhpuri (population 1151) where the road from Murtizāpur to Daryāpur crosses the river. In Akola tāluk Mhaisang (population 1127) was a *taraf* of Akola pargana and has about 25 families of deshmukhs. A number of religious wanderers make a temporary halt here on account of the hospitality of a *sāhukār*, Nārāyan Bāburao Deshmukh. At Kathād (population 571) is a fairly large Gosain *math* with a temple of Kāteshwar Mahādeo and the tombs of 12 *pujāris* outside it. A fair is held on each of the four Mondays in Shrāwan (July-August) and another on Somwati, a Monday which coincides with the last day of the dark fortnight and therefore with the end of the month, a very holy day. At Keli Weli in Akot tāluk is a very interesting school; the headmaster, Suryābhān Jānji, a Koli, has been in charge since 1883. In a village of less than 1400 people he has maintained a school of 150, of whom 50 are boarders. Good fireworks are made in the village, as a display costing Rs. 200 is given annually at the fair held in the name of Gairānboa. In the *gairān*, land set apart for grazing cattle, near the river are some Gosain tombs in connection with which miracles are related. Nānā Sāhib of Pātur wished at one time to build a temple here but found it impossible owing to the displeasure of Deogir, whose tomb is close by. Shiurāmpuri was a prophet, had a miraculous supply of money from which he paid two annas a day for his food, used to get intoxicated with *gānja* and strong drink, was always left dry in a flood, and lived to be 100 years old. Sakhārāmboa has been here for 25 years; he takes no thought about cleanliness, caste prejudices, or the ordinary interests of life. At his bidding a barren bitch suckled puppies, and matches were handed out from an empty tomb; in 1903 plague spared the villagers near him who at his desire remained in their houses; and in a flood he lived three days in a tree, casting down snakes and scorpions without suffering harm. If people ask him for supernatural help and he kicks or strikes them it is thought a sure sign of success. At Pilkāwadi in Akot tāluk a Brahmachāri of unknown name who died in 1905 or 1906 made a great impression. He was fair and very tall and could touch his forehead with his tongue; he ate only in the evening but was hospitable, charitable, ready to talk, and a Sanskrit scholar. He would not have his photo taken, telling people to inscribe his likeness on their hearts. A mango tree at Kāpsi in Akola tāluk was barren for a century but bore fruit, now dedicated to his tomb, when given to him. Once seven days' worship was being maintained in a house where an old woman was very ill; the Brahmachāri came and warned the men to continue, but they fell asleep; suddenly the woman cried out that she had fallen down when being carried to heaven; she lived six months as an invalid and then died. He sent a Bhoi bitten by a snake to sit among people who were worshipping God, which gave immediate relief. Finally a garland fell down when he was hanging it round the neck of Māroti, in whose temple he lived; he understood that his death was near but reminded the god that it was then Dakshināyana and not a good time to die; he went on pilgrimage to Prayāg and returned to die, in the *yogi* attitude, on Māgh Krishna sixth. Various details are told about his last days, for instance that a plover cried and he said he knew the reason, and that he was feverish with anger and said nothing one day but spent the next twenty-four hours in giving wise counsel. People began a *nāmāsapta* service on the day after his death; the place was almost flooded, but a voice cried to them not to fear. Through an oversight *shendur*, the sacred red powder, had not been bought, but a packet was mysteriously found among the stores.

At Ner in Akot tālük is a temple to which Jains go on pilgrimage. The Akola-Akot metalled road crosses the river at Wāgholi and the Shegaon-Akot road at Andurna.

Risod.—Risod, or *Riswad*, is situated 26 miles from Bāsim in the south-west of the tāluk. It was the head of a pargana and has always been a place of some size. Its population was 4716 in 1867, 4609 in 1891, and 3923 in 1901. It is now the second largest place in the tāluk and, as it stands amid very good soil, is perhaps the wealthiest. It has a large tank, put into repair during the famines and used for irrigating garden land. Its institutions include a police station, hospital, post-office, and school; it has also a ginning factory. The soil is good and the neighbouring country pleasant. The last fighting in Berār occurred in this part. During the general disorder of 1857 Rohillas and other unruly people who had been connected with the Nizām's service got out of hand and took up dacoity. In January 1858 a large party under Jalālkhān committed a dacoity at Risod, near which the Inām Commissioner was in camp. It happened that some of the Nizām's Contingent infantry had reached Wākad, 6 miles to the north-west, on their way back from Northern India to their quarters at Hingoli. The Inām Commissioner sent them information and they came in pursuit of the dacoits. The band fled to Chinchāmba Bhar, 7 miles to the south-west, and took refuge inside the village. The troops attacked them at once, but the assault was resisted and Captain Mackinnon was killed, and in the night the marauders escaped into the hills. The name Risod is said to be derived from *rishi wut kshetra*, the place of all the *rishis*.

Shāhānur River.—The Shāhānur river is a tributary of the Pūrna on the northern bank. It rises in the Melghāt and flows right through the Daryāpur tāluk of Amraoti District, passing Surji-Anjangaon and Umri, and enters Akot tāluk at Dahihanda. Its original course took it thence westward, though with a considerable curve round the north side of Kadholi, till it entered the Pūrna at a point 12 miles as the crow flies from Dahihanda. The total length of the river was 70 miles, of which 20 were within Akot tāluk; the channel at Dahihanda was however within two miles of the Pūrna. People on the lower course complained of the damage done by floods to their crops, and the river flowed across the Akola-Akot road, with an awkward crossing. In the famine of 1896-1897 it was determined to divert the river, so as both to prevent floods and to improve the Akot road. A channel was therefore cut, as a relief work, directly from Dahihanda south to the Pūrna. It is said to have been originally only about six feet deep, but more earth was quickly carried away, and people on the original course of the stream suffered from lack of water. Accordingly a dam was built in the second famine to turn the river back into its original course, but this dam was swept away in five minutes when a flood came, and the water again poured along the artificial channel. Now the new cut, called the Nawīn Nadi, forms an absolute gorge, 60 feet deep in parts and of about the same width. In its lower part it is of about the same depth throughout its width, but near Dahihanda it consists of a nullah about 15 feet deep along the bottom of another nullah, itself 30 or 40 feet deep, and the deeper nullah yearly comes further up the stream, its end being now a few hundred yards below the village. The course is practically straight and the banks have not fallen into any appreciable extent, but there may possibly be further developments. One result has been to cause the water to pass Dahihanda in violent floods which prevent people crossing for a day or two and then leave the bed almost dry, whereas there was formerly water for some months and it still remains longer in the higher reaches. The river used to be held up at Dahihanda by an anicut, but this is now useless and people build an earthen *bāndh*, bund, every year. Springs are said to have been uncovered in the deeper part of the cut. It does not appear that any great change has yet been made in the Pūrna at the point where the new cut joins it; the channel of the larger river is no doubt to some extent protected by the fact that it has always a much stronger current than the Shāhānur. It is proposed again to close the new cut.

Sirpur.—Sirpur is a village in Bāsim tāluk 15 miles north-west of Bāsim. Its population was 3515 in 1867 and is now 3809. The population is almost entirely agricultural, includes no very wealthy *sāhukārs*, and maintains no particular daily bazar. Two-thirds of the people are Kunbis and about 40 families more are Marāthas. A great deal of *rabi* is grown. Sirpur was the head of a pargana of 60 villages divided between four deshmukhs, of whom three are Brāhmans and one is a Marātha. Another Marātha is called a Naik and has a large *inām* given him on account of aid rendered to a past Government. The village had once three forts and a wall. It has now a police station, a hospital, two boys' schools, a post-office, and a weekly market on Wednesdays. The chief point of interest is that Sirpur is a very holy spot to Jains. It is sometimes spoken of as their Benāres, and pilgrims visit it from all parts of India. Its sanctity is however chiefly local, as Palidhāna in Kāthiawād and Shamastikar in Bengal are mentioned as having wider fame. Within Berār Muktāgiri in the Ellichpur tāluk of Amraoti District is also a holy place of the Jains. Sirpur has two Jain temples, the chief one in the middle of the village with *dharmshālas* for pilgrims all about it and the Pawali temple outside the village. The great object of reverence is an image of Antariksha Pārasnāth in the chief temple. The story told about this is that two Jain demons called Khar and Dūshan made the image of cowdung and sand and used to worship it. They hid it in a pit beside a river on the side of a hill near Werul, a village near Aurangābād in the Nizām's Dominions. Long afterwards Il or Ilak Rājā of Ellichpur happened to pass the spot and to see a little pool of water, no larger than might be contained in a cow's hoof-mark. He suffered terribly from white leprosy, but on applying this water to his body became immediately whole. He was a Jain, and every night his queen had been accustomed to take the germs of the disease from his body and, not being allowed to kill them, put them in a tin case till the morning, when they were replaced. She now asked how he had been cured, and went with him to the spot, where she prayed the unseen god to manifest himself. That night the image appeared to her in a dream and directed that it should be dug up and conveyed in a cart to Ellichpur, but it warned her that the king, who was to drive the cart himself, must on no account look back. In fact he looked back near Sirpur and the image remained suspended in the air. The king built over it the temple of Pawali—a Hemādpanthi building, having neither arch nor mortar. Presently the god expressed disapproval of this and directed that another temple should be built at the cost of a *panch*, and the present temple was built accordingly. It is not a striking building, but the image, which looks as if it was made of a kind of black stone, has the peculiarity that it is so supported as barely to touch the ground at a single point; a cloth can be passed almost entirely under it. At Pawali it is said that a man on horseback could ride beneath it. The image used to be in the hands of a Kunbi family called

Pawalkar, but for the last five years it has been taken over by a *panch* who pay something to the Pawalkars but control all business arrangements through a Brāhman manager. The image is said to have been set up in the present temple on Vaishākh Shuddh, 3 Vikram Samvat 555, or about 1500 years ago. Two images of Pārasnāth in white marble are said to have been placed in the Pawali temple about 20 years ago. Pilgrims come throughout the year but especially during a three days' fair held in Kārtik (October-November). Digambaris enter the shrine naked, while Shwetambaris wear all their ornaments, or if they are poor at least place *chakshu*, spectacles, over their eyes. The village contains 50 or 60 families of Jains. Mahārs for many miles round also go on pilgrimage to Sirpur, their objective being the tomb of Shāh Dāwal, where a *fakīr* is in charge. Some higher castes, such as Marāthas, also visit this tomb. The writer on Paush Wadya Amāwāsya in January 1909 met band after band of Mahārs on foot, in carts, and on buffaloes, men, women and children, going to the place, while Marāthas filled a whole string of carts. Various explanations are given of the name Sirpur. Some refer it to a saint called Siddha Purush, others to the fact that aborigines here offered a vessel of milk to a *fakīr* who spoke Persian and called the place 'milk-full,' others to a corruption of Shripāl, a second name of Il Rājā who brought the wonderful image, while yet others say the image is a form of Vishnu and the village is named after his wife Lakshmi or Shri.

Telhāra.—Telhāra is a town in the west of Akot tāluk 17 miles from Akot. Its population was 4294 in 1891 and 5160 in 1901; it is thus the third largest place in the tāluk. When Jalgaon tāluk belonged to Akola District an Extra-Assistant Commissioner was stationed at Telhāra and had civil jurisdiction over Akot and Jalgaon tāluks. This has now been discontinued, but during 1908 a Bench of Honorary Magistrates was established at Telhāra with jurisdiction over one-fourth of Akot tāluk. For revenue purposes there are five separate villages adjoining one another, two of them having the name Telhāra and the other three having Muhammadan names. A vague rumour suggests that these three were founded by a Muhammadan Emperor, but there is no account of any considerable Muhammadan settlement in the town. The one noteworthy point about the population is that there is a very large Mārwāri colony here. Muhammadans are said to number about 50 families, Kunbis 125 or 150, but Mārwāris 200, or one-fifth of the whole; almost all of these have come since the Assignment. Many of them are *sāhukārs* and have made large fortunes, so that three-quarters of the land of the five villages is in their hands, but poorer caste-fellows have come to work for these; thus Mārwāri Mochis, leather-workers, amount to about 25 families. The houses of the wealthy have in many cases fronts of carved wood, which form a striking characteristic of the town. The place has no ancient temples of much interest, but several temples of some size have been built during the last fifty years. Harakhchand Gulābchand, Honorary Magistrate, a Swetambari Jain, to carry out a vow of his father's, has at a cost of Rs. 40,000 or more built a temple to Padmaprahu, one of the 24 Tīrthankars of the Jains. It has a golden image, and the building is strikingly coloured and furnished; some of the details, such as the introduction of the figures of British soldiers in the front, seem at first incongruous, but have at least a certain significance. The neighbourhood is rich in large weekly markets, the chief being that at Mālegaon, 3 miles away. One is held at Telhāra on Sundays. During the rest of the week, but not on bazar day, the same site is used as a cotton-market. The demand is that of four gins and two presses in the town, but this is sufficient to absorb all the cotton of the locality and to bring perhaps 200 or 250 carts a day into Telhāra. A police station and a hospital have been situated here for many years, and there is also a telegraph-office; the schools are vernacular only. A library survives from the time of the important courts now removed. The size of the town causes difficulties about its sanitation, and its commercial activity is somewhat hampered in the rains by the lack of good metalled roads, as the road from Telhāra to Adsul is not kept in good condition.

Wādegaon.—Wādegaon is a village in Bālāpur tāluk eight miles south-east of Bālāpur. Its population was 6096 in 1881, 5872 in 1891, and 5825 in 1901. Its prosperity depends almost entirely on agriculture, as it has no cotton factories and its only industry, the making of turbans, is on a very small scale. Land is very much subdivided, people combining a little agriculture with shopkeeping or carting. A good deal of land is either irrigated or used for crops, such as tobacco, which require a good water-supply and careful cultivation. About one-third of the population are Mālis, who are said to be very hard-working cultivators. A made road runs from Pātur through Wādegaon to Bālāpur. The village is situated on the river Nirguna or Bhuikund, and the old men still remember the damage done by a great flood called Dhādya Pur about 60 years ago. It is said that the village was founded by Gaolis and that they made twelve *wādis*, parts, whence the name. The patel holds some high ground in the village but has no fort, *gadhi*. The ruins of an ancient wall and three gates still remain, the Sasti gate on the south being in good preservation. A Māmlatdār was stationed here under the Nizām's Government before 1853 and lived in a large and beautifully finished house. A son of the last Māmlatdār, Sonāji Anaji Mahājan, a Krishnapakshi, is still living in the village and is in his 103rd year. Wādegaon is divided into two *khels* for revenue purposes, but there is no division of the records. A fairly large temple of Mahādeo, with *ghāts* and a resting place for wandering *sādhus*, stands by the river. A small double temple built not long ago by a Māli widow who had lost both her husband and her son stands on a strong platform on the low ground just on the other side. Wādegaon is remarkable in that the villagers have prevented Mārwāris from settling there; it is also famous among one section of the general population alone, the Mahārs. This caste in Berār has five or six places of pilgrimage, of which Wādegaon is one. The sacred object is a tomb above a high strong wall at a bend in the river. It is said that this wall alone prevents the river carrying away a great part of the village. A small rough image is set up under a tree at this spot, and other tombs of less sanctity surround it. A Mahār *guru* with faded vestments is in charge of the whole and receives contributions, generally of one or two annas, from pilgrims. The tomb is said to be that of Dego Mego, but the Mahārs know very few details about him. The general story is that long ago his prayers brought rain in a time of great famine; the name Dego is now associated with the clouds and Mego with falling rain. Pilgrims bathe at a ruined platform at the brink of the water, then climb the steep bank—where there used to be steps—and pour water on the sacred tomb. A small well close by is also brought into the ceremonies.

Wāri.—Wāri Bhairawagarh is a deserted village on the Wān river in the extreme north-west of Akot tāluk. Though remote it is of considerable religious interest, and it is situated amid fine scenery. An image of Hanumān or Māroti, over six feet in height and with a striking face, is said to have been set up 400 years ago by Rāmdās Swāmi, an incarnation of Māroti. About ten years ago a shrine was erected above it by the efforts of a Bairāgi called Hanumāndāsboa, who died and was buried close by three or four years ago. The river Wān has various sacred associations. It was here that according to legend the miraculous Payoshni, generally identified with the present Pūrna, came into existence to maintain the pious hospitality of King Gaya Chakravarti. The point where the Wān river issues from the hills is said to be the place where Draupadi, the wife of the Pāndavas, distributed *halad*, turmeric, and *kunku*, red powder, to women whose husbands were still alive. A deep *doho*, pool, in the river is said to have been made by one of the Pāndavas, Bhīm, when they came here on pilgrimage, and is called Bhīmkund in consequence. The pool is said to be unfathomable, so that when an uncle and nephew once spent six months in making a rope to measure it they still found the rope too short. Near the temple are high cliffs, and it is related that sometimes at midnight a full-grown tiger, which never kills anything, appears on one just opposite the temple and bows in adoration to the image. A religious fair gathers at Wāri every Saturday, and a larger one is held annually for the performance of the birthday ceremony of the image. South-east of the temple are the ruins of a fort called Bhairawagarh together with an image of Kāl Bhairawa. To the south is a tiny village called Sālwan, where there lives a family called Gond Rājās, but no information about them is available.

Wyāla.—Wyāla is a village in Bālāpur tāluk midway between Bālāpur and Akola, that is eight or nine miles from each ; its population is 2460 ; it has fortifications of a very unusual kind and religious traditions of some interest. The fortifications consist of an unusually good *gadhi*, village-fort, and a large stone-lined trench. Both are said to have been built by Khushālji Deshmukh, an officer appointed by the Bhonsla Government but a resident of Jalamb in Khāmgaon tāluk. Wyāla lies in the plain country and has no natural defences, but when fortified it would clearly have been of considerable strategic value from its situation between the Nizām's fortresses at Bālāpur and Akola. The *gadhi* is of the common *māti*-built type, but is large and lofty and has a single small entrance through a brick wall; it has long been in the hands of Government; it was dismantled soon after the Assignment of 1853 and two cannon were removed. The trench, *khandak* or *khai*, surrounds the whole of the older part of the village except for a space on the Bālāpur road; it was apparently left unfinished on account of the death of Khushālji. Its breadth is in one part 45 feet and elsewhere 90 feet; people say that the narrower part was made first, but someone declared that he could jump a horse across it and the rest was consequently made wider. The trench is in parts 18 feet deep and is said formerly to have been deeper and to have been kept flooded; the sides are lined with stone to a thickness in places of 6 feet. A part of the village called *peth*, which is said to have been settled by Khushālji, is some hundreds of yards from the older part, *shahar;* traces of old foundations suggest that both were once included in a town perhaps a mile in breadth. The religious traditions of Wyāla attach chiefly to the *samādh* of a *sādhu* called Ambujiboa Patkar. He was a Kunbi disciple of Nānā Sāhib of Pātur, was married and had two daughters, but maintained himself by begging and took no interest in worldly affairs. He used to worship a cow before taking food and is said to have performed various miracles. Once a Brāhman disciple of his collected Government dues and distributed them to the poor; he was arrested by the Hyderābād authorities, but Ambujiboa offered to make good the loss. When the officers came to collect the money the *sādhu* told them to take it from a heap of cowdung cakes lying in front of his house, but warned them not to try to take too much; they found the money but covetously disregarded the warning, whereon a snake bit them; the *sādhu* took up the snake and would not let them kill it. Ambujiboa used sometimes to drink *mori*, drain, water; at first people blamed him, but presently they saw that a spring of good water had risen in the drain; so they took home some of the water as a sacred gift of the *sādhu*. Water was very scarce in the time of Khushālji, the builder of the fortifications; a Hemādpanthi well still existing close to the present *samādh* was the only source of supply and was so dry that water could be drawn only with a cocoanut-shell. Ambujiboa directed Khushālji, who was a disciple of his, to offer a *bhandāra*, religious feast; and the well became filled with water when preparations were undertaken; during the feast *ghī* ran short, but the *sādhu* directed a pot of water to be brought him, and the water turned to *ghī*. Since that time other wells have been dug and plenty of water has been found. Ambujiboa once placed a basket of flesh on his head; people were scandalised, but presently saw that the flesh had turned to flowers. He was very faithful to Nānā Sāhib; a fair is said to have begun through people coming to Wyāla to see Ambujiboa, but he went to Pātur to cause the fair to take place there in honour of his master. He was buried at Wyāla and people still make vows to him. Religious traditions attach also to a Kunbi family still represented in Wyāla. Mānājiboa, a native of Pāras, came to Wyāla after the time of Ambujiboa. It is recorded that he worked as a labourer and never wore shoes, and that he worshipped a cow and the god Māroti. Once when he was employed to collect thorns he did so by placing his feet upon them, but felt no pain ; in later life a certain Krishnāji Deshmukh asked who it was that told him to collect thorns, whereon he indicated his stomach. He was seen worshipping Māroti at the same time at Wyāla and at Pāras, five miles away, was called *sādhu* from that time, and was honoured at his death by a *samādh* in the temple of Māroti. His son Withoba had the power of relieving people possessed by evil spirits ; he used to give them *tīrth*, water that has been used to bathe a god, and *angāra*, ashes from a sacrifice. Malwithoba, *guru* of Rājā Chandūlāl of Hyderābād, visited Wyāla, taught the wife of Withoba *gurumantra*, and secured for the husband *ināms* for the worship of Māroti. Withoba like his father was buried under a *samādh*, but vows are not made to either, and later generations have lived secular lives and been burnt in the ordinary way. The temple of Māroti is not a striking one. The village also contains a Hemādpanthi temple of Mahādeo which has recently been surrounded with a good stone wall. About 100 families, or one-fifth of the population, are Mālis ; their headman is called a *rājwya*. Both the *patelki* and the *patwāripana* are divided ; one patel is a deshmukh and claims to be a Marātha, while the other calls himself only a Kunbi.

Baptist Mission Press, Calcutta.

Bemrose; Collo., Derby.

TOMB OF BURHANUDDIN AND SHAKKAR TALAO, NARNALA,

Bemrose, Collo., Derby.

GENERAL VIEW OF BOTH CAVES, WEST OF PATUR.

Bemrose, Collo., Derby.

DAHIHANDA GATE, AKOLA.

Bemrose, Collo., Derby.

TEMPLE OF ANTARIKSHA PARSVANATHA FROM NORTH-EAST. SIRPUR.

Bemrose, Collo., Derby.

INNER GATEWAY OF FORT BALAPUR

Bemrose, Collo., Derby.

CHHAṬRI, BALAPUR.

Bemrose, Collo., Derby.

GENERAL VIEW OF TEMPLE OF KALIKA DEVI FROM NORTH-EAST, BARSI TAKLI.

Bemrose, Collo., Derby

INTERIOR OF TEMPLE OF KALIKA DEVI, BARSI TAKLI.

Bemrose, Collo., Derby.

PILLAR INSIDE HALL OF TEMPLE OF KALIKA DEVI, BARSI TAKLI.

Bemrose, Collo., Derby.

GENERAL VIEW OF TOP, SHOWING INSCRIPTION ON MAHAKALI GATEWAY, NARNALA.

Bemrose, Collo., Derby.

RAMA'S TEMPLE AND SHOP FRONTAGE, AKOLA.

Bemrose, Collo., Derby.

VIEW OF FORT FROM SOUTH-WEST, BALAPUR.

Bemrose, Collo., Derby.

GENERAL VIEW OF SOUTH CAVE, PATUR.

Bemrose, Collo., Derby.

TEMPLE OF KAPALESVARA, PINJAR.

Bemrose, Collo., Derby.

FRONT VIEW OF MAHAKALI GATEWAY, NARNALA.

Bemrose, Collo., Derby.

FRONT DOORWAY OF HALL OF TEMPLE OF ANTARIKSHA PARSVANATHA, SIRPUR.

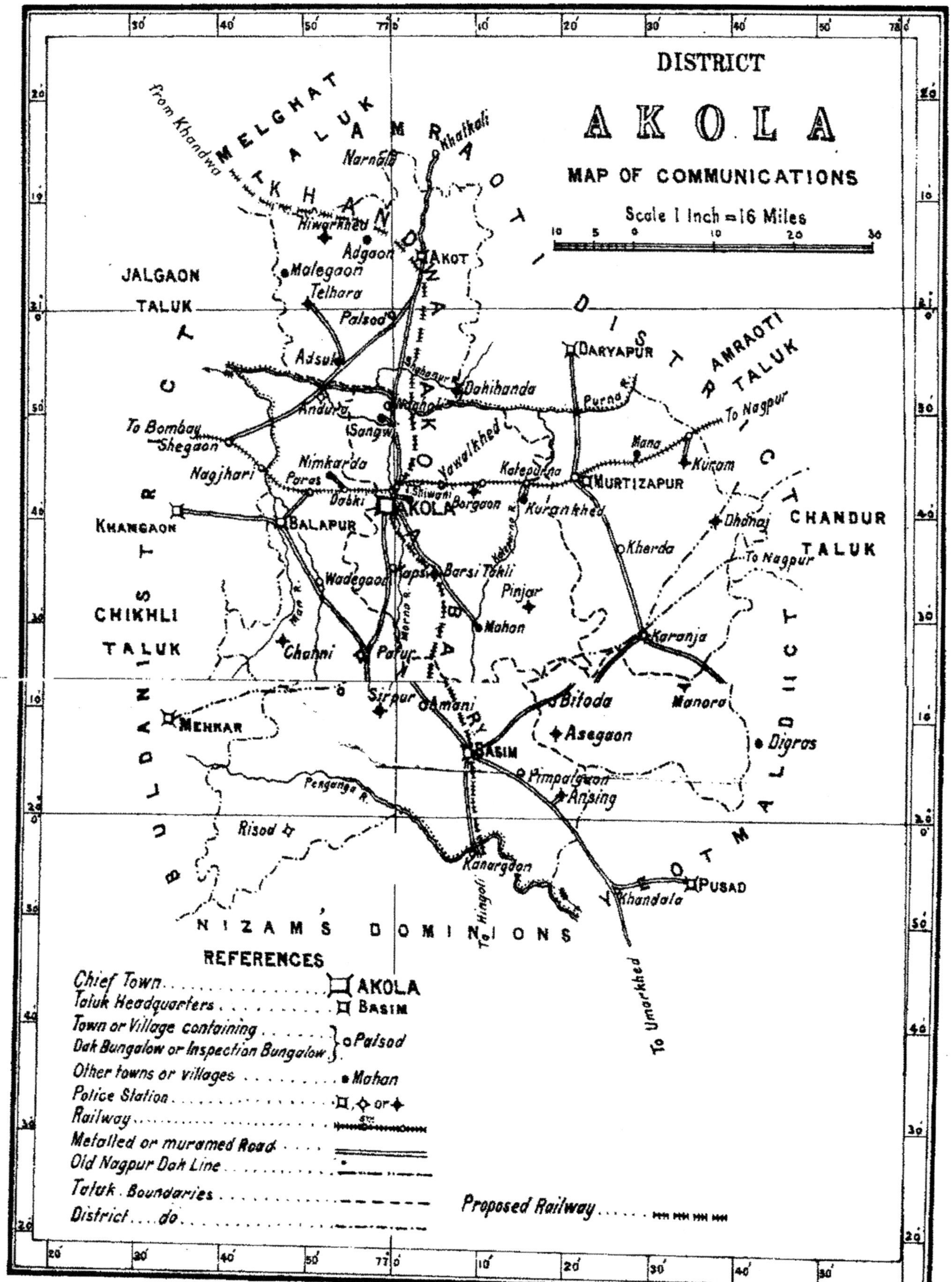

Specially prepared for the Superintendent, Gazetteer, C. P., from an original supplied by him.

Reg. No. 1416 E., 09.—H.—400

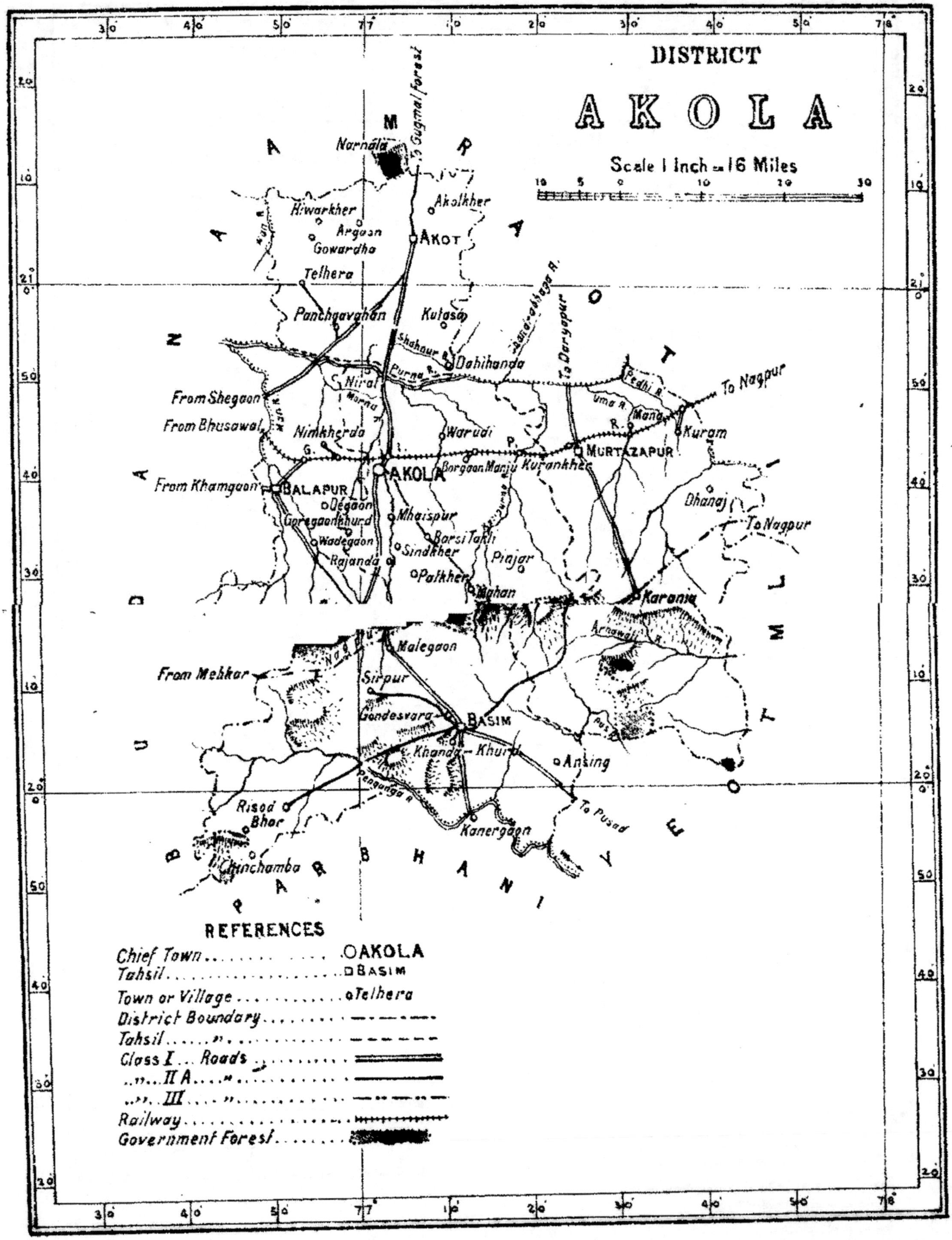

DISTRICT
AKOLA
Scale 1 Inch = 16 Miles
AMRAOTI
NANDAPUR
BUDANA
PARBHANI
YEOTMAL
Narnala
To Gugmal Forest
Akolkher
Hiwarkher
Argaon
Gowardha
AKOT
Telhera
Panchgavhan
Kutasa
Shahaur R.
Dahihanda
To Daryapur
Purna R.
Niral
Pedhi R.
To Nagpur
From Shegaon
From Bhusawal
Nimkherda
Warudi
Uma R.
Mana
Kuram
MURTAZAPUR
AKOLA
Borgaon Manju
Kurankher
From Khamgaon
BALAPUR
Degaon
Goregaonkhurd
Mhaispur
Wadegaon
Barsi Takli
Rajanda
Sindkher
Pinjar
Dhanaj
To Nagpur
Patkher
Mahan
Karanja
Arnawati R.
Malegaon
From Mehkar
Sirpur
Gondesvara
BASIM
Khanda Khurd
Ansing
Penganga R.
To Pusad
Risod
Bhor
Kanergaon
Chinchamba
REFERENCES
Chief Town .... AKOLA
Tahsil .... Basim
Town or Village .... Telhera
District Boundary ....
Tahsil ...... " ......
Class I ... Roads ....
" ... II A ... " ......
" ... III ... " ......
Railway ....
Government Forest ....

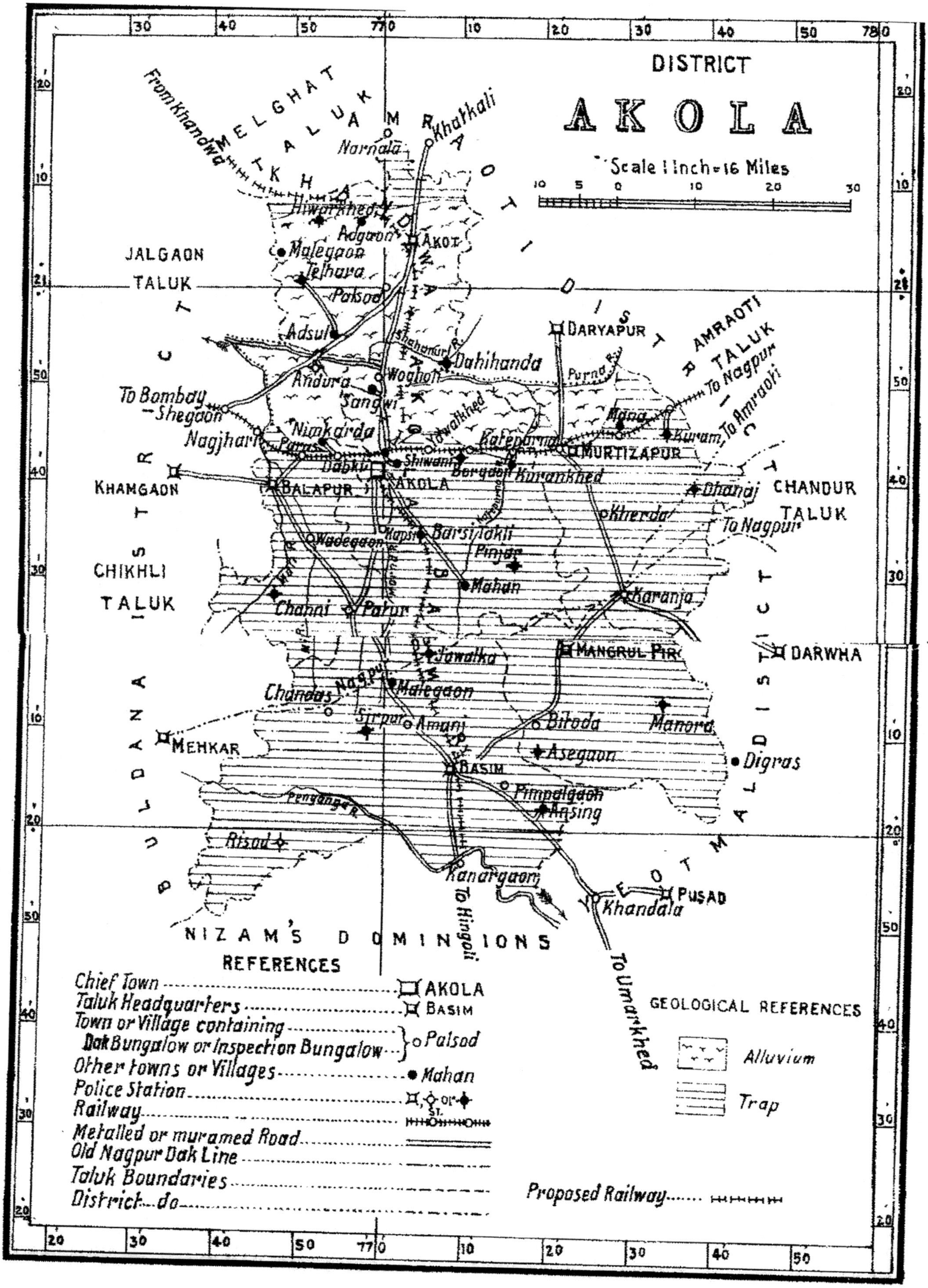

DISTRICT
AKOLA
Scale 1 Inch = 16 Miles
MELGHAT TALUK
AMRAOTI DISTRICT
AMRAOTI TALUK
AKOT
DARYAPUR
MURTIZAPUR
AKOLA
BALAPUR
JALGAON TALUK
KHAMGAON
CHIKHLI TALUK
CHANDUR TALUK
MANGRUL PIR
DARWHA
BASIM
MEHKAR
PUSAD
BULDANA DISTRICT
YEOTMAL DISTRICT
NIZAM'S DOMINIONS
From Khandwa
Khatkali
Narnala
Hiwarkhed
Adgaon
Malegaon
Telhara
Palsod
Adsul
Andura
Woghoh
Sangwi
Dahihanda
To Bombay
Shegaon
Nagjhari
Nimkarda
Paras
Dabki
Shiwani
Borgaon
Katepurna
Kurankhed
Mana
Kuram
To Nagpur
To Amraoti
Dhanaj
Kherda
To Nagpur
Wadegaon
Kapsi
Barsi Takli
Pinjar
Mahan
Karanja
Channi
Parur
Jawalka
Chandas
Malegaon
Sirpur
Amani
Biloda
Manora
Asegaon
Digras
Pimpalgaon
Ansing
Pengange R.
Risod
Kanargaon
To Hingoli
Khandala
To Umarkhed
Purna R.
REFERENCES
Chief Town — AKOLA
Taluk Headquarters — BASIM
Town or Village containing Dak Bungalow or Inspection Bungalow — Palsod
Other towns or Villages — Mahan
Police Station
Railway
Metalled or muramed Road
Old Nagpur Dak Line
Taluk Boundaries
District do
Proposed Railway
GEOLOGICAL REFERENCES
Alluvium
Trap